Taxpayer's Comprehensive Guide to LLCs and S Corps

2023-2024 Edition
(last updated fall of 2023)

by   **Jason Watson, CPA**
Senior Partner

and

WCG CPAs & Advisors

Introduction

About the Author

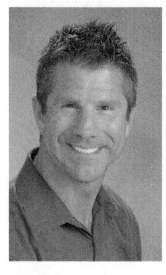

Jason Watson, CPA
Senior Partner

Jason Watson is a Senior Partner for **WCG CPAs & Advisors**, a boutique yet progressive tax, accounting and consultation firm located in Colorado Springs, Colorado. He has owned two small businesses in the past and holds both a Bachelor's and Master's in Business Administration from the University of Wisconsin – Madison.

Aside from carrying the one in accounting class, his desire is speaking with small business owners and creating a dynamic map for the future. Jason enjoys talking about business planning, corporate structures (for elegance and efficiency), S Corp vs LLC concepts, self-employment taxes, health insurance issues and retirement planning. He is quick to point out that while 70% of all situations can be covered with the basics, every business and person is truly unique. One of his Jason-isms is "every house has four walls and a roof, but inside, the things that are personal to you, are different than your neighbor's."

Ask a question and have a dry erase board handy, and you'll see the true passion of a person who not only wants to educate but also wants to see small business owners thrive. While this book on LLCs and S Corporations can be labeled as shameless self-promotion, it truly came from Jason's heart to help small business owners everywhere. And No! He doesn't unnecessarily complicate things; while complication is great cocktail party fodder, most often it is the illusion of precision.

Other than sharing a beer with other Colorado Springs CPAs and drooling on the latest IRS Notice, Jason likes dirt biking, boating in Wisconsin, watching the Packers own the Bears (it never gets old), and running trails in Colorado.

Lastly and most importantly, he is a father of three wonderful, amazing and perfect children (posturing is the new past time in Colorado Springs) and is married to WCG's founder and Senior Partner, Tina Watson, CPA.

You can contact Jason at 719-428-3261 (direct) or **jason@wcginc.com**.

Progressive Updates

The tax law is continuously changing from the acts of our government, from the decisions by the Tax Court and Federal courts, and through notices and private letter rulings from the IRS. In addition to changes, other topics of interest pop up in various trade journals such as Journal of Accountancy, Tax Adviser and Kiplinger's Tax Letter. As we discover other issues concerning LLCs, S Corporations and self-employment taxes, we want to get the word out right away.

More importantly, the frequent business consultations we perform and the questions we field provide a steady stream of new ideas that are worthy of being wormed into this book. So, here's to you- the intellectually curious small business owner helping others.

Currently this book is our 2023-2024 Edition and includes little tweaks here and there. Nothing too crazy like we had the last two editions- between the Tax Cuts & Jobs Act of 2017 and COVID, there were plenty! One of the biggest changes to the paperback version is the removal of the two chapters for Section 199A and the Qualified Business Income deduction. The book was getting too darn thick like Ms. Riley's glasses in My Cousin Vinnie.

We encourage you to visit our website for information on updates-

wcginc.com/book

In addition, please check out our blog from time to time for discussion of current tax issues-

wcginc.com/blog

> Note: As much as we attempt to update our book periodically throughout the year, our blog posts allow us to provide more frequent updates. We encourage you to visit. We are a tax and consultation firm first, and a book-writing firm second; we kindly ask for some patience.

Disclaimer

The information materials and opinions contained on the **WCG CPAs & Advisors** website and in this book are for general information purposes only, are not intended to constitute legal or other professional advice and should not be relied on or treated as a substitute for specific advice relevant to particular circumstances.

WCG Inc. and Jason Watson make no warranties, representations or undertakings about any of the content of our website and this book (including, without limitation, any as to the quality, accuracy, completeness or fitness for any particular purpose of such content), or any content of any other website referred to or accessed by hyperlinks through our website and this book. Although we make reasonable efforts to update the information on our site and this book, we make no representations, warranties or guarantees, whether express or implied, that the content on our site is accurate, complete or up to date.

Please contact us for additional information or seek the advice of other professionals as it pertains to your unique situation.

Shameless Self-Promotion

This book originally was a collection of Knowledge Base articles that were written to help small business owners. The unintended benefit was helping our own small business, **WCG CPAs & Advisors**, grow and thrive through educational marketing. Today, we have 7 partners and over 60 tax and accounting professionals.

Since you probably paid some money for the privilege of being bombarded with shameless self-promotion, we hope you take our comments with a grain of salt (and perhaps some tequila and lime to go with the salt). Our primary focus is to-

▲ educate you,

▲ minimize your tax consequence,

▲ maximize your wealth, and

▲ keep you out of trouble.

If you read this, arm yourself with knowledge and then ask pointed questions of your current accountant and other professionals, we are completely happy. We have done our job with this book.

Having said that, if you want WCG's assistance in whatever capacity necessary, from quick second opinions to full-time service, we are also happy to provide that. Want more information? The Epilogue in the back of this book has all kinds of continued self-promotion and supportive material.

Conversational Tone

This book is written in a conversational tone. If you like perfect prose and editorial exactness that you would expect in a book on brain surgery, then we will be disappointing. We make jokes, some of which are only funny to ourselves. We don't have the best punctuation. We might even have a missing word or a misspelling. We are nerdy accountants who did everything possible to avoid English literature and writing classes. Yuck!

Duplicate Content

You'll see about 15 pages of duplicate content. We did this since everyone jumps into a book at different places, especially with our online Knowledge Base version. Time is all you have on earth to sell, and it cannot be inventoried nor is it refundable; just do a Bob Seger and turn the page if you've seen it before.

How Did We Get Here?

How can I avoid self-employment taxes? This simple question was the inspiration for creating an article describing the benefits of an S Corporation. That original article, which was about four pages long, quickly became a series of Knowledge Base articles on the WCG website. The articles touched on basic topics such as how to elect S Corp status, S Corp vs LLC, shareholder payroll, reasonable salary determination, retirement planning, health care, fringe benefits and liability protection.

Those broad topics demanded much more information, both horizontally by spanning into more related issues, and vertically by digging deeper into the granular yet riveting levels of the tax code. The articles were grouped and relabeled as the **Taxpayer's Comprehensive Guide to LLCs and S Corps** which grew to 39 pages in its first edition. Sorry, all the good titles were taken (remember, the longer the title the less important the material is. Bible, Beowulf, Caddyshack... short and sweet). The Hunt for Red October is one exception, yet we digress.

Time marched on, and more information was added to the first edition such as expanded retirement planning concerns, health care options after the Affordable Care Act and business valuations including exit strategies. Boom, we now had our second edition at over 100 pages. At that point it was suggested by some clients and colleagues to convert the PDF into an eBook as well as paperback.

Specifically, we owe a ton of success to Cherie who writes faith-based books for children. After a consultation on her LLC being taxed as an S Corp, she said, "Hey, make these articles into a book." All we could do is envision pallets of stale outdated books. Thanks to Amazon and their print on demand service, we can update as often as necessary. And of course, Thank you Cherie!

So here we are on our tenth iteration, or the 2023-2024 edition. Unlike Tax Cuts and Jobs Act of 2017 and COVID and the three major pieces of tax law which was the basis for the Ninth edition, these changes are primarily focused on the little things. There are also several examples and little comments that come from the hundreds of consultations we do each year. Nothing tests your bad idea like the public, and people are full of wonderful stories and inquiring minds. All this leads to more fodder for the book!

Each week we receive several phone calls and emails from small business owners and other CPAs across the country who have read our **Taxpayer's Comprehensive Guide to LLCs and S Corps** and praised the wealth of information. Regardless of your current situation, whether you are considering starting your own business or entertaining a contracting gig, or you are an experienced business owner, the contents of this book are for you.

While this book's origins were based on reducing self-employment taxes through an S Corporation election, it has dramatically expanded to sound business advice from entity structures to operational considerations to business tax deductions and retirement planning.

This book is written with the general taxpayer in mind. Too many resources simply regurgitate complex tax code without explanation. While in some cases tax code and court opinions are duplicated verbatim because of precision of the words, this book strives to explain many technical concepts in layperson terms with some added humor and opinions. We believe you will find this book educational as well as amusing.

Enjoy! And please send us all comments, hang-ups and static. This book is as much yours as it is ours, except the tiny royalty part- that's ours. Stop by and we'll buy you a beer with the pennies.

WCG CPAs & Advisors
2393 Flying Horse Club Drive, Colorado Springs CO 80921

719-387-9800 office

support@wcginc.com

Table of Contents

Chapter 8 Section 199A Examples and Comparisons............217

Quick Reference 2023

Single 2023

From	To	Rate	Marginal Tax	Total Tax
0	11,000	10%	1,100	1,100
11,001	44,725	12%	4,047	5,147
44,726	95,375	22%	11,143	16,290
95,376	182,100	24%	20,814	37,104
182,101*	231,250	32%	15,728	52,832
231,251	578,125	35%	121,406	174,238
578,126	forever	37%		

Married Filing Jointly 2023

From	To	Rate	Marginal Tax	Total Tax
0	22,000	10%	2,200	2,200
22,001	89,450	12%	8,094	10,294
89,451	190,750	22%	22,286	32,580
190,751	364,200	24%	41,628	74,208
364,201*	462,500	32%	31,456	105,664
462,501	693,750	35%	80,938	186,602
693,751	forever	37%		

* Start of Section 199A qualified business income phaseout for small business owners.

Standard Deduction Single	13,850
Standard Deduction Married Filing Joint	27,700
Social Security Wage Limit	160,200
IRA Contribution Limit	6,500 + 1,000 catch-up
Roth Income Phaseout Single	138,000
Roth Income Phaseout Married Filing Joint	218,000
401k Employee	22,500 + 7,500 catch-up
401k Employer	43,500
Max 401k Total	66,000 + 7,500 catch-up

Quick Reference 2024

Single 2024

From	To	Rate	Marginal Tax	Total Tax
0	11,600	10%	1,160	1,160
11,601	47,150	12%	4,266	5,426
47,151	100,525	22%	11,743	17,169
100,526	191,950	24%	21,942	39,111
191,951*	243,725	32%	16,568	55,679
243,726	609,350	35%	127,969	183,647
609,351	forever	37%		

Married Filing Jointly 2024

From	To	Rate	Marginal Tax	Total Tax
0	23,200	10%	2,320	2,320
23,201	94,300	12%	8,532	10,852
94,301	201,050	22%	23,485	34,337
201,051	383,900	24%	43,884	78,221
383,901*	487,450	32%	33,136	111,357
487,451	731,200	35%	85,313	196,670
731,201	forever	37%		

* Start of Section 199A qualified business income phaseout for small business owners.

Standard Deduction Single	14,600
Standard Deduction Married Filing Joint	29,200
Social Security Wage Limit	168,600
IRA Contribution Limit	7,000 + 1,000 catch up
Roth Income Phaseout Single	146,000
Roth Income Phaseout Married Filing Joint	230,000
401k Employee	23,000 + 7,500 catch up
401k Employer	46,000
Max 401k Total	69,000 + 7,500 catch up

Chapter 1
Business Entities and LLCs
(updated October 2023)

Basic Business Entities

There are three basic small business entities with variations within. The three basic entities are-

▲ Limited Liability Company (LLC), the crowd favorite

▲ Limited Liability Partnership (LLP) Limited Liability Limited Partnership (LLLP or triple "L" P as the cool kids say), or the legacy dinosaur General Partnership (GP).

▲ C Corporation (for profit), and the Personal Service Corp

There is an additional entity subtype with the "Professional" prefix. Some states require certain professionals, such as doctors, attorneys, accountants and engineers, to be a Professional LLC (the PLLC) or a Professional Corporation (the PC). Since you don't see too many LLPs these days, you don't see too many PLLPs either.

Two notables are missing from the list. First, sole proprietors are not an entity nor is the variant or close cousin of "Doing Business As" (DBA). If you wake up and want to sell used copiers, you can, right now, without any formalized structure. It is not smart, but certainly permissible. At times sole proprietors are interchanged with single-member limited liability companies (SMLLC) since the IRS and most states consider a SMLLC to be a disregarded entity for taxation, and both a sole proprietorship and a SMLLC will end up on Schedule C of your Form 1040. However, they are truly different in several underlying ways.

Also note how an S corporation is not listed. It is not an entity. It is a taxation election. The underlying entity has to be one of the above, and usually it is an LLC (either single-member or multi-member) for the ease of formation including documentation.

> Spoiler Alert: In California, it is preferred to create a C corporation or convert to one if you are also electing S Corp taxation. Why? When you pay a reasonable salary to the shareholders, they must pay into California's State Disability Insurance (SDI) plan. However, as corporate officers, they can opt-out. But! LLCs do not have officers; they have managers and members. As you will learn in this book, when

1

invoking the S Corp election, the underlying entity does not change. Ergo, LLCs taxed as an S corporation in California cannot opt-out of SDI which can save over $1,000 annually.

Let's chat about each of these entities in turn. Here we go...

Sole Proprietorship

We don't want to spend too much time on sole proprietorships since most people reading this book don't want this arrangement. It also behooves us to say that you cannot elect a sole proprietorship to be taxed as an S corporation. Therefore, if you have been in business for several years without an underlying entity, such as an LLC, then you must first create one and then file an S Corp election to enjoy the benefits of an S corporation. What are those mysterious benefits we keep mentioning? Slow down love... we're getting there!

As a sole proprietor you might still need a state registration or some licensing for your particular line of work (such as real estate agent, massage therapy, family counseling), but it is easy to do without needing to form an LLC. Additional downsides to sole proprietorships include zero financial liability protection, poor transfer of ownership upon expansion or death, and the ugly self-employment taxes. Income and expenses are reported on Schedule C and your Form 1040, a separate business tax return is not necessary.

Having said all this, in some cases a sole proprietorship is preferred. For example, in California, there is an $800 annual franchise tax. If your business is barely a side gig and perhaps more of a hobby that might turn into something one day, then $800 annually might seem expensive. You can easily make a business card with some marketing on it and open another personal checking account for the business activities. Done!

Also, be wary of annual Secretary of State filing fees. Nevada is $350. Massachusetts is massive at $500. These are annual fees for just having an LLC. The "pleasure to have an LLC in our state" fee, if you will. Other states vary between $100 to $250, and a few remain free after the initial filing fee like Texas.

Single-Member Limited Liability Company (SMLLC)

Single-member limited liability companies (what we abbreviate as SMLLC) are treated the same way as a sole proprietorship since in the eyes of most taxing agencies SMLLCs are considered a disregarded entity. Just as the name suggests, the entity is disregarded for tax purposes and all business activities are reported on Schedule C with your Form 1040.

The disregarded entity stands in contrast to the pass-through entity (PTE) which are usually partnerships and S corporations.

While the IRS disregards the general SMLLC, several states have a separate form or filing. California uses Form 568. New York uses Form IT-204 LL. Texas has an annual franchise tax filing on Form 05-102 (even with their recent changes in reporting requirements the public information report is still required). We can keep going but you get the idea.

Therefore, SMLLC equals sole proprietor from a federal income taxation perspective and most states. However, keep in mind that a SMLLC enjoys some distinct benefits over a sole proprietor such as liability protection, anonymity and improved transfer of ownership through its Operating Agreement.

Multi-Member Limited Liability Company (MMLLC)

Once you take your single-member LLC and add a member, you are now a multi-member LLC (MMLLC). Boom! Instant increased complexity. The IRS will now call you a partnership since you have more than one member and as a result you will file a Form 1065 Partnership Tax Return.

However, you are technically not a partnership, but rather you are a multi-member LLC with an Operating Agreement as opposed to a partnership with a Partnership Agreement. Adding your spouse typically counts as a MMLLC unless you are in a community property state which is explained a bit later in this chapter (it's underwhelming but important).

Therefore, we must be technically sound on the nomenclature. Smart people rarely interchange the Bears and professional football team, yet many people often interchange 401k and IRA, and multi-member LLC and partnership. This is incorrect. A MMLLC might be taxed as a partnership, but the underlying entity is a limited liability company which has different rules and state statutes as compared to partnerships. Governance, and the rules encompassing that, is different than taxation. Easy to confuse the two.

MMLLCs are similar to sole proprietorships and SMLLCs in terms of income and self-employment taxes, but enjoy a bit more financial protection through the concept of Charging Orders (more on that later in this chapter as well). Transfer of ownership is the same as a SMLLC since you have a member interest that can be gifted, sold, inherited, painted purple, etc. However, most MMLLCs will have an Operating Agreement governing the transaction of each members' interest.

Operating Agreements will also define the sharing of expenses and income. For example, you could be an angel investor at 20% injection but demand 50% of the income. Expanding this concept further, a partnership tax return (Form 1065) generated from a MMLLC will have three "allocations" for each member; allocation of capital, profits and losses. Commonly profits and losses are tied together. Again, you could have a 20% allocation of capital and a 50% allocation of profits and losses (spoiler alert: S Corp blows this flexibility up... standby!).

Operating Agreements also become critical when the entity has value- issues like death, divorce, incapacitation, required distributions, dispute resolution and exit strategies must be handled within the agreement. Perhaps a separate Buy-Sell Agreement is required (usually funded with life insurance- we can help navigate on this).

You and your business partner are besties today, but our job at WCG is to not unnecessarily complicate things. Additionally, our job is to protect your future with a malleable arrangement that endures and provides for a graceful exit.

In terms of self-employment taxes, the taxation of a MMLLC is very similar to a sole proprietorship or SMLLC as alluded to earlier. Partnerships and those mimicking partnerships (MMLLC) commonly require a separate partnership tax return on Form 1065 (with an allowed exception for those living in community property states), which creates K-1s for each member or partner.

This might be your first brush with the term K-1. A K-1 is similar to a W-2 since it reports income and other items for each member, partner, shareholder, owner or beneficiary. It is coded to tell the IRS how the business activities should be treated.

A K-1 is generated by an entity since the entity is passing along the income tax obligation to the K-1 recipient (hence the concept pass-through entity, or PTE for TLA lovers). There are three basic sources for a K-1, and the source dictates how the income and other items on the K-1 are handled on your individual tax return (Form 1040). Here they are-

▲ Partnerships (Form 1065)

▲ S Corporations (Form 1120S)

▲ Estates and Trusts (Form 1041)

All of these are PTEs with the exception of a trust, which might or might not a be pass-through depending on the purpose of the trust. A K-1 is usually filed electronically as a part of the tax return that is generating the K-1. As such, it is preferred to prepare and file your individual income tax return after the PTE's tax return is filed.

We say preferred because it is not absolutely required. However, you run two risks; the first risk is that the K-1 information could change once the PTE's tax return is finalized. The

4

second risk is that too much time lapses between the tax returns, and the IRS sends a tax notice based on a database mismatch (mismatch between what you report and what the IRS has... like a bad game of Go Fish... "Do you have a K-1?" "Go fish.").

A K-1 from a Form 1065 Partnership Tax Return and a K-1 from a Form 1120S S Corporation Tax Return are scarily similar. We could hold two K-1s about three feet from your face and you couldn't tell the difference- heck, we couldn't either. What makes matters worse, is that they both are reported on Page 2 of your Schedule E, and ultimately on line 5 on Schedule 1 of your Form 1040.

But here is the crux of the matter, so please pay attention- one is generally subjected to self-employment taxes and the other is not simply based on which form created it (1065 versus 1120S). Read that again! There is another subtle difference. Expenses associated with K-1 income from Form 1065 are deducted immediately on Page 2 of Schedule E as Unreimbursed Partnership Expenses (UPE) while shareholders of S corporations do not have a place to deduct shareholder expenses.

Sidebar (we love these by the way): In Tax Court Memo 2011-289 McLauchlan v. Commissioner, the court states-

The parties dispute whether the expenses at issue are deductible as unreimbursed partnership expenses. Generally, a partner may not directly deduct the expenses of the partnership on his or her individual returns, even if the expenses were incurred by the partner in furtherance of partnership business. Cropland Chem. Corp. v. Commissioner, 75 T.C. 288, 295 (1980), aff'd. without published opinion 665 F.2d 1050 (7th Cir. 1981). An exception applies, however, when there is an agreement among partners, or a routine practice equal to an agreement, that requires a partner to use his or her own funds to pay a partnership expense. Id.; Klein v. Commissioner, 25 T.C. 1045, 1052 (1956).

Having said that, most S corporation shareholders are also considered employees so they would deduct unreimbursed employee business expenses on Form 2106 and Schedule A. With the passage of the Tax Cuts and Jobs Act of 2017, Form 2106 expenses are no longer deductible on Schedule A.

This can be a surprise to an unaware new S Corp owner. When WCG prepares a business entity tax return, we ask for Accountable Plan reimbursements which include things like home office, mileage, cell phone and internet. At times the business owner figures that we do not need this information since they will deduct home office and mileage, as they've always done, on their 1040 tax return. To make matters worse, the business entity tax return is usually prepared and filed long before the 1040 tax return. We chat about this and other pitfalls in Chapter 10 – Operating Your S Corp (Accountable Plan Expense Reimbursements, page 262.)

Regardless of S corporation or partnership, expenses should be reimbursed by the business through an Accountable Plan and therefore deducted on the business entity tax return. We'll talk about Accountable Plans, and the office politics when you have multiple shareholders, in a later chapter. Good stuff!

As a reminder, entities being taxed as a partnership or S Corp do not pay federal tax- the partners or the members of a MMLLC pay income taxes as individuals (again, hence the pass-through nature). But note the word federal. States can do a lot of crazy things, and there is a whole chapter about the 185 reasons not to elect S corporation taxation that touches on state related issues such as franchise taxes and obscene corporate taxes including what some call the "pleasure to do business in our state" tax.

Limited Liability Partnerships (LLP) and General Partnerships (GP)

General Partnerships (GP) have unlimited liability exposure whereas Limited Liability Partnerships (LLP) have, as the name would suggest, limited exposure for the limited partners. There is also the limited liability limited partnership (LLLP or triple "L" P) which extends liability protection to the general partner as well. Remember, this is financial exposure not necessarily other perils such as tort liability. More about that later.

We won't discuss these entity types much either since they have fallen out of favor lately. Many attorneys are now creating two classes of members within a MMLLC to mimic the different groups that a true partnership would create. So, it walks and smells like an LLP but it is actually a MMLLC without the burden of complication and cumbersome ordering rules. For example, "A Members" are the old-school version of General Partners, and "B Members" are the equivalent of Limited Partners. Most of the attorneys we work with don't create partnerships anymore, including family limited partnerships (FLPs), opting instead for the use of MMLLCs.

Throughout this book we might refer to members as partners. More often than not we are referring to a member of a multi-member LLC. While partner and member are technically different, and the entity type will ultimately decide member or partner, these words are often interchanged by business owners; we are doing our best to reverse the trend.

What gets really obnoxious is shareholder and member. A C corporation has shareholders. An LLC has members. A C Corp taxed as an S Corp has shareholders (that one is easy). But an LLC taxed as an S Corp has members and shareholders. From an entity perspective, we use members. From a tax return perspective, we use shareholders. Why? Historically before the existence of LLCs, an S corporation's underlying entity was predominantly a C corporation.

Being Considered a Passive Business Owner

This is aimed at business owners where they no longer materially participate in the business activity, and as such they are now considered passive investors. Seems easy right, but why would you care? For two big reasons- first, if you have other non-deductible passive losses due to income limitations, such as those from a rental property, you can now have your passive income absorb these passive losses. This allows you to enjoy your tax benefits now rather than delaying the pleasure to future years. Yay!

Second, as a passive owner you might be able to only draw distributions from your business (no salary) rather than salary plus distributions. Since you are pulling money from the business as passive income, this saves you several thousands of dollars in avoided Social Security and Medicare taxes. Every $10,000 in owner salary is about $1,500 in payroll taxes. Yay again!

The world is always trending towards harmony, so here are the passive business owner downsides. It is difficult to claim passive business owner given the material participation tests. The hardest one to overcome is #5 from IRS Publication 925 Passive Activity and At-Risk Rules. Here is the list-

Material participation tests.
You materially participated in a trade or business activity for a tax year if you satisfy any of the following tests.

1. You participated in the activity for more than 500 hours.

2. Your participation was substantially all the participation in the activity of all individuals for the tax year, including the participation of individuals who didn't own any interest in the activity.

3. You participated in the activity for more than 100 hours during the tax year, and you participated at least as much as any other individual (including individuals who didn't own any interest in the activity) for the year.

4. The activity is a significant participation activity, and you participated in all significant participation activities for more than 500 hours. A significant participation activity is any trade or business activity in which you participated for more than 100 hours during the year and in which you didn't materially

participate under any of the material participation tests, other than this test. See Significant Participation Passive Activities under Recharacterization of Passive Income, later.

5. You materially participated in the activity (other than by meeting this fifth test) for any 5 (whether or not consecutive) of the 10 immediately preceding tax years.

6. The activity is a personal service activity in which you materially participated for any 3 (whether or not consecutive) preceding tax years. An activity is a personal service activity if it involves the performance of personal services in the fields of health (including veterinary services), law, engineering, architecture, accounting, actuarial science, performing arts, consulting, or any other trade or business in which capital isn't a material income-producing factor.

7. Based on all the facts and circumstances, you participated in the activity on a regular, continuous, and substantial basis during the year.

Let's look at #5 again, but with some verbiage from the IRS Audit Techniques Guide (ATG) for Passive Activity Losses-

> You materially participated in the activity (other than by meeting this fifth test) for any 5 (whether or not consecutive) of the 10 immediately preceding tax years.

> **IRS ATG:** An activity is non-passive if the taxpayer would have been treated as materially participating in any 5 of the previous 10 years (whether or not consecutive). This test usually applies when a taxpayer "retires from material participation" but maintains an ownership interest in the activity. Yikes (emphasis added).

> **IRS Examination Techniques:** Even if the taxpayer performs no services for a business currently, the examiner should inquire about involvement in prior years and review the returns to see if income or losses were treated as non-passive.

In other words, you need to look back for 10 years and if 5 of those years had material participation by you in the business activity as defined by any of the above, then the IRS will disallow your passive claim. Could you start a brand-new business without the history? Perhaps, but this might be viewed as an end-around especially if the new business magically looks, walks, talks and smells like the old. Transitioning from material participation to passive is certainly tough!

Just because you call yourself a limited partner in a limited liability limited-partnership or some other variant does not matter. It is all about your actions and the reliance on your participation by the entity or enterprise for its success. Should you be considered materially participating in the business, then your income will be typically considered self-employed income and subject to self-employment taxes (Social Security and Medicare taxes). If the entity is taxed as an S Corporation then you would need to be paid a reasonable salary.

A quick recap- you would like to be considered a passive business owner to either-

▲ have passive losses be deductible against your newfound passive income,

▲ to avoid having to pay yourself a reasonable salary in an S Corp environment (and only take shareholder distributions), or

▲ have your income avoid self-employment taxes in a sole proprietor, single-member LLC or partnership environment.

However, the tax code has seen you (and a zillion others) coming a mile away and mostly says No unless you can slip and slide around the rules above.

Rental Partnerships
WCG CPAs & Advisors encourages short-term rentals to be owned by partnerships (ie, a multi-member LLC). Why? For three reasons-

First, the historical audit rate of partnerships (Form 1065) is 0.4%. Super low compared to individual tax returns (Form 1040) which might be 4% to 12% depending on your income levels. Why does this matter? When you have a big cost segregation depreciation plus your big startup expenses such as furniture and supplies, and you then have a big tax deduction against your big W-2 income because your passive losses are no longer limited with your big material participation, it raises some eyebrows. Any large tax deduction raises eyebrows. Cute, electronic AI eyebrows, but eyebrows, nonetheless.

Second, with a partnership tax return, we can mechanically show your capital contribution (at-risk money) including recourse loan debt. Why does this matter? Let's say you invest $250,000 into a new business, and that business loses money. The IRS sees your "partner basis," the $250,000, within your 1040 tax return, and suddenly the $100,000 first-year loss doesn't seem so out-of-whack. A short-term rental is certainly a business activity; sure, you might not have a profit right away, but you will make money someday (otherwise you wouldn't do it, right?).

Conversely, a rental property reported on Schedule E of your 1040 tax return does not present the same way. The mathematical support relative to the allowed rental loss and tax deduction is simply not presented but rather assumed.

Third, all rental activities, including short-term rental (STR) activities, within a partnership tax return are reported on Form 8825. This is another layer of cloaking within the 1065 tax return and allows your rental income and deductions to fly just a little closer to the ground as compared to Schedule E page 1 of your 1040 tax return. There are three degrees of separation... the 1040 to the K-1 to the 1065 to the 8825, all wrapped with nice basis information. Wow, we really geeked out there.

Also, there is an additional reduction in audit rate risk and tax footprint with states. If you have an income-producing asset in a taxing jurisdiction, such as a rental property, then you have a tax return filing obligation even if the rental activity yields a tax loss. Why? A taxing jurisdiction, and in this case, a state department of revenue, has the right to inspect your books and records to ensure your loss is truly a loss. However, if you file a partnership tax return for the taxing jurisdiction, and that results in a tax loss, it is unlikely you need to file an income tax return as a person in that jurisdiction as well. This reduces your personal tax footprint among multiple states.

Other minor benefits include anonymity of the enterprise, orderly transfer of ownership within the LLC's Operating Agreement (versus a trust or will), discounted gifting of interests to others such as your kids, and some enhanced protection with charging orders (super flimsy, but they still exist).

Downsides include the additional tax return preparation fees and perhaps unnecessary state taxes such as California's franchise tax and LLC fee which can be summarized as money-grabs or pleasure to do business in our state fees. You need to consider your exposure versus the cost of reducing your exposure and therefore subsequent risk.

How do you create a partnership? If you are married, this is quite simple. You and your spouse would be members of a multi-member LLC. Not married? There are other options. You could have a sibling, parent or child who hold economic interests in the entity (LLC, for example). They would not hold equity interests, but the arrangement would be considered a partnership, and the rental activities would be reported on a partnership tax return (again, Form 8825 within Form 1065).

Of course, this second method might be more hassle than it is worth, but the first example, the spousal version, is easy. Don't run off and get married just to make a partnership. That's nutty.

> Sidebar: Let's talk briefly about the short-term rental (STR) loophole. If the average stay of your guests over the course of the tax year and only considering actual rented days is 7 days or fewer and you materially participate in the activity (think business owner versus investor), then your rental activity is not deemed passive.
>
> Taking this one step further, and since your investment into the rental property is considered at-risk, losses from this type of activity are not limited and may be deducted against other sources of income such as W-2, K-1 from an S Corp, investment income, etc. Read more here-
>
> **wcginc.com/str**

C Corporations

The big knock on C Corps is that they might be tax inefficient. Wyoming was the first state allowing LLCs in 1970, but most states did not follow suit until the 1990's. Therefore, if you wanted to avoid double taxation you had to first create a C corporation and then elect S corporation taxation.

Thanks to current tax law changes, corporations now enjoy a 21% income tax rate. But… not all that glitters is gold. Dividends are then taxable to you up to 23.8% (which is 15% to 20% capital gains plus 3.8% of Medicare surtax potentially). Therefore, your effective tax rate for using a C Corp as your entity choice ranges from 36% to 44.8% where the top individual rate of an S Corp shareholder is 37%. This is the double taxation part.

We don't run into too many business owners who want to make money but never spend it. Sure, you can enjoy a lasting 21% corporate tax rate, but to spend it you need to be taxed again at your dividend rate.

Read more in our recent blog post-

wcginc.com/8376

If you think you are clever and drive corporate profits down to zero with high owner salaries, this too unnecessarily pays more in overall taxes ultimately (payroll taxes being the main culprit). You will discover in a later chapter that the IRS requires reasonable salaries to be paid to materially participating shareholders in an S corporation (not too low); however, the same is true in a C corporation where an unreasonably high salary is a target for the IRS. Seems odd, but true.

In other words, C corporation plus high salary, Bad. S Corporation plus low salary, Bad. Like Goldilocks, it needs to be just right to the IRS.

Not all is bad with C Corporations.

C corporations generally enjoy better financial liability protection and have much easier transfer of ownership. Taxes are paid at the corporate level to the IRS and states (either through an income tax or a business tax) on Form 1120. Notice the subtle difference; 1120 and 1120S.

Because of the relatively low tax rate as compared to the highest individual tax rate, C Corps can leverage debt reduction at a cheaper rate. How? You buy a piece of equipment with a loan. A portion of the loan payment is principal and is basically paid with after-tax dollars since the interest portion is deducted. Said in another way, you make $1,000 in profits and use $1,000 of it as accelerated debt reduction. You will still pay tax on the $1,000. Yuck.

So, the question becomes, if you must pay taxes on the $1,000, would you rather do it at 21% than 37%? We'll give you a minute to decide with an optional chin rub. Again, this is predicated on smart budgeting and using excess cash to pare down debt versus that European cruise you've been eyeing.

There might be an issue with accumulated earnings tax (AET), but don't get too hung up on that since depreciation will reduce earnings (tax loss or tax neutrality, but cash "gain"). Then later on down the line you elect S Corp tax status on this C Corp and you have the best of both worlds... reduced income tax for some time, and then avoided double taxation as you start pulling out excess cash.

C corporations are also required for any type of self-directed IRA or 401k, and in some cases where a life insurance policy is being paid for by the corporation (and where the beneficiary is the corporation). For example, if you wanted to open a business with a rolled over IRA it would typically need to be a C corporation. However, some IRA trust providers are creating LLCs and funding them with a self-directed IRA. The jury is out on the legality of this, and there are enough attorneys and legal professionals on either side to warrant concern.

If you wanted a life insurance policy on your best sales producer, these are sometimes restricted to C corporations only (essentially, it cannot be a pass-through entity such as a multi-member LLC or partnership, or any entity taxed as an S corporation).

C corporations might also be necessary for exotic stock options, vesting schedules, different classes of voting stock (one share equals ten votes, Class A or one share equals one vote, Class B) and initial public offerings. If you have these needs, seek an attorney. A smart one.

Don't forget the golden rule where the person who has the gold makes the rules. Said differently, if an investor or venture capitalist wants to put their money with you, and they will only do so under a C corporation regime, you are stuck between a rock and a hard place.

Personal Service Corporation

We are not going to spend too much time on this. A corporation will be deemed a personal service corporation if-

▲ Substantially all of the corporation's activities involve the personal of services such as health, law, engineering, accounting, consulting, among others.

▲ At least 95% of the stock is owned by the employee(s) performing the service.

Why do you care? You shouldn't. Personal service corporations are taxed like regular C Corps, but must use cash-based accounting and have a calendar year-end. There is also a bit more pressure on accumulated earnings since the trigger is lower. Without proper justification for the big pile of cash, the IRS might require dividends to be paid or reclassify these earnings as dividends.

Professional Corporations or Limited Liability Company

Several states require certain professions such as accounting, law, medicine, architecture and engineering to be a Professional Corporation (PC). These have the same housekeeping and corporate governance as a C corporation, and they can also elect S corporation status. Other states only require these professions to create a Professional Limited Liability Company (PLLC). Again, PLLCs can also elect S Corp taxation. Not much else to say here.

S Corporations

This book is mostly about S corporations so we saved the best for last. The benefits of an S corporation election include-

▲ A low audit rate of 0.4% as compared to perhaps 3-5% (yawn)

▲ Allowing wages to be paid to the business owner to combat the Section 199A qualified business income deduction phaseout (more on that in a bit),

▲ Leveraging the pass-through entity tax (PTET) deduction, and

▲ The reduction of self-employment taxes (the big elephant).

Read that again. There is very little difference between a garden-variety LLC and an LLC with an S corporation election from an income tax perspective; the savings of an S Corp is from the reduction of self-employment taxes which comprise of Social Security and Medicare.

Recall that Social Security taxes stop at $168,600 (for the 2024 tax year) but Medicare continues into perpetuity. Don't laugh! That 3.8% Medicare tax times a zillion dollars is a lot of money.

> **Spoiler alert:** At $2M in net income after expenses (profit), your S Corp tax savings is still above $60,000 even with a $400,000 salary… all because of Medicare taxes.

Other payroll taxes such as Unemployment, State Disability Insurance (SDA), etc. actually increase by electing S Corp taxation, but they are minor compared to the reduction of Social Security and Medicare (self-employment) taxes.

As mentioned earlier, S corporations are pass-through entities and therefore do not pay federal income taxes directly. However, various states might have different taxes such as a business or franchise tax. Additionally, the shareholders only pay Social Security and Medicare taxes on their salaries, yet do not pay these taxes on the net income after expenses (and shareholder salaries) from an S Corp.

Therefore, you would want a tiny salary and a large distribution from the net income, right? Well, sure, but there is a small little IRS rule called "reasonable shareholder salaries" that we spend an entire chapter on. We'll also show in a later chapter that S corporations have various sweet spots in terms of income versus payroll tax savings from $30,000 to $2 million, between sole proprietorships, LLCs, partnerships and entities taxed as an S corporation.

S corporations are never formed contrary to popular belief. They are spawned from an entity such as a limited liability company, partnership or C corporation that elects to be taxed as an S corporation. After the election is made on Form 2553, you are treated as an S corporation for taxation purposes only. The underlying entity does not change! A lot of business owners rightfully say, "I have an LLC taxed as an S Corp" but they also say, "I have an S Corp." Technically the former is more accurate, but both get the point across.

Oddly enough, the equity section in your balance sheet should then have a Capital Stock account and an Additional Paid-In Capital account. Again, while your underlying entity might be an LLC without stock (LLCs have interest not shares), it is being taxed as an S corporation so the balance sheet and tax return should look like a corporation. Yeah, it seems weird to have equity accounts that are for corporations while the underlying entity is a limited liability company. However, this coincides with representing the entity as a corporation for tax purposes, yet the underlying governance might be different. This is the whole S Corp vs LLC conundrum.

We can help with the journal entry to populate these accounts correctly so your equity section resembles that of a corporation. This also helps the tracking of basis in your S corporation. A later chapter has some examples.

To reiterate, you are in a weird limbo with electing to be taxed as an S corporation. You need to walk and talk like a corporation for taxes, but the underlying entity and what the Secretary of State will have on file is going to be an LLC, partnership or C corporation. More on the election, and the behind-the-scenes stuff in a later chapter plus our thoughts on corporate governance such as Meetings and Minutes.

Again, this book is mostly about S Corps. The last couple of pages were a slamma-jamma description of the basics.

Section 199A Qualified Business Income Tax Deduction

Section 199A deduction also known as the Qualified Business Income deduction arises from the Tax Cuts & Jobs Act of 2017. This is a significant tax break for small business owners but there are rules and limits of course.

Section 199, without the A, is the section covering Domestic Production Activities Deduction. Section 199A is seemingly modeled after this (or at least a portion was ripped off by legislators) since the mathematics and reporting is similar between Section 199A and Section 199.

Section 199A Qualified Business Income deduction is a deduction from gross income on Line 13 on Page 1 of your individual tax return (Form 1040) for the 2020 tax year.

Section 199A Defining Terms

Pass-through entities and structures include-

▲   Sole proprietorships (no entity, Schedule C).

▲ Real estate investors (no entity, Schedule E).

▲ Disregarded entities (single-member LLCs).

▲ Multi-member LLCs.

▲ Any entity taxed as an S corporation.

▲ Trusts and estates, REITs and qualified cooperatives.

Specified Service Trade or Business (SSTB) is defined as-

▲ Traditional service professions such as doctors, attorneys, accountants, actuaries and consultants.

▲ Performing artists who perform on stage or in a studio.

▲ Paid athletes.

▲ Anyone who works in the financial services or brokerage industry.

▲ And now the hammer... "any trade or business where the principal asset is the reputation or skill" of the owner. Why didn't they just start with this since everything else would have been moot. Oh well...

Interestingly, removed from the traditional service profession are engineers and architects. But an engineer operating a business based on his or her reputation or skill might still be a specified service trade or business. In other words, reputation or skill might trump the fact that engineers and architects were purposely left off the list. Every consultant is suddenly going to reclassify themselves as an engineer; software consultant is now a software engineer. Watson Business Engineers has a nice ring to it. Hmm....

Sit on the ledge, sure, but don't jump off a bridge just yet. The specified service trade or business problem only comes up when your taxable income exceeds the limits. So, a financial advisor making $150,000 might still enjoy the Section 199A deduction. Keep reading!

Section 199A Income Limits
▲ Based on taxable income including all sources (not just business income). Also limited to 20% of taxable income.

See Line 15 of Form 1040 to assess your taxable income.

▲ Single is $157,500 completely phased out by $207,500 (adjusted for inflation). $157,500 represents the end of the 24% marginal tax bracket using 2018 as the base year and is indexed each year (see quick reference in the beginning of our book for the current 24% marginal tax bracket).

▲ Married filing jointly is $315,000 completely phased out by $415,000 (adjusted for inflation). $315,000 represents the end of the 24% marginal tax bracket using 2018 as the base year and is indexed each year.

Calculating the Qualified Business Income Deduction
The basic Section 199A pass-through deduction is 20% of net qualified business income which is huge. If you make $200,000, the deduction is $40,000 times your marginal tax rate of 24% which equals $9,600 in your pocket. Who says Obamacare isn't affordable now?

Here is the exact code-

(2) DETERMINATION OF DEDUCTIBLE AMOUNT FOR EACH TRADE OR BUSINESS. The amount determined under this paragraph with respect to any qualified trade or business is the lesser of-

(A) 20 percent of the taxpayer's qualified business income with respect to the qualified trade or business, or

(B) the greater of-

   (i) 50 percent of the W-2 wages with respect to the qualified trade or business, or

   (ii) the sum of 25 percent of the W-2 wages with respect to the qualified trade or business, plus 2.5 percent of the unadjusted basis immediately after acquisition of all qualified property.

There are some devils in the details of course. The best way is to show some examples-

▲ Wilma makes $100,000 in net business income from her sole proprietorship but also deducts $5,000 for self-employed health insurance, $7,065 for self-employment taxes and $10,000 for a SEP IRA. These are not business deductions- they are adjustments on Form 1040 to calculate adjusted gross income. Her deduction is the lessor of 20% of

$100,000 (net business income) or 20% of her taxable income, which could be less (see Pebbles below). This might change as the IRS clarifies.

▲ Barney owns three rentals with net incomes of $20,000 and $5,000, with one losing $8,000 annually. These are aggregated to be $17,000. He would deduct 20% of $17,000.

▲ Barney has passive losses that carried forward and are "released" because he now has net rental income, those passive losses are taken first. With using the same example above with $10,000 in passive loss carried forward, Barney's deduction would equal $17,000 less $10,000 or 20% of $7,000.

▲ Pebbles earns $100,000 from her pass-through business but reports $80,000 of taxable income on her tax return due to other deductions such as her itemized deductions. Her Section 199A deduction would be $16,000 since it limited by the lessor of 20% of $100,000 or $80,000.

▲ Mr. Slate operates an online retailer S corporation which pays $100,000 in W-2 wages and earns $400,000 in net qualified business income. Because he is considered a "high earner" by exceeding the income limits, his deduction is limited to 50% of the W-2 or $50,000 which is less than 20% of $400,000.

▲ If Mr. Slate instead operates as a sole proprietor and earns $500,000 but does not pay any W-2 wages, his deduction is the lessor of 50% of the W-2 wages (or $0 in this example) or 20% of the $500,000. If he paid out $200,000 in wages and had $300,000 in net business income, his Section 199A deduction would be the lessor of 50% of $200,000 or 20% of $300,000.

In other words, he would deduct $60,000 ($60,000 is less than $100,000, even in Canada). He would want to create an LLC, tax it as an S corporation and pay out W-2 wages to maximize his Section 199A deduction.

▲ If Mr. Slate instead operates as a specified service trade as defined previously, he would completely phase out of the Section 199A deduction by exceeding the income limit of $207,500 and $415,000. This is the specified service trade "gotcha."

▲ If Mr. Slate was married and operated a specified service trade, and the taxable income considering all income sources (spouse, investments, etc.) exceeded $315,000 but was less than $415,000, there would be a sliding scale of deduction eligibility. Silly rabbit, tax reform doesn't mean tax simplification.

▲ Fred... yes, we can't neglect Fred... is single and operates an S Corp as an accountant. Days of busting up rocks for Mr. Slate are in the rear-view mirror. He earns $100,000 in net qualified business income after paying $50,000 in W-2 wages to himself.

He is a clearly a specified service trade but because he earns less than $157,500 total ($150,000 in this example) he can take advantage of the full Section 199A deduction of 20% of $100,000. The question of reasonable salary is not being entertained here... focus on the W-2 to income relationship.

▲ Betty becomes a slumlord and earns $500,000 in rental income. No W-2 since she is operating the properties as an individual (and converting passive income into earned income vis a vis a W-2 would be silly). Let's say she purchased the properties for a $1,000,000 (unadjusted basis). The math would go like this-

- 20% x $500,000 is $100,000 (straight calculation).
- 50% of $0 is $0 (W-2 limit calculation).
- 2.5% of $1,000,000 is $25,000 (depreciable asset limit calculation).

Section 199A is limited to the lessor of $100,000 as compared to the greater of $0 (W-2) and $25,000 (depreciable assets).

Section 199A Takeaways

No entity is penalized under this tax law. Some entities and situations might not qualify or be limited in some fashion, but the high-water mark in terms of taxation is the old crummy 2017 tax law.

Taxable income becomes a big deal for two reasons! First, $1 over $157,500 or $315,000 starts the specified service business disqualification and W-2 limitation (and there is also a depreciation component that we are glossing over in this summary). Second, the Section 199A deduction is limited by 20% of taxable income from all sources (what would be reported on your tax returns).

W-2 wages include all W-2 wages, not just those paid to the owner(s). Converting a 1099 contractor to a W-2 employee might be beneficial.

Note: The $157,500 and $315,000 taxable household income limits are the end of the 24% marginal tax rate using 2018 as the base year. These numbers are indexed each year. Said in another way, if your taxable household income exceeds the 24% marginal tax bracket, then you trigger the secondary Section 199A tests and possible limits.

Self-employment taxes will still be calculated on the net business income before the Section 199A deduction since the deduction is taken separately on Line 13 on Page 1 of your individual tax return (Form 1040) for the 2020 tax year. Therefore, you could earn $100,000 and deduct $20,000 under Section 199A, but still pay self-employment taxes on $100,000.

S corporations remain a critical tax saving tool for two reasons. First, the usual self-employment tax savings remains intact for all business owners including specified service trades or businesses. Second, a business owner might need to pay W-2 wages to himself or herself to not be Section 199A limited by income, and only corporations can pay W-2 wages to owners (in other words, an LLC cannot without an S Corp election).

Section 199A Pass-Through Optimization

As you can see, there is some optimization that is necessary for a small business owner to get the most from the Section 199A deduction. On one hand we want to reduce W-2 salaries to shareholders to minimize self-employment taxes. On the other hand, we want to increase W-2 salaries so they do not limit the amount of Section 199A that is deducted.

This seems straightforward since payroll taxes are 15.3% plus some unemployment and other insidious stuff and the Section 199A Qualified Business Income deduction is 20%. However, the 20% Section 199A deduction must be multiplied by the marginal tax rate to obtain the true tax benefit. Even at a 37% marginal tax rate, the additional payroll taxes might exceed the Section 199A deduction tax benefit. Again, optimization is important.

> Spoiler Alert: the optimal salary for Section 199A as a percentage of net business income before salary is 27.9% or about $28,000 salary paid on $100,000 business income.

Section 199A Deduction Decision Tree

Remember that taxable income is all income for the household.

Specified Service Trade or Business-

▲ If taxable income is less than $157,500 (single) / $315,000 (married) then the 20% deduction for your pass-through entity is fully available.

▲ If taxable income is greater than $157,500 / $315,000 but less than $207,500 / $415,000 then a partial deduction is available. The phase-in of the limit is linear.

▲ If taxable income is greater than $207,500 / $415,000 then you are hosed. Sorry.

All Others-

▲ If taxable income is less than $157,500 / $315,000 then the 20% deduction is fully available.

▲ If taxable income is greater than $157,500 / $315,000 but less than $207,500 / $415,000 then a partial deduction is available with the W-2 and depreciable asset limit calculations phase in.

▲ If taxable income is greater than $207,500 / $415,000 then the 20% deduction is compared to the full W-2 and depreciable asset limit calculations (see Betty above).

Please recall that these numbers are from 2018, and represent the top of the 24% marginal tax bracket. As such, these numbers are indexed each year. See the beginning of our book for current tables. Yes, we keep reiterating this concept. Sorry!

S Corp Versus LLC

The next pay per view! UFC #58,723, The Apology... S Corp Versus LLC... Sunday Sunday Sunday!

Since this book is about LLCs and S Corps, and we've already discussed a ton of stuff, we put together a small table to illustrate the S Corp vs LLC contrasts and comparisons; sounds like the start of a college essay. Yuck.

Here we go-

	LLC	S Corp
Self-Employment Taxes	Yes	No
Section 199A Deduction Ability	Max*	Max
Business Tax Deductions	Max	Max
401k Plan	Yes	Yes
Liability Protection	Limited	Limited
Tax Return	1040 / 1065	1120S
Headaches	Yes	Yes

Quiz time! What's the difference between an LLC and an S Corp? None, except the reduction of self-employment taxes and the tax return form number. That's it! Ok, perhaps that is not entirely true.

The little asterisk above is referencing a phaseout of the Section 199A qualified business income deduction where a secondary test is used to determine (or limit) the deduction. Basically, it is 50% of the business income (profit) or 20% of the wages paid, whichever is lower. Since it is frowned upon for a non-S Corp'd LLC to pay wages to its owner(s), at times an S Corp election is required to "open up" the Section 199A deduction.

There are two additional burdens when exploring the LLC vs S Corp comparison.

One is tax return preparation, and subsequent fee. A Form 1120S is a business entity tax return and WCG's fee is typically $1,500 to $1,800. The second burden is payroll processing; as an S corporation you must pay the shareholders a reasonable salary as employees. This too adds a financial burden as well as a series of administrative "touches." But! As you will see, the savings can be significant. For a small increase in chores, you could easily save thousands of dollars. Yes, plural.

LLC Popularity (Hype)

The power of advertising, the ease and the hype have created this fervor surrounding the limited liability company. Note the word company. An LLC is not a limited liability corporation. An LLC is a company and a corporation is a corporation. Woefully different.

Some people think they must create an LLC just to operate a business- not true, you can be considered a sole proprietor the day you woke up, decided to ruin your life and started operating a business. Some people also think they save taxes by creating an LLC- not automatically true unless you take the additional steps to either elect S Corp status and / or implement executive benefits that are otherwise unavailable.

While there are benefits as explained throughout this book, there are also many misconceptions and downright pitfalls to forming and operating an LLC. Don't be fooled, or at least keep it to yourself if you are.

The Formation of an LLC or S Corp

It is very easy to form an LLC and have it taxed as an S corporation. However, an S Corp is not formed by itself; another entity is created and then taxed as an S Corp. If you use a limited liability company as the underlying entity, at times people will refer to this as an LLC S Corp.

While LLC formation is easy, it is also very easy to screw it up. **WCG CPAs & Advisors** can assist with all the filings with the Secretary of State (for any state), and our fee is $625 plus the state filing fees ($50 to $200ish, some states are even $500). Some states such as Nevada require an initial report, and that will typically add $150 to our fee plus the initial report fee.

As an aside, Nevada might have good corporate laws but it is an expensive state to form a business entity in. More on the Nevada hype in a bit.

Sure, you can form an LLC on your own or through LegalZoom, but we will provide consultation and advice during the startup process. You can also use an attorney but be careful since not all attorneys are the same. If you were an idiot before law school, getting a law degree doesn't suddenly make you smart. We have seen many things messed up by attorneys who didn't understand their client's needs, didn't understand the tax code, unnecessarily complicated the heck out of an otherwise simple entity structure, so on and so forth.

Accountants and doctors are not immune. How many quack doctors are there? Plenty. Accountants? Just a bunch of nerdy, socially awkward types. Thanks to Ben Affleck, us accountants are also secret assassins. Thanks Ben, the secret is out. Way to go, wizard.

Some of the kidding aside, we have seen some attorneys do some ingenious things as well. WCG works with business law and corporate attorneys all the time. It is a great relationship since they know corporate governance and contract law, and we know taxation and businesses. Do not think you only need an attorney- you need both an attorney and sharp business consultants (like us).

For your small business formation, WCG will do the following-

▲ Create Articles of Formation or Incorporation, and file with the Secretary of State,

▲ File an initial report if required,

▲ Check on local taxing jurisdictions for registrations (for example, San Francisco which has its own registration form and fee in addition to the State of California),

▲ Obtain your Employer Identification Number (EIN) from the IRS and,

▲ Create an Operating Agreement (for single-member LLCs only since rights are not being represented) or provide a MS-Word template set of Bylaws for corporations.

LLC, Professional Corporation or Corporation
Typically, we will want to form an LLC and later elect S corporation status. However, certain states require certain professions such as accountants, attorneys and doctors to be professional corporations. These entities can also elect S Corp taxation.

Side Note: California allows corporate officers to opt-out of the State Disability Insurance (SDI) tax, which can easily exceed $1,000 annually depending on your salary. However, if you create an LLC and have it taxed as an S corporation, California says No since the underlying entity remains an LLC.

If you create a corporation and elect S Corp taxation, then you can opt-out. Subtle difference, and the fees are virtually the same. Several states have nuances like this that LegalZoom and others might not be aware of since they don't process payroll and prepare tax returns.

Operating Agreements

Multi-member LLCs and Partnerships need agreements between the members and partners respectively. As mentioned through this chapter, there are issues such as death, divorce, incapacitation, spending limits, required distributions (so you have cash to pay taxes), valuation techniques, offramps / exit strategies, etc. that need to be addressed. These agreements are legal in nature and represent rights, therefore WCG cannot assist in drafting these. However, we act in a consulting capacity with attorneys all the time to ensure a quality agreement is drafted that meets the client's needs and objectives from all aspects.

We have more details on Operating Agreements later in Chapter 2 (Operating Agreements, page 89) including deal structures and other way cooler stuff than entities alone. Please review yours for probable missing things.

Accountable Plan

If your underlying entity is a corporation then we also draft Corporate Minutes for your Book of Record to adopt an Accountable Plan which is used for employee reimbursements (see our fun-filled chapter on operating your S Corp).

The days of deducting out of pocket expenses such as mileage, cell phone and home office were not a good idea with S corporations prior to the Tax Cuts and Jobs Act of 2017, but today they are essentially gone. The Accountable Plan allows you to reimburse yourself as an employee, and as such the deduction is taken on the business tax return (which in turn reduces the amount net ordinary income being passed through to the shareholders). We will show you how this is a slick way of pulling money out of your business in the form of employee expense reimbursements.

Corporate Minutes and Books of Record

This is a bit old school. Back in the day, you needed an attorney and a $5,000 check to create a corporation since we didn't have the use of an LLC. The process was very formalized since only large businesses did it, and the states used the process to track the comings and goings of businesses operating in their jurisdiction. Plus, these documents were public and used by shareholders.

However, if your underlying entity is a corporation, we recommend maintaining your Book of Record for three reasons- helps to maintains the integrity of the corporate veil, some banks and other institutions might ask for it to allow you, the controlling shareholder, to act on behalf of the corporation (such as buying an automobile in the business' name), and the IRS from time to time will ask for it during an audit.

Corporate Minutes are generally not required for LLCs; again, because LLCs are not corporations.

Business Banking

The three typical small business formation documents (Articles of Organization / Formation, EIN and Operating Agreement) are required by most banks for a business checking account. An Operating Agreement is not always required. The Patriot Act, Bank Secrecy Act and Homeland Security want to clamp down on illegitimate business accounts and financial holdings. While it might throw off the Feds, Guido's Money Laundering LLC is a no-go for your business checking account name unless you have an EIN, which defeats the purpose if you are Guido.

So, all banks will want either an EIN or a SSN to open a checking account regardless of it is a personal or business checking account. Your business EIN is also tied to your SSN. Follow the money, find the bad guys.

> Note: You can also just get another personal checking account (typically for free from your current bank). However, if you plan on taking checks written in your business name, you'll need a business checking account or a personal checking account with a DBA (doing business as). Then again, most people are utilizing direct deposit or some sort of ACH / EFT deposit which bypasses account names issues.

Remember, you can also create a DBA for your entity name. Therefore, if your business is a franchise but you want a different LLC name on the checking account, you can be Big Bucks LLC dba Starbucks or Bad Coffee dba Starbucks. Remember, friends don't let friends drink Starbucks. Please, find a decent coffee for yourself unless it is wintertime, and Starbuck's chestnut and praline latte is in season. Yum!

We pick on Starbucks, but you have to admit while they might not have the best coffee, they are prolific and consistent throughout the world. You always know what you are going to get.

Oh, and they made drinking $6 lattes fashionable and helped launch hundreds of thousands of small coffee shops. Wow, we really went off there.

S Corp Election
The S Corp election can wait. As mentioned throughout this book, $54,000 net income after expenses (profit) is the break-even point for an S Corp. Not sure? Not to worry, we can elect S Corp as far back as three and a half (3 ½) years using special IRS Revenue Procedure 2013-30 (as opposed to the 75 days provided in the Form 2553 instructions). WCG files about 150-175 late S Corp elections each year, and we are batting 100% on getting them pushed through.

Therefore, if net income is unknown or unpredictable, our advice is to wait until November or December to decide if the election makes sense, and then make it retroactive to the start of the LLC formation or January 1. So, get the LLC in place now and wait on the S Corp trigger until it makes sense- and Yes, we provide this consultation for you. Then again, if you are converting from W-2 to an independent contractor and your revenue is known, then we can form an LLC or corporation, and file the S Corp election right away.

Note that the last paragraph spoke of possibly delaying the S Corp election for an LLC. What if you are required to form a Professional Corporation (PC) because of your business activity (doctor, attorney, accountant, etc.)? Since a PC must file a separate tax return and incur a tax preparation fee, which is large chunk of the break-even analysis, an immediate S corporation election upon PC creation might be prudent.

More on the late election later but here is a spoiler-

▲ You could be in the middle of March 2024,

▲ Elect S Corp status back to January 2023 and

▲ Run a late 2023 payroll event dated 12/31/23 (or simulate Officer Compensation with a one-time 1099-NEC). Boom! You just save 8-10% of your net business income in taxes.

This is all legit, pain in the butt for us, but all legit and successful. Sure, there are some devils in the details in terms of your reasonable cause of the late election, and we will review those with you. **WCG CPAs & Advisors** did this about 160 times last year, and we've been doing this for more than a decade without major hiccups. Not the ideal way in the eyes of the IRS- but then again, hate the game not the player. We are just playing within the parameters of their game.

Not sure if you want to have a full-blown S corporation? As stated earlier, the break-even point where an S Corp makes sense is about $48,000 in net business income after expenses. Why? Simple cost benefit analysis. The expense of running an S Corporation such as payroll and tax preparation equals the savings at $48,000.

How did we calculate that? Our Vail business advisory service package is $4,320 per year. Take this number and divide it by an average savings of 9%, and that equals $48,000. Our business advisory service packages are discussed further, but it is basically your corporate tax return (Form 1120S), individual tax return (Form 1040 and state), payroll events, and unlimited tax planning and consultation.

Let's say you are teetering on that income figure, and not sure about running payroll and all that jazz. You could still run your business income and expenses through your individual tax return (Schedule C on Form 1040) as a sole proprietor, and take the small self-employment tax hit. Then simply file a No Activity tax return for your S Corp. Legal. Legit. Sure, not perfectly elegant but certainly all good in the IRS hood.

If you expect to lose money the first two or three years, the S Corp election becomes a bit more complicated, and more discussion is required- it is generally better to delay the S Corp election so you can avoid the costs and hassles of filing a corporate tax return. More importantly, a single-member LLC or sole proprietor can theoretically have unlimited losses (assuming the money is all at-risk) where a partnership or S Corp cannot because of partner and shareholder basis rules. Briefly, as an S corporation you are both an investor and an employee. As an investor in any business, you cannot lose more than your investment (basis). Same thing here.

[intentional whitespace]

Here are some more gee-whiz stats from 2017 (IRS is slow to release this stuff)-

Industry	Tax Returns	Share
Professional, Scientific & Technical Services	702,282	16.7%
Wholesale & Retail	652,750	15.5%
Construction	544,711	12.9%
Real Estate	461,284	11.0%
Health Care & Social Assistance	354,625	8.4%
Accommodation & Food Service	234,534	5.6%
Waste Management & Remediation	209,690	5.0%
Finance & Insurance	162,832	3.9%
Manufacturing	157,884	3.8%
Transportation & Warehousing	152,086	3.6%
Other	575,000	13.7%
Total	4,207,678	100.0%

Nevada Fallacy of an LLC (or Delaware, or Wyoming, or wherever!)

We just listed out the three most debtor-friendly states, but that's where it ends. You might have heard that you can avoid taxes by forming an LLC in Wyoming or Nevada- is that true? Sure, if tax fraud comes easy to you. Sorry Charlie, your profits will technically be apportioned (fancy accounting speak for allocated or assigned) to the states in which you operate. Here is a super basic rubric on apportionment which some states use to calculate your tax liability-

▲ Payroll- One third of your profits are allocated based on payroll. So, if you have payroll expenses only in Colorado and California, but are incorporated in Nevada, one third of your LLC's profits are split between Colorado and California after applying California's crazy rules. Nothing is allocated to Nevada.

▲ Property- The second third of your profits are allocated based on property ownership and where it is located, such as real estate, inventory, etc.

▲ Sales- The last third of your profits are allocated based on sales and sales nexus, but this can get extremely sticky since the definition of where a sale occurs is grey- is it point of sale (seller's location), point of purchase (buyer's location), title transfer, fulfillment centers, etc.? Where a sale actually occurs is an argument which states and taxpayers can go around and around with- you can only imagine how it will end fighting a state with virtually unlimited resources and time coupled with their presumption of being right.

So, yes, under nexus rules perhaps a small portion of your profit can be attributed to Nevada- yet, this is not because you were incorporated in Nevada, it's because you had a presence in a state that does not impose an income tax. Same would be true for all your sales in Wyoming, Washington, Texas, South Dakota, etc. where strict corporate income taxes do not exist. In addition, several states impose a gross sales receipts tax and other forms of taxation (such as franchise tax) although their corporate income tax rate is zero.

> Note: This is a super simple sample. Some states give sales a larger weight. Others ignore payroll and property entirely. Talk to your apportionment buddies at WCG. As gray tax positions go, income apportionment is right up there with the best of the "well, it depends" accountant responses.

State Nexus

State apportionment boils down to nexus, and states are getting much more aggressive with claiming nexus so that the income generated in that state is taxable. This might make people unhappy, but the reasoning behind it is fair in our opinion. You target a certain group of customers who live in a certain jurisdiction, and you sell computers. Why would Best Buy in the same tax jurisdiction have to pay income taxes in that jurisdiction while you do not? Please don't use the "it's just little ol' me versus the big box store" excuse. Seems a bit unfair if you are Best Buy, or Wal-Mart, or Apple. Go and compete, just make it a level playing field.

Those customers in that jurisdiction perhaps enjoy a smaller tax rate and can have more purchasing power. That smaller tax rate might be offset by higher tax rates for the businesses. Business A (Best Buy in this example) must subsidize the customers in the taxing jurisdiction while Business B (you) does not. Best Buy would be a bit upset in this example.

Avoiding taxes is the American way. We get it. But something about the 14th Amendment and equality and pursuit of happiness comes to mind. Then there's that darn 16th Amendment.

States define economic presence differently. Some states, such as California, use a sales dollar threshold (sometimes referred to as a bright-line) to determine nexus. WCG is getting close to having enough California business to necessitate filing as a foreign entity there just based on revenue. Yuck, since the income tax rate is twice as much as Colorado's. California also has a presence test where if you have an agent working for you in California, then you have income tax nexus.

Remember, this is only income sourced to that taxing jurisdiction. About half the states have nexus rules and thresholds. Can't get enough? Here is a Journal of Accountancy article from 2010 (yeah, it's a little old but so are most accountants, and it provides a good base to learn from)-

wcginc.com/1515

Don't forget the basics such as bank accounts, licenses and permits. If you must be licensed in another state to legally conduct business such as an agent for an insurance business, this in itself might create nexus.

This book dives deep into the issue of nexus in a later chapter, with topics such as sales tax, FBA (Fulfillment By Amazon), throwback rules, and interstate commerce rules. With the recent South Dakota v. Wayfair U.S. Supreme Court case, the sales tax nexus is going to be transformed over the next several years.

> **Massive Word of Caution:** You might not have recognized it, but we introduced two nexus issues alongside each other. Income tax nexus and sales tax nexus. These are wholly different! Just because you have income tax nexus in a state does not mean you also have sales tax nexus, and vise-versa. This is akin to 401k and IRA. People muddy the waters by interchanging these terms, but they are vastly different. Income tax nexus and sales tax nexus is similar in terms of accidentally mixing the terms.

Foreign Qualification

This has nothing to do with international business. When your business has either a physical or economic presence in another state, you must register as a foreign entity. This is usually a formality, but some states might require your business to be in good standing with the home or "domicile" state. Therefore, keep up with your annual filings with the Secretary of State.

Conversely, you might simply want to create another LLC in the satellite state. This allows you to separate financial liability- for example, you might get sued in one state with unfavorable tax laws yet protect your interests in the other state (separate LLC). Bankruptcy laws change by state as well. Something to consider and be reviewed by a competent attorney.

Nevada Fallacy Recap

So, don't believe the Nevada hype. You can probably get away with not paying state income taxes on your own, but as tax and accounting professionals we are bound by such inconveniences like ethics and law. Sorry.

Here is another example to chew on- you have a home office in Maryland. You commute to Washington, D.C. to work for your only client. You incorporate in Maryland since that is where your home office is, and you pay yourself a wage subject to Maryland income taxes. Wait there's more. You also have a presence in D.C. requiring a D.C. corporate tax return as a foreign entity in addition to your Maryland corporate tax return. Thankfully these and other jurisdictions have reciprocity rules, and we can help navigate.

The bottom line is that Nevada tax laws benefit business owners with a presence in Nevada. As Zig Ziglar would say, "You might get a free lunch on consignment, but eventually you'll have to pay." We encourage you to not game the system, and if you want to, WCG cannot be a part of it- we have too many clients relying on us to do the right thing. Please pay your fair share of taxes, just not a dollar more.

Having said that, there are a zillion reasons why forming a corporation or an LLC in a tax friendly state does make sense. But those are case-by-case scenarios. Nothing is a slam-dunk or carte blanche either way. The right questions must be asked and answered to reach the best decision.

Chapter 2
Customized Entity Structures
(updated July 3, 2021 waiting for fireworks)

Your Spouse as a Partner (Happy Happy Joy Joy)

You might be in one of three situations. First, you have a partner in your business already and there's no getting around it unless someone meets with an accident. Or, you work alone like Lone Wolf McQuade (first Chuck Norris reference) and don't see that ever changing. Now the remaining situation allows for a fork in the road- either to add a partner now as you form your business or later after things stabilize a bit. Regardless of having a choice or your spouse allowing you to believe that you do, you contemplate adding your spouse as if it was your idea all along.

Husband and Wife as Owners

Should you immediately form an LLC with your spouse? No. Don't you see enough of each other at the house? All kidding aside, there are two scenarios at play here. First, adding your spouse as an owner and second, adding your spouse to payroll as an employee only. Just because your spouse is an owner does not mean he or she needs a salary, and he or she does not need to be an owner to receive a salary. While those scenarios are commonly combined, it remains a choice, and each has very specific objectives.

We'll look at ownership first, and touch on the payroll component in a later chapter. Two primary reasons for adding your spouse to the business as an owner are-

▲ Leverage the minority owned small business benefits (usually with government contracts). This is getting less and less lucrative.

▲ Asset protection through Charging Orders and the associated rules with multi-member LLCs (attorney stuff).

▲ Your spouse suggests it one lovely evening over dinner, and upon reflection of considerable collateral damage, you surrender. A solely owned small business is still a marital asset in most jurisdictions and as such will be part of any divorce action regardless.

We tricked you there into thinking there were only two primary reasons. Gotta have some fun with this material, right?!

Back to business; please note how tax savings or other big "wow" things are not listed. In other words, adding your spouse as an owner only has two super narrow bands of benefits.

Two Options
If you and your partner are married, and want to become the next power couple, you have two basic options-

▲ Elect to be treated as a qualified joint venture (as defined and allowed by the IRS), and file on Schedule C on your individual tax returns, or

▲ Form an entity, treat the entity as a partnership and file accordingly (either Form 1065 or 1120S).

How you arrive at these two options will vary depending on your state's property laws. There are two types of states beyond red and blue; community property and common law property. Here is some gee whiz information. Community property laws stem from Spanish law whereas common law property states originate from the English law system. Therefore, it makes sense that most of the community property states are in the southwest portion of the United States plus the odd ducks up there in Wisconsin, Washington and Idaho.

Community property states dictate that the income is added into a "community" pot, and then divided equally between the joint taxpayers. Federal laws will usually follow the state laws in terms of income joining and splitting, with some exceptions here and there. On a jointly filed tax return this is moot, but if you need to file a separate tax return this gets complicated (separate tax returns are occasionally needed for second marriages or prenuptial agreements). But regardless of the taxation issues, there are also some procedural issues with business ownership.

Community Property State
Two people, married, in a community property state are not a partnership unless they elect to be treated as such. If you are not electing S corporation status now or in the near future, we would advise not to elect to be a treated as a partnership. Keep it simple.

Electing to be treated as a partnership will complicate things from a tax preparation perspective, does not provide any added tax benefit, and forces you into one of two situations, which are both ultimately equal. You could prepare a partnership tax return and create separate K-1s for you and your spouse at 50% each, or prepare a partnership tax return and create a joint K-1.

Please recall that a K-1 is the byproduct of a pass-through entity tax return which summarizes various business activities that are later presented on the owners' individual tax returns (Form 1040).

What the heck is a joint K-1? Rare, Yes, but the K-1 would be issued to the primary taxpayer's SSN but read "Bob and Sue Smith, JTWROS". When your individual tax returns are prepared, this joint K-1 gets spread among both you and your spouse equally, and therefore the income might be taxed with additional, unnecessary Social Security taxes.

Don't like that idea? Sure, an S Corp election solves the issue above, but here is an alternative that saves you some tax preparation fees since you avoid the partnership tax return but remains "tax expensive-"

A husband and wife owning an LLC in a community property state can be considered one owner, or in the case of an LLC, one member and therefore becomes a disregarded entity as opposed to a partnership. The business activities are then reported on Schedule C of your Form 1040. However, if you properly prepare your individual tax returns, you will split the business activities equally between you and your spouse.

> Sidebar: An individual tax return is a bit of a misnomer. It is synonymous with Form 1040, and may be filed as one person or two married people (married filing jointly). In both situations, the tax return is called an individual tax return. Many of us think of the word individual as numerical such as one or single. But in the case of tax returns, individual is better known as person or human. Furthermore, a married couple is considered one in so many walks of legal life, hence the singular use of individual in referencing a tax return.

Let's run through these three tax return scenarios once more when a married couple own a business together in a community property state-

▲ Elect partnership with separate K-1s at 50% each, or

▲ Elect partnership with joint K-1, or

▲ Remain a disregarded entity (single member LLC) and evenly split activities on two Schedule Cs (you and your spouse), and report them collectively on your individual tax returns (Form 1040).

All three of these scenarios are identical from a self-employment and income tax perspective. Remember, each person has to pay Social Security taxes which is the bulk of the self-employment tax equation up to $168,600 of income (for the 2024 tax year). So, if you are forced to push income equally to you and your spouse, you could easily pay more self-employment taxes than necessary.

You may avoid this by being a single-member LLC. Read that last tidbit again. As mentioned just a bit ago, splitting up your income might actually increase your overall tax liabilities. Remember grammar school; may is permissive and might refers to chance. You may go to the bathroom. It might rain today. It's a bit laughable when flight attendants state that your nearest exit may be behind you as if the exit submitted a proposal for its desired location. Oh well.

Back to more business; two scenarios to drive home this point-

▲ Scenario A- The business earns $300,000 in net income after expenses (profit). You pay Social Security taxes up to $168,600 for the 2024 tax year, and Medicare taxes on the whole amount.

▲ Scenario B- The business earns $300,000 in net income. You and your spouse pay Social Security taxes up to $150,000 each if your spouse is also a member or partner in the business, or about $17,000 in unnecessary taxes which is cash out of your pocket. (Yes, an S corporation could alleviate some this, but you get the idea).

The only way to avoid this equalization in a community property state is to file separate tax returns and claim that you did not know about the community income (seems farfetched, Yes). You could always move to a common law property state such as Colorado which is lovely (we promise).

Or, prove to your family and friends that you are trainable by reading this book, and not add your spouse to the business entity. This is the most elegant and preferred choice when living in a community property state and wanting to avoid the additional Social Security tax as illustrated above.

Or, eclipsing the threshold where an S corporation election makes sense, which we will explore in fascinating detail.

> **Note:** Making an S Corp election can prove problematic if your spouse is a nonresident alien or if your spouse does not consent to the election (even if he or she does not own the business with you). More on this later.

Common Law Property State
Similar to community property states, a husband and wife (or same-sex couples) living in a common law property state have two options- file a partnership tax return or elect to be a qualified joint venture.

Two major differences to note here right away; in common law property states, the presumption is that you and your spouse are a partnership. In community property states, the opposite is true. The presumption is that your business entity is essentially a qualified joint venture.

The other major difference is that in a common law property state, you can chop up the business activities based on a pro-rated basis of involvement / interest in the business. For example, your husband supports your consulting business by handling the books; perhaps his involvement is only 15%. This is converse to community property states which generally divide things equally (whoever thought a marriage was a 50-50 relationship was fooled long ago, but here we are).

Some other details allowing married business partners to be a qualified joint venture include the following-

▲ You and your spouse are the only members (owners) of the joint venture, <u>and</u>

▲ You file a joint tax return (Form 1040), <u>and</u>

▲ You both materially participate in the business operations (which has legal IRS definitions attached to it such as number of hours and activities), <u>and</u>

▲ You are not operating the business as a limited liability company (what?!).

The last one is the deal breaker for most people. According to IRS rules, if you and your spouse operate a multi-member LLC, whereby each of you are members of the LLC, then you must file as a partnership using Form 1065 in common law property states. Most people are confused on this including attorneys and other CPAs. Don't believe us? No worries, refer to these wonderful IRS resources-

wcginc.com/5401

There is a flimsy reason why a qualified joint venture for a husband-and-wife team might make sense over a partnership. A disregarded entity (single-member LLC) or a husband-and-wife team that elect to be a joint venture can theoretically have unlimited losses reported on Schedule C of your joint Form 1040 (assuming the money invested is at-risk).

This contrasts with a partnership where your losses cannot reduce a partner's basis below zero. In other words, if you invest $5,000 in a partnership you can only lose $5,000. Without going into crazy detail, this is different than a partner's capital account (for example, you inject property into the partnership that is worth $10,000 but you only paid $2,000 for it, your capital account will show $10,000 but your basis in only $2,000). Sorry for the diversion.

Having said all this, WCG still prefers to file partnership tax returns even for married couples in community property states since it allows us to track your capital accounts and other basis information. If you sell the business or get divorced or bring on a new partner, then this history is readily available. Otherwise, you must rebuild this information.

Additionally, the audit rate risk is much lower for partnership tax returns than individual tax returns. This does not mean you can be cavalier with your tax positions, but it certainly provides comfort in having a lower risk in defending them. We expand on this in a bit.

If a narrow reason exists, the qualified joint venture election can be made on Form 8832. Here is a quick summary table for married couple teams-

Entity	Common Law Property	Community Property
Sole Proprietor	May be qualified joint venture (Schedule C for each, Form 1040).	May elect to be partnership (Form 1065). May elect to be disregarded entity (Schedule C, Form 1040)
Limited Liability Company	Must be a partnership (Form 1065). May be taxed as an S corporation (Form 1120S).	May elect to be partnership (Form 1065). May elect to be disregarded entity (Schedule C, Form 1040). May be taxed as an S corporation (Form 1120S).

You might be saying to yourself, Yeah, but there have to be some good reasons to add my spouse to the ownership. Here are some considerations.

Disadvantaged Business
Women are a protected class, and therefore might receive favorable government contracts or grants as small business owners. Same sex couples might see increased favorable treatment as well. Don't forget about Veterans and other groups of people whose status might be leveraged.

There are several acronyms out there-

DBE	Disadvantaged Business Enterprise (California uses this often)
MBE	Minority-Owned Business Enterprise
WBE	Women-Owned Business Enterprise
DVBE	Disabled Veterans Business Enterprise
WGBE	White Guy Business Enterprise

Yeah, okay, the last one was a joke. You should always explore these opportunities especially if you are engaging with governments. There are also businesses who will certify your entity as one of the above since there has been a lot of fraud lately. Shocking. Say it isn't so!

Charging Orders
When you have a multi-member limited liability company, and there is a judgement against a member of the LLC, the creditor must obtain what is called a charging order from a court. Theoretically this forces the creditor to only receive distributions from the LLC rather than the LLC's assets. Adding a spouse creates a multi-member LLC situation, but there are some caveats. A later chapter has more information on the concept of charging orders (spoiler alert: it is flimsy legal defense for owners who are married to each other).

Audit Rates
According to IRS data for the 2019 tax year (the most recent data set), 9.3 million partnership and S corporation tax returns combined (Forms 1065 and 1120S) were filed. Of those, 17,543 were audited for an audit rate of less than 0.2%. This further breaks down to 15,852 as a field audit (face to face at your place of business) and 1,691 as a correspondence audit (letters). The IRS is slow to compile and release this data, but we doubt the trend has shifted.

Of those audited by a field audit, 35% resulted in a no-change audit whereas correspondence audits resulted in a no-change audit 52% of the time. This is a blended rate, and digging deeper into the data reveals that partnerships generally result in a no-change audit about half of the time, whereas the same result for an S corporation happens about 33% of the time.

Audit rates for individual tax returns (Form 1040) for the 2019 tax year for adjusted gross income between $50,000 and $200,000 was 0.1%, whereas $200,000 through $1,000,000 was 0.4%. These rates increase to 0.6% and 1.0% respectively with Schedule C and Schedule E. Therefore, if you are in this second band of income range, a partnership or S corporation tax return will have half the IRS scrutiny as your individual tax return. To say half is a bit misleading, right? In practical terms, your audit rate risk goes from microscopic to tiny... both scenarios are favorable, but you get the general idea.

Reduced Salary

Assuming an S corporation, if your spouse is an inactive owner of the business, then the operating spouse's salary might be reduced. For example, one of the criteria the IRS will use to determine if your salary is reasonable is the comparison to shareholder distributions. As we will discuss further in our chapter titled reasonable shareholder salary, one of the jumping off points is 1/3 of net business income after expenses and from there we massage the number to suit the operating spouse specifically.

But if this 1/3 number is based on an ownership percentage less than 100% (such as 80% for the operating spouse and 20% for the inactive / investing spouse), then there might be some savings.

1/3 of 80% of $100,000 is $26,600
1/3 of 100% of $100,000 is $33,300

A $6,000 reduction in salary could save you over $900 in payroll taxes! Again, a later chapter has more information on this within the reasonable salary determination arguments.

Another way to look at this is this; if the IRS uses distributions as compared to salary as one of the determinants of reasonableness, you lower your distribution by shifting some to your inactive spouse. So, your ratio of distributions to salary is lower which is good. Note the words "some" and "inactive." Some being reasonable like 20% or less. Inactive being an owner who does not materially participate in the business and can warrant not collecting a reasonable shareholder salary.

Net-Net Spouse Summary

Again, assume an S Corp. On one hand you have the option of making your spouse an inactive shareholder which theoretically could defend a lower reasonable salary. For mid-range salaries ($30,000 to $50,000), your savings could be $900 to $1,500. Okay, that's one side of the coin.

The other side is adding the spouse as a shareholder and employee (or just employee) and expanding business tax deductions such as business meals, and adding contributions to solo 401k plans. What does that get you in terms of money? At a 24% marginal tax rate, if you were to reduce taxable income by $10,000 because of additional business deductions, you save $2,400.

Therefore, the ultimate answer is weighing the payroll tax reduction (inactive shareholder) versus the income tax reduction (spouse as employee). Remember that the income tax deduction is not generated by solely giving your spouse a wage (assuming you file a joint individual tax return). The income deduction is generated by justifying increased business spending and solo 401k plan deferrals. By the way, a solo 401k plan is available to a married couple team which is contradictory to the word solo... unless you both have one heartbeat and all that mushy stuff T-Swift sings about.

The best trick is to find a legal way to take the money you already spend and turn it into a small business tax deduction. Employing your spouse might help. Thumb through your family expenditures and see if you could have attached a business purpose them.

Married Couple Problems
Staying with the S Corp version of adding your spouse as an owner, if you are trying to classify your spouse as an inactive investor of the business, then you cannot pay a salary. This ultimately prevents your spouse from participating in a 401k plan, and expensing business meals and travel becomes challenging.

Another concern are certain professions- law, medical and accounting do not allow non-professionals to be owners in most states. For example, to be an owner of medical practice requires that you are also a medical doctor. There are some minor exceptions here and there, and each state is different. Over the past several years, however, ownership rules are loosening in all professions. For example, the medical industry has learned that doctors make lousy business administrators and are allowing medical practices to leverage smart Harvard MBA types to run the business.

Here is another example; in Colorado a non-CPA can be an owner of a CPA firm, but the majority (51%) must be CPA's. There are also supervisory and control rules as well. This is a reflection of the times since CPA firms are now offering so many services such as software implementation and real estate consulting. To say that a person cannot be a partner because he or she does have a CPA credential but yet are very valuable to the success of the firm is not equitable.

The overall theme is to double check with your local regulatory agencies first.

Ownership Transfer with Married Couple Teams

If you are concerned about ownership transfer in case of death, we suggest taking care of this issue within your estate planning. Transfer of assets between spouses during death is generally seamless in most states. Contact an estate planning attorney for more comprehensive analysis and advice.

If you are concerned about separation of property during divorce, our experience and observation show that a single owner will still be required to obtain a business valuation from an expert and the business becomes a marital asset. Most courts use a method such as excess earnings to determine the value to the operating spouse, not necessarily the fair market value.

For example, a one-person consultant with a single client might not be able to sell the business because no one else could do the work. However, the business remains valuable to the operating spouse. This is the same as the POS you drove in college- you could sell it for $50, but to you the car was worth a zillion dollars. It ran well, the heater worked, got you to class or work on-time, etc.

Business valuations for divorces sounds like fun, doesn't it? A real hoot. **WCG CPAs & Advisors** is heavily involved in forensic accounting and business valuations, so if you need help let us know. Remember, the goal of any divorce is to ensure both parties are equally upset. No one should be high-fiving as they leave the courtroom.

Family Partners

As mentioned in other areas of this book, your family might benefit from adding children and / or parents to your entity. For example, you could have your children be 10% owners each. They in turn pay very little tax compared to you, and they can either gift the money back to you (good luck) or you can surrender and use this ownership method as a conduit to give them your money which is going to happen anyway but at a reduced tax effect. Imagine helping them pay for basic living expenses, college or savings using business dollars while reducing your overall taxes? Nice, for sure, but it takes some planning.

For example, they are 25 years old making $50,000 on their own. Your business had net profits of $250,000. Because of exemptions and deductions, your child is in the 10% marginal tax rate whereas you are in the 22% marginal tax rate. Not a huge swing, but you get the idea.

Other examples include minor children. Yes, a minor can own shares in an S corporation or generally own interest in an LLC. However, given kiddie tax rates (even with the recent

SECURE Act) this might not be beneficial since your child could be taxed at your rate. What if the minor child materially participates in the business activities? Huh?

There are seven tests for material participation, and the easiest one for your child to meet is 500 hours per year (or about 10 hours a week). The activity must also be regular, continuous and substantial (this is straight out of the ATG – Audit Techniques Guide from the IRS). There are other tests that are preferred when you are needing to claim material participation (such as for the short-term rental tax loophole) but they are not as easy for your child. See the WCG CPAs & Advisors blog for more details.

Back to the issues at hand. If you nail down the material participation with your minor children, they can earn income and be taxed at their own tax rate as opposed to your tax rate. Yes, they can gift the money back to you for your bar bill or make a contribution to their retirement accounts. We prefer the former naturally.

Wait! There's more. You can still claim them as a dependent if you provide over half of their support. How expensive are kids? Really expensive! The word "support" is very interesting. Here is an example; your child could earn $20,000, and puts $15,000 into savings to one day buy a house. They also have $12,000 in living expenses. If you paid $6,001 of those expenses, you are providing over 50% of their support and the child can still be your dependent. Seems a bit silly, but it is good tax planning just the same.

Your Mom and Dad can qualify for this as well where you could siphon income and distributions off to Mom, and she will be taxed at her income tax rate. Also, if you own and operate an S Corp, you don't have to pay a salary to shareholders who do not materially participate in the business activities (inactive shareholders).

Let's recap the idea of children and parents being owners. The practical theory is that if you are going to provide $1,000 for your children or parents, it takes $1,300 or $1,400 in total cash assuming your tax rate is higher than theirs. Moreover, you could "gross up" the $1,000 to account for taxes at their rate and still come out ahead overall in cash (which is what we all care about).

Keep in mind that the juice might not be worth the squeeze. If you are going to deploy these tax strategies, another zero is probably needed.

Family Problems
Yuck but real. Thanksgiving becomes super awkward when the pressures of business ownership span family members including in-laws. A lot of discussion and even

disagreements between business partners are absolutely necessary for successful business stewardship. But retreating to neutral corners is tough with the entire family watching.

Wait! There's more. If you get divorced from your spouse, it is crummy and a bit messy. You own a business interest with your spouse's sibling, and a bit messy becomes a real problem.

Imagine you owning a rental property with an in-law. You might not be able to exit gracefully; regardless of fault, your in-law is sitting on your ex-spouse's side of the room and backing every play. You might not be able to buy him or her out either if the asset has appreciated substantially. Lovely, just lovely.

Real Estate Holding Company and Operating Company

This is one of the most common situations where you own two entities that conduct business between themselves. For example, you are a typical poor accounting firm with the usual high maintenance clients, and you feel that everything would be better if you also owned your own office building. You would create an LLC as the holding company which owns the building, and another LLC (and probably taxed as an S Corp) for the operating company.

This allows for some excellent ownership separation. For example, if you and your father-in-law own the building, he doesn't have a stake in your accounting firm, and vise-versa (didn't we just scare you with this idea, and now we are bringing it up as an example... we're evil). You might also want to make one of your key employees a business partner in your operations, but he or she should not have a stake in the building. Chinese Wall. Can we use Chinese Wall as a separation analogy anymore? We likely offended someone.

Please keep in mind that rental properties including self-rentals are mostly wealth-building strategies and not tax reduction strategies. Yes, depreciation and perhaps even cost segregation can yield some accelerated tax savings, but even that is primarily a wealth building move.

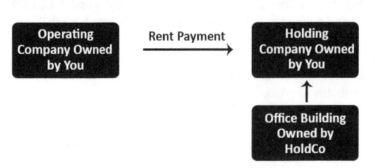

The holding company and operating company arrangement can also reduce self-employment taxes or payroll taxes since this conduit changes the color of money. Huh? As discussed in an earlier chapter, your accounting firm's income is earned income, taxed both at the self-employment tax level (or payroll tax level) and the income tax level. However, you reduce this earned income by the amount of rental expense and that subsequent rental income on the other end is considered passive and only taxed at the income tax level (technically non-passive since it is a self-rental under Section 469, but let's not muddy the waters).

Beauty! You must have a lease and the rent must be market rates; usually a rent appraisal from an independent appraiser will suffice. The rent appraisal is also a good idea in the expansion of ownership. For example, Jason and Tina Watson own the building that WCG leases. As WCG expands its ownership to other partners, the rent payment to Jason and Tina needs to be above reproach; ergo, a rent appraisal. This reduces office politics and hurt feelings. Maybe just office politics.

Parent-Child Arrangement (Income Flows "Up")

You might have two business entities that you want to combine but they are also very different. For example, you are a realtor and your spouse is an IT consultant. We could create a holding LLC called Smith Ventures which owns the realtor LLC and the IT consultant LLC. In other words, the realtor LLC and IT consultant LLC have a single-member, and that single-member is the holding LLC.

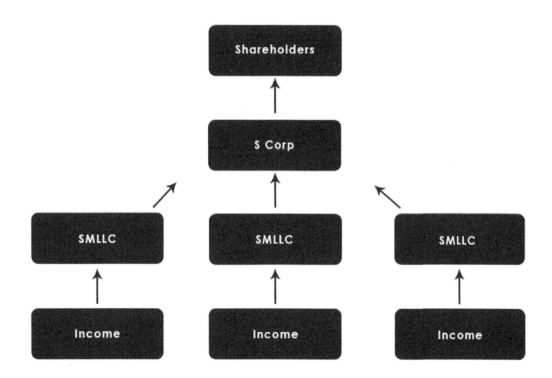

The holding LLC would then make the S Corp election, and all the LLC income (realtor and IT, using the example above) would flow into the S corporation as wholly owned subsidiaries. Remember, single-member LLCs are disregarded entities and are reported on the sole member's tax return. In this case the sole member is a sexy and tax-efficient S corporation. Sexy and tax-efficient... probably went too far with that one. Then again it is called an S Corp election for a reason, and not a U Corp election.

You might be saying, "Yeah, but, why not just have two S Corps?" You can, and in some situations you must (like an attorney and doctor as a married couple). The downside is the additional costs in tax return preparation and payroll processing. Conversely in the arrangement above, all the payroll for the shareholders is handled out of a single S Corp. Each single-member LLC (SMLLC) is a disregarded entity and therefore only a singular tax return is required at the S corporation level.

We rattled that off fairly quickly. Let's break it down with some specifics. An S corporation tax return preparation fee is generally $1,500 to $1,800, and the cost of processing shareholder payroll is about $1,200 annually. Let's call this $3,000. By having two S Corps, you added $3,000 to your overall legal and professional services budget perhaps unnecessarily. Then again if a little division between you and your spouse keeps the pillow talk on the positive side, then perhaps $3,000 is cheap therapy.

Another benefit is that one of these business units, subsidiaries or whatever you want to call them can be carved away and later sold off. You could also expand ownership in one without expanding ownership in the whole structure (we'll show this later in the chapter).

Let's move onto the minor inconveniences. Each entity should have its own checking account and set of books. Common expenses such as an umbrella policy or tax preparation fees would be paid at the S corporation level, while subsidiary specific expenses such as website hosting would be paid at the LLC level.

Also, if you want to take a distribution out of one of the subsidiaries, truly the S corporation would receive the distribution first, and then make another distribution to you, the shareholder. A double hop, and what is referred to as a trampoline in the drug trafficking business (fire up Narcos or Snowfall... great shows!). In other words, transfer money from the SMLLC's checking account to the S corporation's checking account to your checking account. Please don't take it directly from the subsidiary.

Another inconvenience is that each entity might be slapped with high annual fees from the state in the form of filing fees, or franchise taxes (like California) or both. For example, if this arrangement was in California, there would be a minimum of $800 x 3 in franchise taxes. Nasty! The benefits might still outweigh the costs but be careful.

This is a common strategy between husband and wife teams where the business entities are completely different, yet the household wants to enjoy the benefits of an S corporation.

Side Bar: We must analyze limitations in each of the subsidiary LLCs. For example, you cannot have an LLC that would be deemed a hobby tucked under the "protection" of an S Corp. Each LLC must have a profit motive. There might be other limitations at the LLC level, but the hobby loss limitation is a wonderful illustrative point.

Want another? Section 199A Qualified Business Income Deduction has limitations for Specified Service Trades or Businesses (SSTB). Therefore, if one SMLLC is deemed an SSTB and another SMLLC is not, there will be some extra math calculations in determining the Section 199A deduction.

[intentional whitespace]

Expanding Ownership

Expanding ownership will be discussed in more detail in a later chapter, but we quickly wanted to add some more reasons for the compartmentalization of your multiple business units into LLCs. Let's say you have a home inspection business and a home remodel business. Like the real estate holding company / operating company arrangement, you might want to expand ownership in the remodeling business unit and not the inspection business unit.

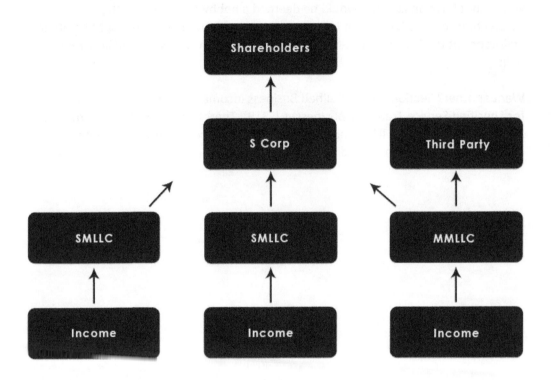

For example, you add a partner to the home remodeling LLC and it suddenly becomes a multi-member LLC (the MMLLC above). This entity would have two members; your S corporation and the other guy. The other guy could be an S corporation as well. In this schematic you would need two business entity tax returns; a Form 1120S for the wholly owned S Corp and a Form 1065 for the MMLLC (Partnership Tax Return). Your S Corp would receive a K-1 from the MMLLC.

A Twist

You could also have the SMLLCs remain owned by each spouse individually. The SMLLCs could then pay the S Corp for services rendered, like a management fee, driving the SMLLC income down to a nominal amount, like $500. Why?

401k plans have all kinds of rules on controlled groups and discrimination rules, and we'll explore more of that later in another chapter. However, if husband owns SMLLC "A" and wife owns SMLLC "B," each business can have a separate 401k plan. One could be filled with employees, and the other is just a solo 401k plan. This is provided that the spouses don't participate in each other's business (again, more on this narrow exception to controlled group rules in a bit).

We discuss holding companies and management companies, and how they are different, later in this chapter.

Parent-Child Arrangement (Income Flows "Down")

Another thought along these lines involves a multi-member LLC where you and another non-spouse partner are the members. Later in another chapter you'll learn that one of the limitations of an S corporation is that distributions must be made in the same percentage as ownership. So, if you are 50-50 with another S Corp shareholder, distributions must also be 50-50.

For now, let's backup for a moment. If this multi-member LLC was not taxed as an S corporation, the Operating Agreement could dictate a different schedule of distributions (we call this special allocation under Section 704). For example, you and another insurance agent team up. But you want an Eat What You Kill revenue model. In this case, you could be 50-50 partners from an ownership perspective, but have the splitting (sharing) of net ordinary business income after expenses and deductions (the profit), and eventual distributions fluctuate based on the production of each insurance agent. Elegant. Simple.

You S Corp elect this thing, and now it blows up. Regardless of the production or income splitting is detailed in your Operating Agreement, or whatever, distributions must be 50-50 since that is the ownership percentage among the two shareholders. Said in another way, the net business income is assigned to each shareholder purely based on ownership percentages and cannot be changed easily.

You could always abandon the S corporation election idea, but you are a taxpaying citizen and want the best of both worlds. You want to save on self-employment taxes as well as having a fluctuating income split. What can be done?

The first solution is to equalize with salaries. Let's say the revenue split based on production for the current year should be 55-45 but you are 50-50 owners. Salaries could be adjusted so that the "55% earner" obtains more of the available cash. This is an easy solution and works reasonably well when the net business income split closely resembles the ownership (or distribution) split.

But if the divergence between net business income and ownership grows too much then equalizing through salaries becomes problematic since the increase in salary for the "high earner" becomes too expensive; keep in mind, and we will reiterate this again later, every $10,000 in salary costs about $1,500 in payroll taxes. Therefore, if an unnecessarily high salary is needed to equalize net business income splits between S Corp owners you might be paying too much in payroll taxes.

Here is an example-

		Batman	Robin
Net Business Income	200,000		
Production Allocation		80,000	120,000
Shareholder Salaries		38,000	38,000
Equalization Bonus		0	40,000
Shareholder Distributions		42,000	42,000
Derived Economic Benefit		80,000	120,000
Extra Payroll Tax due to Bonus		6,120	

In this example, there was $200,000 in profits before shareholder salaries and distributions. Robin needs to get paid $120,000 in some fashion because of a production formula with Batman and the business (let's say they are financial advisors). Salaries were set at $76,000 combined. However, to provide an economic benefit of $120,000 to Robin between salary and distributions, a $40,000 bonus needs to be paid. This creates $6,120 in unnecessary taxes that the business has to pay because of the combination of S Corp rigidity and production-based profit split.

What's plan B then? Easy!

We create three entities. A holding company that is a multi-member LLC (MMLLC), with each member being an S corporation. Each S corporation is owned 100% by each principal involved. Stay with us on this one. The following example shows three S corporations as members of the MMLLC, but just ignore one side if you are a two-person show.

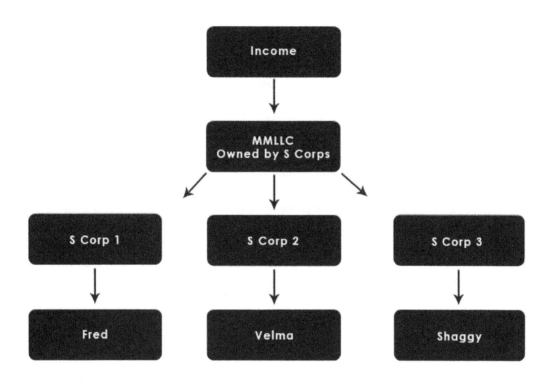

The MMLLC is really a funnel or the "mothership." All revenue goes in, all common expenses are paid out such as internet, copier lease, admin functions, etc., and an Operating Agreement dictates how the distributions are to be handled. K-1s are issued to the MMLLC's members which happen to be S corporations. And then those S corporations pay a reasonable salary to its respective sole shareholder and distribute the remainder.

Let's break this down with an example. $250,000 is earned by the MMLLC after expenses. S Corp 1 receives $125,000 according to the Operating Agreement (yet it remains a 1/3 owner). S Corp 1 pays out a reasonable salary of $55,000 and distributes $70,000. S Corp 2 receives $60,000 and S Corp 3 receives the balance… and both S corporations pay out a reasonable salary and distribute the remainder.

There are some excellent benefits with this arrangement beyond the income splitting and saving of self-employment taxes. Each S corporation is independent, and has autonomy and privacy.

In referencing the previous schematic, there are some intangible yet valuable tax advantages-

▲ Fred could buy whatever business car he wanted. Sure, the MMLLC could establish an allowance that everyone is allowed to spend, and any amount about that is augmented by the members but that gets messy real quick and loses significant tax efficiency.

▲ Velma could work from home and reimburse herself for a home office while others choose not to. Also, consider that Fred and Velma might have different sized home offices and associated expenses, and by leveraging the reimbursement at the S Corps level, you remove office politics and equalization issues.

▲ Shaggy could rent an office since his place is… well… a doghouse of sorts and he needs some space to work.

Each S corporation can run expenses through as it sees fit without upsetting the other business partners. For example, you want to attend conferences in Las Vegas. Another example would be adding a child or spouse to payroll. Each S Corp operates independently and can do what it wants with its money (with some minor rules such as 401k plans). Home office? Buy a car?

We see this arrangement commonly in attorneys, medical groups (surgery groups, physicians, doctors, anesthesiologists, nurse anesthetists, etc.), insurance agents and financial advisors. It is very common in entities where the net business income is not shared equally, but rather on some formula or agreement.

401k plans in this situation are tough since it is a controlled group (technically what ERISA and the IRS call an Affiliated Service Group). More information can be found in a later chapter on controlled groups, and how retirement planning within this scheme works. Controlled group is a commonly overlooked problem with this arrangement; proceed with caution with your 401k plan administrator (spoiler alert: you can have separate 401k plans if you have only owner employees).

Wait! Before you blast off and create the above arrangement, this has fallen out of favor. There is another version of this where the MMLLC is owned by the individuals rather than the S corporations. Why? Let's find out!

Multi-Member LLC That Issues Invoices

A simpler way to accomplish the same thing as above is to create three entities again, but the multi-member LLC is owned by you (the humans) and the other guys, not the S corporations. While we showed the previous schematic, the following is the preferred arrangement for a host of reasons, especially state apportionment of income and business valuation (more on that in a bit).

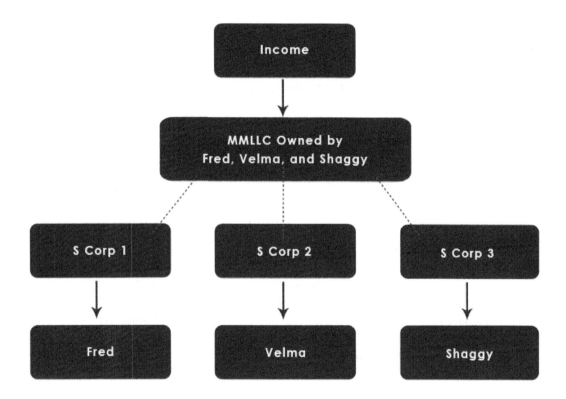

The S Corps issue consultation, fee for service or management fee invoices to the multi-member LLC in the amount of the net business income (profits) split driving the multi-member LLC income down to zero, or some nominal amount like $500. In other words, the payments from the MMLLC to the S Corp would be recorded as Payments for Services Rendered or Outside Contractor or something similar (see dotted lines below).

Therefore, each human would receive two K-1s. One from the MMLLC or "mothership" for a small amount and another from his or her respective S Corp. Additionally, this still accomplishes the Eat What You Kill income splitting objectives and changes the color of money through distributions from each person's "baby" S Corp. Flexibility plus tax efficiency. Brilliant!

This would also be beneficial if you didn't have an Operating Agreement or if you are afraid that an Operating Agreement could be too restrictive from year to year. You would still need some sort of instrument or agreement that dictated how the fees are calculated so there aren't any hard feelings.

Regulated Industries
The above schematic is also preferred for regulated industries like financial advisors or real estate agents where entity ownership must be individuals. In some states and with certain regulatory agencies, the MMLLC may be owned by S corporations provided the named principals are the licensed / regulated individuals... again, this arrangement avoids that issue.

Having said that, the "baby" S Corps typically must register separately with their regulatory body. For example, if you are band of attorneys wanting the mothership baby S Corp multi-entity construct (yeah, we just made that up) with fee for service agreements, each S Corp would probably need to be registered as a law office with the state bar. This is a minor housekeeping detail, but an important one.

State Income Tax Footprint
You might also reduce your exposure to state nexus based on revenue or income. If the MMLLC is a California entity issuing a small K-1 to an individual running an S Corp in Illinois, you will reduce the long-reach risk of California. What do we mean here?

Scenario 1 is where your Illinois S Corp owns member interest in a California LLC. The LLC will issue a K-1 to your S Corp and now you instantly have a very visible tax footprint in California. They will likely be expecting a state tax return for your Illinois entity doing business (as they see it) in California.

Scenario 2 is where your Illinois S Corp provides a service to a California LLC in a business to business (B2B) relationship. You might still have a tax footprint in California, but you are in complete control of the narrative since California does not instantly know about this not-so-visible relationship.

We are not advocating avoiding apportionment (the allocation of taxable income to other states), but at least you are more in control of what California knows and what they don't need to know. They feel like they need to know everything, and they most certainly do not.

No 1099s

Do not issue 1099s in this scenario. First, a 1099 is only required to be sent to non-corporations. Even though you might have created an LLC and then later elected S Corp status, you are now considered a corporation for taxation and your vendors are not required to send you a 1099 (although many do).

> Side Bar: Business tax returns such as Form 1065, 1120 and 1120S are usually prepared by tax professionals, and as such the IRS believes revenue has a much higher chance of being recorded properly, and 1099s are not necessary. It would also be ridiculous for Verizon to receive a million 1099s from its customers. Funny, Yes, but ridiculous.

Second, a 1099 has EINs and possibly SSNs. Since these dots can be connected by the IRS, the issuance of a 1099 might invite unnecessary scrutiny. The IRS agent's question becomes "Why did you issue a 1099 to a partner rather than let the income flow through a K-1?" "To avoid taxes and headaches" is probably not going to go well during the audit.

A multi-member LLC with a zero for taxable income (or close to it) is a no harm no foul tax return. In other words, it flies well below the radar but it also above reproach. As stated previously, Fred, Velma and Shaggy would get two K-1s, one from the MMLC and another from their S Corp.

Here is a brief recap of three possibilities given what we've discussed in the previous two schematics-

▲ The mothership (MMLLC) makes distributions to the S Corp members and issues a K-1, both in accordance with the Operating Agreement's provisions. The S Corps pick up the K-1 as ordinary income plus external income that is earned separately from the MMLLC (moonlighting… or another MMLLC perhaps).

▲ The mothership pays guaranteed payments to the S Corp members, which fluctuate according to the Operating Agreement's provisions. The MMLC distributes the remaining cash to the S Corp members and issues a K-1, both in accordance with the Operating Agreement.

▲ The mothership makes direct payments to the S Corps and those payments are recorded as fees for services. This can be called a corp to corp or business to business transaction. The individuals are the members of the MMLLC, and the external S Corps are recipients of the fees for services.

There are two additional considerations for the mothership baby S Corp construct-

▲ In California, you might want the mothership to be taxed as an S corporation to avoid the franchise tax being calculated on gross receipts. See California Multi-Member LLC S Corp Twist on page 63.

▲ It might be better for the mothership to be a C corporation rather than an LLC. There are some concerns with a member of an LLC being paid as a contractor to provide services that he or she would otherwise be required to provide to the LLC in a fiduciary capacity. There are other benefits of a C Corp as well. See C Corporation as Mothership on page 65.

Things to Work Through with Multiple Entities

There are some things you need to work through with the multi-entity arrangement. Depending on your situation, some of these things might be show-stoppers. However, don't take the first answer as the only answer. A multi-entity scenario is super common among popular groups like doctors, lawyers, accountants and financial advisors. If your tax professional or accountant says No, push a little harder. Same with your vendor (see below).

By the way, **WCG CPAs & Advisors** is a C corporation and pays a fee for service to each of its partners' S Corps. We know firsthand the ins and outs of this arrangement since we live it. Why a C Corp? We also have employees who own shares but are not partners per se.

Health Insurance

Check with your health insurance broker or point of contact on how the health insurance needs to be administered. Do we have the primary entity pay for it, and each S Corp reimburses the primary entity? Can the policies be split up and paid by each S Corp separately, or does that mess up the group policy rates? These are questions that need to be explored; again, just because you have a certain look to your health insurance coverage today does not mean it is cast in stone.

At times when using a professional employer organization (PEO) to administer your payroll and benefits, you might need to process a small shareholder salary or guaranteed payment at the mothership level for each owner to allow for health insurance coverage. This is turn reduces the fee for service or management fee that is paid out (a small payout matrix might be created). The difference between salary and guaranteed payment is whether the mothership is a partnership or an S Corp.

Professional Liability
This is similar to health insurance, but ideally the policy should be maintained at the primary entity level. For example, WCG's errors and omissions policy is held by WCG, but each partner is named as a principal of WCG and as such is covered by the single policy. This took minor coordination with our insurance provider, but since many accounting firms are set up similarly it was easy to add language in our Bylaws and Shareholder Agreements to satisfy. You might also have to name the S Corps as additional insureds.

Licensing and Compliance
We mentioned this previously, but we want to circle back on it again. Licensing and compliance can be a bit larger of a rock going up a bit steeper of a hill. If your trade or profession is governed by a regulatory body, you'll need to ensure the multi-entity arrangement is in compliance. Typically governing regulatory bodies want to ensure two things; first, the people in control are the ones licensed, and second, the licensed people are the ones earning revenue from the practice. In other words, they don't want some murky structure where a faceless business is practicing law or medicine, as an example, without individual licenses.

What has helped other licensed and certificated people is using the words "tax vehicle" when having this conversation. When explaining the multi-entity structure, try to focus on two things; the licensed people are still the people doing the work, and the structure is designed for tax efficiency. Luckily you shouldn't be the first one to introduce this concept to your governing body. Hopefully they give you the "yeah, yeah, yeah... slow down sparky... here's what we need from you to make this work" response.

401k Plans
We discuss this elsewhere, but 401k plans are ideally implemented at the mothership (primary entity) level, and then each baby S Corp adopts the plan as an adopting employer. Your 401k plan administrator should be able to help.

Depreciation
At times with the way the tax code works, especially Section 179, it might be challenging to drive net income down to a nominal amount in the primary MMLLC entity. Don't get hung up on this since it is uncommon; however, it might create a self-employment tax on the residual income.

In addition, Section 179 has limitations at the individual tax return level, and as such it is reported separately on the K-1 to the member or partner. There could be a situation where one member or partner's tax benefit is not proportional to his or her share of the revenue or profits. Don't get hung up on this either since we can probably align this correctly within the tax return; it will just take some mental gymnastics.

As an aside, Section 179 is not as popular with the current landscape of 100% bonus depreciation.

Professional Fees
More tax returns increase tax preparation fees. If you were just a MMLLC with your partner, you had a single business entity tax return. Creating a multi-entity arrangement adds at least two more business entity tax returns (S Corp tax return), and possible more depending on how many partners or owners there are. You might also have additional payroll "systems." One for clerical staff at the MMLLC level, and then one for each S Corp to pay out reasonable shareholder salaries to the owners.

Let's put some math to this conundrum. A three-owner MMLLC without the mothership and baby S Corp setup, would have all-in tax preparation only fees of about $4,500 annually, or $1,500 per person. If the mothership MMLLC baby S Corp strategy is deployed, the all-in business advisory services fee for each S Corp is about $4,320 annually (tax returns, payroll, consulting, planning) and the MMLLC would be about $1,500 to $1,800. This is about $4,800 per person, or a delta of $3,300 per person.

Is the $3,300 in additional fees worth it? Perhaps. It is challenging to put a value on squishy things like flexibility, office politics, varying tax risk profiles, enhanced individualized tax strategies, etc.

Asset Appreciation
This one is goofy, and 99% of the time won't come into play. But! If you owned a bunch of assets in your S corporation including an interest in the primary entity (the MMLLC), upon your death the S corporation would need to be valued to receive what is called a step up in basis. For example, you bought a house for $150,000. You die. The house is worth $500,000. Your heirs sell it for $500,000. There are no capital gains since the heirs receive a step-up in the basis to go from $150,000 to $500,000 upon your death.

The tricky part is valuing an S corporation since we would value the enterprise as whole. Sure, it would comprise of individual assets being assembled into an enterprise value but there could be some complication.

Another concern along these lines, which we also address in a later chapter, is the appreciation of assets. When you revoke an S corporation election or shutdown the business, the assets are distributed at fair market value. So, if your S Corp owns interests in the

MMLLC, and that interest has increased in value, there could be capital gains taxes without a transaction.

We solve this concern using the previous schematic where the interests in the MMLLC are owned individually rather than through an S Corp. We only express this concern should your member interest be held within your S Corp.

> Sidebar: We mentioned this in several different ways throughout this book, and we'll say it again here. There is a strong desire to put everyone you own and do into your S corporation. Don't! The primary purpose of an S Corp is to reduce the amount of earned income subjected to Social Security and Medicare taxes. Holding assets and investments in your S Corp rarely improves your tax position and usually yet unintentionally increases risk.

Recap of Benefits with Multiple Entities

Alright… we just explored some of the pains in the butts with a multi-entity structure. Let's recap the benefits so you can value-assess the pros and cons.

Eat What You Kill

Some people soften this phrase to Eat What You Hunt. It makes no difference to us… the end result is the same. Someone's eating, right? You want to ensure your efforts are rewarded appropriately however that is defined or calculated. A multi-entity arrangement allows for that while keeping your ownership percentage static. As mentioned previously, you can make tweaks with shareholder salaries to equalize or to provide an equitable outcome. Unfortunately, salaries can only do minor equalization tweaks without paying too much in Social Security and Medicare taxes.

Expenses and Fringe Benefits

You and your partner want to buy automobiles. Great! How much are we spending? Perhaps you want a small economic sedan and your partner wants the latest Ford-a-saurus. Sure, you could put a limit on the purchase amount where anything above that the partner or owner has to pay for separately. But what about maintenance? Or finance charges? Or registration fees? These additional expenses might be contingent on value.

Aside from automobiles, there are other fringe benefits that might be challenging. Partner A wants to insure his whole family. Partner B doesn't need insurance. Partner A wants to buy a work laptop for home. Partner B already has a home setup. The list goes on and on, like a Journey song.

Having a multi-entity structure keeps fringe benefits from becoming political hot potatoes around the office.

Reimbursements
Along the lines of fringe benefits comes reimbursements, and specifically Accountable Plan reimbursements (which we discuss in detail in a later chapter). Let's say your home office is 250 square feet and your home is 2,500 square feet. That is 10% business use. But your partner lives in an apartment, and her business use percentage is 25%. But! You have a mortgage and property taxes, whereas your partner pays rent. How do we keep that equitable? Tough!

Similar to automobiles, we can establish a not-to-exceed reimbursement limit but doesn't that hose the owner who has more expenses? It certainly does.

Office Politics
You fly first class and your partner slums it in economy. You want a new computer and your partner thinks a 486 is still the best. And if you know what a 486 is then you are certainly a product of the 90s. A multi-entity structure doesn't necessarily solve all office politics, but it takes away some of the sting since you can spend what you want and get the maximum tax benefit without being crimped by your partner.

Apportionment
As mentioned earlier, if your business activities including the locations of the owners span multiple states, a multi-entity arrangement will allow for less state scrutiny. Yes, you will pay your fair share of income taxes to each state that you have nexus in, but the states will have limited visibility into your world without requesting an audit. Why give them something to bother themselves with unnecessarily?

We expand on this next.

State Apportionment with Multiple Entities
Imagine you and another person want to form a business together, but you live in different states such as Minnesota and North Carolina. Where do you put the entity? In the end, it doesn't matter since you would probably have a foreign filing registration requirement in the other state. So, you domicile the entity in Minnesota but also file as a foreign entity in North Carolina.

What's the big deal? States get all bent out of shape on nexus and income apportionment. We have a whole chapter on this nexus stuff, but let's do a quick preview. Generally, there are two types of nexus triggers, either economic or physical. Economic refers to how much "business" is being conducted commonly based on revenue. Physical nexus is commonly viewed as "boots on ground," such as people or contractors (payroll), furthering your interests or "bricks and mortar," such as offices (property). What makes it slightly confusing is that most states attach a dollar amount to payroll and property; as such the mere existence doesn't necessarily mean you trigger nexus unless it exceeds a dollar amount.

So, the three nexus triggers are revenue, payroll and property. With sales tax nexus (as opposed to income tax nexus), the recent Wayfair decision has upheld the concept of "substantial" economic presence where essentially enough economic activity equals physical presence. Again, the Wayfair decision was about sales tax nexus, and not income tax nexus.

Sidebar on Nexus: This is similar to driving under the influence (DUI). Let's say your state has a 0.08% blood alcohol limit. You can still be considered driving under the influence even if you have less than 0.08%. However, if you are over 0.08% then the state automatically presumes you are driving under the influence no matter how well you walk the line or touch your nose. This is called a "bright line." States may argue you have nexus even if you do not cross the bright line, but if you do cross the bright line then it is automatic without argument or anything else to support it. Does that help?

If you trip the nexus wire, then the entity is on the hook for apportioning the taxable income among multiple states based on various formulas. One of the factors is naturally revenue, so if you trip nexus in two states, you must source revenue to each state. Next, each owner now has an income tax obligation in multiple states and is required to file non-resident tax returns in each state outside of his or her resident state. This is unavoidable, but what is avoidable to some degree is the scrutiny. How's that?

Using our Minnesota and North Carolina example, if the entity is domiciled in Minnesota, you might have to convince Minnesota that a big chunk of the taxable income is not theirs (i.e., the revenue earned in North Carolina). We find ourselves having to connect dots for revenue agents often since you commonly must report all revenues earned, and then split them off to other states. As such, states get to peer into your world and then make you defend it. Yuck.

Solution? We usually create an entity in Wyoming or some other "tax-inert" state, and then also create entities in each resident state of the owners. All revenues pour into the Wyoming entity which in turn pays out revenues as fees for services to the other entities (Minnesota and North Carolina, in our example). Does this allow the Minnesota owner to avoid North Carolina taxes? No. Taxable income is still apportioned between states, and each owner has an income tax obligation in multiple states. What this does, however, is reduce the scrutiny triggers since you only need to "show the cards" that are pertinent to each state.

This also avoids the discussion of K-1 income as well. K-1 income is generally considered investment or passive income, but if you materially participate in the generation of that income, it might be considered non-passive income or for some limited purposes, earned income (like for use with foreign earned income exclusion). What are we getting at here?

Let's run through an example (we explored this earlier, so this might be duplicative to some readers)-

Your Illinois S Corp is part owner of a California multi-member LLC that conducts business in several states. The MMLLC issues a K-1 to the S Corp for the pro rata ordinary business income, and then also apportions that income among the various states. California might argue that all the income to the S Corp is California income since the MMLLC is in California. But in reality, all the income came from other states and only made a pitstop in California. California might want to change the genesis of the revenue based on this alone.

Furthermore, California might consider the K-1 income to not be revenue or sales income at all. In other words, they might consider it investment, passive or non-passive income. Anything but revenue! Having it not be revenue or sales income prevents you from apportioning the revenue among several states, and possibly dipping below the economic nexus thresholds.

In summary, having the multi-member LLC issue payments for services provided to the partners' S corporations reduces the visibility that states have. Again, we are not doing anything wrong or dodging income tax; we are simply controlling the narrative. Why spend a bunch of resources to prove your innocence (unless you're O.J.)?

California Multi-Member LLC S Corp Twist

Sounds like a drink doesn't it? "Oh man, I was up all night pounding Cali Twist."

The problem with the previous MMLLC entity structure that issues invoices or makes fee for service payments, is that this works well in most situations except California. It still works in California as a structure, but the tax expense, namely the LLC fee, makes this egregious.

California's LLCs, including SMLLCs and MMLLCs, have an LLC fee based on gross receipts. Read that again. On gross receipts. If you make a $1,000,000 and have $950,000 in expenses, you still pay a franchise tax, called an LLC fee, computed on the $1,000,000.

The fee is "banded" as we say since it is not a straight calculation based on a percentage.

Gross Receipts	LLC Fee
250,000 to 499,999	900
500,000 to 999,999	2,500
1,000,000 to 4,999,999	6,000
5,000,000 +	11,790

What makes matters worse is if the S Corps receiving income from the MMLLC are domiciled in California, they also must pay a 1.5% franchise tax on the net income after expenses (profit). Therefore, the same dollar might be taxed twice; once at the MMLLC level as an LLC fee, and again at the S corporation level as a franchise tax. Yuck. Super yuck!

What can be done? Simple! We elect the MMLC to be taxed as an S Corp. Hang in there on this one!

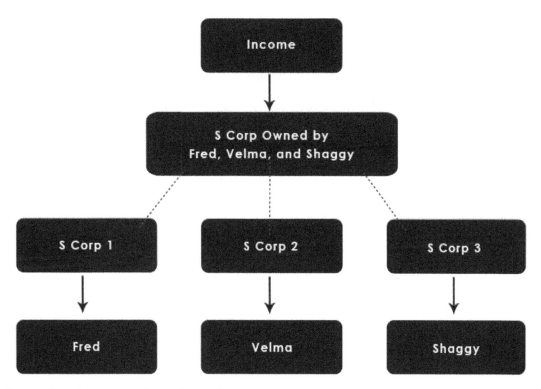

The graphic above is eerily similar to the previous one... except S Corp replaces MMLLC. The MMLLC is now taxed as an S Corp and Fred, Velma and Shaggy remain as shareholders. After paying the other S corporations a fee for Payments for Services Rendered or Outside Contractor or something similar, the MMLLC S Corp will have very little taxable income, such as $1,000. A franchise tax will be computed by California at 1.5% x $1,000 or $800, whichever is higher. Unavoidable.

The MMLLC S Corp would not pay salaries to its shareholders since the income is so low, and there isn't any cash available. In addition, distributions theoretically should be $0 since all the cash is leaving in the form of payments to the other S Corps. There might be some goofiness if the MMLLC has depreciating assets or loans or some other transaction which causes net income to be something other than a $1,000 and shareholder distributions to be something other than $0 (we discussed this previously). The important takeaway here is the reduction of the LLC fee that California imposes.

The other S Corps owned separately by Fred, Velma and Shaggy would carry on as normal. Pay expenses related to themselves, pay salaries, provide distributions, etc. Fred, Velma and Shaggy would get two K-1s, one from the MMLC taxed as an S Corp and another from their respective S Corp. This is exactly the same as our previous schematic in terms of K-1s.

Loan Basis in an S Corporation

This is a relatively common issue and when it pops up it can be brutal. As a partner in a multi-member LLC taxed as a partnership, if you personally guarantee a loan for the business, you create what is called loan basis. In a simple way, this allows you to take out more distributions from the business without creating a "distributions in excess of basis" situation which subsequently creates a capital gain.

If we are in California and want to reduce the egregious LLC fee, we S Corp elect the primary entity or "mothership." But under the auspice of an S Corp, you cannot create loan basis without the shareholder providing a loan directly to the S corporation. Huh? At the risk of belaboring this issue too much, consider the following-

You buy a piece of equipment for $100,000 and took out a loan in the business name including a personal guarantee. You deducted 100% of the purchase price using bonus depreciation. You had cash revenue of $100,000 and a deduction of $100,000 for the equipment leaving $0 at net ordinary business income. Nice! But, you have a $100,000 in the business checking account and like most business owners you sort of kind of would like to spend it.

In a MMLLC taxed as a partnership scenario, you would have created additional basis by guaranteeing the loan allowing you to distribute this $100,000 without creating a capital gain. In an MMLLC taxed as an S corporation scenario, the $100,000 distribution would be in excess of shareholder basis and capital gains taxes might be incurred. Your starting shareholder basis at the beginning of the year would not change since the business had $0 in net income. So, December 31's basis equals January 1's basis, but you have a bunch of cash earned from revenues and you used depreciation to reduce your ordinary business income to $0. Depreciation can be a cashless expense to reduce income. Good and bad, right? No taxable income, good. But no access to the cash without capital gains tax, bad.

Had the S Corp shareholders lent $100,000 to the business personally, then they would have created loan basis. Speak to your lender before doing some of this stuff! If your lender can give the shareholders the cash to lend or inject into the S Corp, and still retain a lien on equipment, that might be preferred.

This is not a showstopper per se, and we definitely geeked out a bit. Having said all this, there is a subtle difference we are not highlighting until right now. The above scenario is only problematic where you have a standalone S corporation. The three previous schematics were multi-entity arrangements with one distributing cash to the S Corp members as distributions and the other two distributing cash to the S Corps as fees for services or management fees or some other business to business mechanism. If the cash leaving the "mothership" is a distribution, this loan basis stuff can be a problem. If the cash leaving is a fee for service, this loan basis stuff is probably a non-issue.

Again, our apologies for getting into the weeds on this. We can always review your unique situation to help avoid this trap.

C Corporation as Mothership

The past handful of sections have discussed the various considerations of the mothership baby S Corp multi-entity arrangement. Another consideration is rather than the mothership being a multi-member limited liability company (MMLLC), it is a for-profit C corporation. Owners would be shareholders versus members / partners. Entity governance would be Articles of Incorporation with Bylaws and Shareholder Agreements versus Articles of Formation or Organization and Operating Agreements. Gee whiz, right?

Hang in there... here are the things to think about with a C Corp as the mothership.

Paying Members for Services
Section 707(a)(1) of the Internal Revenue Code reads-

> (a) Partner not acting in capacity as partner
> (1) In general
> If a partner engages in a transaction with a partnership other than in his capacity as
> a member of such partnership, the transaction shall, except as otherwise provided

in this section, be considered as occurring between the partnership and one who is not a partner.

This doesn't really tell us much, but there is some case law that suggests that the member must provide services to the LLC that are different from the activities for which the LLC was created or operated. For example, let's say a partner provided accounting services to a CPA firm by preparing a tax return for the firm's client. This suggests that the services provided are the same as the activities of the LLC.

However, there is case law suggesting that paying this same partner is not a problem at all. Slightly different facts with slightly different courts with all human nuances you would expect.

Keep in mind that the mothership baby S Corp does not avoid or reduce taxable income and therefore does not impact income taxes. Moreover, self-employment taxes might be reduced, sure, but they are reduced if the mothership elects to be taxed as an S Corp just the same (without the baby S Corps). As such, how is the IRS damaged?

Having said all this, a C corporation where you have shareholders (and not LLC members) might sidestep Section 707's interpretive concern.

No Mothership K-1
Corporations naturally do not issue K-1s. This in itself might not be that exciting, but it does shrink the mothership owners' tax footprint. If the entity is operating in California but one owner lives in Texas, and the entity issues a K-1 albeit a small one it still allows California to snoop around. They love to snoop and make wild assumptions.

Increasing Working Capital
When you increase working capital in a MMLLC, this usually increases net ordinary income on the K-1 issued to each member. As such, there is taxable income without cash, and that taxable income is computed at individual tax rates with the highest bracket being 37% federally. A C Corp would only pay 21% to increase working capital.

Why does increasing working capital increase income? In a mothership baby S Corp environment, profits are driven down close to zero with payments to the baby S Corps. This requires cash. Therefore, retaining cash prevents the mothership from reducing profits with payments to the baby S Corps. Sure, you could accrue the expense as a liability without cash leaving, but that can get challenging to reverse (make the payment) in future years without creating the very problem you are trying to avoid.

Using a line of credit solves might solve the working capital taxable income conundrum since the delta between 37% and 21% is likely to be higher than the tax-effected interest expense. Something to consider.

Ancillary Benefits
As mentioned in other parts of the book, a corporation allows you to issue stock to employees without the mess of member interest and the subsequent K-1 of an LLC.

The corporation might qualify for the Qualified Small Business Stock (QSBS) exemption upon sale. Loosely, Section 1202 of the Internal Revenue Code offers taxpayers (other than corporations) the potential to permanently exclude from taxable income $10 million om capital gains recognized in connection with the sale of the corporation. Yes, there are rules.

Summary
Here is a summary of the various scenarios in a multi-entity arrangement using the mothership baby S Corp construct-

▲ The mothership is an LLC and each member is an S corporation (the baby S Corps holds the interest in the LLC). This can be bad if crossing state lines between mothership and baby S Corp.

▲ The mothership is an LLC and pays a fee for service or management fee to the baby S Corps. This might be bad given some of the interpretations of Section 707.

▲ The mothership is a C corporation and pays a fee for service or management fee to the baby S Corps. All the taste of the mothership baby S Corp environment without the possible calories of Section 707, plus all the benefits above.

Holding Company versus Management Company
We've discussed this in a roundabout way, but this section hopefully ties some concepts together. Holding companies and management companies are not the same thing. One, as the name suggests, holds or owns underlying assets (other businesses). The other offers management services in exchange for fees, and typically doesn't own underlying assets.

The Holding Company
In the holding company scenario, each underlying entity is wholly owned by the holding company. Since these entities are usually single-member LLCs, they are disregarded for tax purposes and their owner (the holding company) absorbs all the revenue and expenses.

This seems simple enough, but it can also open several cans of worms.

Liability Protection

While the liability protection in LLCs is largely contractual (as opposed to torts and bad acts), if an underlying entity gets sued there is a possibility that the holding company gets dragged into the mess and all its assets (the other entities) might be pulled in as well. This is attorney stuff for sure, and you should review your unique situation with a qualified one.

State Nexus

If some of your underlying business activities are operating in multiple states, the holding company might have a multi-state tax footprint. This in itself is not bad, and with a management company, you are not subject to more or less state income tax. However, with a holding company you cannot control the narrative as easily (more on this in a bit).

Credit Worthiness

At times one of the entities might need to obtain credit independently to buy some equipment or enter into a contract such as a lease. While the holding company scenario can easily be explained, at times the underwriters or more aptly said, the sales prevention team, cannot wrap their head around a holding company tax return as it compares to the underlying entity's set of books and financial records. In other words, they want tax returns for the entity, and as a single-member LLC, they don't exist.

Balance Sheet

This is a minor housekeeping item, but it can create some headaches. When a holding company owns other assets such as real estate, portfolio investments or other entities, it books that asset at the historical purchase price. Therefore, if you purchase a house for $500,000 and five years later it is worth $650,000 it will still show as $500,000 on the holding company's balance sheet. No biggie.

However, if a holding company owns a piece of another business, do you record the initial investment? Sure, but what about subsequent fluctuations in the investment / capital account? Do we use a fair value calculation? Mark to market elections for portfolio investments? What if we are using this data to create a personal financial statement (PFS) for borrowing purposes? All kinds of fun, right? Please don't get too worked up on these nuances since they are situational, but they are things to consider.

Not all is bad with a holding company. For rental real estate, it can work well where each rental is owned by an LLC and each LLC is owned by a holding company. Holding companies are also great for the ease of transferring ownership of the underlying assets; instead of each asset being individually transferred or transitioned with various instruments, a holding company is like Santa with a big bag of stuff that moves together as one.

Moving on...

The Management Company

A management company arrangement stands in contrast to a holding company since all the associated entities remain owned by "the humans." For example, you would personally own the home building entity and the hard-money lending company as well as the management company as three separate entities. The home building entity would pay a management fee to the management company, and same with the lending company.

This in essence pumps all the income through the management company which naturally is taxed as an S corporation for tax efficiency and cocktail party bragging rights.

As mentioned above, and elsewhere in our book, state nexus is more controlled. Each entity might have to file a state income tax return or at least have the business activity apportioned to the correct states within Schedule C on your individual tax return. Additionally, the management company might have state nexus based on the fee earned from the underlying entity. Again, this doesn't alter your state income tax footprint, but it does cut down on what the state sees (let's make them work at it a bit, right?).

Some states are very aggressive and proving your calculations can be a pain with the holding company arrangement. No, creating a loss within the underlying entity does not preclude you from having to report the activities to the state (think rentals... a taxing jurisdiction has the right to audit your revenue and expenses even when combined they end in a loss).

An underlying entity with a management company arrangement also allows for a lot of flexibility. In a holding company situation, all the activities are brought into the holding company. You don't have a choice, and there might be times when this is not desirable. With a management company, you dictate how much of a fee is paid and all the underlying activities are encapsulated away from the management company.

The management company arrangement has some warts too.

Schedule C Audit Risk

Using our home building entity example above, this entity would likely be a single-member LLC and as such would be disregarded for tax purposes. In turn, these activities would be reported on Schedule C of your individual tax return (Form 1040). That in itself is not a big deal, but the audit risk of a Schedule C is much higher than the holding company S Corp.

To compound this risk is the fact that we are wanting to shift income to the management company with a management fee. You could tuck this into Advertising or Contract Labor or plainly as Management Fee on the Schedule C. You might even sprinkle it around between these expense categories. Perhaps work Commissions and Fees into the mix. Either way, you are driving income down to a nominal amount with expenses the IRS loves to snoop into like the Pink Panther. If you love audits, call your management fee Meals or Travel; that will get the IRS juices flowing for sure.

A solution to the audit rate risk concern is to have the underlying entities either be partnerships themselves, or in some cases S corporations. This would add the burden of additional tax returns. However, if the S Corp doesn't have material income (let's say $10,000 net ordinary income or less) shareholder payroll can be avoided. The audit rate of partnerships and S corporations is about a tenth of a Schedule C (0.4% versus 4%). Also, for those entities operating in California, you might need each underlying LLC to be taxed as an S corporation to reduce the LLC fee (which is based on gross receipts if not an S Corp).

Business Purpose
This concern is not a massive one, but the arrangement between the underlying entities and the management company must have a business purpose or commercial substance. Said in another way, the management company would likely need a light duty contract outlining the services being provided to the underlying entity, and the associated fee such as an hourly rate which is very flexible.

The cornerstones of business purpose are- the expenditure (for example, the management fee) must be ordinary and necessary. Ordinary is an expense that everyone in your industry incurs and you would argue that owner wages or management fees are synonymous. Necessary is an expense that must be incurred to maintain operations and you would argue that the expertise offered by the management company keeps the lights on.

Hybrid Accounting
Most small businesses are cash-based taxpayers, and record an expense when cash leaves the checking account or a credit card is swiped. The accounting conundrum with the management company arrangement is that you usually don't know the taxable business profits of the underlying entities until well after December 31. So, how do we put toothpaste back in the tube on March 1 when we have everything reconciled and financial statements are prepared?

The accounting industry and the IRS allow for a hybrid accounting system where accruals are used in a cash-based world provided it is consistently applied each year and does not attempt to artificially reduce taxes. The biggest example is employer 401k contributions. It is common to record a 401k Liability (the credit) and the associated 401k Expense (the debit) on a tax return since cash didn't leave until after December 31.

Using the 401k example above, we would record a Management Fee Payable and Management Fee Expense with a date of December 31, and then have the money move at some point after. One of the principles in accounting is the matching principle where expenses associated with revenue are recorded in the same period; the hybrid accounting system described above buttresses this principle.

The Flow of Money
In either situation, holding company or management company, the subsidiary entities or business units have their own business checking accounts to receive direct payments to pay expenses specific to themselves. Next, leftover cash is moved to the holding company or management company. In a holding company, this money movement is referred to an owner distribution since the holding company is the owner (not the humans). In a management company, this money movement is simply a management fee or some similar expense in a business-to-business transaction.

Regardless of holding versus management company arrangement, the money temporarily lands there to pay overall common expenses (such as tax return preparation, legal expenses, Accountable Plan reimbursements, etc.) including owner salaries and / or distributions. What should be avoided in both arrangements is to distribute money directly to the human owners at the underlying / subsidiary entities. Said differently, the money needs to double hop from underlying entity to holdco / mgmtco to humans.

Pure LLC Holding Company
The previous section was about holding companies versus management companies, but this particular LLC holding company variant does not have any commercial activity. What are we talking about here? Let's say two people want to own an airplane. They could title it in their own names such as Buzz Aldrin and Amelia Earhart JTWROS. The fancy JTWROS is joint tenancy with rights of survivorship. This means that should Amelia die before Buzz, typically Buzz would absorb her interest in the airplane.

Time moves along, and Buzz and Amelia want to bring in Pete Mitchell as a third owner. They could add Maverick to the title because no one really knows who Pete Mitchell is, but this gets a bit cumbersome. If you add financing with personal loan guarantees to the mix, it could get messy if the bank wants to re-write the loan docs to add Pete… err… Maverick.

Rather, Buzz and Amelia would create a multi-member limited liability company (MMLLC) called The Little Red Bus LLC. This entity would hold title to the airplane but it would not have any commercial activity. The LLCs's Operating Agreement would dictate how members could come and go, what happens if one member passes away, and other entity governance items. Therefore, when Pete Mitchell wants to be a part-owner, he would simply acquire member interest in the LLC. Title would not change since The Little Red Bus LLC owns the airplane, and Buzz, Amelia and Maverick own the LLC. Loan documents would not change, but perhaps an additional personal guarantee would be required.

LLCs are being used more and more in non-commercial or non-operating environments to make transfer of ownership super easy. We see this with boats, exotic car collections, art, among other things. Also, since there is no commercial activity, a tax return would not be required. Yes, an EIN would be necessary for a business banking account, but that in itself does not trigger a tax return filing requirement.

Economic versus Equity Interests

You can own different interests in an entity, and the most common are economic and equity. Generally, as an equity owner you are an owner of the business's equity which includes its assets (tangible, and intangible such as goodwill) minus the liabilities and debts. This also typically means that your equity interest entitles you to a share of the proceeds upon sale (unless contracts and agreement state otherwise).

An economic interest is generally a share of the profits but does not necessarily entitle you to the equity or value of the entity itself. Many businesses will have a profit-sharing plan which is similar to an economic interest, however these are usually reserved for certain employees or groups of employees, and not necessarily memorialized in a business's Operating Agreement. Here are some examples-

You work for Google and they have a profit-sharing plan where you receive a prorated amount of the allocated profit sharing based on a formula (such as salary and years of service). This is generally not viewed as owning an economic interest in Google, however Google probably has at least a contractual obligation to you.

You work for an accounting firm. You are paid 30% of the gross revenues less direct labor attributed to your efforts. This payment is made directly to you and bypasses payroll (i.e., not reported on your W-2). The Operating Agreement of the accounting firm reflects all this, and you are named a non-voting member. This is commonly regarded as an economic interest, and as such you are technically a partner in the accounting firm and will receive annual K-1s reflecting your earnings.

Subtle difference.

What's the big deal? At times you might not want to immediately give away or sell the net worth of a business to a partner. Rather, you want to split the difference; you want them to feel like an owner, think like an owner and get compensated like an owner, without actually owning the sticks and bricks. Later, down the road and upon reflection, an economic interest can be piggybacked with or wholly converted to an equity interest.

How does the entity structures work with an economic interest? It is not much different than the arrangements discussed in this chapter. You could very easily have a multi-member LLC which has two equity members and three additional economic members. All five members would receive K-1s reflecting their portion of the business activities, however, only the two equity members would have capital accounts.

The previous example does not work where the MMLLC is taxed as an S Corp, and without leveraging S corporation elections the members would be pay unnecessary self-employment taxes. One solution is where the economic member owns an entity taxed as an S Corp, and the primary entity pays a fee for service to the S Corp (see previous section for schematics of how this mothership baby S Corp construct looks visually). Usually, contracts memorializing this fee for service arrangement are also created and executed.

So, a couple of lessons here. Economic interests-

▲   are wonderful tools to provide ownership in a sense,

▲   allow for baby steps of bringing in a new business partner (stress test your relationship), and

▲   can leverage the mothership LLC and baby S Corp concepts for tax efficiency,

Expanding ownership is tricky and it requires legal documents to be safe; but it is also unlimited in terms of buy-in arrangements, splits, vesting schedules, exit strategies, etc. We can help with the imagination! You'll freak out because casting future unknowns in stone can keep you awake at night; we can also help make things malleable without being locked into a once-was-good-but-now-is-bad deal.

Structuring Deals with Angel Investors

We are only going to scratch the surface on the types of deals and arrangements that you might see out there. Our intent with this section is to illustrate some of the considerations. One of the common statements we get from clients at **WCG CPAs & Advisors** is, "I have a guy who is giving me $100,000 to help me start my business." Our next response is, "Will the guy be an investor, lender or both?" Then your response is stunned silence... which is certainly re-assuring. Not!

There are many ways to handle this, and no one way is always the best. It depends on humans, emotions and personal objectives. Don't forget the golden rule where the person with the gold makes the rules (you hear this often in our book, but it is so true).

Here are some ideas and various considerations-

Investor is Truly a Lender
If the investor wants to get paid back first with interest then make him or her a bank, and pay or accrue interest accordingly. Done. This is also finite, right? After the loan is paid back, the cord is cut, and everyone lives on like perfect strangers.

Investor is a Lender with Economic Interest
Same as above, but once the loan is paid back the investor continues in an economic interest capacity and has claim to some of the business profits. Perhaps this claim expires at a predetermined time such as five years following loan re-payment. This is tricky since the investor is both a lender and an owner of sorts which could be conflicted.

This is commonly called a profits interest where you receive a share of the future profits (revenue less expenses) and the appreciation of the assets of the business. There are some rules, with the most common one being "the service partner must receive only a profits interest in the partnership in exchange for the contribution of services." In turn, the profits interest partner cannot be given a share of current capital in exchange for the contribution of services. This makes sense since you usually have tax basis in your capital, and to have tax basis you needed to have paid taxes on that capital at some point in the past.

Investor is a Lender with an Interest Upon Sale
Similar to above, but the lender gets a piece of the action upon sale. Perhaps the loan is paid back as necessary, with the sale option enduring into perpetuity. The thought process is, "hey I helped you get off the ground and now you owe me beyond the 8% interest I charged." Surely these are your inside words and they are presented in a softer way to others.

Some caution is in order too. You might not have any control regarding the sale such as terms, timing, etc. For example, you have an agreement that upon sale you get 10% of the proceeds. Great! What constitutes a sale? What if a 100% owner sells 60% of the business but retains the remaining 40%? Hmmm. In these cases, you could draft the agreement to read that upon sale, partial sale or change in control, there is a payout.

That change in control is a big deal since you probably have a personal connection with the owner, and now you are tethered to someone else. People are pro-marriage, but they generally do not want to be told who to marry.

Back to the original idea. The investor is initially the lender but has a contractual interest should an event occur regardless of the current loan status (paid off or not). These particular arrangements need to be stress tested with various scenarios and contingencies.

Investor is an Owner

Rather than recording a loan on the books, the injected cash is credited to the investor's capital account. The investor may get a return of capital prior to other owners per an agreement. In other words, distributable cash goes to the investor first as a return of his or her original investment. The splits can vary; for example, the investor contributed $90,000 and you contributed $10,000. You could still own 90% of the entity while the investor only owns 10% (an exact flip-flop). We call this special allocation.

Loans Versus Capital

Most lenders want some sort of guarantee from the owners. As such, the angel investor might demand that you guarantee the loan personally which can make a failed business or real estate venture scenario a messy one causing ruined friendships, awkward Thanksgivings and all that fun stuff. Conversely, an investor who wants to be an owner (versus a lender) and injects capital now has a seat at the table so-to-speak and might not fully let you run the venture the way you see fit.

Your Capital as a Loan

While there might be some good reasons, typically you do not personally lend money to your single-owner business. We hear it all the time, "my business owes me money." Unlikely. Rather, what is meant is that you've invested money into the business and / or perhaps you've paid for business things with personal funds (since the business was broke). This is invested capital and not a loan. When there is distributable cash, you can take that capital out of your business generally tax-free.

Keep in mind that a loan requires a loan document, amortization, interest expense (which becomes income to you) among other things. Therefore, while the venture might have your money, it doesn't technically owe it to you. However, you are allowed to take it back when it's sitting on a pile of cash.

S Corp Rigidity

As we have explored in other parts of our book, S corporations can be super rigid with the splitting of distributable cash. At times you also want to get a rip of the action ahead of others. In partnerships, not taxed as an S Corp, these "payments ahead of others" are usually in the form of guaranteed payments. You do not have this option in an S Corp unless it is in the form of increased shareholder salaries which largely defeats the purpose of an S corporation election.

What about varying capital accounts in an S Corp situation? Let's say you and another person are consultants and you ban together to form a 50-50 partnership, and you also want to use the S Corp election to save on self-employment taxes. Furthermore, you have $100,000 to invest and your partner has $1,000 and some average looks. A consideration (not a rule or a must-have) would be to have each of you inject $1,000 in cash as capital, and then you provide the remaining $99,000 to the shiny new S corporation as a loan. This allows for an elegant way for you to get your cash out.

Ineffective S Corp Elections

Limited liability companies are amazingly flexible in structuring a deal. As mentioned elsewhere, you can build an LLC with all kinds of deal structures such as-

▲ Special allocation of income and losses (including qualified income offsets to maintain compliance),

▲ Liquidating distributions made in accordance with positive capital account balances,

▲ Employment agreements,

▲ Buy-sell and redemption agreements, and

▲ Options and warrants, including convertible debt.

This list isn't exhaustive, but what this is telling us is that certain agreements inside and outside the Operating Agreement might make the S Corp election ineffective. Why? Special allocations are simply not allowed in an S Corp. That's easy. However, the outside agreements such as employment, buy-sell, redemption, options, warrants, debt instruments, etc. (all the fun stuff in this section), can create a second class of stock. As you might recall, an S corporation can only have one class of stock (voting and non-voting is allowed, however) according to IRC Section 1.1361-1. Recall? Of course you do!

We talk more about this in a later chapter.

Front-End Back-End

There are two things to consider when bringing in another owner or becoming that new owner yourself. Do you want to make money on the front-end, or the back-end, or both? In other words, do you want to make money along the way as an investor owner getting a return on investment from operations? Or… do you want to forego some money from operations, and put more emphasis on an eventual sale?

> Sidebar: You might hear the term liquidity event. According to Investopedia, a liquidity event is an acquisition, merger, initial public offering (IPO), or other action that allows founders and early investors in a business to cash out some or all of their ownership shares or interest.

Of course, your risk aversion and the risk versus reward thing are going to drive this decision including your current lifestyle and income needs. Are you the person who works hard trusting you'll get paid in the end? Or are you the person who wants money today and is willing to sacrifice the big payday at the end? Everyone is different. Every deal is different. You just need to find one that fits everyone involved.

Venture Capital

As we've mentioned here and there, and at the risk of over stating it, the one with the gold makes the rules. This is the Golden Rule. Some venture capitalists and other "professional" investors have specifications before they will entertain an investment. For example, an investor might require a C corporation domiciled in Delaware. Period. Take it or leave it. Why?

Who knows? Perhaps that is what they have always done, and why change now? Or… perhaps that is how the investor was able to raise capital and the prospectus outlined this detail such as "all equity investments will be made into C corporations domiciled in Delaware only."

By now you should have a good handle on the fact that a C corporation is a lousy tax vehicle and that Delaware only adds to your tax filing headache if you operate in a state other than Delaware. But! If that is what it takes to receive seed money for your big idea, then that is what you do.

Nuts and Bolts of Adding Another Owner

Let's assume you have a single-member LLC, and you want to add a 20% member for $50,000. What are the accounting mechanics behind this transaction? It depends. If you are personally receiving the $50,000 then you are selling a part of your interest directly to the new owner which might create a capital gain to you, as a seller.

Conversely, if the LLC is receiving the $50,000 as a capital injection and carving out a 20% interest to this new member, this is not a taxable event. This also does not mean the business is worth $250,000 (1/5 = $50,000 so 4/5 = $200,000). When a business valuation is performed, the enterprise is valued as a whole, and then discounts are taken for lack of control (minority interest) and then lack of marketability (difficulty in converting ownership into cash).

Therefore, this $50,000 is just a number the two of you came up with based on some data. When that $50,000 is received by the LLC it becomes a part of the capital account of the new owner. This is a tax-less transaction for the existing or original owner(s).

Let's recap this a bit. When adding an owner, you can-

▲ Sell or gift a portion of your interest or shares to them, or

▲ The entity can sell shares or "create" an interest in exchange for consideration (usually money but it could easily be another asset like property).

In the case of an LLC (versus a corporation), the second scenario is preferred. There is an election under Section 754 which allows a new member (partner) to receive a step-up in basis of the entity's assets which might lead to additional depreciation and amortization benefits. The "754 election" as it is commonly tossed around at parties and accounting back alleys aligns the new member's portion of inside basis (the assets inside the entity) with the outside basis (the investment by the new member). This can also occur when you buy out another member (partner).

Sorry for throwing you into the weeds on this little tax code issue.

Injecting Different Property
This is one of those Pet Shop Boys "I've got the brains, You've got the looks, Let's make lots of money" sort of things. The best way of describing this deal arrangement is with a real-life example.

WCG has a client who helped a business (let's call them ABC Co) develop a product. However, he wasn't fully paid for his services (about $836,000) and was willing to get paid on the backend. The product cost about $7.5 million dollars to develop and ABC fronted all the costs.

They wanted to create another entity where our client was going to be a 25% owner and ABC was going to be the remaining 75%. Initial capitalization was low since our client did not want to realize any income until later. In other words, if the injected product was valued at $10 million, our client might have to realize the $836,000 deferred income as part of the $2.5 million capital account. There were a bunch of other basis issues that are not worth going into with this approach.

So, it was abandoned for a different arrangement.

The plan was to keep developing the product and eventually sell out to another business who would take it to market (a liquidity event). If this new entity sold for $12 million, then it would be easy to pay out $7.5 million to ABC and $826,000 to our client, and then split the remainder 75% - 25%. But what if it sold for $5 million? Who gets what and when?

We agreed on various tranches. Tranche 1, ABC received $2,500,000. Tranche 2, our client received $278,000. Then Tranche 3 was 90% ABC and 10% our client for the remainder of what was available. Finally, there was a Tranche 4 should the business be sold for more than $8.4 million or so that was split 75-25 (or along party lines of the member interests).

This was a shared risk approach. Certainly, ABC was the 800lb gorilla and wanted to recoup a big chunk first, but it was also willing to reduce our client's risk as each tranche was satisfied.

These things are unique since they involve humans and emotions, and various risk horizons. But as they say, there are a thousand ways to skin a cat, and as such, only limited imaginations get in the way of a good deal.

Recap of Angel Investors

Are we suggesting avoiding these situations entirely? No. At times they are the only options available. We just want to let you know of the concerns and considerations. Marriage is all about love, and divorce is all about money. Business is no different, and in some respects can be worse.

The cool thing is that you have several options and you can certainly rip off best practices or other ideas, smash them up, and create your own plan.

ESOPs and S Corporations

What happens when you have an S corporation but want to implement an ESOP? First, what the heck is an ESOP. According to a May 2017 article in the Journal of Accountancy-

ESOPs were created by the Employee Retirement Income Security Act of 1974 (ERISA), P.L. 93-406, and have long been used as a vehicle for ownership succession planning. According to The ESOP Association, there are approximately 10,000 ESOPs in the United States, covering 10.3 million employees. While ESOPs exist in a broad range of industries, they are most prevalent in manufacturing and construction companies, as well as engineering and architecture firms.

The basic gist is that the present owners sell their shares to the ESOP and typically take back a note from the ESOP (a loan). The ESOP can also obtain outside financing to purchase the outstanding shares. From there the business provides the funding to the ESOP to pay its debt obligation.

Of course, there are stats everywhere suggesting that employee recruitment, retention and satisfaction all improve with an ESOP... but that can be costly too. According to the National Center for Employee Ownership (**www.nceo.org**) and affirmed by a Journal of Accountancy article, the cost to set up an ESOP which includes the feasibility analysis, paperwork and initial valuation ranges from $40,000 to $80,000 (and higher). As such this requires some careful consideration.

However, succession planning is important in certain businesses. If you are a one-person engineering consultant perhaps succession is simply riding off into the sunset. Like Def Leppard sings, it is better to burn out than to fade away. But if you have a business that you would like to see carry on my wayward son while you fade away, like a smash up of Def Leppard and Kansas, then an ESOP might be the answer.

There is no need to regurgitate information that is readily available elsewhere. Please understand two things; first, ESOPs can provide some immediate tax benefits and second, S corporations have more limitations and annoyances than C corporations with respects to ESOPs. Here are some links-

wcginc.com/6113   NCEO's article on ESOPs and S Corporations

wcginc.com/6111   Journal of Accountancy on ESOPs in a CPA Firm

Another Employee Ownership Situation
WCG has implemented the poor man's version of an ESOP where our primary entity is a C corporation which has a robust Shareholder Agreement for buying and selling of shares. Why do you need a Shareholder Agreement? If you own 5% of a privately held small business, you basically own 0%. Huh?

Unless there is a market (public or private) where the minority shareholder can sell his or her shares, a 5% ownership in a privately held small business is not marketable and therefore not as valuable. In the business valuation world we call this degradation of value a discount for lack of control (DLOC) and a discount for lack of marketability (DLOM).

Therefore, a business needs to create a market both on the buy and sell side. For example, CPA firms typically are valued at about 1.0 to 1.2 times gross revenue depending on the book of business quality (age of clientele, average fee, amount of recurring revenue, etc.). Using our example, you could set up a program where an employee could buy shares using a valuation formula. Let's say you have a CPA firm and you believe the multiple is 1.2, and you also want to give your employees a 10% discount. You are growing and so you also want to use an average revenue number based on the previous two years to smooth out the value.

Your per share value formula would be (90% x Avg Revenue x 1.2) / number of issued shares. This could be used for the buy side, and on the sell side.

On the buy side you could allow employees to purchase shares annually. You could also issue shares as a form of compensation (yes, that would find its way onto a W-2). You could also use this arrangement for a future owner where he or she pays some cash and obtains bank financing for the remainder allowing acquisition of a large chunk of shares. Many business-oriented banks will put together a deal where the new owner puts in 20% and the bank finances the 80% using the original owners as a backstop for collateralization. In other words, the sellers or original owners would promise to buy the shares back from the bank upon default, should it occur. You might have to post collateral to satisfy the bank's risk department.

On the sell side you could allow employees to sell annually as well, and only upon separation from the business. By creating a market, a 5% minority ownership now has value. Some other considerations include that no person or entity other than current employees can own shares, and should an employee get divorced he or she cannot give the marital property to the other spouse.

Another consideration is voting rights. Do the minority shareholders have a vote? Perhaps by proxy? Ownership without a voice might not feel like ownership to your employees. How about wholesale sale? In other words, are the majority owners allowed to sell the entire business including the employees' interests (usually Yes, through drag along rights)? Do the employees get a first right of refusal to buy out the majority owners?

Our example above was straightforward since CPA firms have enough market data to determine a gross revenue or sales multiple. Other businesses use multiples as well such as insurance agencies, financial advisor firms, franchised restaurants among several others. If a market approach to valuation using a gross revenue or sales factor cannot be used, a more complicated valuation approach or agreed-upon formula must be used.

How does the current owner(s) pull money out? Our schematic illustrates an arrangement that could be followed.

In our arrangement, income flows into the C corporation which is owned by you and your employees. A contractual arrangement would exist where the C Corp would pay your S Corp a management fee leaving a small amount of C corporation income behind (near zero).

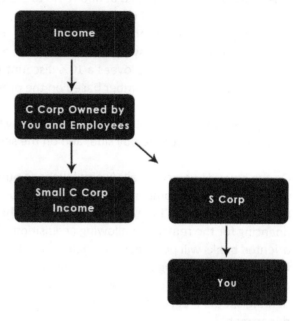

A minor thorn to this arrangement is the accumulation of working capital at the C Corp level. As a business grows, it will need increased working capital. At WCG we peg that to be 5% of the current year's revenue. Whenever you grow working capital, you will pay taxes on the growth since the money is left behind in the C Corp and not paid out as a fee for service to the S Corps.

This is a generalization and proper consultation with a tax professional (us) and an attorney (others) is a must. Under current SEC laws, such as Regulation D, and Colorado Securities laws, WCG does not have to register our stock as a regulated security. Your state might be different.

Medical C Corporation

One the many challenges facing small business owners is health insurance and out-of-pocket medical bills. Generally speaking, self-employed health insurance premiums, including dental and vision, are directly paid by the business and are deducted as Officer Compensation on a business tax return That's good. Health Savings Account (HSA) contributions are also directly paid by the business and are deducted as Officer Compensation. More good news!

As we stated elsewhere, these fringe benefits inflate Officer Compensation but are later deducted on the owners' individual tax returns. We call this an "in and out" since the net change on the individual tax return is zero and the actual deduction takes place on the business tax return. But what about out-of-pocket medical expenses like co-pays, lab fees, prescriptions, etc.?

Health Reimbursement Arrangements (HRA) have been around since the 1960s and became very popular in the 1990s, but they recently went through a transformation as a result of the Affordable Care Act. The 21st Century Cures Act and H.R. 34 established the Qualified Small Employer HRA (QSEHRA, pronounced "Q Sarah" opposite of "Suzie Q"). Beginning in 2017, qualified businesses with fewer than 50 employees who did not offer group health plans could use a QSEHRA to reimburse for health insurance premiums and out-of-pocket medical expenses.

There is a catch! A greater than 2% shareholder of an S corporation cannot participate in a QSEHRA. They can, however, participate in a garden variety Section 105 HRA but still do not enjoy the income tax deduction of HRA reimbursements. Huh? If an S Corp reimburses a shareholder, that amount is added to Box 1 of the W-2 as Officer Compensation just like self-employed health insurance premiums and HSA contributions. The huge difference is that HRA reimbursements are not later deducted on the owners' individual tax returns as they are with self-employed health insurance premiums and HSA contributions. Instead, they are reported on Schedule A as medical expenses subject to all the usual limitations.

There is still a savings however! As we will reiterate many times throughout the book, self-employed health insurance, HSA contributions and HRA reimbursements can be leveraged into providing a lower yet reasonable S Corp shareholder salary.

Let's assume that data support an $80,000 Officer Compensation as reasonable.

Officer Compensation	80,000	
less Self-Employed Health Insurance	11,800	
less Health Savings Account	7,200	max for 2021
less Health Reimbursement Arrangement	10,000	
Salary Needed to be Paid	51,000	

As you can see, we are "building" Officer Compensation by adding wages, health insurance, HSA and HRA components together. How does this help?

Here is a quick table that illustrates how leveraging the non-salary components of Officer Compensation reduces Social Security and Medicare taxes-

Box 1 (Wages Subject to Income Tax)	80,000
Box 3 (Wages Subject to Social Security Tax)	51,000
Box 5 (Wages Subject to Medicare Tax)	51,000
Total Social Security and Medicare Taxes Saved	4,437

Recall that earlier we determined $80,000 was considered a reasonable amount of Officer Compensation (of course, yours will vary). But because of other components, we were able to pay a salary of only $51,000. This $29,000 reduction in salary saved $4,437 in Social Security and Medicare taxes. In the absence of other components, we would have had to pay $80,000 in wages. Yuck.

Back to the HRA. In our example, the S Corp reimbursed $10,000 in out-of-pocket medical expenses. Unlike self-employed health insurance and HSA contributions, there is not an income tax savings, but there is a Social Security and Medicare tax savings as you see above. Specifically, $10,000 x 15.3% or $1,530 was saved by having an HRA.

TASC charges about $600 for HRA plan administration (2021 rates). As such, an HRA in this example put a $1,000 in your pocket. Not too shabby for very little effort.

How could we get an income tax deduction using an HRA? Good question. That is where a C corporation comes into play.

A C Corp is not a pass-through entity and therefore it does not have to worry about the greater than 2% shareholder rules that S Corps face. Therefore, a small business owner could set up a C Corp that offers services to an S Corp in a business to business transaction (such as a fee for service agreement), and then pays medical bills on behalf of the C Corp employee(s). The S Corp's income would naturally be reduced by the fees paid to the C Corp which would have a double benefit; lower income taxes and a possibly reduced shareholder salary.

You would need a business purpose for the C corporation such as providing marketing or management services. To buttress this, you could identify certain expenses to be paid from the C Corp. For example, you would pay for web hosting, SEO services and other marketing expenses from the C corporation, plus the medical expenses.

The savings might be significant. TASC boasts a 20% add-on to your marginal tax rate; this 20% seemingly represents the Social Security, Medicare and state income tax savings added to your federal marginal income tax rate. We don't necessarily agree since the Social Security and Medicare component is already available with an HRA deployed in a standalone S corporation. But… if we play along… if you spent $10,000 in out-of-pocket medical expenses at a combined marginal tax rate of 30% (24% + 6% for state), then you save $3,000 by using the C corporation entity structure. An additional tax return would be required at around $1,000 in tax preparation fees so you pocket $2,000.

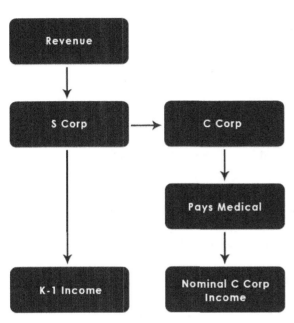

If you have $20,000 in annual medical expenses, then your savings would be $6,000. Those are real dollars.

What about audits? C Corps with under $250,000 in assets have a 0.5% audit rate and S Corps have a 0.4% audit rate. Individual tax returns with a small business are upwards to 2%, and even higher with travel, meals and auto expenses (the low hanging IRS fruit). As a side note, if your C corporation has $20B in assets you audit rate in 2017 was 58%. Luckily most people reading this book are about $20B away from having to worry.

More discussion is required to ensure the C Corp idea fits your objectives, but you can see the basic arrangement.

Fleischer Tax Court Case

Ryan Fleischer tempted fate with an unreasonable salary and brought a case to the Tax Court that has reverberating consequences. In our opinion, had he been reasonable with his S Corp salary we wouldn't be faced with this issue. As the saying goes, Pigs get fed and hogs get slaughtered. We are not comparing Ryan to a hog of course, but we are certainly mindful of the risks people take. Those who try to take too much end up in trouble.

Did Ryan try to take too much? It is hard to say since that is a matter of opinion. So, what is the issue?

Ryan Fleischer was a financial advisor for LPL and Mass Mutual, and he received payments and ultimately a 1099-MISC to himself personally. Per FINRA's Rule 2040 compensation payments cannot be made to an entity unless that entity itself is a registered broker-dealer (and in some cases a Registered Investment Advisor, an RIA).

Ryan would report this income on Schedule C but then have a singular line item for "Other Expenses" resulting in a $0 profit. Too convenient, right? Through a random audit, the IRS issued a tax deficiency for all the years in question amounting to over $41,000.

Here is a summary of his business income and salaries-

Tax Year	Net Income	Salary	%	Distributions
2009	46,775	34,851	75%	11,924
2010	182,498	34,856	19%	147,642
2011	150,323	34,996	23%	115,327

The salaries seem to jump out, don't they? According to the Bureau of Labor Statistics, a personal financial advisor's median 2017 pay was $90,640. Keep this in mind as we explore some other issues. Quick math would suggest that his salary was about a third of what the median salary was in 2017.

The case was docketed as Fleischer v. Commissioner, Tax Court Memo 2016-238.

The Tax Advisor's March 1, 2017, article summarized the crux of the Tax Court's decision-

> The Tax Court stated that, based on precedent going back to the Supreme Court's decision in Lucas v. Earl, 281 U.S. 111 (1930), "the first principle of income taxation is that income must be taxed to him who earned it."
>
> In a case involving an individual and a corporation, the question that the court must ask is, "Who controls the earning of the income?"
>
> For a corporation to be in control of the income, two elements must be present:
>
> (1) The individual providing the services must be an employee of the corporation whom the corporation can direct and control in a meaningful sense; and
>
> (2) "there must exist between the corporation and the person or entity using the services a contract or similar indicium recognizing the corporation's controlling position" (Johnson, 78 T.C. 882, 891 (1982)).

The Tax Court essentially agreed with the IRS since Fleischer was named on the contract with LPL and Mass Mutual, and not his S corporation. However, as mentioned before, FINRA's Rule 2040 was designed to make financial advisors accountable and transparent, but it also created a roadblock from a tax efficiency perspective. In other words, had Fleischer provided consulting services to a singular client, he could have entered his S Corp into a contract with the client and the client could issue a 1099-MISC to his S Corp's EIN.

What can be done? First, the easiest thing to do is amend the contract between the financial advisor and the broker-dealer / investment advisor firm to give the S Corp privity to the contract (or some sort of recognition). The next step is to enter into an employment contract between you, the financial advisor, and your S Corp plus updating the Bylaws and Shareholder Agreement. Please contact us for some sample language that we've seen others use.

There is a company called Succession Resource Group (SRG), Inc. who positions themselves as being able to defend the "Fleischer issue," and their contact information is 503-427-9910 and info@successionresource.com. Give them a shout. Again, according to SRG these provisions satisfy the Tax Court's big gripe. That is the easy stuff, and it might require legal assistance.

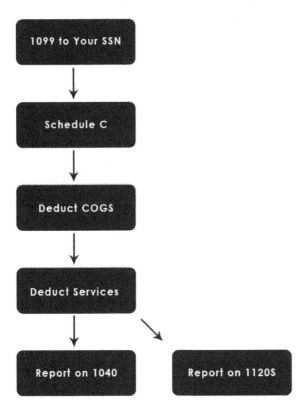

For long-term success consider that the world of financial advisors is changing dramatically. Most are leaving the broker-dealer world of commission sales for the investment advisor world of advisory fees. FINRA generally governs broker-dealer representatives while the SEC governs investment advisor representatives (the B/D versus IA worlds).

Further, a lot of financial advisors, investment advisors, Certified Financial Planners, etc. are creating their own Registered Investment Advisor (RIA) firms and electing those to be taxed as an S Corp. Yes, registering your firm as a broker-dealer or registered investment advisor (RIA) with either the State or SEC (depending on size) can be expensive. Most RIAs can be formed for about $6,000 where broker-dealers are much more cash intensive between the registration fees and the capital requirements.

The other option, as other business consultants have kicked around, is to prepare a Schedule C with the income related to the activities governed by FINRA as issued on a 1099-MISC. From there "cost of goods sold" expenses such as advisor fees, technology fees, insurance and other expenses directly related to the generation of that income are deducted.

Next a consulting arrangement is entered into between the financial advisor and the S Corp to provide marketing and consulting services to the financial advisor. Lastly, the Schedule C has some nominal profits remaining and the S Corp pays out a reasonable salary from the consulting arrangement. See the schematic below.

Does this appear like an end-around? Perhaps. Is it unreasonable? No, we do not believe so but at the same time this position has not been directly tested. Again, the tax discrimination that occurs simply out of a securities rule from FINRA is patently unfair given the financial burden of compliance. Fleischer sells his knowledge as a consultant, good to go. Fleischer sells his knowledge as financial advisor, no good. A technical housekeeping glitch is preventing good tax planning that most small business owners are able to receive.

Ryan Fleischer was well-represented by Howard Kaplan who pitched several good arguments, but in the end he lost. Ryan did not want to appeal to Federal court since he already spent $50,000 in legal fees; he might have also felt like his position was untenable given the current legal landscape. Unfortunately, this case shines a bright light on the common practice among tax professionals to nominate the income from an individual's SSN to his or her S corporation's EIN.

In our opinion, and the opinion of several other legal and tax professionals, had Ryan paid himself a reasonable salary he wouldn't have gotten spanked so hard by the IRS. But that is conjecture, and certainly wasn't an opinion expressed by the Court. However, in conversation with Ryan, he stated that the IRS audit was random yet he strongly feels it was deliberate because of his political party registration. Draw your own conclusions.

Having said that, our recommendation remains to start heading towards registering your business such that you can enter it into a contract with the broker-dealer / investment advisor firm.

Joint Ventures

Using the previous example from this chapter, the two insurance agents could simplify life by entering into a joint venture agreement that allowed for revenue and expense sharing, without the formality of the business entity structure above.

Be careful here however! The IRS could impute that this is a partnership and demand a partnership tax return. Not much more will be said here since WCG is not a huge fan of joint ventures in this fashion, and most attorneys say it is very expensive to draft the necessary agreements. Automobile manufacturers have the budget to enter into large joint ventures with finite timelines (like business flirting), and also have a myriad of highly visible problems (brand, employee groups, regulations, etc.).

Loans or Capital Injections

We broached this from an investor perspective earlier and is largely repetitive. This tiny section expands on the notion of your cash going into the business, and how that might be problematic.

The question comes up from time to time about how to fund the new venture. If you are the only owner, then any money going into the business should be deemed a capital injection and not a loan. For some reason small business owners want their business to owe them money; this typically does not make sense and can set you up for problems down the road.

For example, if you lend your business money and it goes bankrupt, your bad debt deduction might be limited as a short-term capital loss. According to IRS Publication 535, a business loan is comprised of-

▲ Loans to clients, suppliers, distributors, and employees

▲ Credit sales to customers, or

▲ Business loan guarantees

As such the loan to your business might be deemed a non-business loan and limited as a short-term capital loss.

Let's not forget that you must also impute interest expense to the business, and then subsequently pick up interest income on your individual tax return (Form 1040). Issuing a 1099-INT from the business to yourself seems silly, but true!

However, another situation might arise where you are partnering with someone else, and let's assume you have all the money for startup funding. Recall the golden rule where the person with the gold makes the rules. As such, you might want to consider your funding as a loan to the business. This allows you to do two things; you can take money out of the business ahead of others as a loan payment (return of capital) and you can execute a personal guarantee from your other partner collateralizing the loan.

You can also convert your loan into additional equity. For example, you are a 50% owner and lend the business $100,000. Things are going great; however, the business does not have the cash to pay you back since all the cash is being re-invested back into the business. You might have a provision within the loan agreements that allows you to convert the debt into equity.

We talked more about this myriad of possibilities when partnering with others, including adding partners in a previous section. Check it out!

Using a Trust in Your Formation Considerations

While discussion with a qualified estate planning attorney is essential when using a Trust, here are some basics about Trusts to better understand how they mesh with your business world.

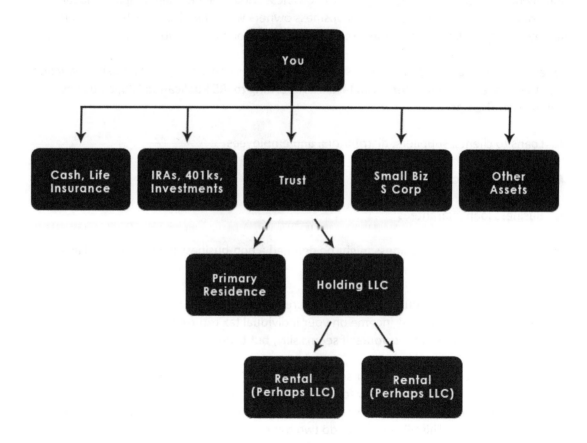

Trusts do two things very well. First, they usually help bypass probate. If you own property in three different states, then probate must be opened and closed in all states. The process is long. It is expensive. It is public.

Second, they help you, the dead guy, dictate policy from the grave. If you want to ruin a 30-year old's life, give Junior a million dollars. A Trust can dole out money according to a schedule. Special needs kid? Drug addict? Nut-job son-in-law? A Trust can protect your interests long after you're cold.

Trusts might also protect your children. Here's an example. You die. Your wife wears a short dress and heels to the funeral, and waits the obligatory 4-6 weeks before dating again. She gets married because your dying words were, "I want you to be happy." She lives another decade and then dies suddenly. Now this dude whom you never met has all the money and doesn't care about your kids. Wonderful.

The only difference for women is that men would only wait 2-3 weeks to start dating, but the rest remains unchanged.

Revocable Trusts are also called Living Trusts. This is where the grantor and the trustee can be the same person. If a revocable trust owns real estate, the grantor can burn the place down, paint it purple or sell it. Since the grantor has ultimate authority over the trust asset, there is no creditor or asset protection afforded. Zippo. None. Don't believe the asset protection hype. If you want protection, you must usually give up control.

Irrevocable Trusts are the roach motel- assets can check in, but they can't check out. The grantor does not have any authority over the trust; only the trustee does. The trustee cannot be you, the grantor. The trustee could be your best friend but cannot be influenced by you. The trustee must make decisions with the Trust's interests in mind as a fiduciary.

Some people try to install poison pills in an Irrevocable Trust where if certain events happen, the assets revert back to the grantor. Be careful on this. The IRS recently ruled in Private Letter Ruling 201426014 that the,

> provision in trust that provides that, in the event that both the children are no longer serving as members of the Distribution Committee or if there are fewer than two serving members, the trust property will be distributed to the grantor, and the trust shall terminate, constitutes a reversionary interest under Code Sec. 673.

This is one example of a poison pill that backfired. This was a Revocable / Living Trust disguised as Irrevocable.

Those items that have built in beneficiaries such as life insurance and investment accounts might be placed in a Trust, but they do not have to be since these assets bypass probate automagically. However, if you want these proceeds metered out according to a schedule, then the Trust needs to be the beneficiary. Get some planning!

Litigious assets are usually encapsulated in an LLC prior to being placed in a Trust. Automobiles are an example of litigious assets, but they are usually directly owned by an individual. Real property such as rental real estate is another great example. But what if you wanted to have your rentals pass through to your estate and skip probate?

Several estate planning attorneys recommend the following arrangement-

Having said all this, many business and corporate law attorneys will suggest only using an LLC with an Operating Agreement, and not rely on a Trust. The new generation of estate planning attorneys are also abandoning the use of Trusts. Some believe that Trusts are being oversold, and while they are necessary, the ideal situations are fewer and farther between.

Operating Agreements

If you are a single-member LLC or if your business partner is your spouse, this information might not apply. But if you are in business with another person, even a brother or sister-in-law, then a beefy Operating Agreement is a must have, at least eventually.

Operating Agreements are like Bylaws for an LLC, and they protect the rights of the members and define the parameters in which the members can operate. In general, attorneys do an adequate job drafting this critical document, but there are some holes that WCG feels compelled to mention.

Death, Divorce, Incapacitation

Death and divorce are easy, and attorneys have this in their templates all the time however incapacitation is often left out, or only briefly mentioned. Look at Donald Sterling who was found mentally unsound and could not run his business. If your business partner is Donald Sterling who is not dead nor divorced much to Clipper fans' chagrin, you might want a contractually obligated and legally enforceable plan to get rid of his member interest.

Do you need one doctor? Two doctors? What is the triggering threshold? Traumatic brain injuries are more common than you think and therefore you need to protect yourself if they occur. It is not just incapacity from a mental perspective either; your business might suffer if a member cannot physically perform the role either.

Accounting, Corporate Waste

Most attorneys draft language allowing any member to request a formal accounting of the expenditures and financial records, and this is commonly afforded in most state statutes that govern corporations and LLCs. However, they often neglect to build thresholds where all members must sign off on an expense. For example, let's say you are a minority member at 25%, and the other three members are also 25% each. Interestingly, the other three members are also a voting block since they are all family members as well. What's to prevent them from buying a business car for someone other than you?

In Colorado we have seen a flood of marijuana investors. This is a cash business of course and all these minority investors are pouring their savings into new pot farms. It is not a bad investment; first to market, stake your claim, build mega farms, control the pricing, etc. However, and this is a big however, it is still a cash business. Don't you want a little assurance that the majority owner is not skimming the till?

Did you know the IRS can determine your sales volume as a bar owner? They look at your purchases which is why most bars must buy from a distributor. Determine the cost of goods purchased slap on a regional markup, and boom, you have sales regardless of what the cash deposits say. Same with divorces; we often look at lifestyle and spending to "back into" the income figures.

There are several other examples that fall under the accounting and corporate waste provisions but we need to move along.

Distributions

Oftentimes the business will have income, but no cash since it is re-investing back into the business. However, as a shareholder of an S corporation or a member of a garden variety multi-member LLC, you will pay taxes on business income (profits) and not distributions. Theoretically you could have a big tax bill based on income but never see the cash. How does this work?

The business has net income of $100,000 after expenses and everyone decides to put the money back into the business such as inventory purchases. Cool, since everyone agrees but all the owners will have a tax obligation based on the $100,000 (inventory purchases may immediately reduce net income but there are rules, so please play along for now). This means that if you are a 25% owner at a 22% marginal tax rate, you will have a cash out-of-pocket tax bill of $25,000 x 22% or $5,500.

WCG CPAs & Advisors recommends two things when it comes to distributions. First, define and calculate working capital for your business. If the entity needs working capital to operate or for future purchases or initiatives (what we call capital expenditures or capex for short), how is that calculated? Second, once working capital is defined, what portion is distributed and what is kept in the business?

Let's run through an example of working capital. Let's say your law firm specializes in personal injury and as such your revenue is lumpy. To be safe, you and the other partners determine that you need 6 months' worth of expenses in working capital. Also, the law firm is moving next year into a new office which needs a build-out. You add that up and determine that excess cash is available for distribution.

> Sidebar: When you grow working capital, you will have a tax consequence. For example, if you want to increase from $100,000 to $200,000 in working capital next year, you will pay taxes at your tax rate (assuming a pass-through entity such as a partnership or S Corp). As you might know or will soon learn, as an S corporation shareholder or partner in a partnership, you are taxed on the profits earned by the business whether you distribute the earnings or retain them for future bills. Therefore, at a 22% marginal tax rate, your $100,000 growth in working capital will take $22,000 in taxes. The good news if you reduce working capital, that distributable cash is tax-free.

From there, the Operating Agreement could dictate that a minimum of 40% is distributed to the owners unless all owners agree to a different figure. This helps reduce some of the tax sting of net ordinary business income after expenses and deductions being allocated to you without the same amount in cash.

What WCG recommends is-

▲ Determine working capital (time-based operating expenses + capex + buffer).

▲ Determine a budget.

▲ Use math to then determine how much you can safely distribute to the owners.

▲ True up each quarter or semi-annually to align reality with budget. In other words, if your interim profit is higher than budgeted, perhaps another off-cycle distribution can safely occur.

Another common example is when you are the minority shareholder or member. The majority elects to increase wages for themselves and not pay distributions, basically starving you out. My partner would never do that! Really? Ok. But everyone else not living in fantasy land, an Operating Agreement can protect from this situation.

Dispute Resolution
Templated Operating Agreements usually have language about dispute resolution, and specifically mediation. Mediation is fine, and some courts have a standing order that parties will attend mediation prior to trial. However, mediation is not binding and parties don't necessarily have to enter into mediation with good faith. Trials take a long time- anywhere from 12 to 24 months, just to get to opening statements.

Arbitration is like mini-court and the rules of discovery and evidence are usually more relaxed including procedure. They can be expensive since you are paying for your attorney plus the arbiter who is usually a retired judge or attorney. However, they can also be efficient.

Regardless of mediation, arbitration or trial, make sure your Operating Agreement has expeditious dispute resolution provisions, and incentives for all parties to be efficient and bargain in good faith.

Business Valuation
If a member wants out, no problem, but what is the value of the business? Should you use a formula to determine the value? Perhaps something based on revenue? A full-blown business valuation (our retainer is $3,000 for a conclusion of value business valuation engagement)? What if you and your business partners cannot agree on the selection of the business valuation expert? Make sure there are provisions in your Operating Agreement.

As a side note, if the value cannot easily be derived from a formula, we often see language where the exiting member and the remaining members each pick a business valuation expert. Then those two experts pick a third as a neutral, or some other seemingly detached and disinterested selection mechanism.

As we've said in the past, just because you are working with an attorney or an accountant doesn't mean you are working with a smart person. **WCG CPAs & Advisors** can act as a consultant with your attorney when drafting these documents.

Exit Plans, Business Succession
Nothing lasts forever, even the Cubs eventually won a pennant. If your business partner is not your spouse, understand that you could suddenly find yourself in business with his or her spouse or children. Imagine you and your partner. Happy as a clam. Successful. Cement truck. Dead. She left everything she owned to her whacked out children including her portion

of the business. Now you and her kids are partners. Wonderful. Do scenes from Horrible Bosses come to mind?

But valuation and funding are the biggest hurdles. For example, the business might be worth a zillion dollars, but has no cash. Or the value is all tied up in assets, such as houses, buildings or machinery. Exit plans or Buy-Sell Agreements really make sense only when the business has value.

In many cases, especially specified service trades or business such as accountants, financial advisors, etc., the remaining partner or partners can simply start up a new business in a different name, and carry on as usual. Huh? Example time. Let's say you and your partner are accountants. Living the high life, declining Robin Roberts interviews, driving fancy cars, etc. One day you decide to call it quits. In this situation, both partners could simply split the office equipment and break away with his or her book of the business and move on as individuals.

Liability Protection Fallacy of an LLC

Can you be sued personally if you operate an LLC? Yes. And you can easily lose on both a business and personal level. There are several myths out there regarding the use of an LLC as a shelter from potential lawsuits and litigation. Some of the hype has been created by attorneys who used to charge upwards of $1,000 to form an LLC. Need to pay for condos in Maui, presumably. We accountants tease attorneys that LLC really means Lawyer's Likely Choice.

> Sidebar: LLCs are quite powerful. As we've already discussed, the deal structures within the entity are endless and the flexibility is strong within multi-entity arrangements. Let's not forget solid estate planning can be achieved with an LLC as well.

Back to picking on attorneys. Remember, attorneys are not necessarily smart because they went to law school. People are smart, and smart attorneys are people who were already smart and then chose law as a profession. To be fair, the same is true for accountants and doctors.

While consultation with an experienced attorney is strongly recommended for your unique situation, as business owners ourselves we feel the excitement of the LLC has overshadowed the reality of our litigious society. In other words, if your acts, errors or omissions injure someone even though it was under the auspice of your LLC, there is a good chance you will be personally named in the lawsuit and held liable as the owner of the LLC.

The word liability in the LLC truly refers to financial liability. Please read on.

For the matter of this liability discussion, LLCs, S Corps, C Corps and limited partnerships are considered the same. No liability protection is asserted for sole proprietorships, general partnerships and general partners in limited liability partnerships (don't forget the old timer LLLP which limits everyone's liability even the general partner). Sure, this is a huge generality, and exceptions always exist depending on agreements and state law.

Types of Liability
There are three areas where you can be held personally responsible- criminal, contractual and torts.

Torts is probably most people's concern, and torts can either be-

▲ negligence where you have a general duty to act in a reasonable way and you didn't (like drive your car safely), or

▲ intentional torts where there was a purposeful act to harm.

There are other tort buzzwords like gross negligence, careless disregard, defamation, etc. Remember, negligence is the opposite of diligence.

Piercing the Corporate Veil
Officers and directors of corporations are routinely held liable for the actions of the corporation. This is called piercing the corporate veil. Can you say Enron?

Piercing the corporate veil typically is most effective with smaller privately held business entities (close corporations) in which the corporation has-

▲ a small number of shareholders (owners),

▲ limited assets, and

▲ separating the corporation from its shareholders would promote fraud or an inequitable result.

While this is referring to a corporation, the same philosophy is applicable to a limited liability company. Does that sound like your LLC? Yes. Could it happen to you? Yes. Is there a small chance of this happening? Who knows? We say risk it, put it all on red and let it ride. Just kidding. No one bets on red.

Even a two-member LLC would easily be considered a closely held entity. If those members were grossly negligent in the way they managed the business, separating the corporation from its shareholders (or LLC from its members) would certainly promote unfairness from a liability perspective. This is our opinion of course, but we want to share with you some of the behind-the-scenes perspectives from the courts and law that might not be readily considered when forming an LLC.

Another perspective- if you owned shares of Ford Motor Company, you were not personally responsible for the damage caused by the Ford Pinto even if you were a shareholder. However, if you were a corporate officer who ignored (gross negligence) the potential for harm, you could be held responsible, even criminally. In other words, fix that loose railing before your tenant hurts himself (using an LLC owning a rental as an example).

The general rule across the country is that individuals acting on behalf of a business are personally liable for their tortious conduct even if they did so on behalf of the business. So, to protect your personal assets you need to fund the LLC with enough resources to pay for a lawsuit. This defeats the purpose of not having to pay personally since you are personally doing the funding.

There might be situations where an investor has a lot to lose personally as compared to his or her smaller co-investors. Therefore, perhaps funding the LLC on an equal basis to hedge against potential lawsuits or to have similar language in an Operating Agreement or Partnership Agreement can mitigate some exposures.

Furthermore, if you own multiple investments and LLCs, and you think you can protect the other assets in the event of a lawsuit on one, think again. In our non-legal opinion and observation of surrounding events, if you face a credible lawsuit arising out of your acts or omissions there is a chance everything you have is going to be pursued by the injured party's attorney including your personal residence, cars, college funds, LLC's assets, Snuggie collection, etc. Yes, even the leopard one.

Other Things to Think About

You are a reasonable person. Does it seem reasonable for someone to hide behind the auspice of an LLC or a corporation when they do bad things? Of course not. Public policy shouldn't allow this. Therefore, it follows that if you maintain an unsafe rental property or if you are reckless while driving the business car, you should be sued, and you should lose.

Some attorneys will argue that if you mix personal and business funds together, even accidentally, you might erode the separation of you, an individual, and the business. For example, a business owner will pay for car insurance through the business. The car is owned personally by the business owner, and the owner is getting reimbursed for mileage. On the books, the car insurance is not a deductible business expense, and is coded as an owner draw or shareholder distribution. In this scenario, a court might determine that the "veil" between you and the business is getting thin, and might be determined to be too thin.

Same with minutes and other business governance. Some argue that if you do not keep up with the housekeeping of your business, you can chip away at the corporate or LLC protection. There is a natural human response to pile on once a defect is discovered. "In closing your honor, on top of Exhibits A through AJ, this LLC failed to record basic business governance." While we doubt how much weight this would be given, it certainly helps buttress a level of carelessness or disregard. As mentioned elsewhere, LLCs generally do not document meetings or minutes unless the state requires it.

Protecting Yourself
After all the gloom and doom, there are some small elements of protection. If your employee's conduct creates a liability for himself and one for the LLC, the owner of the LLC may be absolved. This can get tricky depending on the conduct, and any instructions the LLC provided to the employee. This is attorney type stuff.

So, what do you do? In addition to your general business liability insurance, you should secure a decent umbrella policy both at the personal and commercial level. This is our strong recommendation for liability arising from your acts, errors and omissions. General umbrella policies are $1,200 to $2,000 per year depending on the limits. Something to note is that your liability limits on the underlying assets such as buildings, rental properties and cars might have to increase to reach the floor (starting point) of the umbrella policy. This prevents gaps in insurance.

Errors and omissions insurance varies depending on your profession (realtor versus financial advisor versus insurance sales).

It appears that many credible lawsuits will sue to the limit of coverage to avoid lengthy and expensive trial litigation. Again, please consult your attorney and insurance agent for your unique situation.

LLC Protection in Borrowing
In addition to the above, there is also a small element of financial protection. LLCs and corporations protect the owners from being personally responsible for the business's debts and obligations unless the owners or officers personally sign for the loan (called a recourse loan).

However, in today's lending climate it will be very difficult to get a business loan in the name of the LLC without having to sign a personal guarantee on the note. In other words, you will more than likely need to sign twice- first, as the person directing the business to borrow and second as an individual promising to pay should the business fail to do so.

Business debt without a personal guarantee is called a non-recourse loan since the bank or lender does not have a recourse against the individual. Tough to get, expensive at times and requires significant equity (60% loan-to-value is the general rule of thumb using real estate as an example).

> Quick Recap: In personal worlds including small businesses, loans are typically collateralized twice. First, property is attached with a lien so you cannot sell it without paying the lender. Second, your promise to pay. Lenders can sue to foreclose on the property, and they can also sue based on your now-broken promise to pay.

How this works is straightforward. Let's say you own three businesses, one is an LLC operating a pizza joint, another LLC owns a rental with a ton of equity, and another LLC is used to trade stocks, bonds and options. The rental was purchased with a non-recourse loan. The rental house has extensive mold, is un-insured for mold, and eventually is foreclosed leaving some creditors holding the bag. Picture the poor guy in Monopoly. Those creditors cannot attach or seize your pizza joint or your portfolio since they are held in other LLCs. This is an overly simplified example, and there are probably some rare and narrow instances where you could still be in trouble, but generally this strategy affords some protection according to most attorneys.

A common arrangement is the self rental which is discussed in more detail later, but here's a glimmer. You operate an LLC as a business and you also buy the office building with another LLC, of course with a non-recourse loan (the only collateral is the building itself and not your personal promise to pay). The business also has a line of credit. Depending how all the debt is structured, each of these assets (the business and the building) has a Chinese Wall between them. Don't laugh; that wall served well for nearly 3,000 years.

Again, banks are smart. You are not the first Tom, Dick or Harry to come around. We should probably update the names to reflect the current smattering- how about you're not the first Parker, Logan or Dakota to come around with your androgynous name and lofty schemes. Most lenders require personal guarantees on every loan.

Asset Protection in Equity Stripping

Another asset protection strategy that is older than dirt is equity stripping (it does not necessarily need an LLC either). It is a process of encumbering your assets to the point where there is no value for lack of equity. In the simplest of forms, you pull cash out against your assets, and separate your cash from the assets. Be very careful. There are "bogus friendly lien" triggers where a person will use a Nevada corporation to file a lien against the asset, however the asset and corporation are owned by the same person (or some related party). This lien is subsequently pierced or tossed as self-serving or deemed to lack commercial merit.

Equity stripping can be a good asset protection strategy, but it requires careful planning with a skilled attorney. And No, it is not older than dirt but it has been around for quite some time.

LLC Protection in Contracts

There is some wiggle room on financial shielding using a limited liability company. If you sign a contract for internet service, or for a copier lease, or some other commitment, you might be able to get away with executing the agreement under the LLC. So, if your business or real estate investment fails, the LLC might be liable for the remaining contract obligation but not you personally. Keep in mind, however, the judgement and foreclosure process could still get you- if someone gets a judgement against the LLC, they can later attempt to foreclose on the distributions or future income of the LLC, and they can also later foreclose on the equity (ownership) of the LLC. On top of all that, your business bank account might be seized to the amount of the lien.

How about we just keep our promises and pay our bills, huh?

Liability and State Nexus

We'll chat about nexus from an income tax perspective in the next few pages- this little tidbit is about nexus from a liability perspective. Several business entities are created in what some people perceive as business friendly states, such as Delaware or Nevada. But when it comes to liability especially tort liability, you will generally be sued in a jurisdiction where you have an economic and / or physical presence.

Yes, an attorney will show up and attempt to fight jurisdiction. But he or she might lose. Now you must hire an out-of-state attorney to fight your out of state lawsuit. Sounds like a grand plan.

So, if you file Articles of Formation, Organization or Incorporation in another state such as Delaware, maintain a presence in Kansas and cause damages in Kansas, you will probably be sued in Kansas. Yes, you can write contracts that clearly dictate the forum of law, but now you are asking a Kansas court to possibly understand and enforce Delaware law. According to several attorneys that we work with, if you march into court pinning your hopes on Delaware law being enforced by a Kansas court, you have already lost. Mediate, settle and move on down the line.

Also, most parties will want the jurisdiction to be in their backyard. You trip and fall in a Wal-Mart and sue Wal-Mart, you are not having to fly to Bentonville, Arkansas to file the lawsuit. Although Table Rock Lake to the north of Bentonville is amazing, you want to sue in your local town, using local courts and jurors. After your big fat judgement, fly to Table Rock Lake in your private jet. Good stuff!

If you have a presence in all 50 states, using Wal-Mart as an example again, you have to pick a state to call home regardless (your domicile), and then file as a foreign entity in all the other states. Picking a more business friendly state makes sense if your operations span several states. Attorneys call this forum shopping. This can be leveraged when you are a large business who enters into several contracts per year, and your attorneys are exceptionally crafty and completely (and only) understand a certain state's laws.

For 99% of the small business owners out there, keep it simple- organize in your home state. You truly have only two major concerns. Where contract disputes will be argued, and that can be dictated within the contract. The other concern is tort liability, and that is usually mitigated with insurance and being a diligent human being.

Yet another example. A lot of real estate investors will incorporate in Nevada (for example) because of the seemingly friendly business laws, and then buy rental properties in Colorado. This requires a foreign entity registration in Colorado. It is a near guarantee that if you are grossly negligent in the maintenance of your rental, you will be sued in Colorado. So why the heck are we forming in Nevada? Or Wyoming? Or Delaware? The theory is that a Colorado court would then interpret and enforce the other state's law in your lawsuit. Good luck with that.

Please don't believe the hype. Do your homework! Do you know of anyone in all your walks of life and circles that fought a lawsuit based on some other state's law? Perhaps, but sleeping at night solely based on this layer of protection might not be that comforting.

There are some situations such as several remote principals collaborating on a business where the "home state" becomes murky. For example, WCG has a client where three brothers own a hotel in a Caribbean country. We formed a Florida LLC since two brothers were residing in the foreign country and the third was residing in New York.

We have another client where the three principals lived in Oregon, Texas and New Jersey. We formed the entity in Wyoming and filed as a foreign entity in each state.

Charging Orders

If you are financially in trouble, and a creditor wants to take your assets, your multi-member LLC and its assets might be safe. Instead of taking the LLC directly, a court can issue a Charging Order which allows the creditor to receive any distributions from the LLC. The theory is quite simple- if you are in business with another person, and that person has financial trouble, why should it be your problem? Your only problem should be where to send the profit distribution check for that person's distributive share.

A Charging Order puts the creditor in line for any financial rights that the debtor has but does not convey any management rights. Therefor the creditor cannot order the LLC to make a distribution. However, many states have allowed the creditor holding the Charging Order to foreclose on the membership interest of the debtor. Yuck. This is done under the auspice that the debtor will not be able to re-pay his obligation. So now the creditor is the permanent owner of the financial rights of the debtor's portion of the LLC, but the creditor still does not own any member interest in the LLC. This results in the debtor owning a portion of an LLC that he will never receive any money from since his financial rights are now in the hands of the creditor.

It doesn't stop there. Some states and certain courts can also assign the full interest (ownership and financial, or some would say equity and economic) to the creditor. This creates a big mess for the other members of the LLC who suddenly need to scrape up enough money to pay off the creditor so as to not be tethered to them as a co-owner.

What does all this mean? Some attorneys want to automatically add a spouse to the LLC so it suddenly becomes a multi-member LLC with the financial protection of a Charging Order. Sure, why not? There is some protection there with very little effort.

As a side note, here is Delaware's verbiage about Charging Orders under Title 6, Section 18-703-

> (d). The entry of a charging order is the exclusive remedy by which a judgment creditor of a member or a member's assignee may satisfy a judgment out of the judgment debtor's limited liability company interest and attachment, garnishment, foreclosure or other legal or equitable remedies are not available to the judgment creditor, whether the limited liability company has 1 member or more than 1 member.

Makes you want to run out and form your LLC in Delaware doesn't it? Again, if you are marching into court with a boatload of financial woes and hanging your hat on Charging Orders for your financial protection, you might have bigger problems. Creditors are wise to this, and they usually make you personally guarantee the financial obligation as an individual.

Also, if you form an LLC in Delaware and operate in Colorado, you will need to file as a foreign entity in Colorado. If you receive process of service in Colorado for a lawsuit, you are now asking a Colorado court to interpret and enforce Delaware law in your matter. Courts and judges are not fond of this ask. We keep mentioning this concept is several spots just to drive it home (and because small business owners jump into our book at various spots).

Using a Self-Directed IRA or 401k to Buy a Rental, Start a Business

Since this chapter is about unique or custom entity structures, there's no better place to talk about self-directed IRAs. What the heck is a self-directed IRA? Just because you make investment choices within your retirement accounts, does not mean they are self-directed. Sure, in a practical sense they are. But a self-directed IRA in the context of this section is about a very specific investment vehicle.

Why would you consider this option? Let's assume that you want to invest into rental properties (which is a great augmenting retirement strategy by the way... we are huge fans), but all your money is tied up in an IRA. You are 50 years old and can't touch it without penalty. The bank won't let you borrow against it. You might be hosed.

However, if you set up a self-directed IRA and roll your existing IRA into it, you can have the IRA invest into the rental property. But there is another reason why this might make sense. The S&P 500 index since inception has returned 9.22%. Not bad. Yet in some situations, rental properties might beat or in some cases, crush, the returns of the stock market. And it creates some diversification within your financial planning.

The other option with a self-directed IRA is to start or purchase a new business. A new business might need cash to invest into equipment, franchise fee, marketing, operational cash, etc.

If you want to expand your horizons into real estate notes, equipment leasing, livestock, private debt and equity placements, and oil and gas you can also use a self-directed IRA. Be careful here. Suitability might be your biggest hurdle. Talk to your financial team before squandering your life savings on ocean front property in Arizona.

A 401k may be used as well but it is slightly more complicated. At times you might hear the term ROBS (rollover business startup) plan.

Here is a blurb from the IRS website-

A ROBS transaction therefore takes the form of the following sequential steps:

An individual establishes a shell corporation sponsoring an associated and purportedly qualified retirement plan.

The plan document provides that all participants may invest the entirety of their account balances in employer stock.

The individual becomes the only employee of the shell corporation and the only participant in the plan. Note that at this point, there is still no ownership or shareholder equity interest.

The individual then executes a rollover or direct trustee-to-trustee transfer of available funds from a prior qualified plan or personal IRA into the newly created qualified plan.

The sole participant in the plan then directs investment of his or her account balance into a purchase of employer stock. The employer stock is valued to reflect the amount of plan assets that the taxpayer wishes to access.

The individual then uses the transferred funds to purchase a franchise or begin some other form of business enterprise.

After the business is established, the plan may be amended to prohibit further investments in employer stock. This amendment may be unnecessary, because all stock is fully allocated. As a result, only the original individual benefits from this investment option. Future employees and plan participants will not be entitled to invest in employer stock.

A portion of the proceeds of the stock transaction may be remitted back to the promoter, in the form of a professional fee. This may be either a direct payment from plan to promoter, or an indirect payment, where gross proceeds are transferred to the individual and some amount of his gross wealth is then returned to promoter.

The IRS is also quick to point out that self-directed IRAs and 401k plans including ROBS face a lot of compliance concerns and are generally very risky. The funded businesses also have a high failure rate.

These steps all seem straightforward. What's the catch? There's always a catch. Here are the things to look out for.

No S Corps or Partnerships
The way these entities are structured, business profits are returned to the shareholders. Profits cannot fall into the hands of the IRA account owner or 401k plan participant (you). Tainting of retirement dollars is the big thing here.

Prohibited Transactions
The business cannot invest directly in collectibles, art, rugs, antiques, metals other than gold, silver and palladium bullion, gems, stamps, coins (except certain U.S.-minted coins), alcoholic beverages, and a few other tangible items related to personal property. Ok- there goes half your list for sure. Yup, cross palladium off your list.

In addition, friends, business associates and siblings may invest in the business via a self-directed IRA or 401k plan, but your parents, children or spouse may not. The strict arms-length perspective of the business dealings must be maintained.

Key Employee / Investor
You cannot be the key employee and key investor in the business. Nor can you own a controlling interest in the business. Basically, someone else must have the right to hire or fire you such as a Board of Directors. The "someone else" is the grey area in all of this and warrants more discussion.

Having said all this we must fully disclose that WCG CPAs & Advisors are not experts. While we could be, we choose not to and leave a ton of room for exceptions and other workarounds to these rules. There are several wealth and trust advisor firms who do this work all day every day, and are full of competent people. We have worked with Equity Trust and New Direction Trust in the past, and also use KKOS Lawyers.

As you work through all this, the net-net is that the IRS does not allow you personally to receive money that was slated for retirement (at least without penalty until you are 59.5 years old).

To reiterate, a self-directed IRA or 401k is very cool. It allows you to move money you normally could not use into an account that can now be used to get yourself into a rental or a hot franchise. All without having to find cash elsewhere.

Not to throw a big wet blanket on your dreams, but we also see a high failure rate. It is a combination of many things; business ownership is tough. Period. But! There is also a feeling generated from using your IRA or 401k funds where the money doesn't seem real... like it is Monopoly money or something. Regardless of where your money is coming from, your business always needs a solid plan, a budget and a little bit of good fortune.

Chapter 3
S Corporation Benefits
(updated October 2023)

Avoiding or Reducing Self-Employment (SE) Taxes

A common complaint from those who own their own business is self-employment tax. Can you avoid, reduce, eliminate or lower your self-employment taxes or SE taxes? Ok, we just said two things that mean the same thing twice. Yes, you may reduce self-employment taxes to a large extent, but it takes some effort starting with an S Corp election (let's not get ahead of ourselves yet).

If you own a business as a sole proprietor or as a garden variety single-member LLC (one owner or member) your business income will be reported on your personal tax return under Schedule C and is subject to self-employment tax (currently 15.3%) and ordinary income tax. So, you could easily pay an average of 40% (15.3% in SE taxes + 24% in income taxes) on all your net business income in federal taxes. Wow, that sucks!

A similar taxation exists for partnerships / multi-member LLCs too since the issuing K-1 will identify the income subjected to self-employment taxes (and of course income taxes, just like the example above).

The "double" taxation should not be a stranger to you. When you were paid a W-2 salary of wage, you had Social Security and Medicare taxes taken out of your paycheck, and you also had income taxes withheld based on some payroll table. Only income taxes were "negotiated" by deductions and credits; Social Security and Medicare taxes were not.

Back to the sole proprietors and LLCs. We are all humans, and we generally spend what we make. If you are not prepared for 30% to 40% in taxes for your business income, it could be a shocker on April 15.

The recent tax reform and specifically the pass-through taxation changes in Section 199A do not alter the theory of self-employment tax savings. The additional pass-through deduction afforded to small business owners complements the benefits of an S corporation. Please bear with us as we go through the mechanics of saving self-employment taxes with an S Corp.

How SE Tax Is Computed

A bit of disclosure is in order. Self-employment taxes are 15.3% which is derived from the "employer" portion at 7.65% and the "employee" portion of 7.65%. However, a small business gets to deduct its portion of payroll taxes from income before determining the taxable income. Huh?

Think of your last job where you received a W-2. The employer might have paid you $100,000 and withheld your portion of Social Security and Medicare taxes on your behalf. The business also had to pay its portion of Social Security and Medicare taxes, so its total expense was the $100,000 salary plus $7,650. Similar concept with sole proprietorships and LLCs.

Here is an illustrative table-

Net Business Income	100,000
less SE Tax Adjustment at 7.65%	7,650
Taxable Business Income	92,350
SE Tax at 15.3%	14,130
Tax Deductible Portion	7,065

Do you see the $14,130 or 14.13% of $100,000? That is essentially your effective rate of tax on self-employed business income because of the deductible portion of 7.65%. Probably doesn't make you feel any better but there you go.

Quick Analysis of S Corp Savings

If you own a business and have elected to be treated as an S Corp (Subchapter S) for taxation, the business now files a corporate tax return on Form 1120S. We will detail this out with a fancy graphic, but basically an S corporation chops up the net economic benefit to the owner between salary and net ordinary business income after expenses and deductions. This split is important. Why?

The salary is subjected to Social Security and Medicare taxes; the net ordinary business income is not. The salary is paid to the employee (you). The net ordinary business income may be paid to the investor (also you). You'll see several references to this concept that as an S corporation owner you are both employee and investor.

Let's look at some quick numbers. These are based on using a salary of 40% of net ordinary business income after expenses and deductions for amounts up to $500,000 and then decreased incrementally to 30% for the millionaire at $2,500,000 below (real case actually).

The 40% / 30% is for illustration (we will discuss reasonable shareholder salary in silly detail in a later chapter dedicated to only reasonable salary determinations).

Here is our summary table-

Income	Total SE Tax	Salary	Total Payroll Tax	Savings $$	Delta %
30,000	4,239	12,000	1,836	2,403	8.0%
50,000	7,065	20,000	3,060	4,005	8.0%
75,000	10,597	30,000	4,590	6,007	8.0%
100,000	14,130	40,000	6,120	8,010	8.0%
150,000	18,711	60,000	9,180	9,531	6.4%
200,000	20,050	80,000	12,240	7,810	3.9%
300,000	22,972	120,000	18,174	4,798	1.6%
500,000	29,991	200,000	20,494	9,497	1.9%
1,000,000	47,537	350,000	24,844	22,693	2.3%
2,000,000	82,630	600,000	32,094	50,536	2.5%
2,500,000	100,177	750,000	36,444	63,733	2.5%

Chart Notes

Let's review some interesting things about the data on the previous page.

The bulk of payroll taxes are Social Security and Medicare taxes, which are combined to be called FICA taxes when payroll specialists are kicking it around the water cooler. You might have other payroll taxes such as unemployment (Yes, some states require it even for one-person corporations) and state disability insurance (SDI).

As mentioned, salaries started at 40% through $500,000 and then reduced to 30% at $2M and $2.5M. This is a jumping-off point. The IRS standard is "reasonable shareholder salary" which includes all sorts of non-qualitative things such as your expertise, Bureau of Labor Statistics, comparison of salary to distributions, zodiac sign, favorite color, etc.

Social Security taxes of 12.4% stop at $168,600 (for the 2024 tax year) of net ordinary business income for LLCs and partnerships who do not elect S corporation status. It also stops at $168,600 for salaries.

Medicare taxes of 2.9% continues into perpetuity. Not only does this go on into perpetuity, it also goes on forever (yes, that is supposed to be a joke). This is one of the major components of savings in the upper incomes since Medicare taxes are capped at the amount of salary with S Corps. In other words, if you earn $1M you will pay Medicare taxes on the entire net ordinary business income, but if you elect S Corp status and pay yourself a $400,000 salary you only pay Medicare taxes on the $400,000.

The Medicare surtax starts for those earning $200,000 and filing single, and $250,000 for those filing jointly. This too continues into perpetuity for LLCs and partnerships. In the data, we assumed a joint tax return. For example, at $500,000 net ordinary business income there is a $1,906 Medicare surtax. But if this business elects S corporation taxation and pays $200,000 salary, there is not a Medicare surtax. There is not a net investment income (NII) tax on the S corporation ordinary income either (more on that loophole later) since you materially participate; in other words, your investment into your S Corp is not passive.

Savings as a percentage of income starts to drop off at $168,600 which makes sense given the Social Security cap for the 2024 tax year. And those savings bottom out around $300,000 net business income and then begin a decent climb rate. Without getting into excruciating details and mental gymnastics, there is an interesting dynamic at $300,000 between Medicare taxes including the surtax on the LLC / partnership income, the salary being paid within an S Corp election, and Medicare taxes associated with that salary.

The Source of the Savings
The S Corp election of your Partnership, LLC or C corporation changes how the business reports income to the IRS. An S Corp prepares and files a Form 1120S which is a corporate tax return. That in turn generates a K-1 for each shareholder. Remember, shareholder, investor and owner are synonymous terms for our discussions.

This might be your first brush with the term K-1. A K-1 is similar to a W-2 since it reports income and other items for each member, partner, shareholder, owner or beneficiary, and is coded to tell the IRS how the business activities should be treated.

A K-1 is generated by an entity since the entity is passing along the income tax obligation to the K-1 recipient (hence the concept pass-through entity, or PTE for TLA lovers). There are three basic sources for a K-1, and the source dictates how the income and other items on the K-1 are handled on your individual tax return (Form 1040). Here they are-

▲ Partnership / MMLLC (Form 1065)

▲ S Corporation (Form 1120S), and

▲ Estate or Trust (Form 1041)

There are two types of K-1s for the purposes of our self-employment tax conversation- one is generated from a partnership tax return and the other is generated from an S corporation tax return. These K-1s look nearly identical and both are reported on page 2 of Schedule E in conjunction with your Form 1040. Schedule E is the tax form used for rental properties, royalties and other investment income including business income from a partnership or an S Corp.

However, a K-1 generated from a partnership tax return which has ordinary business income in box 1 and / or guaranteed payments in box 4 will typically be subjected to self-employment taxes for an active partner or member. Conversely, ordinary business income in box 1 on a K-1 from an S corporation will not be taxed with self-employment taxes. The S corporation election changes the color of money (we love this saying).

> Note: S Corps do not have guaranteed payments like partnerships might- S Corps would call these payments wages or salary. A partnership (and an LLC for that matter) cannot pay its partners or owners a wage or salary. The IRS frowns on this. Any periodic payment that is recurring in a partnership to one of the partners is called a guaranteed payment and is reported separately from partnership income. Both might be subjected to self-employment taxes.

You just heard the term "pass-through entity" and you might also hear the term "disregarded entity"- a disregarded entity is a single-member LLC. As the terms suggests, it is disregarded for tax purposes, and therefore does not have to file its own tax return since the taxable consequence is reported on the owner(s) individual tax returns (Form 1040) as a sole proprietorship (Schedule C).

A pass-through entity passes its federal tax obligation onto the partner of a partnership, the member of an LLC, the shareholder of an S corporation or the beneficiary of an estate or trust. States might impose a business tax or a franchise tax on the partnership, LLC or S Corp directly (they legally cannot impose an income tax... more about interstate commerce rules later).

Quick Recap, The S Corp Money Trail
So, when your partnership, LLC or corporation is taxed as an S Corp you are considered both an employee and a shareholder (think investor). As an employee being paid a salary, your income is subjected to all the usual taxes that you would see on a paystub- Federal taxes, state taxes, Social Security taxes, Medicare taxes, unemployment and disability.

However, as a shareholder or investor, you are simply getting a return on your investment. That income, as the Romneys, Gates and Buffets of the world enjoy, is a form of investment income and therefore is not subjected to self-employment taxes (tiny exception for income over $200,000 (single) or $250,000 (married) where Medicare surtax is charged).

As you recall, when we say self-employment taxes, we are really talking about Social Security and Medicare taxes. From a sole proprietor perspective, they are self-employment taxes. From an employee perspective, they are Social Security and Medicare taxes. Same thing.

Let's look at another visual in terms of how the money travels-

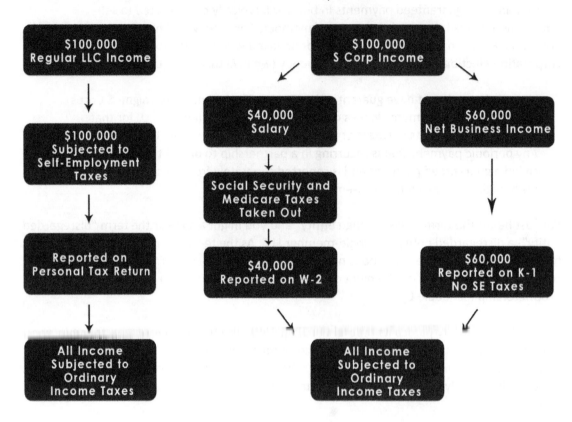

We love this graphic! It was our first one, and it remains the most important one.

The four boxes on the left are the money trail of your sole proprietorship, LLC or partnership. The series of boxes on the right is the money trail of your entity being taxed as an S corporation. Note the $60,000 chunk of income on the far right-hand side that is not being taxed at the self-employment tax level. This is the source of your savings.

Also note that all your $100,000 is being subjected to income taxes. This is a common misconception- a lot of business owners believe there is a magical income tax reduction with an S Corp election. Not true. The only reduction is in self-employment taxes. All other tax deductions such as operating expenses, home office expense, mileage, meals, 401k plans, etc. are equally deductible with or without an S corporation.

Still not sure or not convinced? No problem... please check out Line 4 on Schedule 2 on your 2022 Form 1040 tax return. This number reflects the self-employment taxes paid on your business income.

We want to reduce this by 60 to 65%. If you see $15,000 then we can save $9,000 ($15,000 x 60%). This makes sense right? $100,000 in biz income would be $15,000. 8 to 10% of $100,000 is $9,000.

The previous table showed significant savings using a 40% salary without self-employed health insurance (SEHI). Again, we are only focused on the self-employment tax and payroll tax savings at this point. Section 199A from the Tax Cuts & Jobs Act of 2017 will be wormed into overall tax savings in a later chapter dedicated to qualified business income deduction. While reducing overall taxes and leveraging the pass-through tax deduction cannot be ignored, we are isolating payroll taxes to drive home a critical point.

Multiple Owners Savings
We have been discussing a one-person band in terms of savings and the flow of money. However, let's briefly chat about the killer savings for a more than one owner situation. If the business had net ordinary business income after expenses and deductions of $150,000, and was split down the middle, each owner (two in this example) would pay nearly $7,000 in unnecessary self-employment taxes or $14,000 combined. A big number for sure, but consider the following.

WCG recently had a 9-person consulting firm being taxed as a partnership where each member earned about $125,000. The before and after analysis yielded a savings of just over $100,000 combined. Our fee for the S Corp administration (Vail Business Advisory Service) plus all the tax returns and tax planning was about $14,000 or approximately $1,550 per owner. And each owner saved about $12,000 in taxes and therefore pocketed $10,000 each.

The super sad part of this is that this entity was in place for over a decade with similar income and owners. Over a million dollars was wasted in unnecessary taxes. When you look at it that way, it makes you gulp a bit.

What happens when the business pays for your health insurance? Let's find out how this can really soup up your tax savings.

Tax Savings with Health Insurance

When your S corporation pays for your self-employed health insurance (SEHI) and dental / vision premiums, including coverage for your family, that amount is added to Box 1 Wages on your W-2. So, your income is artificially increased by the annual amount of premiums. However, there are two huge concepts you need to love and embrace.

First, Box 3 Social Security Wages and Box 5 Medicare Wages do not get increased by the amount of premiums paid. Here is a silly looking, but illustrative W-2.

Box 1 Wages	50,000	Box 2 Federal Tax Withholdings	21,735
Box 3 Social Security Wages	40,000	Box 4 SS Withholdings	2,480
Box 5 Medicare Wages	40,000	Box 6 Medicare Withholdings	580
Box 16 State Wages	50,000	Box 17 State Tax Withholdings	4,347

Don't get tweaked on the federal and state tax withholdings. We'll explain that in a later chapter.

> Spoiler alert: When WCG processes shareholder payroll, we increase income tax withholdings to help budget for the K-1 income that is combined with your W-2 income on your individual tax return). This allows you to land on tax neutrality as a household without needing separate estimated tax payments. Beauty!

Back to the W-2. Your focus should be on Box 3 and Box 5- these are the boxes that we want to reduce to the best of our abilities and with reasonableness.

Subsequently Box 4 and Box 6 is the calculation of the social security and Medicare taxes based on the amounts in Box 3 and Box 5. As you can see, your compensation is $50,000 but only $40,000 is being used to compute Social Security and Medicare taxes. Why is this? Some taxable fringe benefits, such as health care benefits (self-employed health insurance premiums and HSA contributions), are only added to Box 1 Wages, and not Box 3 or Box 5. Boom!

Explained another way; if we all decide that $50,000 is reasonable shareholder salary, and your self-employed health insurance premiums are $10,000, then only $40,000 is ran through payroll. But, the $40,000 and the $10,000 are combined to reflect total shareholder salary.

How does this translate to the corporate tax return? Line 7 of Form 1120S is "Compensation of officers" and the $50,000 in Box 1 above would be entered there (we'll chat about the effects of solo 401k plan deferrals in a bit). Line 21 of Form 1120S is "Ordinary business income." Line 7 as compared to Line 21 is one of the ways the IRS will consider a challenge of your S corporation with respect to reasonable shareholder salary (the IRS also looks at your K-1, specifically Box 16 Code D, as compared to your W-2, both connected by your Social Security Number).

Got it? Good. Next concept.

The second concept is that self-employed health insurance (SEHI) premiums are effectively deducted on Line 7 of Form 1120S as Officer Compensation. Therefore, the salary paid to the shareholders plus health insurance directly reduces Line 21 on Form 1120S which is your taxable ordinary income generated by the S corporation.

However, your W-2 shows $50,000 in taxable wages and this will appear on Line 1 of page 1 on your Form 1040. Hmmm... how does that work? We know what you are thinking- you are paying income taxes on the full $50,000 since the W-2 shows $50,000 but you were paid $40,000. Where are the tax savings?

This concern would be true except that you are considered self-employed as a greater than 2% shareholder, and therefore the health insurance premiums are deducted on Line 16 on Schedule 1 of your Form 1040 as an adjustment to income. This is a dollar-for-dollar reduction in your gross income to arrive at your adjusted gross income (AGI) on Line 8b.

Just to reiterate- the deduction and subsequent tax benefit of self-employed health insurance (SEHI) is done on the S corporation tax return. The deduction also appears on your individual tax return, but it is a net zero as we've illustrated above (we accountants call this an in and out... income comes in, but is adjusted out for a net zero effect).

Said in another way; salary and health insurance end up as Officer Compensation and are deducted together on the S Corp tax return. This amount appears again on your individual tax return, but you get a "reduction" for the health insurance component. Deduction on business return. Net zero on individual tax return.

If this doesn't resonate quite yet, don't worry. However, we have seen this screwed up several times when clients run their own payroll and / or prepare their own individual tax returns. Be aware and know that you should have a Line 16 entry on Schedule 1 of your Form 1040 if you are paying self-employed health insurance premiums.

To make things even stranger, a lot of taxpaying citizens are accustomed to health insurance either being 100% provided by their employer or a payroll deduction in some fashion. This works well for employees since the payroll deduction is usually pre-tax and therefore the tax benefit is immediate However, for the employee turned S Corp owner, this can be a small derailment during the transition.

To recap- we have an artificial increase in salary by the amount of SEHI and our reasonable shareholder salary testing is improved, but Social Security and Medicare taxes are computed on a lessor amount. Winner winner chicken dinner!

Another way to view your self-employment health insurance is that it is costing you about 60 cents on the dollar. 15 cents in less payroll taxes and another 25 cents in income tax savings. This might not make you feel better given the massive cost of health insurance, but here it is just the same.

There are more examples of this stuff in a later chapter dedicated to reasonable shareholder salary. Also, the handling of self-employed health insurance in this manner is encouraged by the IRS as outlined in Fact Sheet 2008-25.

Here is the blurb if you can't get enough-

> The health and accident insurance premiums paid on behalf of the greater than 2 percent S corporation shareholder-employee are deductible by the S corporation as fringe benefits and are reportable as wages for income tax withholding purposes on the shareholder-employee's Form W-2. They are not subject to Social Security or Medicare (FICA) or Unemployment (FUTA) taxes. Therefore, this additional compensation is included in Box 1 (Wages) of the Form W-2, Wage and Tax Statement, issued to the shareholder, but would not be included in Boxes 3 or 5 of Form W-2.

> A 2-percent shareholder-employee is eligible for an AGI deduction for amounts paid during the year for medical care premiums if the medical care coverage is established by the S corporation. Previously, "established by the S corporation" meant that the medical care coverage had to be in the name of the S corporation.

> In Notice 2008-1, the IRS stated that if the medical coverage plan is in the name of the 2percent shareholder and not in the name of the S corporation, a medical care plan can be considered to be established by the S corporation if: the S corporation either paid or reimbursed the 2percent shareholder for the premiums and reported the premium payment or reimbursement as wages on the 2percent shareholder's Form W-2.

> Payments of the health and accident insurance premiums on behalf of the shareholder may be further identified in Box 14 (Other) of the Form W-2. Schedule K-1 (Form 1120S)

and Form 1099 should not be used as an alternative to the Form W-2 to report this additional compensation.

That was IRS Fact Sheet 2008-25 which can be downloaded here-

wcginc.om/8247

Big Alert: If you have access to health insurance through your spouse, you generally cannot do two things. You cannot get your own health insurance coverage and have it be a tax deduction for the business. You also cannot consider the additional premium paid by your spouse as a reimbursement and therefore deduction for the business (typically this is already tax-advantaged since it deducted pre-tax by your spouse on their paycheck).

[intentionally blank to keep two cool tables together for comparison]

Here is a summary of the savings assuming a 40% salary and a $10,000 annual health insurance premium.

40% Reasonable Salary, With Health Insurance
The following table highlights the significant savings when factoring self-employed health insurance into the reasonable salary calculations.

Income	Total SE Tax	Salary	Total Payroll Tax	Delta	Delta%
30,000	4,239	2,000	306	3,933	13.1%
50,000	7,065	10,000	1,530	5,535	11.1%
75,000	10,597	20,000	3,060	7,537	10.0%
100,000	14,130	30,000	4,590	9,540	9.5%
150,000	18,711	50,000	7,650	11,061	7.4%
200,000	20,050	70,000	10,710	9,340	4.7%
300,000	22,972	110,000	16,830	6,142	2.0%
500,000	29,991	190,000	20,204	9,787	2.0%

35% Reasonable Salary, Without Health Insurance
As mentioned, the previous illustrations are based on a reasonable salary that was 40% of the net ordinary business income after expenses and deductions. If your reasonable S Corp salary is less than this, your savings increase. For grins, the table below shows the results and subsequent savings using a 35% reasonable salary figure. Check out the $150,000 figure! $10k in savings.

Income	Total SE Tax	Salary	Total Payroll Tax	Delta	Delta%
30,000	4,239	10,500	1,607	2,632	8.8%
50,000	7,065	17,500	2,678	4,387	8.8%
75,000	10,597	26,250	4,016	6,581	8.8%
100,000	14,130	35,000	5,355	8,775	8.8%
150,000	18,711	52,500	8,033	10,679	7.1%
200,000	20,050	70,000	10,710	9,340	4.7%
300,000	22,972	105,000	16,065	6,907	2.3%
500,000	29,991	175,000	19,769	10,222	2.0%

The salary calculation part of running an S Corp is one of the biggest challenges, but it also allows for most wiggle room for argument if necessary. Our chapter on S Corp salary will touch on the various tools we use to determine a reasonable shareholder salary including-

▲ IRS Revenue Ruling 74-44

▲ IRS Fact Sheet 2008-25

▲ Tax Court Cases

▲ Bureau of Labor Statistics / Risk Management Association Data

▲ RCReports

▲ Rules of Thumb (Biz Valuation, 1/3 1/3 1/3)

Here is some initial food for thought from a 2013 Tax Court case-

Sean McAlary Ltd. Inc. v. Commissioner, TC Summary Opinion 2013-62- the IRS hired a valuation expert to determine that a real estate agent should have been paid $100,755 salary out of his S Corp's net income of $231,454. Not bad. He still took home over $130,000 in K-1 income and avoided some self-employment taxes. The valuation expert had used Bureau of Labor Statistics data to determine the average salary for real estate agents in the taxpayer's zip code.

Here is the entire Tax Court summary opinion-

wcginc.com/8244

Please don't be that guy who extrapolates or basically twists the previous Tax Court case into something else. BLS data is only one aspect of determining a reasonable salary. As mentioned, there is more on the salary stuff in a later chapter and pinning your entire argument on BLS data might leave money on the table.

Until then, consider the following summary which outlines the savings using various net ordinary business income after expenses and deductions, and reasonable shareholder salaries paid (including one with self-employed health insurance)-

Net Biz Income	40% Salary No Health Ins.	40% Salary $10k Health Ins.	35% Salary No Health Ins.
30,000	2,403	3,933	2,632
50,000	4,005	5,535	4,387
75,000	6,007	7,537	6,581
100,000	8,010	9,540	8,775
150,000	9,531	11,061	10,679
200,000	7,810	9,340	9,340
300,000	4,798	6,142	6,907
500,000	9,497	9,787	10,222

Good stuff!

Why are we belaboring the heck out of this? In other words, does payroll really need to be dialed in this tightly? Consider that paying a salary which is $10,000 too high will cost you $1,530 in unnecessary payroll taxes. Read that again. If you paid yourself $100,000 when a reasonable salary could have been $80,000, you paid $3,060 too much in payroll taxes. What would you rather spend $3,060 on? Lots!

So, payroll calculations need to be just a bit tighter than bar napkin quality and just a hair below NASA precision.

[more intentional blank space]

S Corp Hard Money Facts, Net Savings

Sales pitch alert! WCG specializes in small businesses which have a small number of owners, and often just a one-person show. Did you know that 95% of all S Corps have only one shareholder, and 99% of all S Corps have three or fewer shareholders?

Common S Corp candidates and current clients for **WCG CPAs & Advisors** are consultants, attorneys, financial advisors, insurance agents, physicians, chiropractors, doctors, surgeons, anesthesiologists, nurse anesthetists, real estate agents, contractors, photographers (the profitable ones), online retailers, FBA retailers and good ol' fashion widget makers, among several others. We also have several medical groups and financial advisor teams operating multi-tiered entity structures.

The tax savings of an S corporation is not in dispute. But what does it cost to have tax preparation, payroll, tax planning and consultation done? Because small businesses are a core competency for us, we have created Business Advisory Services packages that includes the following-

Tax Planning and Preparation	Vail	Telluride	Aspen
Pro-Active Household Tax Planning	✓	✓	Advanced
Pro-Active Business Entity Tax Planning, PTET	Add-On*	✓	✓
Annual Tax Reduction and Deferral Analysis	✓	✓	✓
Small Business Tax Deductions Optimization	✓	✓	✓
Section 199A QBI Tax and Salary Optimization	✓	✓	✓
Estimated Tax Payments (done thru payroll)	✓	✓	✓
Business Entity Tax Prep	✓	✓	✓
Individual Tax Prep, One Owner	✓	✓	✓
Expat / Foreign Income Calcs, Forms	Add-On	Add-On	Add-On
Tax Resolution, IRS Audit Defense	As Req'd	As Req'd	As Req'd
Situational Tax Law Research (up to 3 hours)			✓

Payroll and Accounting Services	Vail	Telluride	Aspen
Reasonable Shareholder Salary Calculation	✓	✓	✓
Monthly Shareholder Payroll Processing	✓	✓	✓
Employee Payroll Processing	Add-On	Add-On	Add-On
Annual Payroll Processing (includes ten 1099s)	✓	✓	✓
Accounting Services (bookkeeping + analysis)	Add-On	Add-On	Add-On
Quarterly QuickBooks Consulting, QuickStart	Add-On	✓	✓

Business Advisory Services	Vail	Telluride	Aspen
Consulting			
Consultation, Periodic Business Reviews (PBR)	Annually	Routine	Routine
Complimentary Quick Chats (CQC)	Routine	Routine	Routine
Interfacing with Other Professionals		Routine	Routine
Financial Analysis			
Fractional Controller	Add-On	Add-On	Add-On
Financial Statements Analysis, Comparisons		Quarterly	Quarterly
Cash Flow Management and Analysis			Annually
First Research, Industry-Focused Consulting		Annually	Annually
National and Metro Economic Reports			Annually
KPI Analysis, Benchmarking, Trend Analysis			✓
Budgeting, Forecasting, Goal-Setting			✓
Strategy and Maintenance			
C-Level Financial Advice and Strategic Planning			✓
Succession Planning, Exit Consultation			✓
Annual Business Valuation			✓
Annual Corporate Governance, Meetings		✓	✓
Annual Fee*	$4,320	$7,560	**Custom**
Monthly Fee*	$360	$630	Custom
		(prorated based on onboarding date)	

Custom! Unlike the modern-day new car packages where you have to spend $8,000 for the moonroof, our Business Advisory Service plans can be customized specifically for you. The array above is simply a starting point. If you need more from us, let's chat about it!

Tax Patrol Services

We also have Tax Patrol! This is a wonderful tax service for those who don't need all the business advisory bells and whistles above, but from time to time want some love from an experienced tax consultant and business advisor. Have a quick tax question? Need to know the depreciation rules as you buy that new car? Wondering what your April tax bill is going to be in August? Tax Patrol is like ski patrol... you might not use it, but you sleep better knowing you have it.

Tax Patrol	Keystone	Copper	Breck
Individual Tax Prep)	✓		✓
Business Entity Tax Prep		✓	✓
Tax Planning, Tax Projection Worksheets	Streamlined	Pro-Active*	Pro-Active*
Estimated Tax Payments Calcs	✓	✓	✓
Tax Resolution, IRS Audit Defense	Add-On	Add-On	Add-On
Complimentary Quick Chats (CQC)	Routine	Routine	Routine
Annual Fee	**$1,500**	**$2,100**	**$3,180**
Monthly Fee	$125	$175	$265

(prorated based on onboarding date)

*The Tax Planning Asterisk

Yeah, we all dislike the little asterisk. The gotcha! The fine print! Well, here is one of those situations. Pro-active and Pro-active Biz are different. Pro-active tax planning is limited (for individuals and households) and does not include business-entity tax planning and payments (California's Franchise Tax, New Jersey's BAIT, Portland's overall madness, NYC, etc.), pass-through entity tax (PTET) calculations and payments, among other things. Not every business entity needs separate tax planning! Please see our Tax Planning Services webpage and Master Service Agreement for more information.

wcginc.com/msa

[intentional white space]

Accounting and Payroll Services

Accounting fees are based on 2 bank account with less than 250 monthly transactions and include the QBO fee from Intuit. Custom quote is available if you have a lot going on such as third-party integrations (POS, time billing system), accrual accounting method, extensive benefits packages and / or industry specific issues (e.g, job costing in construction).

Employee payroll can be added to shareholder payroll for $100 per month if already using our Business Advisory Service plans above (e.g, Vail), or $175 for standalone. Custom quote for more than 5 employees and a referral to therapy.

Accounting, Payroll

Monthly Accounting	starting at $500 / month
Bi-Monthly Accounting	starting at $250 / month
Quad-Monthly	starting at $175 / month
Sales Tax, Personal Property Tax	typically $75 / month, or $150 / quarter
Employee Payroll (up to 5, bi-weekly)	1 employee, $100 / month 2-5 employees, $175 / month

Prorated Fees

Some more things to consider- when a partial year remains, our usual annual fee is pro-rated to not charge you for services you didn't use (like payroll and consultation). However, a large chunk of our annual fee is tax preparation which is typically a built-in fixed amount of $1,600 (both business entity and individual tax returns). Whether we onboard you in January, July or December, we have to prepare a full year tax return. This increases the monthly fee for the remaining months of 2021 but the monthly fee will later decrease in January of 2022 to reflect the amounts above. Yeah, we make it sound like 2021 is just around the corner.

Payroll Processing

We make very little profits on payroll processing... we offer it as a convenience to our clients. One throat to choke with a single call can be reassuring but if you want to run your payroll, go for it! Everyone thinks payroll is a piece of cake; write a check and done. Nope... we see a lot of mistakes being made by clients especially the handling of health insurance and HSA contributions since there are special rules for greater than 2% S Corp shareholders. Then again, we don't mind fixing what was broken.

Tax Returns
You can prepare your own individual tax return as well... but the benefit WCG preparing both individual and business tax returns is that we slide things around depending on income limitations and phaseouts.

> Note: An individual tax return is what the IRS calls Form 1040 and refers to the entity filing the tax return (you, the individual, are the entity). However, a married couple are deemed to be one entity for the sake of an individual tax return. So, when we say we will prepare your individual tax return, it is meant to include your spouse in a jointly filed tax return.

Break-Even Analysis (does an S Corp make sense?)
Break-even analysis is based on our annual fee of $4,320. If an S corporation saves you 8% to 10% (on average) in taxes over the garden-variety LLC, then $4,320 divided by 9% equals $48,000 of net ordinary business income after expenses and deductions.

More sales pitch! Keep in mind that our fee of $4,320 includes your individual tax return which you might already be paying another tax professional to prepare. WCG has a handful of clients who are right at the break-even point of $48,000 but leverage an S Corp and our services to get tax preparation, tax planning and consultation.

You can always find someone to do it for less- we know that. At the same time, we have a vested interest in your success and provide sound tax and business consultation as a part of our service. Here is a link to our Periodic Business Review agenda that we cover throughout the year so our consultation to you is comprehensive-

wcginc.com/PBR

We also have written a webpage on end of year tax planning-

wcginc.com/EOY

And, to see our entire fee structure (transparency)-

wcginc.com/fee

Ancillary Benefits with S Corporations
As we've discussed, the big benefit with an S Corp is the reduction of self-employment taxes. There are some other benefits that we touch on throughout our book, but they are also recapped here-

Section 199A Qualified Business Income Deduction
Once you hit the 32% marginal tax bracket, your QBI deduction either a) phases out if you are deemed to be a Specified Service Trade or Business (SSTB), or b) has a secondary test based on W-2 wages paid and / or qualified property. If you are a sole proprietor, an LLC or a partnership, and not taxed as an S corporation, you cannot pay owner wages. As such, an S Corp election might be necessary allow wages to be paid to the shareholders to resolve the QBI phaseout due to W-2 wages paid.

The quick Section 199A secondary test math goes like this- 20% of net business income (profits) or 50% of wages paid including employee wages, whichever is lower. 50% x $0 is $0, even in Canada.

Pass-Through Entity (PTE) Tax Deduction
Way back in 2017, the Tax Cuts and Jobs Act was passed with a lot of cool tax deductions like the Section 199A qualified business income deduction. But life is one big equalizer, and Congress wanted to limit state and local taxes (SALT) to $10,000. This means either state income taxes or real estate taxes, or both, were severely muted.

So! States got creative and created a state tax that was deducted on partnerships and S corporations tax returns (otherwise called pass-through entities) resulting in lower federal taxable income. This tax is in turn credited on the business owner's individual tax return for the state. In other words, the business pays for the human's state income taxes and this lowers the federal income associated with the business.

This also called the great SALT work-around. Cash is cash to a business owner whether it is spent by the business or the human.

Why is the PTE tax deduction considered an S corporation benefit? Your single-member LLC is not considered a pass-through entity, but if you slap an S Corp election on it, you suddenly have this deduction available to you (you can also add another member and tax your LLC as a partnership).

There are all kinds of rules, and not every business owner will benefit from the PTET deduction.

Lower Audit Rate Risk
Travel, meals and auto expenses are the big triggers for a Schedule C audit of your 1040 individual tax return. This is why the IRS calls them out specifically on the tax form. However,

with an S Corp (and partnership or C corporation), these expenses are generally tucked away into other deductions. Home office is also tucked away.

S Corporations enjoy a 0.4% audit rate risk versus 3-5%. The best way to win an argument with the IRS is not having the conversation in the first place.

California's LLC Fee
Without an S Corp election, California's LLCs fee is based on gross receipts regardless of actual net income after expenses (profits) earned. With an S corporation, this tax is based on 1.5% of the net income (with an $800 minimum).

QSubs
A Qualified Subchapter S Subsidiary, also known as a QSub or QSSS, is simply an S corporation that's owned by another S corporation. A QSub is treated as a subsidiary of the parent S corporation. Why do you care?

At times you want to merge two businesses, but the assets are immoveable (think of a Medicare certification or a specialized defense contract). You might need to S elect one before the combination because of certain rules with the merger. You might also want to combine gross receipts for the passive investment income test, or combine basis between stock and loan basis, or combine to release accumulated earnings and profit (AE&P). This is a bit technical, but just a little awareness as you move along in business life.

Officer Compensation with Solo 401k Plan Deferral
Previously we showed you a mock-up of a W-2 with self-employed health insurance premiums added to Box 1 as Wages. When you have a solo 401k plan and make employee (you) deferrals, that reduces Box 1 of your W-2. However, Line 7 of the corporate tax return will still show the gross salary paid plus self-employed health insurance premiums as Officer Compensation.

In other words, contributing to a 401k plan does not reduce your Officer Compensation below a level where the IRS might challenge your reasonable salary determination. If you worked for Google making $100,000, and Google collects $23,000 and sends it off to the 401k people on your behalf, Google's wage expense remains at $100,000. Same thing here.

Let's geek out with a journal entry assuming $50,000 reasonable salary calculation with a $10,000 self-employed health insurance premium and an $23,000 employee pre-tax deferral-

DR Shareholder Wage Expense	40,000	
DR Self-Employed Health Ins.	10,000	
DR Payroll Taxes	3,060	(7.65% of $40,000)
CR 401k Liability		23,000
CR Cash		30,060

Line 7 Officer Compensation would read $50,000, but Box 1 of your W-2 would read $50,000 less $23,000 for 401k or $27,000. Your adjusted gross income on your individual tax return would be $27,000 less $10,000 for health insurance or $17,000. Yes, we would have K-1 income of some mystery number but you get the idea.

We will give you more examples including a table showing how this shakes out in our chapter on S Corp salaries. Super fun!

W-2 Converted to 1099

One of the biggest pushes into the S Corp world is when your employer decides to convert you from W-2 to 1099. You are fired on Friday and brought back on Monday as a contractor. Now what?

To refresh your memory, when you are paid a W-2 salary your employer pays for half of the Social Security and Medicare taxes associated with your income. Conversely when you are paid as a 1099 contractor, you pay both halves of the Social Security and Medicare tax.

Another nice feature of being paid a W-2 salary is the built-in budgeting since your taxes are taken out before the direct deposit into your checking account. On the other hand, 1099 income is raw- just a big ol' fat check ready to spend.

Businesses like to have contractors versus employees since it cuts down on cost and offers more flexibility. Some businesses can easily exceed a factor of 1.5 for a fully burdened labor rate. For example, if you are being paid a $100,000 salary, the cost to the employer could be $150,000 after you factor in payroll taxes, 401k contributions, pension funding, health insurance, vacations and sick pay, office resources, etc. This would be a factor of 1.5.

Another benefit of deploying contractors is when a business needs to shrink, it simply ends the contract or reduces it dramatically without much hoopla. If Northrop Grumman laid off

10,000 workers there would be congressional hearings. If they cancel 10,000 contracts with sub-contractors, no one pays any attention to it.

Some employers, such as Verizon, have recently gotten in trouble by converting too many W-2 employees into 1099 contractors. The IRS and several states see it as an end-around. Many one-person S corporations are probably disguised W-2 employees so this is a sensitive subject.

Regardless, when entertaining being converted from W-2 to 1099, consider the fully burdened labor rate of your employer. If you were making $100,000, you really need to make at least $130,000 or more to come out ahead. You win, they win.

Don't forget that as a 1099 contractor you now can rifle a bunch of expenses through your business that were otherwise limited or not allowed. Wait! What? Let's take mileage as an example. If you are paid as a W-2 employee, you cannot deduct mileage expenses since 2017. But if you are paid as a contractor, your business can either own the car and deduct actual expenses, deduct mileage (Schedule c) or reimburse you for mileage (S Corp). Not just one option, baby, but a 3-pack of 'em.

Being converted from a W-2 employee to a contractor is risky since the connective tissue is reduced dramatically, but generally it is a good thing since it puts you in a better tax position (and you might actually make more money). However, don't leak that out during negotiations.

Lastly, create an LLC and tax it as an S corporation, or at least consider it. In another chapter we'll review some of the reasons an S Corp election is not good. In yet another chapter, we take the W-2 Converted to 1099 one step further when considering a reasonable shareholder salary.

Net Investment Income, Medicare Surtax and S Corps

To help fund the Affordable Care Act (Obamacare), an additional Medicare surtax is tacked on to your net investment income. Recall that as an S corporation owner, you are both employee and investor. When you trigger the high-income threshold for the Medicare surtax, then you could pay 3.8% (2.9% Medicare plus 0.9% surtax) on some portions of your income.

The tax is calculated by multiplying the 3.8% tax rate by the lower of the following two amounts:

▲ net investment income for the year; or

▲ modified adjusted gross income over a certain threshold amount ($200,000 for single filers and $250,000 for married filing jointly).

Again, whichever is lower (how nice of Congress?).

The IRS defines net investment income for the purposes of calculating the Medicare surtax as interest, dividends, capital gains, annuities, royalties, rents, and pass-through income from a passive business such as S Corps and partnerships. Yuck. Why did they have to pointedly name S corporations?

But! And this is a big but! Like a Mama June butt. If you materially participate in your S Corp this income is not included in the net investment income calculation. 99% of the small business owners out there who elect to be treated as an S Corp will also qualify as materially participating. In other words, your income is not considered passive which would otherwise be subject to the Net Investment Income Tax. Yeah baby!

Here is the laundry list the IRS uses for testing material participation-

To materially participate in a business for a particular year, the shareholder must meet one of the following seven tests discussed in Temporary Regulations Section 1.469-5T(a)-

▲ The shareholder participated in the activity for more than 500 hours during the year;

▲ The shareholder's participation in the activity constituted substantially all the participation of all individuals in the activity;

▲ The shareholder participated for more than 100 hours in the activity, and the shareholder's hours were not less than those of any other participant in the activity;

▲ The activity is a significant participation activity for the year, and the shareholder's aggregate participation in all significant participation activities exceeded 500 hours;

▲ The shareholder materially participated in the activity for any five of the past 10 years;

▲ The activity is a personal services activity where the shareholder materially participated in the activity for any three years preceding the tax year; or

▲ Based on all the facts and circumstances, the shareholder participated in the activity on a regular, continuous, and substantial basis.

This list is an "or" list, therefore you only need to fit into one of the buckets to trigger the material participation designation. Interestingly, these regulations are titled Temporary Regulations but they have been around for a very long time. Like forever. Maybe even forever and ever.

Material participation is a common theme with the IRS, and in some respects, it changes the color of money similar to an S Corp election. A silent investor in an S corporation will have passive income and might be subject to Medicare surtax on that income. That same investor now materially participates, and the same income is now considered non-passive (or quasi-earned but without self-employment taxes) and is sheltered from the Medicare surtax.

While we are here, let's chat about being a passive business owner.

Being a Passive Business Owner

This is aimed at business owners where they no longer materially participate in the business activity, and as such they are now considered passive investors. Seems easy right, but why would you care? For two big reasons- first, if you have other non-deductible passive losses due to income limitations, such as those from a rental property, you can now have your passive income absorb these passive losses. This allows you to enjoy your tax benefits now rather than delaying the pleasure to future years. Yay!

Second, you might be able to only draw distributions from your business rather than earned income (i.e., reasonable shareholder salary) + distributions. This saves you several thousands of dollars in avoided Social Security and Medicare taxes. Every $10,000 in owner salary is about $1,500 in payroll taxes. Yay again!

The world is always trending towards harmony, so here are the passive business owner downsides. It is difficult to claim passive business owner given the material participation tests. The hardest one to overcome is #5. Here is a blurb from our Real Estate Professional webpage which is applicable to all business owners, not just real estate related-

> 5. You materially participated in the activity for any 5 (whether or not consecutive) of the 10 immediately preceding tax years.
>
> IRS Audit Techniques Guide (ATG): An activity is non-passive if the taxpayer would have been treated as materially participating in any 5 of the previous 10 years (whether or not consecutive). This test usually applies when a taxpayer "retires from material participation" but maintains an ownership interest in the activity. Yikes (emphasis added).

IRS Examination Techniques: Even if the taxpayer performs no services for a business currently, the examiner should inquire about involvement in prior years and review the returns to see if income or losses were treated as non-passive.

In other words, you need to look back for 10 years and if 5 of those years had material participation by you in the business activity (as defined by the IRS and Treasury Regs), then the IRS will disallow your passive claim. Could you start a brand-new business without the history? Perhaps, but this might be viewed as an end-around especially if the new business magically looks, walks, talks and smells like the old. Transitioning from material participation to passive is certainly tough!

Three Types of Income

Let's back up a bit. Our book loves to spill the beans so-to-speak with the net-net fun facts, and then dig a hole under the house for the foundation. Wow. All kinds of metaphors. There are three types of income- earned, portfolio and passive. There is also a small subset of passive income called non-passive income.

Earned Income

Earned income is income that is a direct result of your labor. This income is usually in the form of W-2 wages or as small business income reported on Schedule C of your individual tax return (Form 1040), both subjected to Social Security and Medicare taxes (self-employment taxes). There are other areas such as Schedule E or F where income can come into your individual tax return and be subjected to self-employment taxes, but Schedule C is the most common.

Portfolio Income

Portfolio income is income generated from selling an asset, and if you sell that asset for a higher price than what you paid for it originally, you will have a gain. Depending on the holding period of the asset, and other factors, that gain might be taxed at ordinary income tax rates or capital gains tax rates. Interest and dividends are other examples of portfolio income.

Capital gains are not a form of income per se. Capital gains simply defines how your portfolio income will be taxed. Income is income, and is therefore taxed. This income might be taxed at capital gains rates or ordinary rates. Subtle difference.

Portfolio income is not subjected to self-employment taxes, but as illustrated earlier it might be subjected to net investment income (NII) Medicare surtax.

Passive Income

We touched on this in a previous section. Passive income bluntly is income that would continue to generate if you died. Morbid. How about this? Passive income is income that would continue to generate if you decided to do nothing and sunbathe on some beach. That sounds better. Passive income includes rental income, royalties and income from businesses or investment partnerships / multi-member LLCs where you do not materially participate.

Passive income is also not subjected to self-employment taxes. But similar to portfolio income, it might be subject to the Net Investment Income tax. So, if you own a rental house, the income generated from the rental house is considered passive income although your participation might be considered active. If you take this same rental, and provide short-term rental periods and offer certain services, your income might be considered earned income. Rentals pose all kinds of problems.

> Sidebar: Taxpayers used to label themselves as Real Estate Professionals under IRS definition to allow passive losses to be deducted; now we are seeing the same label to avoid Net Investment Income tax on rental income.

Additionally, if you wrote a book and receive royalty checks, that income is also passive and not subjected to self-employment taxes. But, if you write several books or make updates to an existing book (like this one) then you are materially participating in your activity and your income is earned income. And Yes, you would pay self-employment taxes on that income.

Non-Passive Income

But there is another funny thing. K-1 income generated from an S Corp where you materially participate is considered non-passive income. It is not necessarily earned income and it is not passive income. It is something in between, but definitely without the Social Security and Medicare tax element.

As an aside, expatriates, or expats for short, can exclude up to $126,500 (for the 2024 tax year) of earned income while working overseas. Many establish S corporations stateside for their contract gig- both the W-2 and K-1 income up to $126,500 are excluded from income tax.

Therefore, as a shareholder in an S corporation you will receive a K-1. How this income is labeled can change depending on your involvement. Material participation makes your K-1 income non-passive, otherwise it is passive income. As mentioned earlier, this changes the color of money in certain tax applications.

Where is this all leading to? Good question.

More Net Investment Tax, Self-Rentals and S Corps
The Net Investment Income Tax was a topic that was briefly broached earlier. Generally, passive income such as long-term rental income will be considered net investment income and subject to the Medicare surtax. Why do you care? Yes, we ask that a lot.

It is common for a business owner who relies on machinery or equipment to have two business entities. One entity is an LLC that owns the assets. The other entity is an S corporation which leases the assets from the LLC to use in the business. This directly reduces the S Corp's net operating business income, and might possibly reduce the amount of salary required to be paid by the business to the shareholders. Good news.

Here is an example-

	S Corp Owns Building	LLC Owns Building S Corp Rents from LLC
Gross Income	100,000	100,000
Rental Expense	0	30,000
Net Income	100,000	70,000
Reasonable Salary (assumed at 40%)	40,000	28,000
Payroll Taxes	5,640	3,948
Savings		1,692

This is an overly simplified example and leaves out depreciation, etc., but you get the idea. In addition, we used a 40% salary calculation simply for the sake of presentation. Your actual salary might be different in your situation. Regardless, the apples to apples comparison shows a nice little savings of $1,692. As mentioned in a previous chapter, the arrangement also allows you to have different partners in each entity allowing you to expand ownership in the operating entity while retaining full ownership in the leased asset (building).

More good news. The LLC's activities are considered self-rental activities which means that you are creating a transaction with yourself. Provided that this arrangement is at market rates, the IRS accepts this relationship. Moreover, the self-rental income is not considered passive and therefore not subjected to the Net Investment Income Tax calculations.

We know what you are thinking... wait for it... Yes, this changes the color of money (how many times have we said this?).

Here is the code. Regulations Section 1.469-2 boringly read-

> (f)(6) Property rented to a non-passive activity. An amount of the taxpayer's gross rental activity income for the taxable year from an item of property equal to the net rental activity income for the year from that item of property is treated as not from a passive activity if the property-
>
> (i) Is rented for use in a trade or business activity (within the meaning of paragraph (e)(2) of this section) in which the taxpayer materially participates (within the meaning of Section 1.469-5T) for the taxable year; and
>
> (ii) Is not described in Section 1.469-2T(f)(5).

Read that first paragraph again. Only attorneys and legislators could have taken a simple concept and made it unnecessarily complicated. Let's summarize. If you have a self-rental situation with a business where you materially participate, that income is not considered passive income.

Self-rental situations are not just limited to buildings. You could lease your car to your S corporation. No, this isn't the same as leasing a car from a dealership. This is where you own a piece of equipment, let's say an automobile, and you lease it back to your business for your business's use. Sounds exotic, but it is quite simple. More about this in a later chapter dedicated to fringe benefits and tax deductions.

This is about the equipment used in your trade or craft. Field engineers and landscapers are just a few that come to mind who benefit from a self-rental situation.

Wait! There's more. There's always more.

Interest income generated from loans to the S corporation are also excluded from the Net Investment Income Tax calculations to the extent of your allocable share of non-passive deduction. Huh? Example time.

Jim Smith and Sharon Jones own JS Toys as 60-40 partners. Jim received $1,000 in interest income from the business because he lent the business money. Jim owns 60% of the business. Therefore, Jim can exclude $600 from his net investment income since that is his allocable share of non-passive income. The remaining $400 would be subjected to the Net Investment Income Tax calculation. Yes, we accountants love a stupidly convoluted tax code- keeps you confused or bored, and keeps us employed.

Make sure this stuff is handled correctly. You might be paying a Medicare surtax gratuitously.

Here is a little teaser: you would never want to own real estate in your S corporation, or any appreciating asset for that matter. We'll explore this in our next chapter.

Income Types Recap
We talked about a lot of things regarding the type of income and how it is treated. Here is a brief recap-

▲ Earned income is subjected to self-employment taxes for self-employed, or payroll taxes in the form of Social Security and Medicare taxes for the W-2 employee. Easy.

▲ Portfolio income is generated by selling assets and is taxed at the capital gains rate or ordinary income tax rate depending on how long you owned the asset. Interest and dividends are also considered portfolio income. Also easy.

▲ Long-term rental income is considered passive income which is taxed at the ordinary income tax rate only (as opposed to being taxed twice, once with self-employment taxes and again with ordinary income taxes). Rental losses are considered passive losses.

▲ Passive losses can only be deducted from passive income, generally. But there are exceptions, of course.

▲ Passive losses might be deducted against other forms of income such as earned income, portfolio income and non-passive income up to a $25,000 limit. This requires your participation to be considered active, which is a much easier threshold than material participation. Usually 100 hours will do it.

▲ The deduction of passive losses with active participation becomes limited when modified adjusted gross incomes exceed $100,000 and are reduced to zero at $150,000. Those disallowed losses are carried forward into the future to be used when incomes or dispositions of assets allow.

▲ Non-passive income cannot be offset or reduced by passive losses except the magical $25,000 figure. So, if you have $100,000 in passive losses from your rental properties and $100,000 in income generated from your self-rental to your business, your non-passive income can only be reduced to $75,000.

▲ There are PIGs (Passive Income Generators) which have been under IRS scrutiny as abusive tax shelters since their sole purpose is to generate passive income in the beginning to offset other passive losses.

Tilt. This can be confusing. Please contact WCG for more assistance and hopefully clarification.

Chapter 4
The 185 Reasons to Not
Have an S Corp or LLC
(updated October 2023)

Chapter Introduction

Not everything that glitters is gold so there are a handful of downsides, some manageable, to the S Corp election or having an LLC. A lot of these examples stand alone, and some of these depend on the net income of the business and other external factors. **WCG CPAs & Advisors** can help guide you through the decision-making process.

And No, there are not 185 reasons- it was just a self-proclaimed catchy number. Most of these reasons in the beginning of this chapter focus on S corporations. However, there are some general pains with having any type of formalized entity, and those are near the end.

Specifically, in this chapter we will review these disadvantages to having an S corporation-

▲ Increased cost (tax preparation, payroll taxes)

▲ 401k or SEP IRA limitations

▲ Trapped assets

▲ Disparate distributions not allowed (but we have a work-around)

▲ Other W-2 income

▲ Deducting losses, trapped cash

▲ Expanding ownership

▲ State taxes

▲ Among other smaller issues

Specific to S corporations, we ask these general questions of each business owner before diving into the nitty-gritty-

▲ Does your business earn over $48,000 net income after expenses (profit)? Say Yes.

▲ Are you located in New York City or Tennessee where S corporation tax rates are egregious and suck up all the federal tax savings? New Hampshire? Say No (unless you are being limited by Section 199A for lack of wages).

▲ Do you have other W-2 income that exceeds or comes close to exceeding the Social Security limits of $168,600 (for the 2024 tax year)? Say No. If you say Yes, we need net ordinary business income after expenses and deductions to exceed $250,000 in #1 above.

▲ Are your state and local taxes limited on Schedule A of your individual tax return? If so, an S corporation might create what has been deemed the SALT work-around where state income taxes are paid and deducted by the business. Say Maybe.

▲ Is this a going concern? In other words, is the business going to continue to earn the same income or more each year? Say Yes.

▲ Do you have an LLC or some other entity in place that can be elected to be taxed as an S Corp? Say Yes. If you say No, we have options just not elegant ones.

Are you still here? Excellent news... then read on!

Additional Accounting Costs

Paying shareholders through payroll and filing a corporate tax return costs money- but with a potential 8% to 10% savings of net income, the benefits will exceed the costs especially if the net ordinary business income (profit) after expenses and deductions exceeds $48,000. This is net income after expenses (profit)- not gross revenue. So many business owners think in terms of gross income- we don't care about gross income necessarily when contemplating an S corporation election, and the IRS doesn't care about gross income when it comes to taxable income.

Since the cost of payroll services and corporate tax return preparation is relatively fixed, the more profit you earn the more you'll save. Something to discuss and consider.

Quick Numbers: Let's say $100,000 in net income saves you $9,000. WCG charges $4,320 ($360 per month) for business entity and individual tax returns, payroll and estimated taxes, income tax modeling and planning, and business consultation under our Vail Business Advisory Services plan. Therefore, a $100,000 S corporation saves you close to $5,000 after our fee, and we do all the work (and give you wonderful tax planning, the forgotten art of most accountants).

Here is a link to our transparent fee structure including our Business Advisory Service plans (a CPA firm who publishes fees?!)-

wcginc.com/fee

If you already have a partnership or multi-member LLC, and you file a partnership tax return (Form 1065) your break-even point is about half, or $20,000 based on the sunk cost of the business entity tax return preparation.

> Sidebar: The savings illustrated here and throughout our book is per person. If you have a multi-member LLC with three partners, and the business has profits of $300,000 (as an example), an S Corp election could easily save the group $27,000 as a whole.

If you also run payroll within your business because you have a staff, then the annual cost of having an S Corp could be zero. So, now your $100,000 actually puts $8,000ish in your pocket (there are some other expenses like unemployment taxes, keep reading).

In other words, a large chunk of the $4,320 is business tax return preparation and payroll (about $2,700). Therefore, if you already pay for these services within your business then they are considered sunk costs when contemplating the S Corp election.

> Sidebar: Consideration of sunk costs should be removed from decision making. One and done costs, like business formation and set up fees should be amortized over the projected life of the business. Yes, it is real money. Yes, it hurts especially all at once. Yes, the pain goes away with time. Just ask a Jets or Browns fan.

If you break-even on the fees as compared to your savings, keep in mind the additional benefits. With our business advisory service packages you are getting individual tax return preparation plus routine tax planning and consultation. There is value there, so if you break-even in terms of cost-benefit analysis, you might actually be ahead.

We are not considering the huge benefits from pass-through qualified business income tax deductions as outlined in Section 199A of the Tax Cuts & Jobs Act of 2017. At this point, in this chapter, one of our primary focuses is the delta between a non-S Corp and an S Corp.

Real numbers and real examples used to be contained in this book, but are now parsed out to be a separate addendum.

Additional Payroll Taxes

The IRS will expect unemployment taxes (FUTA) on all W-2 wages paid, including corporate officers. According to IRS Topic Number 759, for the 2024 tax year the first $7,000 will be taxed at 6% with a credit of up to 5.4% for unemployment taxes paid to your state (SUTA). This $7,000 has not changed since 1983. Crazy!

Some states such as Alaska, Kansas, Minnesota, Nebraska, Oregon, Washington state and Washington D.C. will allow you to opt out of state unemployment.

Before you opt out of your state unemployment taxes, consider two things. First, you get a credit for the state unemployment taxes paid when you file your federal unemployment taxes on Form 940. This is a big deal. Here is how it works-

Minnesota (for example) has a wage base of $40,000 (for the 2023 tax year). Let's say the average SUTA rate is 2.6% and your salary is $42,000. You would pay $910 to Minnesota for unemployment. Then, because you paid into Minnesota's unemployment system, the IRS only charges you 0.6% of the first $7,000 or $42. So... $910 + $42 = $952. If you opted out, you would only pay 6% of the first $7,000 or $420. Opting out in Minnesota at this wage base makes sense.

In Colorado, where you cannot opt-out but provides a good illustration, the wage base is $20,400 (for the 2023 tax year). If your SUTA rate was 2.1% then you would pay $428 to Colorado and $42 to the IRS for a total of $470. If you could opt out and did opt out, the IRS would charge you 6% of the first $7,000 or $420. A tiny savings, but a savings nonetheless (you just covered 10% of your wine pairing dinner at Ski Tip Lodge in Keystone).

Some states, such as California, were in arrears with the federal government on unemployment debt payments and as such the credit the IRS provides was reduced. For example, the FUTA rate is 0.6% if you pay SUTA, but for California businesses the FUTA rate is 2.7% in addition to the SUTA rate. California caught up on its federal unemployment debt in 2018 thanks to the backs of resident taxpayers, and the FUTA rate will revert to 0.6%.

Note the subtle difference- full FUTA rate is 6% and the reduced rate is 0.6%. The simple decimal move is sneaky.

The COVID unemployment craziness will certainly put more states into arrears with the federal government. It will be interesting to see how this plays out. There could be debt payments made on the backs of small businesses as they see a higher unemployment tax. Remember, unemployment is a payroll tax that is wholly paid by the employer.

Second... and this one you might laugh at... second, if you shut down your S corporation you might be eligible for unemployment benefits. Remember, unemployment benefits are administered by the state and if you opt out because of your corporate officer exemption, you could be limiting yourself unintentionally. Yeah, this is crazy but beware just the same.

Pre-COVID and from direct experience with some of our clients, Colorado fights the heck out of a former business owner collecting unemployment benefits; the business owner must show that his or her business suffered a catastrophic event; one that prevented future business income. Many other states are similar. During 2020 and 2021, all kinds of nutty things were happening with small business owners and unemployment benefits being paid to them. It'll take some time to unravel and settle back into a predictable future.

COVID also shined a light on sick pay and disability, including medical leaves. Therefore, many states recently passed legislation to fund various state-ran programs to address these issues.

For example, California, Hawaii, New Jersey, New York and Rhode Island impose a state disability insurance (SDI) payroll tax when you run payroll on the shareholders (as of 2022). Colorado has the FAMLI program which stands for Family and Medical Leave Insurance. As of October 2023, over 20 states have some sort of paid family leave.

> Critical Note: Specifically, California charges 0.9% with a maximum of $1,378 (0.9% x $153,164). Starting in 2024, however, California's SB 951 eliminated the wage limit but lowered the tax to 0.9%. Yuck.
>
> You can opt-out of California's SDI if your underlying entity is a corporation or if you obtain voluntary disability insurance from an approved insurance provider. Read that again. This is for corporations. An LLC taxed as an S Corp remains an LLC with the Secretary of State and as such cannot opt-out of SDI. A C or professional corporation taxed as an S Corp may. Subtle difference, but one that bites people all the time.

But there is an interesting situation with California (and perhaps other SDI states). In California, employees pay into the insurance fund and not the employer. So, if you were paid a W-2 salary of $100,000 and then was converted to a 1099 contractor, you are suddenly saving $1,000 in state disability insurance taxes. Then again, if you create a corporation and also elect S Corp status, you suddenly pay at least $800 in franchise taxes. They get you... always... eventually.

To summarize some of these various terms that you might hear-

▲ FUTA and SUTA- unemployment tax. Unavoidable. You might be able to opt out, and as the Minnesota example above illustrates, there is a tax savings by doing so.

▲ SDI- state disability insurance. Might be able to opt out for single-owner corporate officers in California or with supplemental insurance.

▲ Workers Compensation Insurance- has nothing to do with unemployment or state disability insurance, and is not interchangeable with those terms. This is purely insurance coverage for on-the-job injuries and is provided by private insurance such as State Farm, All State, Farmers, etc.

Washington state runs their own program but allows business owners to opt-out. Ask your local insurance agent if you can opt out. Typically, you can since you don't plan on suing yourself for a paper cut or a rogue paperclip stabbing.

Be aware that additional payroll taxes can nibble at the S Corp savings, but frankly it is relatively small at approximately $500. We are not trying to value-assess your money since $500 is still a big number. However, it is dwarfed by the savings.

SEP IRA Limitations
If you earned $100,000 in your garden-variety LLC, your SEP IRA deduction is $18,587. How do we get there?

Net Business Income	100,000	
Reduction for Biz Portion of SE Tax	7,650	(100,000 x 7.65%)
Self-Employment Income	92,350	
SE Tax at 15.3%	14,130	(92,350 x 15.3%)
Deduction for Half of SE Tax	7,065	
Net Business Income	100,000	
Deduction for Half of SE Tax	7,065	
Income Base for SEP IRA Calcs	92,935	
20% SEP IRA Contribution	18,587	

It is a two-step process. First, we need to calculate the deduction for half of the self-employment tax ($7,065). Second, we take the net business income and subtract half of the SE tax. This difference ($92,935) is then multiplied by 20%.

The 7,065 number should mean something. If you recall in a previous chapter, the self-employment (SE) tax rate is 15.3% but the effective rate is 14.13%. This is because of the reduction of the business income subject to the SE tax by the "employer" portion of SE tax. 7,065 x 2 is 14,130 or 14.13%. In other words, if you made $100,000 you would pay $14,130 in self-employment taxes.

Therefore, the SEP IRA calculation in our example is reduced to $100,000 x (1- half of 14.13%) x 20% = $18,587. Or simply $100,000 x 0.9294 x 20%.

Wow, did we belabor the heck out of that? Admit it; you're better for it... you can wow your friends at the next cocktail party... or... proudly announce on Jeopardy, "I'll take self-employment retirement calculations for $200 please Aaron." We certainly miss you, Alex. Sorry, Aaron, not many miss you.

Back to the issue at hand- if you elect S corporation taxation, your SEP IRA is now 25% of your W-2. Let's say you paid yourself $40,000 in wages, your SEP IRA contribution would be $10,000 versus $18,587. That is a huge difference!

However, if you leveraged a solo 401k plan instead, your total contribution is now $23,000 (for the 2024 tax year) plus 25% of your W-2 or $33,000. Another way to look at the SEP IRA versus 401k calculation is 401k = SEP IRA + $23,000+ $7,500 (if 50 or older).

The reduction in what you can save in your SEP IRA or solo 401k cannot be viewed in isolation. In the $100,000 example above, your S Corp savings might exceed $9,000. Also recall that tax deferrals are merely little IOU's to the IRS. As such, the small reduction in contribution limits and the small tax deferrals and even smaller ultimate tax savings (provided your retirement marginal tax rate is less than your current tax rate) are shadowed by the savings of an S corporation.

Sidebar: While **WCG CPAs & Advisors** defers to your financial planner, we usually recommend Roth (post-tax) deferrals into your solo 401k plan. Yes, pay taxes now, but then your growth and distributions are tax-free later in life. Tax savings is a lifelong perspective. Also, keep in mind that the discretionary employer (your business) contribution must be pre-tax. Therefore, you are achieving some immediate tax savings and hedging your tax bets at the same time. If you going to have a tax bill, would you prefer it today during your working years or when you are watching Matlock reruns? More about this in our retirement chapter.

Trapped Assets

As the only shareholder of an S Corp, you might think that everything the business owns you also personally own. Not true. The relationship you have with your S Corp is not a marriage where mine is mine and yours is mine too.

Part 1

If you want to move assets out of an S corporation or convert them to personal use, you will trigger a taxable event. A potentially big one. When assets are distributed to the S Corp shareholders, they are distributed at fair market value. Cash is easy. An automobile is generally not a big deal. But real estate can kick your butt.

We recently had a consultation with an S Corp owner whose business owned a hotel building. On the advice of an inexperienced CPA he revoked his S corporation election. This triggered a distribution of business assets at fair market value. The basis in the hotel building was $400,000 and the fair market value was $2,000,000. This sparked a $320,000 capital gain tax event reported on his K-1. Capital gains is a success tax, right? But when you don't actually get the cash from the transaction, this tax could be impossible to pay. Keep appreciating assets out of an S corporation people (or at least have eyes wide open on the risk)!

Sole proprietors and garden-variety LLCs enjoy a bit more flexibility under certain circumstances when distributing property or assets out of the business.

Part 2

Assets within your S Corp can also be problematic upon death. If you own an asset at the time of death, the asset is re-valued and your heirs get a step-up in basis (cost). So, when they sell the asset their gain is lower. For example, you buy a painting for $5,000 and when you die, the painting is valued at $20,000. If your heirs sell the painting for $22,000, they will only realize a $2,000 taxable gain.

If the asset is sitting in the S Corp upon your death, the S corporation's stock value might get a step-up in basis through an appraisal. However, it might prove harder to demonstrate than the increased value of one particular asset. Look at it another way. S Corps don't die, and therefore assets within the business don't get a step-up in basis upon a shareholder's death.

We'll acquiesce. This trapped asset problem is super rare yet so many owners love to have personal stuff owned by the S Corp.

Distributing Profits, Multiple Owners

S Corp shareholders are allocated net ordinary business income (profits) as a percentage of ownership whereas multi-member LLC's use an Operating Agreement. Electing S Corp status in certain situations can create headaches for silent partner or angel investor situations, and other non-traditional ownership structures.

Fluctuating Income Splitting

Recall in a previous chapter, an S Corp election can be problematic for partnerships or multi-member LLCs who have an Eat What You Kill revenue and profit arrangement. For example, WCG has a client where the entity was comprised of two insurance sales agents. They created a multi-member limited liability company to share in some of the costs and to gain some economies of scale by working together. After common expenses were paid, the Operating Agreement allocated remaining profits as a percentage of revenue generated by each of the partners. So, one year could be 60-40 and the next year could be 45-55. This worked fine with no problems.

However, if this multi-member LLC elected to be taxed as an S corporation the arrangement blows up since shareholder allocations and eventual distributions must be made on a pro-rata basis of ownership. In using the above example, an insurance agent might be a 50% shareholder but should only receive 40% of the distributions according to the income split agreement. This is no bueno which is Spanish for no bueno.

Here is why this is a problem-

Net Business Income   100,000

	Batman	Robin
Beginning Shareholder Basis	5,000	5,000
Allocated Income	50,000	50,000
Ending Shareholder Basis	55,000	55,000
Shareholder Distributions	60,000	40,000
Ending Shareholder Basis	-5,000	15,000

In this example, Batman is receiving 60% of the distributions as a 50% shareholder. The negative ending basis cannot happen without ugly consequences in S Corps (we call this a shareholder distribution in excess of shareholder basis which causes a capital gains tax event).

You could solve this by changing salaries- however this usually creates unnecessary additional payroll tax burdens in the attempt to equalize the income. Let's say you must pay Batman $15,000 more in salary to "equalize" the eat what you kill income split. This would cause about $2,000 in additional payroll taxes to be paid unnecessarily. Furthermore, the equalization calculation is circular since as you increase wages for one shareholder it reduces the remaining income for both shareholders. Yuck.

A more elegant way to solve this problem, as mentioned in our chapter dedicated to customized entity structures, is to simply create two more S corporations who are 50-50 members of the multi-member LLC (MMLLC). The Operating Agreement will still dictate the pro-rata share of distributions on a fluctuating basis yet the ultimate income is sheltered by the taxation of an S Corp. We did this in the insurance agency example, and each insurance sales agent was 100% owner of his or her respective S Corp.

Also, in that chapter on customized entity structures, and specifically the mothership baby S Corp construct, we recommended a fee for service or management fee arrangement in contrast to the S Corps being members of the MMLLC.

Here is that schematic again from a previous chapter (there are all kinds of good stuff in there).

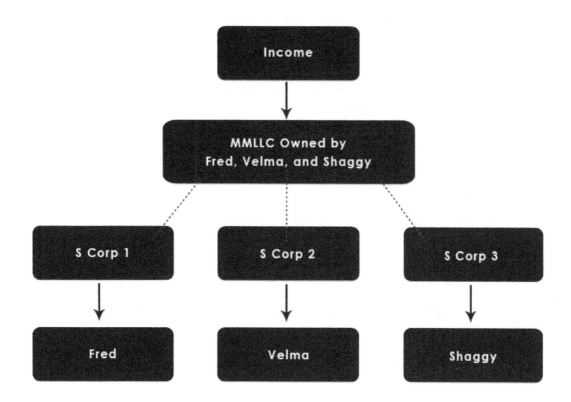

Minority Shareholders

Similar problems occur with minority shareholders or silent investors. The author, Jason Watson, served on a jury trial in 2003 when 50 Cent was singing In Da Club. An S corporation was formed with three people. One owner was a 10% shareholder, while the other two were split evenly as a husband-and-wife team. Not looking good from the start.

The minority shareholder, the 10% guy, was constructively ousted from the daily operations of the business. He was not paid a salary. He did not receive any money from the business. Distributions were not made to any shareholder, but the husband-and-wife team paid themselves a salary and used expense reimbursements as a way to funnel money out.

The business began earning money, lots of money, and the minority shareholder was getting K-1s showing taxable income of several thousands of dollars. Good right? No. Not good. He had to report taxable income, but never saw any money in the form of a shareholder distribution. The husband-and-wife team were upset too since they could not take distributions without having to pay the minority shareholder. No one was willing to budge.

Sidebar: Had this entity had a strong Operating Agreement which forced distributions, minority problems can be avoided. One of the provisions we advocate for when working with attorneys is to establish a cash reserve (working capital) for operations and then distribute 40% of the remaining amount periodically throughout the year. This forces the entity to at least cover the shareholders' typical tax obligation associated with the K-1 income.

Other W-2 Income

You might not reap all the benefits of an S Corp election and subsequent self-employment tax savings if you have other W-2 income. But there is a lot to unpack here-

▲ You have Medicare savings versus forfeited Social Security taxes.

▲ You have the pass-through entity tax (PTET) deduction that is only available in an S Corp or partnership environment.

▲ You have the qualified business income deduction (QBID) that might be wage limited once you hit the 32% marginal tax bracket.

These all interplay. We'll start with forfeited Social Security taxes first.

Medicare Tax Savings

Let's say you are an IT consultant for ABC Company, and you also do some outside consulting. If ABC Company pays you $170,000 in wages, you are already max'ing out your Social Security contributions, and therefore any supplementary income regardless of your entity will automatically avoid additional Social Security taxes.

You still obtain a small savings in Medicare taxes, which is generally immaterial at 2.9% or 3.8% of the side gig income. Then again, a tiny number multiplied by a big number can be a big number. We'll talk more about when forfeited taxes exceed the reduction in Medicare taxes in a bit.

We find this very common among medical professions. Many times, a surgeon or anesthesiologist will be full-time for a hospital or medical group, but also moonlight on the side for smaller towns with smaller hospitals with even smaller budgets.

The problem with piling extra W-2 salary from your S corporation onto W-2 salary from your main job is the S Corp's portion of payroll taxes. While both salaries might exceed your individual Social Security cap ($168,600 for the 2024 tax year), any salary in excess will unnecessarily increase the tax burden of your S Corp by 6.2% (the employer portion of Social Security taxes). Huh?

In other words, your main job will stop collecting and paying Social Security taxes once you reach the annual limit. However, since Social Security taxes are paid by both the employee (you) and the business, when you run payroll with your S corporation, the business will collect and pay Social Security taxes just like your main job.

On your individual tax return, you will get your portion of excess Social Security taxes refunded to you on Line 11 on Schedule 3 of Form 1040. That's the good news. The bad news is that the S Corp's portion will not be refunded. This is lost forever, and we call this a forfeited tax.

Here is yet another table to explain this further-

Salary from Main Job	170,000	
Income from Side Gig Business	200,000	
Medicare Tax w/o S Corp	7,600	
Salary	66,000	
Payroll Tax w/ S Corp		
ER Social Security	4,092	
ER Medicare	957	
EE Medicare w/ Surtax	1,551	
Total Payroll Taxes w/ S Corp	6,600	
Initial Savings	1,000	(7,600 less 6,600)
Fees for Payroll, Tax Prep (typical)	2,700	
Net Savings (loss)	-1,700	

Ok... here we go. Let's say you had a main job that earned $170,000 and you also run an online retailer business where you plan to make $200,000 net income after expenses. You eclipsed your Social Security maximum with your main job salary, so the $200,000 is only subjected to Medicare taxes plus the surtax, or $7,600 ($200,000 x 3.8%).

Now we elect S Corp for your business and pay a salary of $66,000. The total taxes paid not considering your portion of Social Security which will be refunded is $6,600. ER is shorthand for "employer" and EE refers to "employee." The initial savings is $1,000. However, now you must run payroll and file a corporate tax return. Therefore, the savings are gobbled up by normal professional fees.

Therefore, in this situation perhaps a garden-variety LLC is more prudent from a cost-benefit and headache analysis. Having other W-2 income, however, could actually work in your favor- more on that later.

> Sidebar: Having multiple sources of income can mess up your withholdings. Each source of income on its own might withhold correctly, but when combined, the total income will be in a higher tax bracket and unfortunately will have under-withheld as a household. Again, payroll tables don't know about other jobs or sources of income and can only make assumptions. Some tax planning is a must. More about tax planning within your S corporation payroll in a later chapter.

Here is an internal table that we use during business consultations to determine the tax-efficiency of an S corporation when combined with high "day job" W-2 income.

	28% Salary		33% Salary	
Salary	28.0%		33.0%	
ER Social Security	6.2%		6.2%	
Forfeited Tax	1.7%		2.0%	
K-1 Income	72.0%		67.0%	
Medicare	3.8%		3.8%	
Medicare Savings	2.7%		2.5%	
Delta	1.0%		0.5%	
Net Biz Income (profit)	200,000	275,000	200,000	275,000
Salary	56,000	77,000	66,000	90,750
Forfeited Tax*	3,472	4,774	4,092	5,627
Medicare Savings	5,472	7,524	5,092	7,002
Delta (cash savings)	2,000	2,750	1,000	1,375

Tilt. We have four scenarios; salaries of 28% and 33%, and business incomes of $200,000 and $275,000. Let's take one and quickly dissect it.

▲ The forfeited tax is your S Corp's portion of Social Security taxes that must be paid but cannot be refunded. This is 28% x 6.2% or 1.7%. This 28% will be meaningful once we get into the Section 199A deduction.

▲ The Medicare savings is the remaining S Corp income that will now avoid this tax. This is 72% x 3.8% or 2.7%. The 72% is in the inverse of the salary percentage.

▲ The first delta is simply the forfeited tax less the Medicare savings, or 1.0%. The second delta is the calculated savings, and it ties out to the first delta since $200,000 x 1.0% is $2,000.

Wait! There's more to consider when your main W-2 exceeds the SSA wage base.

Pass-Through Entity Tax (PTET) Deduction

We touched on this in an earlier chapter, but we need to bring it up again here. As you recall, with the Tax Cuts and Jobs Act, Congress wanted to limit state and local taxes (SALT) to $10,000. This means either state income taxes or real estate taxes, or both, were severely muted on their deductions.

States got creative and created a state tax that was deducted on partnerships and S corporations tax returns (otherwise called pass-through entities... or PTE if you are a cool kid) resulting in lower federal taxable income. This tax, paid by the PTE, is then credited on the business owner's state income tax return (or in some cases the taxable state income is reduced by the PTE's income). This is also called the great SALT work-around.

Cash is cash to a business owner whether it is spent by the business or the human, right? There are all kinds of rules, and not every business owner will benefit from the PTET deduction. Shocker, we know.

Bottomline is this- does it feel better to pay your state income tax with personal dollars or business dollars? It's a bit rhetorical... no need to say it out loud or call us. However, you need to have a pass-through entity, which is either a partnership or an S Corp. A single-member LLC disregarded for tax purposes or a sole proprietorship does not qualify! Read more here-

wcginc.com/ptet

Qualified Business Income Deduction (QBID)

You are likely getting tired of this section, but there is one more consideration. As mentioned elsewhere, once your household taxable income reaches the 32% marginal tax rate, your QBID has a second test. If you are a specified service trade or business (SSTB) such as attorney, accountant, physician, consultant, etc. you are mostly hosed. But if you are not an SSTB such as a retailer or an architect or realtor or the zillion other business owners, then read on.

The qualified business income deduction is 20% of your business income. Easy. Once you hit the 32% marginal tax rate, then your QBI deduction is 20% of your business income or 50% of wages whichever is lower. Lower. As such, if you do not pay wages (complete with payroll filings and W-2s), you might be limited on your QBI deduction. Keep in mind that you cannot pay wages to yourself in a sole proprietorship or a single-member LLC that has not elected an S corporation election. You also cannot pay partners a wage in a partnership.

As such, you might have regular W-2 wages that exceed the Social Security wage base and you might still need to S Corp elect your business entity just to capture the full effect of the qualified business income deduction.

Net Net

What do we do with all this data? We compare all the possible savings to the additional fees associated with an S Corp which are specifically business entity tax return preparation (Form 1120S) and payroll processing. From there, a simple cost-benefit analysis is done.

Make $200,000 with your W-2, and $150,000 with your used copier sales gig, and you live in California? S Corp is not shabby with about $7,500 in savings (factoring in franchise tax too by the way).

It is not all dollars and cents, however. Please recall from another chapter that S corporations enjoy a significantly lower audit rate risk than plopping all this side gig income and expenses on Schedule C of your 1040 tax return.

Ok, enough of that nonsense. Please contact us if you want your unique situation projected and analyzed.

State Business Taxes (Not Just Income Taxes)

State tax laws might not treat S Corp income and subsequent K-1 income in the same benevolent manner as the IRS. Recall that S corporations do not pay a federal income tax directly. Rather the income is passed onto the shareholders who are then taxed on that income at their individual tax rates. However, some states impose an additional tax. For example, California imposes a 1.5% franchise tax on S Corp net ordinary business income (profit) after expenses and deductions with a minimum of $800. Yuck. So, your 8% savings in federal tax turns into 6.5% after you pay California.

Other income tax free states, such as Texas, have similar taxations and various exemptions too. Franchise tax is another buzzword you might come across. Why do they call it a franchise tax, or a business and operating tax as they do in Washington State? They can't call it an income tax because of the Interstate Income Act of 1959. Yup. Way back when, and it is battled every year in court, in various representations. Consider that in 1959, interstate commerce was quite small compared to what we have today with Amazon and all the interwebs. States are tired of businesses skirting local income taxes.

Before we get into that, there are two issues at play here and we'll pick on California to illustrate some points. One, if you are an S corporation headquartered in California you will be subjected to the franchise tax. Period. End of story.

But the other side of the coin is state nexus (which was broached earlier) where you are not physically headquartered in California but have a nexus either physically or economically in California. This too would subject your income sourced from California to the franchise tax.

In some cases, you might have nexus in California but not have any California sourced income, and you will unfortunately be subjected to the minimum franchise tax of $800 (for the 2024 tax year). Nutty. You have nexus, but no taxable income, and you still pay the minimum franchise tax? Yes. This happens when you create an LLC, but all your income sources are outside California and they exceed certain thresholds. There are other situations where this can happen.

Conversely, if you are a sole proprietor in California (and not an LLC or corporation), you do not pay a franchise tax. Yes, you will be subjected to federal self-employment taxes which is why you want to consider an S Corp election. So therein lies the rub. Franchise tax versus self-employment tax.

About half of the states have some sort of franchise, business or excise tax. Back to the Interstate Income Act of 1959- it is against Federal Public Law 86-272 for states to charge an income tax on foreign businesses in certain circumstances. Remember, foreign does not mean domestic and international. Foreign is a business registered in Nevada doing business in California, as an example.

Here is a snippet of Federal Public Law 86-272-

> No state, or political subdivision thereof, shall have power to impose ... a net income tax on the income derived within such state by any person from interstate commerce if the only business activities with in such state by or on behalf of such a person during the taxable year are either, or both, of the following-
>
> 1. The solicitation of orders by such person, or his representative, in such State for sales of tangible personal property, which orders are sent outside the State for approval or rejection, and, if approved, are filled by shipment or delivery from a point outside of the state; and
>
> 2. The solicitation of orders by such a person, or his representative, in such State in the name of or for the benefit of a prospective customer of such a person, if orders by such customer to such person to enable such customer to fill orders resulting from such solicitation are orders described in paragraph (1).

States are therefore prevented under Public Law 86-272

▲ from taxing out-of-state businesses on income derived from activities within the state

▲ if the activities are limited to mere solicitations of tangible personal property, and

▲ the orders are processed from outside the state.

Note how this focuses on tangible property and not services. Huge distinction! Is internet hosting a service or tangible personal property? How about an eBook? This is discussed more in a later chapter, and the current news is not great. The future isn't good either.

Let's have California's Franchise Tax Board offer a few words on Public Law 86-272-

> Public Law 86-272 (15 USC Section 381) prevents States from asserting their right to impose a tax based on net income, such as the corporate income tax or franchise tax. Public Law 86-272 protection is available to out-of-state business entities that:
>
> ▪ Sell tangible personal property in this state
>
> ▪ Who's in-state activities are limited to the solicitation of orders for their goods

As a result, if a taxpayer is protected by Public Law 86-272, they will not be required to pay the franchise tax or the corporate income tax, as both are measured by net income. However, even if protected by Public Law 86-272, an out-of-state entity that is doing business (R&TC Section 23101) in California is still obligated to file a tax return and pay taxes that are not measured upon net income, unless certain exceptions apply, such as:

- The minimum franchise tax

- Annual limited liability company tax

- The limited liability company fee

You are probably asking, "What does this mean, how does this work?" First of all, protection under Public Law 86-272 does not apply to businesses that derive in-state income from the solicitation or sale of:

- Intangible property

- Services

- Any combination of goods and services

Technical Advice Memorandum: 2018-03 addresses the application and interpretation of Public Law 86-272 in the context of delivering goods by company owned delivery vehicles. This memorandum concluded the delivery via a private delivery truck is protected activity under Public Law 86-272. However, any activity that goes beyond the scope of delivery, such as backhauling, is not protected activity.

For example: Corporation C, an out-of-state corporation that does not file a combined return, sells tangible goods over the internet and qualifies for protection under Public Law 86-272. For the 2019 taxable year, Corporation C has $1,000,000 of California sales but no property or payroll in California. Corporation C, though considered doing business in California because it has $1,000,000 in California sales, will not be subject to California's franchise tax as it is protected under Public Law 86-272. This is true even if the tangible goods are delivered using Corporation C's vehicles. However, Corporation C must still file a California return and pay the minimum franchise tax of $800. If Corporation C's vehicles are used for any other business activity along with the delivery, such as backhaul of goods (like hauling off the customer's old items), this activity would go beyond the solicitation of orders and would no longer be protected.

California has a lot to say!

So, the wizards at various states came up with a tax that is not based on income or at least not called an income tax. Some states tax your gross receipts, no matter what your expenses are! Amazing. It is also noteworthy that Public Law 86-272 does not protect businesses located in and doing business in the respective state (only interstate activities, not intrastate activities). But it appears that states keep things consistent, and impose a franchise tax, a business tax or an excise tax on local businesses just the same. Genius.

Here are some sample state links-

wcginc.com/1304	California
wcginc.com/1302	Oregon
wcginc.com/1307	New York City
wcginc.com/1311	Tennessee
wcginc.com/1314	Texas

New York City S Corp tax rate is 8.85%. Tennessee is 6.5%. Texas is about 1% on gross receipts exceeding $1 million. Washington DC has a tax it imposes on S corporations, but tax is exempt if over 80% of the revenue is from personal service. All kinds of rules!

Do you want more wrinkles? Here you go- California (we just love to pick on them) has a unique rule to their franchise tax. As a garden-variety LLC, you are taxed on gross receipts in addition to the $800 franchise tax. For example, you could have $1,000,000 in gross receipts and $1,000,000 in expenses. Your franchise tax would be $800 + $6,000 (for the 2023 tax year) although you do not have any net income. Yuck.

However, if this LLC is taxed as an S corporation, then it would pay 1.5% of the net income (profits) or $800, whichever is higher. Using the example above California's franchise tax would be $800 versus $6,800. Therefore, the lesson is that you might be forced into electing S corporation status in California just to avoid its silly gross receipts tax.

To complicate things even more, you must apply nexus rules to all this. You might not be subjected to another state's franchise or business tax if you don't have an economic or physical presence in that state.

The issue of state business taxes and nexus is discussed in nauseating detail later in a chapter dedicated to state nexus. More buzzwords such as economic presence, throwback rules, tangible personal property, commerce and due process clauses, etc. Bottom line- talk to your nexus experts at **WCG CPAs & Advisors** to nail this down. It is extremely tricky, and states are extremely aggressive.

Before that, here are some big takeaways with this section-

▲ Income tax nexus and sales tax nexus are woefully different, and one doesn't invite the other to the nexus party. Income tax cannot just show up with a plus 1.

▲ Each state is unique and different, like snowflakes, but without the innocence and the ability to be shoveled away.

▲ Tripping nexus wires can unwittingly expose your business to additional taxes beyond income taxes.

Deducting Losses, Trapped Cash

With an S corporation or partnership you need sufficient shareholder / partnership basis in your business to deduct losses. For example, if you invested $10,000 into your business but the business lost $30,000, as an S Corp shareholder you can only deduct losses up to the amount of your shareholder basis (in this example, $10,000).

Think of Google. You invested $10,000 into Google stock and they go out of business, you only lose $10,000. Remember that with an S corporation you wear two hats- one as an employee, and one as an investor (shareholder).

Section 179 Depreciation Losses

How does a loss in a small S corporation happen? A lot of small businesses are cash based and don't have a lot of equipment (dentists are a common exception). However, for the sake of argument we will assume you bought a piece of equipment for $100,000 and borrowed $100,000 to pay for it. The equipment also qualified for Section 179 depreciation deduction allowing you to deduct (or attempt to deduct) the full amount against business income. Great! The benevolent IRS king is alive and well.

Let's assume that the business income prior to depreciation was $60,000 (and Section 179 depreciation was $100,000). The S corporation tax return would still show a $60,000 net business income amount, but your K-1 would show a $70,000 amount for Section 179 deduction. Why $70,000? You had $10,000 in basis (using the example above) plus the

$60,000 net business income. 10k + 60k = 70k, even in Canada. Sorry Canada... just too easy to pick on.

You would be able to deduct $70,000 as a loss. The $30,000 remainder of the Section 179 deduction that was not taken or used would be carried forward to future years. Yuck! Sorry, the once-benevolent IRS king is now asking you to be patient and wait.

Here is a table to demonstrate the depreciation conundrum more clearly. We love tables.

Taxable Income Prior to Depreciation	60,000
Section 179 Depreciation	100,000
Beginning Shareholder Basis	10,000
Net Biz Income (profit) on K-1	60,000
Section 179 Depreciation on K-1	70,000
Loss Taken on 1040 Tax Return	-70,000
Section 179 Depreciation Carryforward	30,000

Bonus Depreciation Losses
Here is another example, that is just slightly different and shows a small difference between Section 179 and bonus depreciation. Similar example to above, but you used bonus depreciation.

Starting Shareholder Basis	10,000
Net Income Before Depreciation	60,000
Bonus Depreciation (80%, 2023)	80,000
Net Income (loss) on K-1	-20,000
Available Cash in Business	60,000
Allowed Losses	-10,000
Ending Shareholder Basis	0
Disallowed Losses Carried Forward	10,000

What we are showing here are two things- first, your losses created by the bonus depreciation will be limited because of your shareholder basis. You started with $10,000 but didn't have any net business income (profits). Rather, you had a $20,000 loss. $10,000 of this $20,000 was allowed and the remainder will be carried forward to future years.

The second thing we are showing is how your cash is trapped. You had profits before bonus depreciation of $60,000 and for the sake of argument this also is your ending cash balance in your checking account. This cash is trapped since you cannot distribute it without creating a distribution in excess of basis.

We will expand on this some more in a bit. The big takeaway is that business losses created by depreciation created by a financed equipment purchase can be painfully and unknowingly limited.

Wait! Looks like we talk about shareholder distributions and basis next. Yay!

Distributions in Excess of Shareholder Basis

We broached this little devil in a the previous section, but we want to expand on it. If you buy Google stock for $100 and later sell it for $150, you have a $50 gain. Easy. The first $100 represents a return of your capital and the next $50 represents your gain. Done. How does this to relate to S corporations?

If you inject $5,000 into your business, your business earns $100,000 and your business checking account has $105,000, you have $105,000 in shareholder basis. You can take all $105,000 out without trouble.

There are at least four scenarios where this breaks down, and we'll review each one.

Depreciation

Please forgive us for reiterating this little issue, and to make matters worse we use a different data set for the example.

Depreciation bites people all the time, and bites hard! Same situation as above. $100,000 in net business income (profit) but you also financed a brand-new Ford F150 pickup truck for $60,000, and used 60% bonus depreciation to deduct it (for the 2024 tax year). Therefore, you have $105,000 in the business checking account and $64,000 in net ordinary business income after expenses and deductions (you had $100,000 in initial profit but deducted $36,000 in truck depreciation).

Your shareholder basis is $5,000 (original injection of cash) plus $64,000 in net business income, or $69,000. If you take out $100,000 as a shareholder distribution, you have $31,000 of the $100,000 exceeding your shareholder basis and that portion will be taxed as a capital gain on your individual tax return. Yuck!

How do you fix this? Easy. You can either not take the cash out in the form of a shareholder distribution, or don't use bonus depreciation on the new truck and pay more immediate income taxes. Wow. Not desirable at all!

You could use another depreciation method that spreads the deduction across several tax years. Sure, you will pay more income taxes in the year of purchase, but you won't have the capital gain on the excess distributions. Moreover, you have a nice depreciation deduction in the future to offset hopefully increasing incomes (and associated tax rates).

Loans

This one can bite too! WCG has a client who is a very successful Amazon reseller. To add to the excitement, Amazon offered a low-cost $250,000 loan to the business presumably with the hopes that the business would buy more stuff to sell on Amazon. The business didn't. The sole shareholder took the loan proceeds plus some extra cash out of the business as a shareholder distribution. Let's breakdown what happened using our basic example above.

You inject $5,000 into your business and the business earned $100,000 in net ordinary business income after expenses and deductions. The business also took on a $250,000 Amazon loan and received cash. Therefore, your business checking account reads $355,000 but your shareholder basis is only $105,000. You can only take a $105,000 distribution leaving $250,000 behind without triggering a distribution in excess of shareholder basis. Another yuck!

When cash loans like above happen and the shareholder has a distribution in excess of his or her basis, we advise the client to return the cash to the business.

Recall that a business loan made directly to an S corporation from an external lender does not create shareholder basis even if the shareholder personally guarantees the loan. This is contrary to a partnership where each partner personally guarantees the loan, and adds to his or her partner basis. However, a shareholder who lends money directly to the S corporation does add to his or her basis (we typically suggest not making this is a loan, but rather a capital injection from the shareholder).

Business debt and capitalization must be handled carefully.

Payables

Along the same lines of loans are payables. Let's say you record a $25,000 employer 401k match expense on December 31, but you haven't sent the check yet. This would be recorded as a debit to 401k Company Contribution as an expense and a credit to a 401k Payable liability account. Additionally, this payable isn't due until March 15 the following year, so you have some extra cash in your business checking account that is earmarked for the 401k payment. But it's Christmas, and baby needs new shoes, so you pull this $25,000 as a shareholder distribution knowing that you'll earn enough between January 1 and March 15 to make the 401k payment.

This distribution could exceed your shareholder basis as well. How? You reduced the amount of business profits by recording the 401k Company Contribution expense, but didn't use cash to do so. You used a payable or an IOU if you will, freeing up some cash albeit temporarily. This cash-less reduction of business profits combined with a distribution can be bad.

Credit cards can create this little fiasco too and are very similar to the 401k example above. The IRS allows you to recognize the expenses as soon as you are liable for the payment (swipe the credit card, and boom you are liable). This is true even in a cash-based accounting system. Therefore, if you rack up a bunch of deductible business expenses in December with your credit card, you will have a gaggle of debits (expenses) and a Credit Card Payable as the corresponding liability (credit) on your balance sheet.

This in turn reduces your net business income (profits) but creates an artificial sense in available cash (since you haven't paid the credit card bill yet). Here is what we mean-

Starting Shareholder Basis on Jan 1	5,000
Net Income Before Credit Card	100,000
Expenses Paid with Credit Card	25,000
Net Income (profit) on K-1	75,000
Available Cash in Business on Dec 31	100,000
Ending Shareholder Basis	80,000

If you take $90,000 out as a shareholder distribution on December 31, you will have exceeded your shareholder basis by $10,000.

What can be done here? Wait until January 1 to take the money out rather than December 31. Show the cash on the books for the ending cash number which is a part of your business entity tax return, wait 24 hours, and then do the money-grab.

Bad Basis Data

Most tax software will maintain shareholder basis using worksheets and other supporting documentation within the tax return. This information is typically not filed with the IRS or state, but it is a part of the tax return documents. Cool, right? If you switch tax professionals, your new person can easily take this data and enter it into the tax software to preserve your shareholder basis data. More cool.

This sounds great until it isn't. Let's say you've been in business for 20 years, and for some reason or another you've had four different tax professionals over the years. What if in year 4, a tax professional messed something up which caused your shareholder basis to get slightly out of whack; nothing huge, but certainly wrong. Your next tax professional simply took last year's worksheets... did a quick sanity check... and plopped a number in as your shareholder basis that was too low. Ten years later, you are pulling some money out as a distribution and get hit with long-term capital gains.

Everyone is scratching their chin asking What happened here?

What makes matters worse is that a lazy tax professional who doesn't want to dig into the numbers or have an awkward conversation with the business owner might create a shareholder loan to avoid the capital gain conundrum. In other words, he or she will take the portion of the shareholder distribution that exceeds the basis and call it a loan to the shareholder. Great, now we've taken a dumpster fire and threw a 55-gallon drum of gas on it. The IRS cannot stand shareholder loans since they are usually disguised distributions.

Lazy might be a strong word. And why are dumpster fires considered bad? They are safely contained in a thick metal box, no? We should say that someone is a camp fire in high winds. We digress...

What can be done? We usually advise pumping the brakes on the current year's tax return and re-building the shareholder basis data from business inception. WCG just recently did this for a client who owned a bunch of Arby's over several years; the shareholder basis on the worksheet from the previous CPA was understated by over $240,000. Yeah, a big number.

The lesson here is to be careful on seeing a bunch of cash and thinking you can do a money-grab without pain. Better yet! The lesson is to engage a team of wonderful Certified Public Accountants and business consultants to keep you out of trouble. We can fix things during the year. After the year is over, it might be hard to put toothpaste back in the tube.

Tax Planning Opportunity

But wait! There's more. There might be a tax planning trick to welcome this capital gain on distributions in excess of shareholder basis. Huh? Well, the capital gain is considered long-term and as such has favorable tax rates versus ordinary income tax rates. In other words, if you are going to pay taxes on the income your business earns anyway, do you want to do it at ordinary income tax rates or capital gain tax rates?

You might have long-term capital losses that are quite large and might take a long time to recoup. For example, and for whatever reason, you have $100,000 in capital losses that are being carried forward. In addition, you don't see yourself using these losses anytime soon. Under current tax law, you can only deduct $3,000 per year so quick math suggests needing 34 years to fully deduct these capital losses. Sounds like a long time, right? As such, having a shareholder distribution in excess of your basis which in turn causes a capital gain just to be absorbed by these losses doesn't seem so bad.

We are saying this in the abstract, but there could also be tax planning opportunities when allowing this capital gain to occur.

Stock Classes

One of the rules of an S Corp is to only have one class of voting stock, and this can be a problem at times if you are trying to bring in a new partner or create a vesting schedule for future owners. You can have two classes of stock as long as the only difference is the voting rights between the stocks. See IRC Section 1361(c)(4). Quite the page turner.

So, if you want to provide distributions to a person but not give them control, assign him or her nonvoting stock (such as a retired parent who needs some money and enjoys a lower tax bracket than you).

Truly stock classes don't trip up many S corporations. What can prove to be tricky and expensive to solve is expanding the ownership of the S Corp through key employees or other graduated buy-in situations. Keep reading.

Vesting and Expanding Ownership

You, or someone you know, might have had a job where the company-match to your 401k was vested over time or the business had a restricted stock grant that only triggered after so many years of service. For most of our readers this concern is moot since the idea of expanding ownership is not on the radar. However, life is funny, and you never know how your path might change directions with left turns at right angles.

If the transfer of stock and subsequent ownership is not handled correctly within your S corporation, this could be considered a second class of voting stock which nullifies the S Corp election. Therefore, if you are contemplating bringing in other owners or partners please read on. If you are not considering it, please read anyway so you have some basic knowledge of the problems.

Basis Problems

If you have a successful S Corp and you sell 10% of your stock to a key employee, you suddenly create a zillion headaches. First, what is the valuation of the stock? A valuation too low might be considered compensatory triggering an income tax obligation for the employee buyer.

What is the cost basis of the shares? This is arguably easier since we would just look at your shareholder basis to determine the capital gain (if any). However, many business owners freak out when they are faced with a capital gain when selling a minority interest in the business.

For example, WCG has a client who established a value of his business based on a long calculus. His basic argument was that he injected intellectual property into the business and therefore his shareholder basis was $250,000. Look at the big brain on Brad! No doubt, this guy was smart and his business was probably worth $250,000 from the beginning. However, he neglected some accounting basics and IRS law.

In its simplest form, you cannot create basis in a business without paying income taxes on the money used to establish the basis. Huh? Let's say you have $1,000 in your pocket. You paid income taxes on that $1,000. You buy stock for $1,000 and sell it for $1,500. Your basis is $1,000 and your gain is $500. Piece of cake.

Same with a business. You wrote a check for $250,000 and you paid income taxes on that money. When you sell your business for $400,000 you will have a $150,000 gain because the $250,000 was already taxed.

Therefore, you cannot create basis out of thin air. In the case of intellectual property, the owner would have had to pick up $250,000 worth of income on his individual tax return somewhere in the past in order to have $250,000 of basis in his business. Same with a loan. If the bank gives you a loan, either through the business or through you personally, the principal payments are not tax deductible since it is essentially a return of capital. As such, if the personal loan is your injection to create basis in your business, it too is done with after-tax dollars.

Another way to look at this is your personal home. You borrow $300,000 to buy a $300,000 house. Over the course of 30 years, you paid over $500,000 in total payments but when you sell the house, your basis remains at $300,000 (and hopefully the $200,000 in interest was tax deductible).

Does this make sense? No? Crud. Perhaps have a nice Dale's Pale Ale and give us a call. We can try walking through it another way. We might need a Dale's too! Yum.

Back to the headaches of selling 10% of your business to someone else. This 10% owner now gets a K-1 with 10% of the S Corp's net business income as taxable income. All shareholder distributions must be allocated among all shareholders. So, if you want to pull out $9,000 to pay for your family vacation, you also need to write a $1,000 check to your new 10% shareholder buddy. Cancel the flights. You might have to drive to vacation.

Death, divorce and incapacitation. Does your Operating Agreement (LLC) or Shareholder Agreement (C Corp or Professional Corp) deal with death, divorce or incapacitation? You need to. What is incapacitation? Do you need two doctors to sign off? If the remaining shareholders have first right of refusal on the re-purchase of the crazy man's stock, how is that valued? It will be hard to negotiate in good faith with someone who is incapacitated.

We touch on various other traps and pitfalls in an earlier chapter when expanding ownership.

Speaking of value, 10% of the shares issued to the new shareholder have very little value. Since the S corporation is closely held, there is not a market to establish the value of the shares. A bank would probably not use the shares as collateral. The majority shareholder (you, in this string of examples) could run the business into the ground or simply shut the business down. The 10% shareholder has very little recourse outside of dissenting shareholder lawsuits (unless there is some contractual obligation governing these possibilities).

Lastly, the 10% shareholder might want to be involved with daily decisions or long-term decisions. Sure, the majority doesn't technically have to listen or even care, but that isn't the most professional way to foster the new relationship. Office politics suddenly become a reality in a business in which you never had to consider it. Want to buy a business car? Might have to get permission. Yuck.

So, what can you do? You have several options to bring in new owners without creating immediate problems, and you can get creative.

Employee Stock Ownership Plan (ESOP)
We mentioned this in an earlier chapter but we expand a bit to illustrate the challenges of expanding ownership and offer ESOPs as a solution for your S corporation. ESOPs are a great way to reward and incentivize employees. They also create a market for the shares of a departing owner or an owner who wants to expand ownership to the employees. Remember, if you have a growing business and you want to start working on an exit strategy or transition plan, using your own staff as future suitors might be the best idea. They have been vetted over time and know the business very well.

Here are the basics of an ESOP. A business creates a trust where shares or cash to buy shares are contributed to the trust account. Each share is allocated to individual employee accounts. You can discriminate based on years of service, full-time versus part-time and age. There are rules on this of course. The default is 1,000 hours of service in a plan year and 21 years old.

You can also create vesting schedules. For cliff vesting where the employee has either 0% or 100%, the maximum vesting schedule is three years. And for graded vesting schedules, the maximum is six years. This is because an ESOP is a qualified defined contribution plan and must follow the rules.

Here is a sample schedule-

3-Year Cliff Schedule			6-Year Graded Schedule	
Year	**Vested %**		**Year**	**Vested %**
1	0%		1	0%
2	0%		2	20%
3	100%		3	40%
			4	60%
			5	80%
			6	100%

You can find vesting rules in IRC Section 411(a)(2)(B).

Here are some other takeaways on ESOPs. The percentage of ownership held by the ESOP of an S corporation is tax-deferred. For example, the S Corp earns $500,000 and the ESOP owns 40%. $200,000 of the taxable income should be added to the ESOP and allocated to each employee participant. This is a tax deferral not a tax deduction. When the employee sells or withdraws the shares (such as retirement) there will be a taxable event based on the individual's tax rate.

This makes sense since an S corporation is a pass-through entity. So, if an ESOP trust owns a portion of the stock, the beneficiaries of the trust (employees) will have a deferred tax obligation.

As an aside, a common theme in income taxation is one person's deduction is another person's taxable income (mortgage interest is a great example). A great exception is charitable donations- your deduction is not a taxable gain to the charity. Back to the ESOP- if a business may deduct the cash or stock contribution into an ESOP, the taxable income is later picked up by the ESOP participants when the money is taken out.

Here are some more takeaways. The law currently does not allow ESOPs for partnerships or professional corporations. Departing employees' shares must be re-purchased. Costs of these plans can be substantial (as much as $40,000 depending on complexity, according to the National Center of Employee Ownership).

If you are seriously considering this please review Section 401(a) of the Internal Revenue Code in between P90X reps at the gym, contact the NCEO (**www.nceo.org**) or contact us.

Here is quick link to NCEO's article-

wcginc.com/6113

Hybrid Purchase Schemes

If the ESOP doesn't suit your needs and if you are afraid of introducing additional ownership through a simple stock sale, the sky is the limit on creating your own scheme. Time to put your thinking cap on.

Again, this is under the auspice of the problems of having an S corporation and wanting to expand ownership. Expanding ownership in a multi-member LLC does not have the same problems with distributions and allocations as an S Corp.

WCG recently consulted on a buy-in scheme involving several millions of dollars. A trust was created and funded with profit incentives. In approximately ten years, if profit goals were achieved, the trust would be fully funded, and a partnership would come to life. The funds would be directed by the trust and trustee to purchase a large chunk of the business for the benefit of the new LLC.

Initially the attorneys involved had an arrangement set up where three key employees would eventually be the members of the LLC (in other words, partners in a partnership). However, it was suggested by us that even key employees might come and go. Instead, each employee invited to participate would be granted units from a pool depending on years of service. Units could also be re-deposited back into the pool upon departure of a key employee.

This allowed seniority and longevity to become valuable, but the owner could also assign additional units as he saw fit depending on an employee's individual contribution. The owner was also able to grant some units to his children to ensure their long-term legacy and wealth transfer.

In addition, the funding was augmented by cash value whole life insurance to protect the current owner's interests and to help fund the transfer of ownership.

Recap of Expanding Ownership Issues

Creating ESOPs, buy-in schemes, Buy-Sell Agreements, and the like, for an S corporation requires a talented business law attorney in concert with business consultants who can draft the corporate governance documents correctly. This stuff is state-specific but also must follow national guidelines within the IRS, ERISA, DOL, etc.

Moreover, and we will expand on this in a bit, you need to be aware of ineffective S Corp elections because of side pot deals and extraneous contracts / promises made to others.

Let us know if you need help in selecting a proper attorney, and adding some creativity and protection to your scheme.

Bad Loans to the S Corp

If your loan is not in writing or does not have a firm schedule for repayment, it might be labeled as a second class of stock which will nullify your S Corporation. We know it's a pain but please go through the hassles of creating a proper instrument when lending money to your business. See IRC Section 1361(c)(5)(B). More amazing information! Or is it spellbinding?

As with most things in the IRS world, there are exceptions and many exceptions are called Safe Harbor provisions. In this situation, there is a straight debt safe harbor which allows for a loan by a person who is eligible to hold stock in an S Corp or is a business engaged in lending. The loan must not be convertible into stock, and there are some other rules. Let's not muddy the waters quite yet since this is rare.

As mentioned earlier in this chapter, shareholder loans are generally a bad idea and might not be as elegant as basic cash injection.

Social Security Basis

If you believe Social Security will remain funded by the time you retire, you might be short-changing yourself since your salary will be used to gauge future retirement benefits. Remember, K-1 income from your S Corp is not subjected to self-employment taxes and therefore will not count towards your Social Security benefits basis.

Conversely the tax money you save today can make excellent retirement investments which can counteract the loss in Social Security benefits. In other words, the savings in Social Security taxes today might exceed the loss in future Social Security benefits if those savings are invested correctly.

The maximum Social Security benefit for 2021 is $3,957 per month for those who delay until age 70, or $3,135 for those who start benefits at full retirement age (FRA). Our apologies for not updating this data in a while, yet it remains relevant.

Using SSA.gov's calculator, at $60,000 in salary with an age of 50 your benefit would be $1,955 at age 67 in today's dollars. A $100,000 salary would have a benefit of $2,675.

Social Security Wage Limit (2021)	142,800
Max Benefit Retiring at 67 Years Old	3,135
Max Benefit Retiring at 70 Years Old	3,957

		Retire at 67 years Old			Retire at 70 years Old		
Salary	% of Max	Benefit	% of Max	Delta	Benefit	% of Max	Delta
20,000	14%	1,037	33%	19%	1,306	33%	19%
40,000	28%	1,496	48%	20%	1,897	48%	20%
60,000	42%	1,955	62%	20%	2,487	63%	21%
70,000	49%	2,185	70%	21%	2,782	70%	21%
80,000	56%	2,415	77%	21%	3,078	78%	22%
90,000	63%	2,567	82%	19%	3,227	82%	19%
100,000	70%	2,675	85%	15%	3,365	85%	15%
120,000	84%	2,890	92%	8%	3,642	92%	8%
142,800	100%	3,135	100%	0%	3,957	100%	0%

Whoa! Look at those deltas between salary and benefits right around $90,000 to $100,000 in salary. This would suggest that salaries above $90,000 have a steep diminishing return on increasing SSA benefits. Or, said differently, salaries below $90,000 have a good retirement benefit for your salary buck. Additionally, consider that paying $140,000 costs about $7,500 in additional taxes without a corresponding strong future benefit ($50,000 x 15.3%). We'll explore this more in our chapter on reasonable shareholder salaries.

Of course, there are a ton of assumptions in terms of age and consistency of earnings, but the table above illustrates some interesting points. You can probably imagine that this gets tricky right quick. Can I parlay my self-employment tax savings into better retirement benefits than the Social Security Administration? Probably. Are SSA benefits going away? Probably not, but they might become means tested and restricted in other ways.

Here is a link to SSA's online calculator-

wcginc.com/6115

Payroll Taxes on Children

Children do not pay any Social Security or Medicare taxes until they reach 18 years of age if he or she-

▲ works for a parent who owns a sole proprietorship or partnership (recall that a multi-member LLC is taxed as a partnership),

▲ works in domestic service (babysitting, chauffeurs, etc.), or

▲ delivers newspapers (the law really lists newspapers.. who does this anymore?)

However, with an S Corp election this blows up because the child is now working for a corporation, and not the parent. In other words, when you run your business as a sole proprietor, you and the business are one in the same. Same thing with a single-member LLC and a partnership. But an LLC with an S corporation election now becomes a corporation for taxation purposes, and your child loses this exception.

For example, your sole proprietorship or LLC could pay your child $13,000. He or she would not pay payroll taxes (Social Security and Medicare), and neither would you as the employer. Your child could then gift the take-home money back to you and your spouse. It is presumed that his or her tax rate would be lower than yours, and therefore you created some tax arbitrage. There is not a kiddie-tax issue since this is earned income. Furthermore, depending on how fruitful you are or your religion, you might have a hefty amount of salaries being paid to your gaggle of children bypassing a lot of payroll taxes.

Yes, he or she would have to file a tax return. But you would still claim the exemption as a dependent. No, having babies is not good tax advice. Kids are expensive. Really expensive.

There are creative types out there who will set up a single-member LLC which is solely owned by the Mom or Dad. Then, this LLC charges a consulting fee to the S Corp and then pays out the proceeds as salary to the children. In theory this bypasses payroll taxes (Social Security and Medicare) since it is an LLC that is paying the salary rather than the S corporation. This is sometimes referred to as a Family Management LLC.

We do not know how this would play out in Tax Court. Oftentimes we see theory making sense on paper just to have it be viewed as an end-around by the court. However, if we can document the business purpose of the Family Management LLC as it pertains to its business-to-business relationship with the S corporation, then let's document the heck out of it and deploy immediately. But please understand the risk. Even Forbes says Go for it, but then again, they aren't going to pay your penalties and interest.

Conversely, there might be several situations where paying your children a salary from your S corporation continues to make a lot of sense. More in this and other fringe benefits in our chapter on tax deductions.

C Corp to S Corp Problems

There are several potential problems when electing a C corporation to be taxed as an S corporation. First is called the built-in gains tax, or BIG tax for short. If the C corporation has net unrealized gains on appreciated assets, you must track these assets for a certain period of time. This also means your assets need to be appraised as of the conversion date.

For example, if an S Corp that was recently converted from a C Corp sells some real estate that increased in value when owned by the C Corp, the S Corp will probably pay taxes on the appreciation even though the corporation is now an S Corp. The BIG tax is for any asset sold within 5 years of S Corp election (it was a 10-year look back period, then whittled down to 7 due to the American Recovery and Reinvestment Act of 2009 and then 5 thanks to the Small Business Jobs Act of 2010). Here is an example-

MyCorp was a C corporation for several years until it recently made an S Corp election following some good advice. The only asset had a value of $100,000 at the time of election and its basis was $20,000. Two years later the asset was sold for $140,000 without consulting with MyCorp's accountant.

Because there was a net built-in gain at the time of the S Corp, it will be subject to corporate income tax on $80,000 of its gain. The remaining $40,000 of its gain is not subject to corporate tax.

However, the entire $120,000 gain ($140,000 less the basis of $20,000) is taxed to the shareholders of the S corporation (but it is reduced by the amount of tax that MyCorp had to pay on the gain).

See Sections 1366(f)(2) and 1374 of the Internal Revenue Code (IRC) if you find yourself in the unique position of not having enough information on the BIG tax.

More bad news- Normally, Net Operating Losses (NOLs) can be carried forward and used in future years for C Corps. On the other hand, unused NOLs will be lost forever with an S corporation election unless the C Corp can use it for previous years through amended tax returns. Otherwise the NOL cannot be used by the S Corp nor its shareholders.

Other issues arise from accounts receivable, inventory, and rents, royalties and investment income. More discussion is always required when dreaming of converting your C Corp to an S Corp. And don't worry, we won't judge you on the reasons you were a C corporation from the beginning (there aren't many legitimate reasons short of funding the startup or seed money with a self-directed 401k or paring down debt with excess cash).

Going Concern

Is your S Corp going to be needed next year, or the year after that? While an S Corp might make sense in the immediate future, the costs and hassles of startup and shutdown need to be amortized or spread out over a handful of years at the minimum. In other words, if your consulting gig might turn into a W-2 job next year, perhaps wait or defer the S Corp election.

Marriage in itself is not a reason to elect S corporation status. But an S Corp is like a marriage- easy to get into, hard to get out. The S Corp election needs to be revoked, the business needs to reclassify itself as an LLC, a final tax return needs to be filed, payroll accounts need to be closed, etc. At times it is easier to shut down the entity and re-light another one.

We are not trying to alarm you or dissuade you, but at the same time many people forget about the back-end issues. Yes, WCG can take care of all this.

Recap of S Corp Downsides

There are several issues where an S Corporation election does not make sense. Be wary of all the accountants and other business owners who automatically check the Yes box when asked about making the election. Attorneys screw this up was too often as well. As you can see in this chapter, it is not for everyone or every situation.

As always, **WCG CPAs & Advisors** charges $250 for 40 minutes of consultation where A Tax Manager or Partner will ask questions to ensure the fit is correct and that it makes sense. If you decide to engage us for future services, we credit back the $250. So… not no risk, but certainly low risk in terms of how you spend your money.

Three options exist from the consult-

▲ A solid Yes, or

▲ A solid No, or

▲ Another appointment to dig deeper into the facts and your objectives to ensure the fit is right.

Business Advisory Service plans is our core competency. We suggest taking advantage of it (Yes, more shameless self-promotion but in our heart of hearts we just want to help you avoid a mistake or a series of mistakes). We see too many costly decisions, and even worse, decisions that cannot be retroactively fixed. Buy yourself some information… buy yourself some peace of mind; if not with us, then with another competent small business consultant.

Growing Business, Debt Service

Another problem a business entity might face, regardless of S Corp status, is debt service.

In a perfect world, if you had a $10,000 K-1, hopefully you received close to $10,000 in cash. But growing businesses might be re-investing all their cash back into the business and if a business has high debt service, taxable income might be present without cash. For example, your business made a $65,000 loan payment. Perhaps $60,000 of this was principal payment since the loan is near the end of its term, and the remainder was interest.

If the business has $100,000 in net ordinary business income after expenses and deductions but before accounting for debt service, it will only have $35,000 in cash but have $95,000 in taxable income. This in itself is not bad, but the business might not be throwing off enough discretionary cash flow for the owners. Huh?

Example time.

Net Business Income	100,000
Principal Payments	60,000
Interest Expense	5,000
Cash Available	35,000
Taxable Business Income	95,000
Effective Tax Rate	30%
Tax Due	28,500
Cash Surplus / Deficit	6,500

The tax rate above of 30% is high and is artificially inflated to illustrate the point. In this example you have $35,000 in cash available for a shareholder distribution, and $28,500 will be eaten up on your individual tax return for taxes leaving $6,500 for happy meals and taco Tuesdays.

Loans are one thing. Buying a bunch of inventory can also cash-strap your business. Remember inventory is not deducted until it is sold or depleted, or deemed shrunk or obsolete. There are some newer accounting methods thanks to recent tax code changes to might allow for inventory purchases to be treated as cost of goods sold immediately.

Another concept to point out is that depreciation of an asset is supposed to alleviate some of this problem. Let's say you purchased some equipment for $100,000. Similar to the example above, you had a high portion of your debt payment being applied to the principal amount of the loan. This reduces your cash yet taxable income is left unchanged.

However, depreciation steps in and saves the day by being a non-cash reduction in taxable income, and helps alleviate the principal loan payment problem.

Here is an example using the same table above.

	Without Depreciation	With Depreciation
Net Business Income	100,000	100,000
Principal Payments	60,000	60,000
Interest Expense	5,000	5,000
Depreciation Expense	0	25,000
Cash Available	35,000	35,000
Taxable Business Income	95,000	70,000
Effective Tax Rate	30%	28%
Tax Due	28,500	19,600
Cash Surplus / Deficit	6,500	15,400

The depreciation amounts and effective tax rates were made up numbers to illustrate this point. As you can see, depreciation can alleviate some of the cash crunch. Then again, if you elected to depreciate it instantly with a Section 179 deduction, then you are back to square one. This is one of the examples where the bird in the hand is not worth two in the bush- the pleasure of an instant tax deduction via Section 179 which lacks the stamina to help you in future years (which presumably are at a higher income).

Note: This really isn't a reason not to elect S corporation status- it is a problem for any business entity.

Cash is king. Plan ahead before paring down debt.

Chapter 5
State Nexus Problems
(updated February 2020, not much has changed)

Introduction

This in itself is not a reason to avoid the S corporation election, but there is not a better place for this material. State nexus stuff is getting very complicated so we decided to make this a separate chapter since it will continue to grow over time.

Every year all 50 states plus the District of Columbia and New York City participate in a survey conducted by Bloomberg. Here is the link for the latest results, but a warning is in order first. The 2017 report is 523 pages (yet the table of contents is rich with detail to find your particular area of interest).

wcginc.com/1744

There is also an executive summary for 2018 available from Bloomberg, and it is only 20 pages (nice!)-

wcginc.com/1746

There are several concepts here and a ton of material. Here is the mini table of contents-

▲ Disclaimer

▲ Wayfair Case Part 1

▲ Nexus Theory

▲ Constitutional and Legislative Standards (*Commerce and Due Process Clause, and Public Law 86-272*)

▲ Sales Tax, Income Tax

▲ Physical and Economic Presence, Nexus Attached

▲ Wayfair Case Part 2

▲ Services and Tangible Personal Property (TPP)

▲ Costs of Performance, Market-Based Approach

▲ Allocation and Throwback

▲ FBA, Drop Shipments, Trailing Nexus Revisited

We will explore each of these in turn, and then attempt to bring it all together with a recap. The operative word is attempt since this stuff is changing all the time and will continue to evolve through court decisions, state legislation and the impending congressional moves.

Disclaimer

This section is not designed to address all your nexus concerns or be a solution. We are merely shining a light on all the angles to this massive problem. Our darn forefathers couldn't imagine internets (yes plural), and other things like trains, planes and automobiles. State nexus is a massive issue both on the sales tax and income tax fronts, and states are becoming increasingly aggressive. Again, our chapter is full of generalities and summations to give you the landscape. Your particular situation will need specific attention from us and other professionals, including your own research.

> Caution! As mentioned elsewhere in our book, state income tax nexus and state sales tax nexus are vastly different. We touch on income tax nexus a little bit, but this chapter is dedicated to sales tax nexus. Having one does not mean you have the other. Frankly, income tax nexus is very murky, and it depends on various factors such as revenue, assets and payroll. We could write a book just on income tax nexus, and by the time we published it, it would be like an eight track cassette player.

Wayfair Case Part 1

The United States Supreme Court in a 5-4 decision in South Dakota v. Wayfair changed the sales tax nexus landscape dramatically. Until then, Amazon retailers and other online resellers were partially safe as a result of the 1992 Quill v. North Dakota decision where the Court required nexus through physical presence before states could demand sales tax collection. But with Wayfair, the Court changed this to "substantial nexus."

Here is the U.S. Supreme Court opinion-

wcginc.com/1788

We will explore the significance of this court decision throughout this chapter, and some concepts are moot but remain for legacy and illustrative purposes. Keep referring to our blog posts for updates-

wcginc.com.com/blog

Nexus Theory

Nexus is a Latin word meaning to bind, join or tie. Simply stated, tax nexus is the minimum amount of contact between a taxpayer and a state, which allows the state to tax a business on its activities. Every state defines nexus differently using terms such as physical presence or economic presence, and those concepts will be discussed in a bit.

There is also a concept called trailing nexus where an entity that once had nexus in a state ceases activities that created nexus in the first place. This is a point of contention between taxpayers and states, and is commonly created by Fulfillment By Amazon (FBA) and other online retailers since product (and therefore physical nexus) is continuously moving around.

The theory behind the trailing nexus concept can be better illustrated with an example. If your business sent a sales rep to Washington for several months to solicit orders, it is safe to say that after the sales rep leaves a residual effect would remain. This in turn would generate sales (business activity). As an aside, Washington is one of the few states that defines trailing nexus explicitly. Pot + Coffee = Progressive Law.

Constitutional and Legislative Standards

Time to go back to school. The Due Process Clause of the United States Constitution requires the seller to have some "minimum contacts" with the taxing state. The seller must reach out and purposefully avail itself of the benefits of that state. Historically, courts have held that a physical presence is required to meet the Due Process Clause, but that was dramatically changed in the Wayfair case.

Once this is satisfied, which is no easy task for a state, a four-part test of the Commerce Clause must be met.

Article 1, Section 8, Clause 3, of the Constitution empowers Congress to prohibit a state from unduly burdening interstate commerce and business activities. The law authors were very concerned with states colluding or combining forces near major trade hubs and routes, and thus created the Commerce Clause. A vision of gangs holding up covered wagons in California.

The United States Supreme Court in *Complete Auto Transit v. Brady (1977)* stated that a seller must meet the following four-part test to be forced to collect a tax:

▲ The seller must have substantial nexus (was physical presence with Quill and now it is substantial nexus with Wayfair) in state;

▲ The tax cannot discriminate against interstate commerce;

▲ The tax must be fairly apportioned; and

▲ The tax must be fairly related to services provided by state.

The common theme after nexus is fairness. The only time a tax is fair is when you pay the minimum amount, right?

Moving onto legislative standards. Public Law 86-272 was quoted earlier in this chapter and basically prevents a state from imposing income tax on businesses whose only activity in the state is the solicitation of orders, provided the orders are accepted and delivered from a point outside the state (interstate commerce). And this only refers to tangible personal property (TPP) and not services. At the time of this law, services were inherently personal and required a close, physical presence to perform (proximity). That has changed with telecommuting and the pure definition of a service (more on that in a bit).

So we have three standards yet states vary across the board based on the definition and triggering of nexus.

Sales and Use Tax, Income Tax

There are two issues at play, and they are not necessarily connected. First is sales and use tax which frankly receives the most attention because of online retailers. Some theory first. When you purchase a computer at your local Best Buy, the seller is collecting sales tax in a fiduciary role. In other words, it is collecting your sales tax obligation for you on your behalf, and remitting it to the authorities. Nice of them, right?

If you buy this same computer from an Amazon retailer, the seller might or might not collect sales tax on your behalf. If the retailer does not collect sales tax, it is still your responsibility to pay this sales tax along with your state income tax return. No one does this of course. We have asked 25,000 times in the past decade, and we have never heard a Yes from a client. But understand that you are required to pay sales tax if not collected by the online seller.

States are getting tired of the under-reported sales tax obligations. Therefore several are going after businesses with strong internet presence. Here is a summary about New York's "Amazon Law" from Cbiz.com (Corrente, 2011, yeah a bit outdated but provides context)-

> In practice, such an online selling scheme may work as follows. A retailer selling neckties has a shop in Florida, and it wants to increase sales by selling over the internet. The retailer sets up a website, and decides that to generate traffic on its website, it will partner with other online websites. In this example, the retailer places an ad on the website of the New York Times. When a customer reaches the retailer's website by clicking on the link at newyorktimes.com, the "click-through" is logged. If the retailer makes a subsequent sale as a result of the click-through, the New York Times is paid a commission. As a result of the Amazon law, New York assumes that the relationship has created nexus for the online retailer.

According to Avalara.com (one of the first experts in sales tax nexus), Amazon does not have fulfillment centers in New York. As of 2016, they further listed about 25 states with similar click-through nexus legislation or policies.

The other issue is income tax. Just because a retailer has an obligation to collect sales tax does not necessarily mean they have an instant income tax obligation. Some states have a fruit of the poisonous tree mentality where sales tax nexus creates an income tax nexus and vice versa. Don't forget that states cannot impose an income tax per se, but they can impose a business tax or a franchise tax or a whatever tax that smells, walks and talks like an income tax but isn't call an income tax.

Remember too that Public Law 86-272 protects TPP only from a strict income tax. However states are the using the same "non-income tax" tax as a work around for everything from tangible personal property to services.

Physical and Economic Presence, Nexus Attached

In a 1992 U.S. Supreme Court case docketed as Quill Corporation v. North Dakota, the court established a physical presence test for sales tax nexus. The court did not address income tax, and since this decision states have varied quite a bit on attaching nexus to taxes other than sales and use tax.

Several appellate courts have limited the Quill case to sales and use tax nexus, and have deferred income tax nexus to economic presence rather than physical presence. According to

Bloomberg's Multi State Survey from 2015, only 7 states applied the physical presence test in determine an income tax nexus leaving 43 states to apply an economic presence test for income tax nexus. That was 2015 and prior to the Wayfair case.

Let's consider California's economic presence rules. A business is considered doing business in California under Revenue and Taxation Code Section 23101 (enacted in 2011) if it meets any of the following conditions-

▲ They have sales in California, in the amount of $500,000 or 25% of total sales, whichever is less.

▲ They have property in California, with a value of $50,000 or 25% of total property, whichever is less.

▲ They have payroll in California, in the amount of $50,000 or 25% of total payroll, whichever is less.

California's numbers above are a bit out dated since they are annually adjusted for inflation. According to their website as of this writing, they state, "For taxable years beginning on or after 1/1/2019, the amounts are $601,967, $60,197 and $60,197, respectively."

These hard numbers are called bright-line nexus, and are used in income tax nexus. You simply meet a numeric threshold, and you magically have nexus in that state. Several states have a preponderance of the evidence set of rules using phrases such as "businesses earning significant income." Really!? Sounds like fun trying to defend that.

> Sidebar on Nexus: Having these hard numbers is similar to driving under the influence (DUI). Let's say your state has a 0.08% blood alcohol limit. You can still be considered driving under the influence even if you have less than 0.08%. However, if you are over 0.08% then the state automatically presumes you are driving under the influence no matter how well you walk the line or touch your nose. This is called a "bright line." States may argue you have nexus even if you do not cross the bright line, but if you do cross the bright line then it is automatic. Does that help?

More bad news. Your business might not have income associated with California but be deemed as doing business in California. Seriously! And, in this case you would be subjected to the $800 minimum franchise tax regardless (as of the 2024 tax year). Yuck.

Here is the direct language from California's Franchise Tax Board website-

An out-of-state taxpayer that has less than the threshold amounts of property, payroll, and sales in California may still be considered doing business in California if the taxpayer actively engages in any transaction for the purpose of financial or pecuniary gain or profit in California.

Partnership A, an out-of-state partnership, has employees who work out of their homes in California. The employees sell and provide warranty work to California customers. Partnership A's property, payroll, and sales in California fall below the threshold amounts. Is Partnership A considered to be doing business in California?

Yes. Partnership A is considered doing business in California even if the property, payroll, and sales in California fall below the threshold amounts. Partnership A is considered doing business in California through its employees because those employees are actively engaging in transactions for profit on behalf of Partnership A.

Corporation B, an out-of-state corporation, has $100,000 in total property, $200,000 in total payroll, $1,000,000 in total sales, of which $400,000 was sales to California customers. Corporation B has no property or payroll in California. Is Corporation B doing business in California?

Yes. Although Corporation B's California sales is less than the $500,000 threshold, Corporation B's California sales is 40 percent of its total sales which exceeds 25 percent of the corporation's total sales ($400,000 ÷ 1,000,000 = 40%.)

And to make matters worse, your business might be protected by Public Law 86-272 if you are simply soliciting orders for tangible personal property in California. But if you are selling services in California, even with independent contractors, there is no protection and the income will be taxed if you meet one of the three criteria above.

More direct language from California's FTB Publication 1050-

PL 86-272 still applies to sellers of tangible personal property. As a result, if a taxpayer's activities in California stay within the protections of PL 86-272, a taxpayer also remains protected from the imposition of those taxes that are computed based on net income, namely, the California franchise and income tax. Nevertheless, if a taxpayer is considered doing business in California either under R&TC Section 23101(a) or (b), it still has a filing requirement and will be subject to the minimum tax, because that tax is not computed based on net income and therefore is not subject to the protections of PL 86-272.

Corporation C, an out-of-state corporation, is a seller of tangible goods over the internet and qualifies for protection under PL 86-272. For taxable year 2011, Corporation C has $1,000,000 of sales but no property or payroll in California. Is Corporation C considered doing business in California?

> Yes. Corporation C is considered doing business in California because it has sales of $1,000,000 in California. Therefore, Corporation C must file a California return to pay the minimum tax. However, since Corporation C is protected under PL 86-272, it will not be subject to California franchise tax.

Corporation D, an out-of-state corporation with no property or payroll in California, is a service provider that has sales of $2,000,000 to purchasers who receive the benefit of Corporation D's services in California. Those services are from income-producing activity that is performed outside of California and Corporation D uses the four-factor formula (property, payroll, and double-weighted sales) to apportion its income to California. As a result, none of Corporation D's income is apportioned to California. Is Corporation D considered doing business in California?

> Yes. Sales of services and intangibles are sourced under R&TC 25136(b) for purposes of applying the doing business test of R&TC 23101(b) regardless of whether those sales are sourced under R&TC 25136(a) for income apportionment purposes (that is, regardless of whether taxpayer elects single sales factor apportionment). Accordingly, Corporation D is considered doing business in California because it has sales of services here of $2,000,000. Although Corporation D has no California source income, it is still liable for the minimum tax because it is doing business here. PL 86-272 does not protect the taxpayer, because it does not apply to service providers, nor does it protect against the minimum tax (because that tax is not income-based).

California is a fun state to research since they are usually on the forefront of legislative changes and updates, and there is so much economic activity. The following link is California's FTB1050 (updated 2017) where they outline in plain language a list of protected activities and unprotected activities as they relate to Public Law 86-272 (tangible personal property).

wcginc.com/1751

As of February 28, 2020 this is the current FTB1050 from California (they require you submit a form and they email you the PDF… not sure why it just doesn't sit on their web server. Oh well).

There are 50 other examples aside from California (including Washington DC and New York City). Please do the homework!

Some more fodder for your consideration. In two U.S. Supreme Court cases, Scripto v. Carson (1960) and Tyler Pipe v. Washington Department of Revenue (1987), the court affirmed that a third-party can create nexus. The court specifically stated what matters

> "is whether the activities performed in the state on behalf of the taxpayer are significantly associated with the taxpayer's ability to establish and maintain a market in this state for the sales."

This third-party connection is detrimental to Amazon and eBay retailers (and the like) and discussed in more detail later.

To recap, what we are doing here is setting the stage for Wayfair. States have established numbers from a sales, property and payroll perspective to say, "hey, based on math alone you have substantial presence in our state and as such you must pay income tax." Keep this in mind as we shift back to sales tax.

Wayfair Case Part 2

As mentioned before, the U.S. Supreme Court ruled on June 21, 2018 in favor of a South Dakota statute enacted in 2016 that defined substantial nexus (remember that word from Complete Auto Transit v. Brady in 1977) as-

▲ Deliver more than $100,000 of goods and services in a year, or

▲ Have 200 or more separate transactions for the delivery of goods or services

Note the Or! Interestingly the suit was brought against Wayfair, Newegg and Overstock collectively. More interestingly, the court noted that other functions of ecommerce like cookies being left behind by browsers and customers downloading retailer apps may be introduced as proof of physical presence. Holy smokes!

Another tidbit was Kennedy, who wrote the majority opinion, admonished Wayfair by stating they could not have a customer base attracted to images of beautifully decorated homes if it weren't for a stable local and state government. Kennedy was just piling on like the cop giving you a ticket, and a lecture. You can read the full opinion here-

wcginc.com/1788

Our little home state of Colorado is famous in the sales tax arena too (not just the Dakotas). In 2010, the state of Colorado passed a law that required out-of-state vendors to collect and provide information to its citizens regarding their total purchases, so that the residents could determine their tax liability for the state. Direct Marketing Association v. Brohl was a U.S. Supreme Court case that essentially upheld Colorado's statute. DMA was a trade group and Barbara Brohl was the Executive Director for the Colorado Department of Revenue.

This stuff is changing all the time. Keep referring to our blog posts for updates-

wcginc.com/blog

Also, we encourage any interstate seller of goods and services to seek the advice of professionals who handle sales tax every day. Our referrals are TaxJar, Avalara and Peisner Johnson.

Services and Tangible Personal Property (TPP)

Public Law 86-272 protects TPP as we previously mentioned. But services are fair game for states to tax. Generally speaking states do not impose a sales tax on services but they can impose a franchise, business or privilege tax.

To make things more interesting, the definition of a service is expanding in light of ecommerce and cloud computing. For example, most states characterize cloud computing as a sale of intangibles or services, but Utah considers cloud computing as the sale, lease or license of TPP. Subtle difference, yet important.

Let's say what you do is a service. What is the standard for determining nexus for your business? Read on please.

Costs of Performance, Market-Based Approach

Prior to Al Gore inventing all the internets, most states used the costs of performance as the method to determine nexus. If your butt was in Colorado and you provided a service to people in California, the costs of performing the service would be in Colorado and therefore you would not have nexus to California. You would only be subjected to Colorado income taxes.

Given the latest Bloomberg survey, there is a growing minority of states that are using the market-based approach. This can be loosely defined as the assignment of revenue based on the location of either

▲ the service provider's customers, or

▲ where the customers received benefit from the service provided.

Consider a web server. As of 2016, 38 states plus the District of Columbia and New York City would consider a web server physically located in their taxing jurisdiction as enough of a presence to find income tax nexus. And most would find sales tax nexus as well. Wow. 38 is a high number, and it is old.

There is an executive summary for 2018 available from Bloomberg, and it is only 20 pages (nice!)-

wcginc.com/1746

Allocation and Throwback

Allocation of the sales and subsequent income is at the top of this heap of nexus mess. States don't want to unnecessarily complicate things, but they do want money.

Throwback is a common concept but not every state uses it. Again, we'll pick on California. Under the old rules, when a California business ships TPP to another state, and that business does not have nexus in that state, the sales are "thrown back" to California since it is considered a California sale.

Interestingly enough, there are cases where a sale would not have a tax home at all. Let's say you sold a service to a customer outside of California. Using the market-based approach and under California's new rules of bright line nexus (turn back a few pages to review), sales exceeding $500,000 in another state are not thrown back to California. So, if you had sales in another state that did not trigger a filing in that state, these sales could arguably be allocated outside of California but disappear into a black hole. Sounds crazy, but true.

Allocation issues such as these can create tax arbitrage and there are other examples of the same dollar being taxed twice by different states. It truly is a mess. States recognize this growing problem and are working together to eliminate the loopholes. In about three perhaps four hundred years we'll be good to go.

FBA, Drop Shipments, Trailing Nexus Revisited

Fulfillment By Amazon (FBA) and other fulfillment services add a new dimension to the nexus conversation. States are scrambling to figure it out so tax revenue can keep up with population growth and resource use.

Avalara is a consultation business who specializes in sales tax issues, and they re-printed a wonderful article on FBA and what it means to you. It was originally written by Michael Fleming of Peisner Johnson & Company and it is a bit outdated since it was the voice before Wayfair, but it provides excellent backdrop of the issues. We will attempt to paraphrase some of the concepts here, but if you want the full details use the following link-

wcginc.com/5858

The first concept is nexus, which we've beaten to death. But here is a different spin for those selling products online. There are four common nexus creating activities-

▲ Your Location

▲ Inventory

▲ Warehouse Use, and

▲ Fulfillment Services

The common theme to these four activities is Where is your stuff? More importantly, is your stuff in a state that ships within the state, and if so, does that state have a sales tax obligation? In other words, if a competitor located in the same state that you are selling your tangible personal property (TPP) through an online channel is collecting sales tax, then you probably have a similar obligation. Location. Location. Location.

There is guilt by association as well. If the distributor, warehouse, fulfillment center, storage facility or whatever else you want to call it stores and ships your stuff, then you also have nexus by the fact of their physical presence. The essence of the facility argument for a state is that the facility is helping you create a marketplace for your goods.

There are some fine lines with who holds title and when does title transfer. For most online retailers and sellers, title arguments probably won't do much good unless there is a lot at stake and you have a war chest to spend on attorney fees.

The next concern is materiality. If you've determined that you have nexus and are required to collect sales tax, is the obligation material? If you sold $200 worth of stuff to a Colorado Springs consumer, is the $16 in tax worth the headaches? Remember, if you do not collect sales tax from a consumer, he or she is still obligated to pay sales tax on his or her individual state income tax return. Unless, of course, your nexus and materiality tips the scale, and you have the responsibility to collect sales tax on behalf of the consumer.

States can spend some time on going after the head of snake, such a medium-sized online retailers or states can spend a lot of time going after the consumer. Drug user versus drug dealer.

There are voluntary disclosure initiatives to allow online sellers to come clean with their dirty sales tax deeds. Several states will waive the penalties and limit the lookback to only three years. You must weigh the chance of the hammer versus the certainty of a light tap. Peisner Johnson and co-hosted by TaxJar held a wonderful webinar in 2016 on the Multi-State Tax Commission amnesty program. You can see the slide deck from Michael Fleming here-

wcginc.com/5863

The issue of trailing nexus must be considered as well. For those familiar with Amazon and FBA services, you understand that your inventory is continuously being shifted to different states. Just because your inventory no longer exists in a state does not mean your nexus is instantly cutoff. This concept was broached in the beginning of this chapter, and is reiterated here to stress the importance of keeping up with the Kardashians and the location of your stuff, and who you owe an obligation to. Good luck.

Recap of State Tax Issues

We attempted to provide several angles and concepts to the state taxation issue. There are very few hard and fast solutions. There are tax attorneys and consulting firms who do nothing but argue and litigate state nexus issues.

If there is nexus, is there allocation? If there is allocation, who gets what? If there is a sales tax obligation is there an income tax (or franchise tax or business tax) obligation? Can you have one and not the other? Are your services considered tangible personal property by some states?

Be careful. States are taking on the bigger online retailers like Wayfair, Newegg and Overstock, and now they now appear to be shifting their focus to those businesses who do not have deep pockets to fight or pay fines. If what you are doing smells wrong or keeps you up at night, it probably is worth looking into.

Our philosophy at WCG is not popular among online retailers, but we believe our position is solid. We are 100% in favor of capitalism and free markets. We are also 100% in favor of fair competition. If another tax and business consulting firm "beats us" then we learn and move along. But if a competitor beats another player in the market because the playing field is not level, then that is not winning... it's cheating.

Selling the same stuff as Best Buy but not charging a sales tax to make yourself look more attractive is not fair competition. Sure, the responsibility is ultimately on the consumer to pay sales tax, Yes, we get it. But a consumer cannot get out of Best Buy without paying a sales tax, and to make matters even worse Best Buy has to collect sales tax even on internet orders. What bugs us the most is the resistance from Amazon and other big online retailers.

Times are changing. Sure, the small retailer might get squeezed, but that's life. Survival of the fittest. Eat or get eaten.

Chapter 6
S Corporation Election
(updated October 2023)

Formation (Election) of an S Corp

There is a misconception floating around out there that an S Corp is a standalone entity. Not true. There are several entity types, and the three most common are-

▲ Limited Liability Companies (LLCs), either as a single-member or multi-member

▲ Partnerships, including all the variants (LP, LLP, LLLP, etc.), and

▲ Corporations (C Corps), including Professional Corporations (PCs).

Each of these entities can elect to be treated as an S Corp for taxation purposes under subchapter S of the revenue code.

So, while we might talk about your "S Corp", we are truly talking about your LLC, partnership or C Corp being treated as an S Corp for taxation. Also, the words member and shareholder are synonymous as well from a conversational perspective- for an LLC, the state considers owners to be members, but the IRS considers the owners to be shareholders when issues like distributions, basis, etc. are discussed. Same is true for equity accounts on the balance sheet.

Electing S Corp Filing Status, Retroactive for 2023

Yes, you are able to engage in revisionist history and retro activate your S corporation election to January 1, 2023, and have your income avoid a large chunk of self-employment taxes. First things first. You must be eligible to become an S Corp for taxation purposes-

▲ you must have an LLC, partnership or C Corp already in place (basically an entity that is recognized by your state's Secretary of State),

▲ your entity must be domestic,

▲ have 100 or fewer shareholders,

▲   have shareholders who are individuals, estates or exempt organizations, and not have any non-resident alien shareholders, <u>and</u>

▲   have only one class of stock (you are allowed to have voting and non-voting as one class).

There are some other devils in the details, but 99% of the LLCs, partnerships and C Corps out there qualify for an S Corp election.

If you do not have an entity already in place, there are organizations that sell shelf businesses. Note the word shelf- not shell. These shelf businesses, with an f, have EINs and file tax returns, and all their history sits on a shelf hence the name shelf company. How this works is beyond our book and usually requires a conversation. In other words, it gets a bit hairy.

Late S Corp Election, Oops
Form 2553 (the S Corp election form) must be filed with the IRS. It is typically due within 75 days of forming your business entity (right around March 15 of the following year). However, in typical IRS fashion there are 185 exceptions to the rule and the late S corporation election is another example. The IRS provides relief for the late filing of Form 2553. Historically, IRS Revenue Procedures 2003-43 and 2004-48 were the governing rules but the IRS has simplified it (imagine that!).

IRS Revenue Procedure 2013-30, effective September 3, 2013, allows an entity to get relief and elect S Corp status within 3 years and 75 days from the date the election was originally intended to be effective. Holy cow. Three years!

The IRS is basically saying that if you walk and smell like an S Corp, then you are an S Corp

So, if it is November 2023, and you want to go back to January 1, 2023, no problem. If it is March 2024 (tax season) and you are freakin' out because you forgot to make the election earlier, you can still go back to January 1, 2023. No that is not a typo... we are talking about going back to the previous year's January 1!

With the preparation and filing of a late Form 2553 for your S corporation election, a reasonable cause letter must be attached. We have a template that we've used successfully at least 1,500 times, and we can guide you through it. Additionally, your reasonable cause cannot be "hey IRS, I just learned of this S Corp thing, and man, it sounds amazing. I would like to do this retroactively so I can save a bunch of taxes."

Beyond the reasonable stuff, there might be other hiccups. Isn't hiccups such a friendly word? Sort of like bumps in the road. Bruises is another word that is about as hollow as hiccups and bumps. No one says pitfalls or disasters anymore, just hiccups. The bottom line is that we can engage in some revisionist history on March 1, 2024 to take effect for all of 2023. Boom!

If your current CPA or tax professional says No, we kindly and very politely suggest you find a new accountant. **WCG CPAs & Advisors** has been doing this for over a decade (there was relief provisions prior to the 2013 IRS Rev Proc as well) without major problems. Given the timeline as it compares to the filing deadlines, you might incur some late filing penalties. However, these are usually abated under the First Time Abatement statutory relief program. Aside from that, the late S corporation election is straightforward.

Once the facts and circumstances are reviewed, and everyone thinks the S Corp election is the way to go, there are three things that happen simultaneously-

▲ Fax Late S Corp Election Form 2553 to the IRS

Fee: **$600** or $1,200 after Jan 1, 2024 which includes late filing abatement efforts since your tax return will unlikely be extended electronically. A timely filed S Corp election is $450.

▲ Open Payroll Accounts for 202<u>4</u> (to be compliant in the future)

Fee: **$550 to $650** (depending on state, CA, CO, TX easier... NY and PA, rough, like a stucco bathtub)

▲ Issue a 1099-MISC as Officer Compensation for 202<u>3</u> (in lieu of a late payroll)

Fee: **$650** (this includes tax planning and estimated tax calculations)

▲ Prepare 202<u>3</u> (due spring 2024) S Corporation Tax Return on Form 1120S

Fee: **$1,500** (typically, most are $1,500)

So, you will spend about $3,200 however you will be saving anywhere from 8% to 10% of your net ordinary business income after expenses and deductions depending in your situation. Also remember that the late S Corp election and payroll account setup is a sunk cost. In other words, you would need these things done regardless of late S Corp election for the previous year or waiting until next year. Bite the bullet now. Get it done.

Said differently; if we isolate 2023 only, your costs are about $2,150. If you have $50,000 in net business operating income after expenses, you will still save well over $2,000 after our fee.

In the past, to obtain relief with a late S Corp election during the tax season, we would prepare and paper-file Form 1120S (corporate tax return) and physically attach Form 2553 (S Corp election) to it. Today, there are three paths-

▲ If we are chillin' around Thanksgiving, then we can likely submit the S Corp election via fax and have it processed by the IRS in time for the March 15 filing. Normal ops.

▲ If we are after December 1, then we prepare the S Corp tax return (Form 1120S) by March 15 and we electronically attach Form 2553. Clean. Nice.

▲ If we are after December 1 and we are wanting to extend the S Corp tax return, then we have some problems since we cannot electronically file a tax return extension. Rather, we attempt to file the extension which will be met with a likely rejection. Next, we deal with the late filing penalty with the First Time Abatement program with a massively high 99% success rate. Messy, but common.

Everyone once in a while the IRS loses its mind and rejects the late S Corp election. We always get it pushed through. Always. Unfortunately, the rejection or some other nasty gram of a notice arrives on your doorstep at 5:01PM on a Friday. Briefly freak out, send the documents to us, and then have a Coke and a smile- it'll be OK.

At the very worst we have to obtain a Power of Attorney from you, call the IRS and give them a "see... how it works is..." spiel. We have a 100% success rate in getting these late S Corp elections pushed through. While your mileage might vary, we are also very successful with getting late payment penalties abated with the IRS. Each state is different, and some are unsympathetic. Again, the savings will outweigh the costs (or we wouldn't let you do it).

Another Option, Dormant S Corp

Not sure if you want to have a full-blown S Corporation? Break-even analysis is based on our annual fee of $4,320. If an S corporation saves you 8% to 10% (on average) in taxes over the garden-variety LLC, then $4,320 divided by 9% equals $48,000 of net ordinary business income after expenses and deductions.

Let's say you are teetering on that income figure, and not sure about running payroll and all that jazz. You could still run your business income and expenses through your tax return as a sole proprietor or another single-member LLC, and take the small self-employment tax hit. Then simply file a No Activity tax return for your S Corp (this assumes you already filed an S corporation election, and now regret the cost of running payroll or some other expense).

Conversely, if you break-even on the fees as compared to your savings, keep in mind the additional benefits. With our Business Advisory Service packages, you are getting individual tax return preparation plus routine tax planning and consultation. There is value there; so if you break-even in terms of cost-benefit analysis, you might actually be ahead with the value received. We'd like to think so (of course we would, right, we're the one collecting the check).

Missing Payroll, Now What?

There is a near certainty that we can make the S Corp election retroactive to January 1 of 2023. As mentioned earlier, one of the pillars of S Corps is to pay a salary to the materially participating shareholders. If you are reading this after Thanksgiving dinner and yet another tragic Cowboys loss, it is time to step on the gas and get payroll setup so a payroll event can be processed before the end of the year.

But if it's 2024, and 2023 is all over, there are three options (in descending order of elegance)-

Issue a 1099 to Yourself

Really?! For real? Hang in there on this one (in all fairness we did allude to this earlier). What we can do is issue a 1099-NEC for a portion of the business net income to yourself which will be reported on Schedule C of your individual tax return (Form 1040). In turn, this income will be subjected to self-employment taxes. Remember self-employment taxes and Social Security and Medicare taxes are the same thing.

The amount of the 1099-NEC is entered into Line 7 of Form 1120S as Officer Compensation. Therefore, from an Officer Compensation to net business / K-1 income comparison, this technique still satisfies the reasonable salary sniff.

While the IRS might frown upon this option, at the end of the day they are typically satisfied since employment taxes are essentially being paid. Again, this is not as elegant as the W-2 option, but it certainly works for the first year.

Additionally, if you were to lose an IRS challenge on reasonable salary determination the IRS would impute income on Schedule C. We are simply following what they would eventually do anyway. Again, this is a first-year mulligan. A one and done. Payroll must be set up for the following year, and normal W-2 and other filings must be done.

Who should lose their mind with this solution is the state since unemployment and other insidious taxes such as state disability insurance (SDI) is not being paid. Then again, we've never heard of a state challenging this either.

Manual Late Payroll Event
WCG used to do late payrolls since we processed payroll manually, in-house. Currently, we are partnered with ADP to handle all our payroll processing (we still consult with you on a reasonable shareholder wage and make the payroll entries into ADP). ADP is wonderful, but they are rigid. As a result, no late payrolls.

We list this option is case you or someone else wants to run a late payroll event after December 31, but we advise against it. If you want to see a flurry of IRS and state notices, and waste time wading through it all, then go for it.

Roll the Dice
As paid tax professionals, WCG cannot advise this course of action. Having said that, we have observed several taxpayers labeling the first year as a mulligan, not creating a W-2 or a 1099, and taking his or her chances. Audit rates are about 0.4% for S Corps, and currently the Treasury Inspector General of Tax Administration (TIGTA) is charging the IRS with the task of auditing S Corps that do not pay a salary and who report losses for three or more years. As a result, profitable S Corps appear to be flying under the radar especially if you only miss one year of paying a salary (your first year).

What could happen? The IRS could simply impute wages, create payroll liabilities and send you a bill. We've seen S Corporations get these types of notices. This is not ideal since the state is not getting its share of things such as unemployment and disability, and the IRS is sharing data with states.

Again, rolling the dice is not our professional advice, even if it rhymes. We do not want some stray bullet from the IRS hitting us while trying to hit you- we will decline the engagement if you want to roll the dice. We don't want your problems to become our problems (sorry).

Conversely, let us do it right. You sleep well at night. More rhymes. Everyone wins.

Of course, we can take care of all this paperwork for you!

> **Huge Emphasis:** We cannot stress enough that having an LLC in place is cheap insurance even if you don't ever elect to be an S Corp. While IRS guidance is hazy, it is our recommendation plus the recommendations of tax attorneys and other

consultants that the effective date of the S Corp election should not occur before the earliest date that the LLC has members, acquires assets or begins conducting business.

Mid-Year Payroll

It's July and your golf game is just as crummy as it was in May, so you start focusing on your business. You talk to us, and we decide that the S corporation election is the way to go. We don't go back to Q1 and Q2, and process late payroll events for those quarters. That is an unnecessary can of worms. We simply open payroll accounts for Q3, determine your reasonable salary for the year, compute your tax obligation through mock tax returns and planning, and chop it up for the remaining months.

For example, let's say shareholder payroll is set to start on August 1 and continue each month. There are five payroll events left (August, September, October, November and December). As such, if your salary is $60,000 for the entire year, we will set up payroll to be $12,000 per month for the remaining months, and then $5,000 starting January of next year.

No, the IRS does not get alarmed when you start payroll in the middle of the year. No, they are not concerned about the lopsidedness of your payroll events. Yes, there might be some underpayment penalties if you haven't made any estimated tax payments. But wait! The super cool thing about payroll is that a singular event on December 31 is considered to have been paid evenly throughout the year, including income taxes. Therefore, you should not incur underpayment penalties if your withholdings encompass your tax liabilities. Nice!

More on withholdings and tax liabilities in another chapter. Also, more on why a singular payroll event on December 31 is strongly discouraged (spoiler alert: humans are humans and spend money they don't truly have… shocker, we know).

Nuts and Bolts of the S Corp Election

Let's take a step back and talk about some of the underpinnings of the S corporation election. Some of this is boring legalese and some of this is nerdy accountant-ese, but you'll be better for it. Perhaps.

Business Entities

Treasury Regulations Section 301.7701 discusses all sorts of things about business entities and the default tax classification. The IRS website has a nice summary-

A Limited Liability Company (LLC) is an entity created by state statute.

Depending on elections made by the LLC and the number of members, the IRS will treat an LLC either as a corporation, partnership, or as part of the owner's tax return (a disregarded entity).

A domestic LLC with at least two members is classified as a partnership for federal income tax purposes unless it files Form 8832 and elects to be treated as a corporation.

For income tax purposes, an LLC with only one member is treated as an entity disregarded as separate from its owner, unless it files Form 8832 and elects to be treated as a corporation. However, for purposes of employment tax and certain excise taxes, an LLC with only one member is still considered a separate entity.

This simply means that unless you do something extra (which the IRS refers to as Check the Box elections), you will default to the tax classification above. Therefore, and as summarized by the IRS above, three possible tax classifications exist for business entities- corporation, partnership or disregarded entity. As we've discussed elsewhere, community property states usually follow the single member LLC disregarded entity rules above.

Treasury Regulations Section 301.7701-2 expands this a bit and defines business entities separately from corporations. We'll move along unless you are starting a bank or insurance company.

Form 8832
Form 8832 allows you to change the tax classification of an entity. Treasury Regulations Section 301.7701-3(g)(1) outlines the various re-classifications, and we've summarized them here-

1. Partnership to an association (corporation). The partnership contributes all of its assets and liabilities to the association in exchange for stock in the association, and immediately thereafter, the partnership liquidates by distributing the stock of the association to its partners. Woohoo!

2. Association (corporation) to partnership. The association distributes all of its assets and liabilities to its shareholders in liquidation of the association, and immediately thereafter, the shareholders contribute all of the distributed assets and liabilities to a newly formed partnership. Exiting!

3. Association (corporation) to disregarded entity. The association distributes all of its assets and liabilities to its single owner in liquidation of the association. Riveting! This

would be the aftermath of revoking an S Corp election and electing the association to now be taxed as a single-member LLC.

4. Disregarded entity to an association (corporation). The owner of the eligible entity contributes all of the assets and liabilities of the entity to the association in exchange for stock of the association. Neat! This would be part of the process of electing S corporation tax status (more on this in a bit).

Is Form 8832 necessary when electing S Corp tax status? No. In fact, you should avoid filing Form 8832 if your true intent is to be taxed as an S corporation. Why? If you file Form 8832 and the IRS accepts that, you are now going to be taxed as a corporation. If you then file Form 2553 and that is rejected for whatever reason, you are stuck with being taxed as a corporation. This is not the worst thing on the planet; the Bears winning a Superbowl naturally is. However, this "8832 no man's land" is certainly an avoidable annoyance.

Rather, if you only file Form 2553 and that is rejected for whatever reason, your tax classification remains as-is. Want to know more? Of course!

Treasury Regulations Section 301.7701-3(c)(1)(v)(C)... yeah... way deep into the indentation... states in part (we saved you from some of the extra verbiage)-

An eligible entity that timely elects to be an S corporation under section 1362(a)(1) is treated as having made an election under this section to be classified as an association.

Ah! This basically says that if you have an eligible entity and you timely file Form 2553, you will be treated as making the election to be classified as an association (corporation) alongside being taxed as an S Corp (a two-fer if you will). Don't get freaked out about the "timely elects" part. As discussed, IRS Revenue Procedures 2013-30 allows for late S corporation elections and as such considers them timely if certain rules are followed.

Tax Free Transfer
The transfer between LLC and association (corporation) is tax free of course unless the LLC's liabilities exceed its assets. Additionally, IRC Section 351(a) applies which generally states, "No gain or loss shall be recognized if property is transferred to a corporation by one or more persons solely in exchange for stock in such corporation and immediately after the exchange such person or persons are in control (as defined in section 368(c)) of the corporation."

Don't get too hung up on the control piece. For most small business owners, this is not a big deal. However, the liabilities exceeding assets part can be a trap especially if you fully depreciated an asset while having a loan (think automobile). If this applies to you, please consult with us.

Timely Election

An election is considered timely if filed within 15 days and two months of January 1 or the entity's activation. Activation is the earliest date of an entity having shareholders / members (owners), acquiring assets or begins conducting business.

Form 2553

Completing Form 2553 for the S corporation election is straightforward. The form asks for basic business information such as name, EIN, date of incorporation (activation date) and date of election. Keep in mind that this form was built for a C Corp electing to be taxed as an S Corp, so some of the form boxes use words like "incorporation." LLCs are not incorporated; rather they are usually formed or organized depending on your state's nomenclature.

It also requires signatures from all owners. Again, the form references shareholders, but an LLC has members. Don't get too hung up on this, but please understand some of the subtleties. For sanity, members = shareholders = owners. Additionally, use ownership percentages rather than shares.

Another way to view the references to incorporation and shareholders is to recall that as Form 2553 is being processed and approved by the IRS, the entity's classification is changing to association (corporation) as it is also being taxed as an S Corp (Treasury Regulations Section 301.7701-3(c)(1)(v)(C)).

Housekeeping

If your LLC has an existing Operating Agreement, it might need to be amended or restated so it aligns with your entity being taxed as an S corporation. We can help guide you on this. We will also explore ineffective S corporation elections because of problems generated by Operating Agreements.

If you are using a corporation (C Corp or Professional Corp), a corporate resolution might need to be drafted and signed allowing for this tax election. However, Form 2553 references this implicitly within the signature blocks of each shareholder.

States

Five states require a separate S corporation election form to be filed- Arkansas (really?!), New York, New Jersey, Ohio and sometimes Wisconsin. Generally nothing needs to be done with your state's Secretary of State in terms of notification or housekeeping stuff.

If you live in a community property state such as Arizona, California, Idaho, Louisiana, Nevada, New Mexico, Texas, Washington and Wisconsin your spouse might need to sign the Form 2553 even if he or she is not an owner.

> Side bar: Community property laws originate from Spanish property laws which is why most of our bordering states are community property states (red does not mean Republican). Wisconsin has no excuse, and Idaho was just caught in some peer pressure from Washington and Nevada.

Ineffective S Corp Elections

Limited Liability Companies (LLCs) are amazingly flexible in structuring a deal. As mentioned elsewhere, you can build an LLC with all kinds of deal structures such as-

▲ Special allocation of income and losses (including qualified income offsets to maintain compliance),

▲ Liquidating distributions made in accordance with positive capital account balances,

▲ Employment agreements,

▲ Buy-sell and redemption agreements, and

▲ Options and warrants, including convertible debt.

This list isn't exhaustive, but what this is telling us is that certain agreements inside and outside the Operating Agreement might make the S Corp election ineffective. Why? Special allocations are simply not allowed in a S Corp. That's easy. However, the outside agreements such as employment, buy-sell, redemption, options, warrants, debt instruments, etc., can create a second class of stock. As you might recall, an S corporation can only have one class of stock (voting and non-voting is allowed, however) according to IRC Section 1.1361-1.

Let's use buy-sell or redemption agreements as an example. It is common for business owners to enter into agreements where shares or interest may be redeemed upon a certain event such as a change in ownership or change in control. This in itself does not create a second class of stock. However, if the purchase price is significantly above or below the fair market value of the shares or interest, it might invalidate the S Corp election.

In continuing with our example, there is a safe harbor where book value may be used. In other words, if the purchase price is somewhere between fair market value and book value, this would be a strong argument that the buy-sell or redemption agreement does not create a second class of stock.

The big lesson is that having an entity taxed as an S Corp suddenly truncates some of the flexibility offered by various deal structures and Operating Agreements (and the like). The determination of a second class of stock is largely based on the governing documents. However, whether all shares have equal rights to distribution and liquidation proceeds is ultimately the deciding factor.

Please don't get too hung up on this. It doesn't affect 99% of the businesses out there who are exploring an S Corp election.

What happens if you made an S Corp election but perhaps shouldn't have? There are several Private Letter Rulings from the IRS that are littered with all kinds of examples. Here are some recent ones-

PLR 202053005 (Oct 6, 2020)
PLR 202110002 (Nov 2, 2020)
PLR 202111011 (Dec 22, 2020)
PLR 202124002 (Mar 19, 2021)

A lot of these are after-the-fact "oopsies" where the entity is now asking for relief from the IRS for electing S Corp status when in fact their Operating Agreement or other agreements made the S election ineffective. As a side note, the user fee charged by the IRS can range from $3,000 to $12,600 (and sometimes as high as $38,000). This does not include your attorney's fee. So, Yes, these PLRs had some big reasons to ask for forgiveness.

What can be done if your entity has "some hair" on its agreements and overall governance? First, you can amend or re-state your agreements to become compliant prior to electing S corporation tax status. But more importantly, the question should be asked, "Why do you need an S corporation election here?"

We don't want to get too far into the weeds with discussions of Q Sub elections where two S corporations are combined (parent is an S corporation and an eligible subsidiary wants to be taxed as an S corporation as well). That's another book, or at least a thick pamphlet for sure, discussing all the reasons why.

> **Small Spoiler:** Most small business acquisitions are an asset sale versus a stock sale, but if the entity you are acquiring cannot transfer its assets easily, then you might have to purchase the stock and file a Qualified Subchapter S Subsidiary election for

the combination. An example would be an entity who has a lucrative long-term government contract that cannot be re-assigned. In this case you would buy the entity as a whole, warts and all, versus just the assets (e.g., government contract).

However, if the objective is pass-through taxation and the avoidance of self-employment taxes associated with the entity's income, a multi-entity arrangement as discussed in Chapter 2 (Multi-Member LLC That Issues Invoices, page 52) might be your best bet.

S Corp Equity Section

Massaging of the equity section of your balance sheet is required when being taxed as an S corporation. But what if the underlying entity is an LLC? Good question. We believe, for elegance sake, that an LLC being taxed as an S corporation should walk, talk and smell like a corporation on the tax return. Ultimately this does not alter the ownership; the IRS calls you a shareholder since that is what the K-1 reads, but if you are an LLC you truly remain a member and your ownership is called an interest (not a share or a stock).

So, you are living two worlds. You have the governance of your entity (LLC - Operating Agreement versus Corporation – Bylaws / Shareholder Agreement) in one world, and the tax election in another.

A lot of people will tell us, "I have an LLC S Corp," or "I have an LLC taxed as an S Corp" or something similar. This is great since it helps us understand the business acumen of the owner in terms of their understanding of the S corporation mechanics. Ok, upward and onward...

Here is some nauseating accountant jargon. On January 1st, or the effective date of the S corporation election, the equity section would have five accounts-

▲ Capital Stock

▲ Additional Paid-In Capital (for each shareholder)

▲ Shareholder Distributions (for each shareholder)

▲ Retained Earnings, and

▲ Net Income

Unlike a C corporation, an entity being taxed as an S corporation can only have one class of stock, so preferred stock is not allowed, yet common stock within an S corporation structure

207

can still have voting and non-voting rights. This section of our book is regarding an LLC but if a C corporation elected to be taxed as an S corporation (for example), Dividends Paid would still be tracked within the equity section purely for legacy purposes. However, S corporations do not pay dividends. Rather shareholders receive distributions.

The challenge becomes how to "fund" the Capital Stock and Additional Paid-In Capital accounts. Typically, an LLC will be initially funded with the owner injecting cash and perhaps some equipment to start the business. This would have been a debit to Cash and Equipment separately, and a Credit to the owner's Capital account. Upon S corporation election, the Capital account would be closed out to Capital Stock using a pre-determined par value such as $10 per stock and a nominal number of shares such as 100, or $1,000 in Capital Stock.

We recommend keeping the Capital Stock account as small as possible because it provides the most flexibility in taking future Shareholder Distributions without affecting Capital Stock. The remainder would be a credit to the Additional Paid-In Capital account(s). Yup we are geeking out.

Generally, when taking a C corporation and electing S Corp status, existing Retained Earnings needs to be recorded separately. Why? Theoretically these earnings would have been subjected to dividends taxes paid by the shareholders if distributed. Therefore, the IRS is wise and doesn't want you to enjoy a 21% corporate tax rate as a C Corp, elect S Corp status and then distribute the prior earnings tax-free. There are some devils in the details and there are some things like Built-In Gains taxes, ordering rules and stuff, but that is rare for most small businesses converting to an S corporation. A ton more discussion is required for each person's unique situation and is beyond the scope of this book.

Since it is common for small businesses to operate as LLCs for several years and to have incomplete records (shocking), the "funding" of the equity accounts might have to wait until the end of the first year of S corporation election to maintain sanity. For example, on December 31st Capital Stock and Additional Paid-In Capital are zero, including Retained Earnings.

The following three journal entries would be made-

▲ Net Income would be closed out with a credit to Retained Earnings, and

▲ Shareholder Distributions throughout the year would be closed out with a debit to Retained Earnings, and

▲ A correcting entry would be made with credits to both Capital Stock and Additional Paid-In Capital using the same guidelines of keeping Capital Stock a nominal value such as $1,000, and a debit to Retained Earnings.

You really don't care about this, do you? No worries, we provide these journal entries during tax preparation.

Another technique where historical records are incomplete would be using the amount of cash in the business checking account on January 1 of the first year of S corporation election as the initial capital injection. The entry would be a debit to Cash, and credit to Capital Stock and Additional Paid-In Capital. The adjusted cost basis of injected assets would be handled similarly.

For example, you have a piece of equipment that you purchased for $28,000 and $20,000 was already depreciated on previous tax returns. The adjusted cost basis is $8,000. The journal entry would be a debit to equipment for $28,000, a credit to accumulated depreciation for $20,000 and a credit of $8,000 to Additional Paid-In Capital. If you were already carrying this information on an LLC's balance sheet, then there might be some other entries to true things up.

> Sidebar: If you are an LLC and have assets, they are probably detailed on your fixed asset listing as part of your Schedule C and Form 1040. Holding periods and future depreciation schedules do not change when electing S Corp status. Keep in mind that the underlying entity does not change; just the tax election. This section highlights how we would set up the equity section to simulate a corporation when the underlying entity was an LLC (especially since we now have to represent all this on your S Corp tax return).

While these techniques are not as elegant as tracing the capital structure from the beginning, it does create efficiencies and simplicity within a small business. Shareholder basis would also be the beginning cash, unless there are some other issues at hand (like transfer of depreciated assets, shareholder loans to the S corporation, etc.).

Terminating S Corp Election

S Corps have relished being the class favorite for all kinds of reasons as stated in this book. However, the original C Corp could be making a comeback based on flawed logic from the Tax Cuts and Jobs Act of 2017.

The primary motivation is the seemingly attractive 21% tax rate for C corporations and while this might be lower than some taxpayer's marginal rate, this is a sucker hole for business owners for two painfully obvious reasons. First, your marginal rate might be 22% or 24%, but your effective tax rate (or blended tax rate) is much lower. We'll show you... not to worry.

Second, there is a little thing called double taxation where the C corporation pays a tax and then the shareholders pay a dividend tax on the money that is distributed. And... if you think you're a smarty pants and say, "Yeah, but, I'll just keep all my money in the C corporation for a rainy day and lower tax rates," there is another little thing called accumulated earnings tax.

Buckle up buttercup 'cause here we go-

S Corp Income	100,000	200,000	300,000
Salary	40,000	80,000	120,000
Payroll Tax	6,120	12,240	18,360
Income Tax	6,980	24,150	44,266
Total Tax S Corp	**13,100**	**36,390**	**62,626**
C Corp Income	100,000	200,000	300,000
C Corp Tax	21,000	42,000	63,000
Dividends	79,000	158,000	237,000
Dividend Tax	0	23,700	44,556
Total C Corp Tax	**21,000**	**65,700**	**107,556**
S Corp Tax Rate	13.1%	18.2%	20.9%
C Corp Tax Rate	21.0%	32.9%	35.9%
Delta (lost tax)	7.9%	14.7%	15.0%

As you can see, a C Corp does not make sense after you add in capital gains tax on the dividends. Also note the effective tax rate (or labeled as tax "pain") for the S corporation owner. At $100,000 in net business income, the total tax pain including payroll taxes is 13.1%, and at $200,000 it is only 18.2%. This is still well below the C corporation tax rate of 21%.

One more thing that is not computed above; C corporations do not get the Section 199A deduction which is 20%. 20% times the marginal tax bracket of 15% is another 3% savings; 20% times the marginal tax bracket of 37% is another 7% savings. So, please pump the brakes on the "I wanna dump my S Corp for the magical tax arbitrage offered by a C Corp" nonsense. Wow, that was harsh. We did tell you to buckle up but then we offended you by calling you buttercup. Safety with an insult.

Sidebar: In a previous chapter we highlighted several reasons why a C corporation makes sense. Paring down debt, employee stock plans, funding with a 401k, keep income off your individual tax return, among many ideas.

Let's say there are other reason to revoke S Corp election. Yes, you can change back and the present-day solution is accomplished by either liquidating, or terminating the S Corp election.

Liquidation is the more complicated of the two. In a nutshell, the process begins with a unanimous vote to close the business. Once that decision is made, it's a complicated process of contacting creditors, assessing receivables, distributing or selling property and closing up the books.

Termination, moderately more elegant. Terminating the S Corp election can happen one of two ways. Preferably by revocation, or the next best alternative, violating one of the S Corp rules. Violating one of the S corporation rules is not an elegant option, however.

Therefore, revocation is the preferred direct route and is as simple as writing a statement to the IRS revoking your S Corp election. In this manner, obtaining written consent from more than 50% of your shareholders is required. Simple for one or two owner S Corps, but community property states, tenants in common, and majority shareholders could complicate that. Again, if the underlying entity is an LLC then the members will be bound by the Operating Agreement in terms of voting and other requirements.

When your S corporation election is revoked, either intentionally or not, your business will more than likely revert to a C Corp for taxation. We can then file a Form 8832 which will reclassify your business back to an LLC or partnership, again for taxation. Remember, the underlying entity does not change with the Secretary of State. There might be some accounting headache and subsequent tax consequences with capital accounts or other assets, but we can advise you on those concerns once all the details are vetted out.

Why would you want to revoke your S Corp election? There are many reasons- business closed or is shrinking to a point where it doesn't make sense, lost the contract gig, got converted from 1099 to W-2, foreign investors, etc. are among the most frequent. We can help guide you as these situations arise.

Notice how making too much income wasn't on the list of possible reasons. Of course, there are exceptions, but generally speaking if you make $30,000 or $300,000 or even $3,000,000, the S Corp election is going to be your friend.

Distributed Assets

When you revoke S corporation status, you will trigger a taxable event. A potentially big one. Upon revocation, assets are distributed to the S Corp shareholders at fair market value. Cash is easy. An automobile is generally not a big deal. But real estate can kick your butt. Therefore, before we put out the flame, a review of the assets and fair market values must be done. To pay capital gains on appreciated assets when you have cash from a transaction is easy. To pay capital gains on appreciated assets when a cashless revocation occurs is brutal.

5 Year Rule

S Corps that lose their "S" status must typically wait five years before being able to re-elect it. As mentioned, deliberately violating one of the rules, such as transferring stock to an ineligible shareholder, is not a good thing. What happens if it was unintentional? The IRS in private ruling letters has on a case-by-case basis allow S Corps to remain as such if the event causing termination was not reasonably within the control of the owners. This is hard to demonstrate, and by the way, private letter rulings (PLRs) can cost thousands of dollars to submit.

In other cases, the IRS has relented and allowed an S Corp to continue when there is a more than 50% change in ownership. Details. Details. So, a business becomes an S Corporation. Revokes the election. Then has a greater than 50% change in ownership within five years. Begs to the IRS. Perhaps is granted an early S Corp election.

Another option is to relight with another entity. You have LLC A, and tax it as an S corporation. You bounce along, and then decide to revoke the S Corp election. A few years later, you want to re-elect S Corp status. Not good. One solution we see is a small business owner starting LLC B, taxing it as an S Corp, and then moving upon things over to this new entity. More discussion is required of course; one of the problems is if LLC A had a government contract (such as defense or transportation) or an approval (such as Medicare), these cannot be easily transferred.

Life Cycle of an S Corporation

Here is a summary of the life cycle of an S Corporation in terms of startup and shutdown-

▲ LLC Formed

▲ S Corp Election Made, Form 2553

▲ Payroll Accounts Opened

▲ S Corp Revoked, Letter to IRS

▲ Reverts to C Corp for Taxation

▲ Revert to LLC for Taxation, Form 8832 (Entity Classification Election)

▲ Distributions and Tax Consequences Dealt With

▲ Payroll Accounts Closed

▲ Final S Corp Tax Return Filed, Form 1120S

Chapter 7
Section 199A Deduction Analysis
(updated February 28, 2020)

This material is fairly static and is also scheduled (and expected) sunset at the end of 2025. To reduce the obnoxiousness of the printed book (currently over 380 pages), Chapter 7 and Chapter 8 were removed, and are available in PDF and online using these links-

wcginc.com/107 (for the PDF for both Chapters 7 and 8)

wcginc.com/207 (for the online Knowledge Base version)

Here are the following section headers of what you can expect-

Section 199A S Corp Considerations

Calculating the Qualified Business Income Deduction

Section 199A Defining Terms

Specified Service Trade or Business (SSTB) Definitions

Trade or Business of Performing Services as an Employee

Services or Property Provided to an SSTB

Section 199A Deduction Decision Tree

Section 199A Reasonable Compensation

Section 199A Pass-Through Salary Optimization

Cost of Increasing Shareholder Salary

Section 199A Rental Property Deduction

Negative Qualified Business Income

Qualified Property Anti-Abuse

Aggregation of Multiple Businesses

Section 199A W-2 Safe Harbors

Additional Section 199A Reporting on K-1

Section 199A Frequently Asked Questions

Chapter 8
Section 199A Examples and Comparisons
(updated February 28, 2020)

This material is fairly static and is also scheduled (and expected) sunset at the end of 2025. To reduce the obnoxiousness of the printed book (currently over 380 pages), Chapter 7 and Chapter 8 were removed, and are available in PDF and online using these links-

wcginc.com/108 (for the PDF of both Chapters 7 and 8)

wcginc.com/208 (for the online Knowledge Base version)

Here are the following section headers of what you can expect-

S Corp Section 199A Deduction Examples

Section 199A Side by Side Comparisons

Section 199A Basic Comparisons

Section 199A Health Insurance Comparison

Section 199A 200k Comparison

Section 199A 250k Comparison

Section 199A Specified Service Trade or Business Comparison Part 1

Section 199A Specified Service Business Comparison Part 2

Section 199A Phaseout

Section 199A Comparison Recap

Section 199A Actual Tax Returns Comparison

Chapter 9
Reasonable Shareholder Salary
(updated November 2023)

Chapter Introduction

Calculating reasonable S Corp officer compensation and shareholder salary is like nailing Jell-O to the wall. If you want to eliminate (not just reduce) the risk that the IRS will disagree with your calculations, you can pay out your entire economic benefit from the business in shareholder salaries. That seems silly, right? This would make the S corporation's efficacy zero. How do we approach this then?

As you go through this chapter, keep two simple things in mind. First, the word reasonable has an antithesis, and can be defined in the negative. In other words, while it is hard to define reasonable, we can confidently define what is unreasonable. Paying $5,000 in shareholder salaries on $100,000 in net business income (profits) for a one-person consultant S Corp is unreasonable. Most people would agree with that sentiment.

One more stab using different words to convey this concept- rather than eclipsing the reasonable threshold, perhaps view determining an S Corp salary as not wanting to trip the unreasonable wire.

To be certain, the IRS and others use the word reasonable, but they too cannot define what is precisely reasonable and then what is precisely not reasonable. While the sparring of reasonable and unreasonable presents as a binary situation with a winner and a loser, it is anything but binary. As such, we are back to hammers, nails and Jell-O.

Second, we encourage you to embrace the fluidity of reasonable shareholder salary. If you like straight lines and clean garages, this will bug you a bit. At the same time, when you always have the option to pitch an argument with reasonable salary calculations, or anything else in life, that puts you in a favorable position. So, you're saying there's a chance. Yes! We are!

This is our favorite chapter not because we like Jell-O shots, because we certainly do at any age or life stage, but because it is the most cerebral S Corp topic and the one we get asked about the most.

In this chapter we will review-

▲ IRS Stats

▲ IRS Revenue Rulings and Fact Sheet 2008-25

▲ Tax Court Cases

▲ Risk Analysis, Investor Perspective

▲ Assembled Workforce, Developed Process

▲ Converting from W-2 to 1099 (revisit the risk analysis)

▲ RCReports, Risk Management Association (RMA), Bureau of Labor Statistics (BLS) and Salary.com

▲ Rules of Thumb, Jumping Off Point

▲ Multiple Shareholders, Spouse Salary, and

▲ Additional Considerations (Section 199A QBI, 401k optimization, etc.)

Here we go!

IRS S Corp Stats

Let's jump right into some numbers first before going through reasonable S Corp salary theory developed from IRS revenue rules and Tax Court cases. The following table is a summary generated from IRS statistics on S corporation tax returns for the 2017 tax year (we will update next go-around, but this remains stable and relevant for discussion).

Annual Receipts	Gross Receipts Per Return	Net Income Per Return	Officer Comp Per Return	Officer Comp % of Net Income
$25,000 to $99,999	63,669	7,967	9,096	53%
$100,000 to $249,999	170,884	24,796	24,405	50%
$250,000 to $499,999	365,715	43,505	43,917	50%
$500,000 to $999,999	718,876	67,243	68,015	45%
$1M to $2.5M	1,581,150	130,244	106,072	45%

First some quick observations. Officer compensation is added back to net income to determine officer comp as a percentage of net income after expenses (profit). Next, this is all industries from capital intensive manufacturing to personal services business such as attorneys, doctors, consultants, engineers and accountants. More data to follow in a bit.

Also, this includes S Corps who lost money, and whether they lost money and continued to pay a reasonable shareholder salary (Officer Compensation) is unclear. In other words, if losses were teased out would Officer Compensation be reduced as a percentage of net income? We cannot quickly determine from the IRS data.

Here is one more nugget to chew on. As compared to 2013, the Officer Compensation as a percentage of Net Income (far right column) has decreased 2-3% for each Annual Receipts category.

The following tables are from 2013. The IRS has stopped bifurcating gross receipts per return on an industry basis alongside groupings of gross receipts. While this data is seemingly stale, it adds more perspective to the previous table. First one is $100,000 to $249,999 in gross receipts-

$100,000 to $249,999	Gross Receipts Per Return	Net Income Per Return	Officer Comp Per Return	Officer Comp % of Net Income
Finance and Insurance	160,359	34,408	23,213	40%
Real Estate	165,375	38,231	28,193	42%
Professional, Scientific	163,151	32,910	35,404	52%
Health Care	174,383	24,622	36,026	59%

And now for $250,000 to $499,999 in gross receipts-

$250,000 to $499,999	Gross Receipts Per Return	Net Income Per Return	Officer Comp Per Return	Officer Comp % of Net Income
Finance and Insurance	366,533	77,518	62,329	45%
Real Estate	359,163	65,419	51,151	44%
Professional, Scientific	355,693	71,136	74,493	51%
Health Care	378,147	51,553	75,382	59%

The following table is from 2017 data (again, we will update next go-around) but it is aggregated regardless of gross receipts-

Industry	Gross Receipts Per Return	Net Income Per Return	Officer Comp Per Return	Officer Comp % of Net Income
Manufacturing	7,325,298	651,340	166,177	20%
Retail	4,616,094	167,040	60,663	27%
Securities, Finance	1,735,986	525,809	167,658	24%
Professional, Scientific	998,564	142,927	85,487	37%
Holding Companies	2,618,030	1,358,171	114,661	8%
Health Care	Not Reported	149,366	126,903	46%

Some comments-

▲ Certainly, aggregating all businesses regardless of gross receipts skews the data. As businesses grow, they have an assembled workforce who contribute to the revenue more than the officers (shareholders).

▲ The IRS had a footnote on Health Care (and other industries) where because of privacy concerns, certain data is not reported. Additionally, Securities, Finance is not the same as Finance and Insurance (close, but not the same).

▲ Check out Manufacturing and Retail as compared to Professional, Scientific and Health Care. Professional, Scientific and Health Care industries will generally have officers (shareholders) who are more impactful to the overall revenue generation and operations of the business.

▲ Professional, Scientific has the second lowest average officer compensation, but the second highest as a percentage of net ordinary business income after expenses and deductions. This would suggest this sector is highly fractured with several smaller businesses (all S Corps however).

▲ Do not read too much into the Officer Compensation Percentage of Net Income figures. These are illustrative only, and do not purport to be a rule or recommendation.

There you go. Remember that Officer Compensation includes all fringe benefits such as self-employed health insurance and HSA contributions, and it might be influenced (increased) by those who want to maximize 401k deferrals, profit sharing plans and defined benefits pensions / cash balance plans. In other words, people with more discretionary cash wanting to defer taxes might increase salaries to do so.

Reasonable S Corp Salary Theory

Determining a reasonable salary is the hardest part of running an S corporation. What the heck do I pay myself? Before we get into that, let's discuss why shareholder salary needs to be just above bar napkin quality and just below NASA precision.

Scattered throughout this book we've stressed that the only tax savings an S Corp provides is the reduction of self-employment taxes, and in the case of shareholder wages we are talking about Social Security and Medicare taxes (payroll taxes). When your business pays you $10,000 in shareholder wages, 7.65% is withheld from your paycheck for the employee's portion of payroll taxes. This is broken down into 6.2% Social Security tax and 1.45% Medicare tax. The business also must pay 7.65% for a combined percentage of 15.3%. Since the business deducts its portion of payroll taxes, the effective tax rate is 14.1%, but we'll use 15.3% since that is the big number everyone knows.

Therefore, a $10,000 shareholder salary costs you $1,5300 in additional taxes beyond income taxes. Said in a different way, if you pay yourself $50,000 when $40,000 could have been a reasonable shareholder salary, you just wasted $1,530. Even a $5,000 delta equates to $765.

Truth be told there is some philosophical issues with the reasonable salary element where your labor is the only material income-producing factor for the business. Some would argue that all the S Corp's income should then be considered shareholder wages and subjected to Social Security and Medicare taxes, since if you died the business would die. Do we see this "loophole" being re-defined and shrinking over the next several years? Yes. But at the same time, we say let it ride until we can't use it. The IRS and Congress move at glacial speeds- let's worry about next time, next time.

Conversely, there might be times where your business would continue without you. When WCG performs business valuations, especially in divorce proceedings, we assign a value to goodwill. We do this by taking a number called seller's discretionary cash flow (SDCF) and we subtract the cash flow that is derived from tangible assets (cash, equipment, etc.). This leaves us with a theoretical number that is considered goodwill which can be used as a proxy to determine your "value" to the business.

We further tease out personal goodwill and enterprise goodwill since in some jurisdictions personal goodwill is not marital property. This might seem like an odd tangent, but a similar argument can be made for a business that does not rely on you. One great example is a financial advisor that has a small team supporting him or her- typically the fee income continues well into the future without the direct involvement of the advisor (enterprise goodwill). In this situation, an argument for a smaller salary could be warranted since enterprise goodwill exceeds personal goodwill. Consider this-

Business Type	Owner Participation
Software developer who has gone to market	10%
Amazon retailer, a lot of drop shipments, no inventory	20%
Financial advisor with small team	30%
Doctor who is a partner in an emergency clinic	40%
Consultant, Attorney, Accountant (solo operator)	90%
Actor with no endorsements or couch-jumping events	100%

Of course, this is all theoretical and is open to debate, but you get the idea.

Not to go too far into the weeds, but when performing business valuations we also consider investor value. What rate of return would an investor need to earn after paying you a reasonable salary? In other words, what would someone be willing to pay you to continue running the business after they acquired it from you?

Take this one step further. What would an investor be willing to pay a person other than you, yet who is also capable of running the business? Perhaps your contribution to the business was developing procedures and workflows to make it hum, and someone with less skill and experience can do the same work and produce the same results. Just a thought as we head into all this.

Naturally, a lower salary to you results in a higher rate of return for the investor. We could also look at the earnings generated from capital investments such as machinery or internally generated assets, and other non-owner employees versus shareholder labor. Think of that software developer from the previous table. We digress here but explore this more in a bit.

IRS Revenue Rulings and Fact Sheet 2008-25

In 1959, IRS Revenue Ruling 59-221 held that amounts of S corporation undistributed taxable income which are required to be included in each shareholder's gross income do not constitute net earnings from self-employment to shareholders. However, in 1974, IRS Revenue Ruling 74-44 stated that "dividends" paid to shareholders will be recharacterized as wages when such "dividends" are paid to shareholders in lieu of reasonable compensation for services performed for the S Corp. The word "dividends" is in quotations because in reality we call these shareholder distributions, but in 1974 they referred to them as dividends.

This makes sense. Dividends being used to pay for services are truly wages. If Google or Amazon pays out a dividend to its shareholders, it is considered investment income. If your S corporation does the same thing to its only shareholder without an accompanying shareholder wage, then it is considered self-employment income and subject to the gaggle of taxes with that type of income.

Also, consider the words "in lieu of reasonable compensation." This is to suggest that if shareholder salary is not processed and only shareholder distributions are paid, those distributions will be recharacterized as shareholder salaries. In other words, paying reasonable shareholder salaries protects shareholder distributions from being recharacterized as salary. But keep on an eye on that word "reasonable." It is the kicker.

Moving on... There are several factors to consider when coming up with a reasonable salary to pay shareholders. The IRS through Fact Sheet 2008-25 released the following laundry list (last update was in 2008 when Flo Rida was singing Low... apple bottom jeans, boots with the fur, the whole club was looking at her. How time flies!)-

▲ Training and experience.

▲ Duties and responsibilities.

▲ Time and effort devoted to the business.

▲ Dividend history (IRS nomenclature, really this should be shareholder distributions-however back in the day it was C corporations who later elected to be taxed an S corporation, so dividend history still has some historical merit).

▲ Payments to non-shareholder employees.

▲ Timing and manner of paying bonuses to key people.

▲ What comparable businesses pay for similar services.

▲ Compensation agreements.

▲ The use of a formula to determine compensation.

Clear as mud. This is the best the IRS can come up with? What is even more frustrating or perhaps embarrassing is that this list was the final draft after probably several meetings and rough drafts. Having said that, this is how our tax system operates in many ways- leave lots of wiggle room for interpretation so the law and the standards can evolve to meet the needs of today.

This list actually has two applications. Since C corporations have had a historically high tax rate including being double-taxed, many small C corporations want to drive corporate income close to zero by paying high salaries. The IRS and the Tax Court will use this list to say your salary is too high as a C Corp.

Conversely, S corporations want to increase corporate income (and available cash for shareholder distributions) by paying small salaries. The IRS and the Tax Court will talk out of the other side of their mouths by using this list to justify a higher salary. Yes, they get to have it both ways.

Here is a link to IRS Fact Sheet 2008-25-

wcginc.com/8247

Tax Court Cases for Reasonable Salary

The Tax Court has provided some guidance over the years in several well-known cases. Here is a quick reference bulleted list, and later we'll dive into the finer details-

Ulrich v. United States, 692 F. Supp. 1053 (D. Minn., 1988)

Sole shareholder of an accounting firm whose only income was dividends. The court held "Under both the weight of the case law and under the treasury regulations, a corporate officer is to be treated an employee if he renders more than minor services."

Spicer Accounting v. United States, 918 F.2d 90 (1990)

Spicer was the only accountant working for the firm and it was owned 50-50 with his wife. He only received dividends, and claimed to donate his services to the S corporation. The court held "The Federal Insurance Contributions Act and Federal Unemployment Tax Act both define 'wages' as 'all remuneration for employment... that the form of payment is immaterial... [therefore] the only relevant factor being whether payments were actually received as compensation for employment."

Watson v. Commissioner, 668 F.3d 1008 (8th Cir. 2012)

No relation to Jason Watson or WCG CPAs & Advisors! (Jason is a bit crazy from time to time, but not this cra-cra). In this case, David E. Watson was an accountant in a firm he owned. He drew a salary of $24,000 even though the firm grossed nearly $3 million in revenue. Watson was a Certified Public Accountant with advanced degrees. The 8th Circuit Court ruled that a reasonable person would consider the dividends paid to Watson to be "remuneration for services performed" as opposed to a return on investment. To support its position, the IRS successfully asserted that the $24,000 shareholder salary was not enough to support Watson's lifestyle. As such, his dividends were reclassified as wages and the firm was assessed huge employment taxes plus penalties and interest.

JD & Associates, Ltd. v. United States, No. 3:04-cv-59 (District Court, North Dakota, 2006)
Dahl, an accountant and sole shareholder, paid himself a small salary. The IRS hired a valuation expert who used Risk Management Association (RMA) data to determine what other accountants were paid for similar services. The RMA data was damning enough, however what really sent this case over the edge is the Dahl paid himself less than his staff including clerical positions. Admins cannot make more than you.

These darn accountants are out of control! Here are couple of "wins."

Davis v. United States, 1994 U.S. Dist. LEXIS 10725 (District Court, Colorado, 1994)
A husband and wife team owned a corporation. The husband worked elsewhere and the wife performed clerical duties (12 hours per month). Her accountant said her services were worth $8 per hour. The IRS did not challenge the value of the time commitment and therefore Davis won this case because the wife was able to prove her minimal hours.

Sean McAlary Ltd. Inc. v. Commissioner (Tax Court Summary Opinion 2013-62)
In a recent Tax Court case, the IRS hired a valuation expert to determine that a real estate agent should have been paid $100,755 salary out of his S Corp's net income of $231,454. Not bad. He still took home over $130,000 in distributions, and avoided self-employment taxes (mainly Medicare) on that portion of his income. Then again, this makes sense. Real estate oftentimes sells itself thanks to the internet, and the real estate agents are merely facilitators. In other words, the actions of the real estate agent were not solely responsible for $231,454 in income.

There are two tests that Tax Courts have used in the past. In **Label Graphics, Inc. v. Commissioner, Tax Court Memo 1998-343** which was later affirmed by the 9th Circuit Court in 2000, the court came up with-

▲ The employee's role in the business.

▲ A comparison of the compensation paid to similarly situated employees in similar businesses.

▲ The character and condition of the business.

▲ Whether a relationship existed between the business and employee that may permit the business to disguise nondeductible corporate distributions as deductible compensation.

▲ Whether the compensation was paid pursuant to a (1) structured, (2) formal, and (3) consistently applied program.

In **Brewer Quality Homes, Inc. v. Commissioner, Tax Court Memo 2003-200**, the court reiterated several points from another Federal court case (Owensby & Kritikos, Inc. v. Commissioner, 819 F.2d 1315 (5th Cir. 1987))-

▲ The employee's qualifications.

▲ The nature, extent, and scope of the employee's work.

▲ Size and complexity of the business.

▲ Comparison of the employee's salary with the business's gross and net income.

▲ Prevailing general economic conditions.

▲ Comparison of salaries with distributions to stockholders.

▲ Compensation for comparable positions in comparable concern.

▲ Salary policy of the business as to all employees.

▲ Amount of compensation paid to the employee in previous years.

Similar to IRS Fact Sheet 2008-25, no single factor controls. It really is a preponderance of the evidence as civil courts like to say. Tax Court judges will go through these lists, depending on the case and the jurisdiction, and will apply the facts and circumstances to each of these factors. They essentially make a list of plusses or a minuses.

For example, the criterion might be "Payment to non-shareholder employees." The Tax Court will analyze the evidence to determine the plus or minus. Let's say the S corporation owner provides evidence that her star employee is the rainmaker, and therefore the employee's salary including bonuses exceeds the S corporation shareholder. Let's also say that the Tax Court finds this argument to be compelling. This would a "plus" for the S corporation owner since the criterion of "Payment to non-shareholder employees" favors the S Corp shareholder.

Continuing with this example, assume the owner had $300,000 in net income after expenses, but only paid $30,000 to herself as an S corporation salary. The IRS and Tax Court would place a "minus" next to the "A comparison of salaries paid to sales and net income" criterion as they did in K & K Veterinary Supply, Inc. v. Commissioner, Tax Court Memo 2013-84.

Risk Analysis to Reasonable Shareholder Salary

We raise the risk issue throughout our chapter on reasonable shareholder salary, but let's touch on it some more. Please recall that shareholder distributions are financial rewards to the investor. While the detached abstract investor and the employee are the same person (you), it doesn't change the theoretical demands of an investor. When a business valuation is calculated, discretionary cash flow is determined and then a risk premium is assigned to it. Simply stated, cash flow divided by risk (capitalization rate) equals value.

Here is a sample build-up method to determine risk-

Discount Rate Element	Risk Value	Source
Risk Free Rate of Return	1.37%	20 Year Treasury Rate, Spot 11/30/2020
Equity Risk Premium	5.60%	Duff & Phelps, 2017 Valuation Handbook
Small Stock Risk Premium	5.59%	Center for Research in Security Prices
Industry Risk Premium	1.00%	First Research Data
Company Specific Risk Premium	5.00%	
Total	18.56%	

Company specific risk includes things like (just naming a few)-

▲ Operational History

▲ Volatility of Earnings

▲ Product or Service Concentration

▲ Customer Concentration

▲ Ability to Affect Pricing

Look at this list again, and compare it to your business. Are you relatively new? Are your earnings volatile (such as real estate)? Even 10% swings could be considered volatile. What would happen if Walmart stated in their shareholder meeting that they were predicting being off 10% next year? Heads would roll.

What about your service concentration? Think of an attorney- they pass the bar exam as a generalist, but quickly become a specialist (and forget all the other law he or she learned). Can you take your current skillset and find a whole new gaggle of customers in a different industry or sector? Maybe. Maybe not.

What about customer concentration? Are you a 1099 contractor who has one client who also happens to be your former employer? Huge risk, right? Heck, they've already fired you once.

What is your ability affect pricing? Usually none. Perhaps Apple but probably not you the mighty solo operator holed in your home office.

What are we getting at here? Would you consider a 19% return on investment (see table above) to be high? Not sure? Walk into your financial advisor's office and ask for investments that only return 19% or higher. After the laughter, he or she might loosely show you some private equity investments or other syndicates that might return 19% if everything, and they mean everything, goes right.

What does all this mean? This means that any small business owner assumes a ton of risk, and that risk should demand a higher return on investment. In other words, a higher return on investment should demand higher shareholder (investor) distributions, and therefore lower shareholder salaries. This is a like a teeter-totter.

The entire economic benefit of the business can only be paid out in salaries and distributions (and perquisites or what we call "perks"). As such, if distributions are higher because of investor risk and the subsequent demand for more return on investment to meet the risk profile, then salaries must be reduced.

Reasonable Salary Labor Data

Among several things, the Tax Court and the IRS will attempt to support a reasonable salary calculation based on your peers and colleagues. They will use an expert who specializes in vocational valuations, and this person might use Risk Management Association (RMA) and Bureau of Labor Statistics (BLS) data, including local and regional data.

Our previous real estate agent benefited from this type of valuation since his S corporation earned significantly more than the average real estate agent's salary. But what if the opposite was true? So, instead of earning $231,454 and only paying out $100,755 in salary, what if you earned $110,000. Would you have to pay out $100,755 in salary just because you are a real estate agent in an area where other agents earn $100,755?

The answer is a true accountant or lawyer response- it depends. There are several factors that mitigate the calculus. Perhaps you work part time. Perhaps you simply are not as good as your peers. Perhaps you focus on a different type of customer. Review the previous IRS and Tax Court laundry lists, and as you go through each item ask yourself if you could safely use it to justify a lower salary than your peers- we bet you can find several instances.

Statistics attempt to homogenize a population so we may draw correlations and eventual conclusions. Certain professions that appear to be slam dunks are not as they appear. Attorneys and accountants come to mind- we know some attorneys that make $150,000 a year while others make $450,000. It is very tough to jam these two square pegs into the same round hole. Accountants, same thing. IT consultants, same thing. Even physicians doing the same line of work (such as anesthesia) range between $80,000 and $400,000. Same work, at least on paper, yet wildly different incomes!

There is another lesson to be learned here. As your S Corp income increases, the reasonable salaries paid to the shareholders do not necessarily increase on a pro rate basis. In other words, if you peg your salary at $60,000 and that is supported with labor data, your salary does not double just because your net business income (profit) in your S corporation doubles. Your salary is based on you, and the data surrounding you. Yes, the courts look at distributions and net income, and Yes, your salary would probably be increased if your net income doubles, but it is not tethered in a lockstep, $1 for $1 pattern (more on this in a bit).

Salary.com and the like also do a great job of compiling labor data. RMA and BLS is going to be much more authoritative in court, but RMA (as an example) requires an expensive subscription and is usually reserved for valuation experts who rely on their data multiple times to justify the cost.

Assembled Workforce or Developed Process Effect

As alluded to earlier, the business's ability to earn revenue without the direct involvement of the owner(s) can be huge. Consider an actor or an on-air personality (WCG has a handful of these clients). Would revenue continue after the owner stopped working?

Assembled Workforce

For example, you start off as a one-person engineering firm earning $150,000 net ordinary business income (profit) after expenses and deductions but before shareholder salary. You pay yourself $65,000 and pocket $85,000 as shareholder distributions. Done.

Time moves along, and you've hired eight other engineers and they are paid $90,000 each but contribute $60,000 to the bottom line of the business (using the $150,000 number above as a proxy). Even if you increase your salary to $150,000, you still have $480,000 ($60,000 x 8) available for shareholder distributions.

Yes, this is overly simplified, but it illustrates a huge point. Should you sell your engineering business to an investor, he or she would hire another person for $150,000 to run the business and use the remaining $480,000 as a return on investment because of the assembled workforce effect. You are no different. As mentioned several times throughout our book, you are both employee and investor when you own and operate an S corporation. You must consider both interests, and at times they are competing.

Using the example above, the employee and investor are the same person when you own it, but we must always bifurcate these worlds because they are not directly related to each other in terms of the split. Granted, if you saw your boss (the investor) making $480,000 perhaps you would ask for more than $150,000 to run the business. Then again, if $150,000 is the going rate, that is what your boss will pay you regardless of what he or she makes as a return on investment.

Developed Process
Using our previous question about the actor or on-air personality, would your answer change if this person developed a process such as podcasts, videos, merchandising, likeness licensing, etc.? Of course, it would. An actor who earns $300,000 from acting and $200,000 from other sustainable sources is much different than the surgeon who earned $500,000. As such, reasonable S corporation salaries would certainly vary.

Here's another one to make you go hmmm. How about a financial advisor who has been in the business for 25 years? A lot of their present-day income is truly deferred earnings from multiple decades of hard work. Sounds more like an investment, doesn't it? And as we've discussed, a return on an investment is more of a shareholder distribution argument than a reasonable salary argument.

We could go on and on with this.

RCReports
For several years now, **WCG CPAs & Advisors** has leveraged RCReports or Reasonable Compensation Reports which is a consulting firm out of Denver, Colorado. They send out a survey to you which asks a bunch of questions about qualifications, time spent on various tasks, regional data, etc. From there, and in their words, "RCReports synthesizes a

proprietary blend of IRS criteria, Court Rulings, geographic data and our EXCLUSIVE database of wages to accurately assess Reasonable Compensation for S Corp, Small & Closely Held Business Owners." Cool!

You can view a sample here-

wcginc.com/8257

If you visit this link and read the report, RCReports does a wonderful job coming up with a number and then putting a bunch of data behind it. The report looks official and uses sources; this is a critical consideration since reasonable compensation is such a squishy thing. In other words, the IRS might challenge your reasonable S Corp salary much like a mall cop with a badge but no gun, and certainly no evidence. When you roll up with a 7-page document that has numbers, data and sources scattered about, it is super hard for the IRS to say No. For lack of better evidence, the IRS would be forced to use your evidence.

Two more considerations with RCReports. They use a typical appraisal approach similar to home appraisals, business valuations, etc. using cost, market and income approaches. This is pretty cool, and lends additional credibility to their work.

Here is a blurb from their website about the approaches-

Cost (AKA Many Hats Approach)

Cost Approach (AKA Many Hats Approach) - The Cost Approach breaks the duties of the business owner into its components such as: business administration, accounting, finance, marketing, advertising, engineering, purchasing, etc.

The Cost Approach breaks down the time spent by the business owner into the various duties performed and quantifies the amount of time devoted to the different duties. Next, salary surveys are used to determine a comparable wage for each job duty performed by the business owner, then added up to arrive at the total "cost" to replace the services of the business owner.

The Cost Approach generally works best for small businesses where the business owner provides multiple services for the business (wears many hats).

Market (AKA Industry Standard Approach)

Market Approach (AKA Industry Standard Approach) - Compares the business owner's compensation to compensation within the same industry. The market approach focuses as much as possible on the owner's business and the specific position being analyzed (often the CEO or General Manager who also owns the business). The question to be answered is: How much compensation would be paid for this same position, held by a non-owner in an arms-length employment relationship, at a similar business?

The Market Approach generally works best for medium and large businesses where the business owner provides only one duty: management of the business.

Income (AKA Independent Investors Test)

Income Approach (AKA Independent Investors Test) - Seeks to determine whether a hypothetical investor would be satisfied with their return on investment when looking at the financial performance of the business in conjunction with the compensation level of the owner.

The income approach can only be correctly applied when the Fair Market Value (FMV) of the company is available for each year that compensation is examined.

The rationale behind the Independent Investor Test is that investors pay employees to work to increase the value of the assets entrusted to their management. A high rate of return indicates that the assets' value increased and that the employee provided valuable services. Thus, if investors obtain returns above what they should reasonably expect, an employee's salary is presumptively reasonable.

The Income Approach generally works best when there is no comparability data available.

A large part of the calculus is predicated on the business owner wearing multiple hats. At times you are a janitor cleaning your office. At times you are a bookkeeper balancing your checkbook. At times you are performing clerical duties. These tasks might have a lower salary than your primary task, which creates a blended rate for an overall Officer Compensation.

The other consideration is that just because RCReports comes up with a salary does not mean you must pay that salary. There might be circumstances which would drive down a reasonable salary such as rapid growth, unsteady earnings, etc. There might be circumstances, such as 401k and other external reasons, to increase your salary.

Recently **WCG CPAs & Advisors** had a foot and ankle physician group in Rhode Island complete two different RCReports interviews to determine a reasonable salary for their S Corp, and the results are worthy of further discussion. The first draft yielded a shareholder salary of $193,762 yet the second draft returned $112,728. That is an $81,000 difference!

What changed? Good question. In the updated report, all three components changed-

▲ 2,080 hours went to 1,820 which is either 35 hours a week or just over 45 weeks per year.

▲ Time spent went from 80% to 75% when the S Corp shareholders dug a little deeper into their time allocations.

▲ Proficiency went from above-average to average. This was HUGE! It changed the hourly rate from $104 to $66.

Therefore, think of the pinball bouncing around in your RCReports pinball machine. The first bounce was reducing the hourly rate from $104 to $66. Next, the annual hours went from 2,080 to 1,820 given vacations, golfing, holidays and general screwing-around. Lastly, less time was spent performing doctor tasks (80% to 75%). In other words, the time spent was less valuable and the amount of time spent was reduced. Double dip!

Please keep in mind too that reasonable compensation includes self-employed health insurance and HSA contributions (and health reimbursement arrangements, and long-term care and disability premiums too). Therefore, if RCReports comes up with $80,000 but your self-employed health insurance including dental and vision is $10,000, then your shareholder salary should be $70,000. This alone saves you $1,500 in unnecessary payroll taxes (we had some tables in a previous chapter showing this arbitrage as well).

> Sidebar: Health Reimbursement Arrangements (HRAs), Long-Term Care and Disability should be paid by the business. No, they are not income tax deductions. No, your benefits are not taxable should you receive them. However, these payments buttress your reasonable salary calculations. In simple math, you save 15% of these amounts through the reduction of salary which reduces your Social Security and Medicare taxes. We expand on this in a later section.

We can do a reasonable compensation analysis for you. Yeah, we charge you about $400 but it gives you a defensible salary and some peace of mind. Bargain!

W-2 Converted to 1099 Reasonable Salary

So, you are bumping along and one day your employer decides to convert you from a W-2 employee to a 1099 contractor. Fired on Friday. Same duties on Monday. Aside from this being a load-shedding sham that the IRS and most states believe to be an end-around, several large businesses continue to reduce their workforce in favor of contractors.

You say, no problem, and eventually create an LLC taxed as an S corporation. Now what? Do you peg your salary to the same salary you had before? Hardly. Labor burden rates for businesses can vary from 1.4 to 2.0. What does this mean? This means if a business is paying you a $100,000 salary, your actual cost to the business might be as high as $200,000. Why?

Health insurance, dental insurance, paid time off, vacation, sick pay, holiday pay, payroll taxes, workers' compensation insurance, disability, group life insurance, office rent (smaller workforce smaller office footprint), overhead, etc. Yeah... read that again. There are a ton of direct costs that gets tacked on to you as an employee. Don't forget profits too. No wonder the business just converted you from W-2 to 1099. Mo' money! Just not for you.

How does this factor in the reasonable salary conversation? Let's say your business's labor burden rate is 1.8 which is not far off most big, fat corporations. This would suggest that a $100,000 salary costs the business $180,000. If you are paid $100,000 as a contractor (which would be a crummy deal), then your relative salary could be $55,000. You shouldn't get penalized if you run a leaner operation than your former employer.

What about the risk of this new arrangement? As a shareholder in an S corporation, you are assuming a ton of risk- equity risk, industry risk, small business risk and business-specific risk. If we perform a business valuation where the business has a singular client, the risk of the future economic benefit (income stream) is huge.

As mentioned elsewhere, as risk increases, we as the investor demand a higher rate of return, or as the shareholder, increased distributions. Makes sense, right?

Mini recap- labor burden rate plus increased risk of singular client can suggest a lower salary than the old W-2 job. And... being converted is not a bad deal- business car, your own 401k, various other deductions that were mostly unavailable to you, business casual means PJs, etc.

S Corp Salary Starting Point

There are plenty of professions that have great data from the Bureau of Labor Statistics (BLS), Risk Management Association (RMA) or RCReports. But let's say your job is some odd-duck, whacky thing for which comparable data doesn't exist. Where do we start quantitatively? At the end of the day, we need a number!

One argument that we and others have made is the concept of 1/3, 1/3, 1/3-

▲ 1/3 paid as shareholder salary, plus

▲ 1/3 retained for expenses (if necessary, otherwise flushed out at end of quarter), plus

▲ 1/3 distributed as return on investment (distributions)

Where the heck did we get this? A rule of thumb for service trades or businesses such as accountants, attorneys, consultants and the usual suspects is to bill three times the salary. For example, if WCG pays a CPA $100,000 per year we hope to bill $300,000. 1/3 of this goes to salary, 1/3 goes to expenses and 1/3 goes to Jason's new boat in a land-locked state. Most professional firms should have net profits of about 30 to 35%.

> Sidebar: This is why CPA firms sell for about 1.0 to 1.1 times gross revenue. This translates to a 3-year payback period at 100% retention or about 5-6 years with the usual 60% retention. This is an acceptable return on investment as compared to other investments and the accounting industry. Remember the rule of 72? Divide 72 by the rate of return, and that is your payback period (or the time it takes to double your money... same thing). 72 divided by 6 is still 12% which is not super great given the risk (oh well). We digress...

Even if your profession is easily teased out from labor data, this 1/3 concept can still be used. The middle 1/3 above is allocated to expenses- why should you be penalized for running a leaner, meaner firm than the bloated clowns down the street?

Using the 1/3 concept is just a starting point- since we must start somewhere, using a mathematical formula makes it easy. From there, and similar to the "plus" and "minus" approach by the IRS and Tax Court judges, we massage this salary to be reasonable for you and your business's situation.

What does **WCG CPAs & Advisors** do?

▲ If we don't have good data from BLS.gov or other resources, and

▲ RCReports is not available, and

▲ We are not affected by other influences (max out 401k, defined benefits pension, etc.), then

▲ WCG starts off at around 35% to 45% depending on the profession (based on observations), and then

▲ Massages the number with the client using IRS guidance.

From there, we-

▲ Create a payroll plan with monthly Processing, and

▲ Create a tax plan for the household to project tax obligations (holistic tax planning), and

▲ Increase income tax withholdings to land on tax neutrality for April 15 (no surprises) and try to avoid estimated tax payments, and

▲ Re-tweak May, June and July, maybe in November

We expand on this in the next chapter. Yay!

Multiple Shareholders Payroll Split

Many S corporations have multiple shareholders, and several are husband and wife teams. In these cases, we determine a starting point as a collective and then massage from there. Using $60,000 as an example, perhaps one spouse should be paid $40,000 and the other spouse be paid $20,000 commensurate to his and / or her individual worth to the business. In other words, don't double the salary once you determine your starting point because you have two shareholders. The starting point is for all aggregated shareholders, and from there you can divvy it up, massage it, increase it, etc.

Your spouse should be considered an officer within the corporate governance or documentation. Otherwise, splitting the salary between the two of you results in a lower overall officer compensation since non-officer salaries are placed on Line 8 versus Line 7 of the S Corp tax return (Form 1120S).

Remember, this would only be for materially participating shareholders. You could have your spouse be an inactive investor in your S corporation at 20% and you would remain at 80%. As we've mentioned previously, one of the reasonable salary tests is the relationship between salary and shareholder distributions. Therefore, if you own 80% of a business taxed as an S corporation, you are receiving 80% of the distributions. Subsequently, your salary could be possibly reduced (but your salary is still ultimately dependent on you and your value to the business).

Here is a table assuming a 35% jumping off point for salary with a column at 100% ownership and 80% ownership to further explain-

Income	Salary at 100%	Salary at 80%	Payroll Tax Savings
30,000	10,500	8,400	321
50,000	17,500	14,000	536
75,000	26,250	21,000	803
100,000	35,000	28,000	1,071
150,000	52,500	42,000	1,607
200,000	70,000	56,000	2,142

To reiterate, the $100,000 line above would be $100,000 x 80% x 35% = $28,000 resulting in a payroll tax savings of $1,071. Note that is a savings of payroll taxes, and not income taxes since the 80% and the 20% would flow presumably onto a jointly filed individual tax return.

Additional S Corp Salary Considerations

Beyond the reasonable salary theories and jumping off points, there are some things to keep in mind as Officer Compensation is determined.

Social Security

As mentioned before, the 35-40% salary is just a jumping off point. There are several factors that need to be considered and they can be competing. For example, you might want a higher salary to add to your Social Security basis. We demonstrated this in Chapter 4 (Social Security Basis, page 167), and a snippet of that is reprinted here.

The maximum Social Security benefit for 2021 is $3,957 per month for those who delay until age 70, or $3,135 for those who start benefits at full retirement age (FRA). Using SSA.gov's calculator, at $60,000 in salary at an age of 50 your benefit would be $1,955 at age 67 in today's dollars. A $100,000 salary would have a benefit of $2,675. Yes, we need to update this data but the illustration remains substantive.

Here is a lovely table-

Social Security Wage Limit (2021)	142,800
Max Benefit Retiring at 67 Years Old	3,135
Max Benefit Retiring at 70 Years Old	3,957

		Retire at 67 years Old			Retire at 70 years Old		
Salary	% of Max	Benefit	% of Max	Delta	Benefit	% of Max	Delta
20,000	14%	1,037	33%	19%	1,306	33%	19%
40,000	28%	1,496	48%	20%	1,897	48%	20%
60,000	42%	1,955	62%	20%	2,487	63%	21%
70,000	49%	2,185	70%	21%	2,782	70%	21%
80,000	56%	2,415	77%	21%	3,078	78%	22%
90,000	63%	2,567	82%	19%	3,227	82%	19%
100,000	70%	2,675	85%	15%	3,365	85%	15%
120,000	84%	2,890	92%	8%	3,642	92%	8%
142,800	100%	3,135	100%	0%	3,957	100%	0%

Whoa! Look at those deltas between salary and benefits right around $90,000 to $100,000 in salary. This would suggest that salaries above $90,000 have a steep diminishing return on increasing SSA benefits. Or, said differently, salaries below $90,000 have a good retirement benefit for your salary buck. Additionally, consider that paying $140,000 costs about $7,500 in additional taxes without a corresponding strong future benefit ($50,000 x 15.3%).

Do you pay yourself $90,000 just to get the most SSA benefit relative to the increased Social Security and Medicare taxes? Consider this

If you paid yourself $60,000 instead of $90,000 you would lose $612 in SSA benefits per month, or about $146,880 assuming 240 months (or 20 years of life remaining at 67 years old).

However, you would save $4,590 in Social Security and Medicare taxes per year with a $30,000 lower salary. If you worked for 30 years, and those tax savings earned 5%, you will have over $320,000 accumulated. Accumulated wealth can also be transferred or spent, where future benefits are just that- future benefits and not money in the bank.

Again, something to consider.

Maximize Your 401k Contributions
You also might want a higher salary to maximize your i401k plan or solo 401k plan. You can contribute up to $23,000 (for the 2024 tax year) plus $7,500 catch-up if 50 or older. Therefore, if you are 50 years old you might want your salary to be at least $33,100 (this leaves room for your portion of Social Security and Medicare taxes). There are instances where a $345,000 salary (for the 2024 tax year) might be the best solution given age-based profit sharing and defined benefits pensions.

Oftentimes, these small business retirements plans are added to the traditional 401k plan to "turbocharge" them. It seems crazy to want to pay a $345,000 salary when one of the resounding themes is to have a low salary, but there could be significant tax savings. See Chapter 12 which is dedicated to self-employed retirement plans for more details or this link-

wcginc.com/turbo

Health Insurance Floor
Another competing interest, or at least a factor, is health insurance and HSA contributions. Generally, you must have income subject to Social Security and Medicare taxes that are equal to or higher than your health insurance premiums. Huh?

Let's say you have not elected S Corp tax treatment on your LLC, and your LLC has a net ordinary business income after expenses and deductions of $10,000. This is subject to self-employment taxes (Social Security and Medicare). If your health insurance premiums are $15,000, only $10,000 would be deducted as self-employed health insurance (a direct adjustment to income) and the $5,000 remainder would be deducted on Schedule A subject to those limitations.

Same thing in S Corp land. If your self-employed health insurance is $15,000 per year, you must pay yourself at least $15,000 in salary to be able to fully deduct the premiums as self-employed health insurance. Your $15,000 salary is subject to Social Security and Medicare taxes just like your $10,000 LLC income above.

Reasonable Salary Recap
Keeping your salary low is what drives the savings in an S corporation. Recall that $10,000 in salary costs you about $1,530 in payroll taxes. However, through the IRS Fact Sheet and several Tax Court cases, the assignment of reasonable shareholder salary becomes qualitative in relation to several factors such as your role and qualifications, and the relationship to net income and distributions (just to name a few).

Labor data such as Risk Management Association (RMA) and Bureau of Labor Statistics (BLS) including RCReports can be hit or miss. Homogenized populations cannot definitely tell the IRS or the Tax Court what you should be paid. It could be a tool in your toolbox, or it could be one of the many nails in your coffin.

Don't forget the assembled workforce effect and return on investment arguments.

Also recall that self-employed health insurance and Health Savings Accounts (HSA) add to your Box 1 wages on your W-2. Let's say your reasonable salary is $60,000 and you pay $12,000 in health insurance premiums. You would pay yourself a $48,000 salary but your W-2 Box 1 and Line 7 (Officer Compensation) on your S corporation tax return would show $60,000, but only $48,000 is subjected to Social Security and Medicare taxes.

One of the best ways to win an argument is to not have the conversation in the first place. The IRS is focused on S corporations who do not pay any salary, or who pay a ridiculously low salary. For them, it is an easy analysis. Line 7 versus Line 21 of the S Corp tax return (Form 1120S). They can also look at the K-1, Box 1 (ordinary income) and compare this to Box 16, Code D (distributions). There's probably an app for that.

IRS scrutiny will only increase over time, but they also want winnable cases. The low hanging fruit is the S Corp without any reasonable shareholder salary. Why go after someone who is paying themselves $50,000 in salary just to settle on $60,000 after negotiation? An extra $1,530 in the IRS pocket for arguably a tough audit might not be worth it to them. This scenario is contrasted to the person who pays themselves $10,000 and it should be $60,000. There's some cash in that IRS challenge!

There is a calculated risk when determining reasonable compensation for S corporations. You can eliminate the risk by paying yourself 100% of the net business income but then again that completely defeats the purpose of an S Corp. You can pay yourself 0% and wait for the audit. Or... ideally... you can operate in the soft middle.

Chapter 10
Operating Your S Corp
(updated November 2023)

Chapter Introduction
Operating your S Corporation is generally a no muss no fuss situation, but there are several considerations to be aware of. Here is the order of business for this chapter-

▲ Costs or Fees for Having an S Corp

▲ I Just Got an S Corp Puppy, What Do I Do?

▲ Processing Payroll, Tax Planning

▲ Shareholder Distributions

▲ Other Considerations and Tricks

Tax deductions and fringe benefits including retirement planning are in Chapter 11 and Chapter 12.

Costs of Operating an S Corporation

Sales pitch alert! WCG CPAs & Advisors specializes in small businesses which have a small number of owners, and often just a one-person show. Did you know that 95% of all S Corps have only one shareholder, and 99% of all S Corps have three or fewer shareholders?

Common S Corp candidates and current clients for WCG CPAs & Advisors are consultants, attorneys, financial advisors, insurance agents, physicians, chiropractors, doctors, surgeons, anesthesiologists, nurse anesthetists, real estate agents, contractors, photographers (the profitable ones), online retailers, FBA retailers and good ol' fashion widget makers, among several others. We also have several medical groups and financial advisor teams operating multi-tiered entity structures.

The tax savings of an S corporation is not in dispute. But what does it cost to have tax preparation, payroll, tax planning and consultation done? Because small businesses are a core competency for us, we have created Business Advisory Services packages that includes the following-

Tax Planning and Preparation	Vail	Telluride	Aspen
Streamline Tax Planning, Tax Projection	✓	✓	✓
Small Business Tax Deductions Optimization	✓	✓	✓
Section 199A QBI Tax and Salary Optimization	✓	✓	✓
Estimated Tax Payments (done thru payroll)	✓	✓	✓
Business Entity Tax Prep	✓	✓	✓
Individual Tax Prep, One Owner	✓	✓	✓
Expat / Foreign Income Calcs, Forms	Add-On	Add-On	Add-On
Tax Resolution, IRS Audit Defense	As Req'd	As Req'd	As Req'd
Situational Tax Law Research (up to 3 hours)			✓

Payroll and Accounting Services	Vail	Telluride	Aspen
Reasonable Shareholder Salary Calculation	✓	✓	✓
Monthly Shareholder Payroll Processing	✓	✓	✓
Employee Payroll Processing	Add-On	Add-On	Add-On
Annual Payroll Processing (includes ten 1099s)	✓	✓	✓
Accounting Services (bookkeeping + analysis)	Add-On	Add-On	Add-On
Quarterly QuickBooks Consulting, QuickStart	Add-On	✓	✓

Business Advisory Services	Vail	Telluride	Aspen
Consulting			
Consultation, Periodic Business Reviews (PBR)	Annually	Routine	Routine
Complimentary Quick Chats (CQC)	Routine	Routine	Routine
Interfacing with Other Professionals		Routine	Routine
Financial Analysis			
Fractional Controller	Add-On	Add-On	Add-On
Financial Statements Analysis, Comparisons		Quarterly	Quarterly
Cash Flow Management and Analysis			Annually
First Research, Industry-Focused Consulting		Annually	Annually
National and Metro Economic Reports			Annually
KPI Analysis, Benchmarking, Trend Analysis			✓
Budgeting, Forecasting, Goal-Setting			✓
Strategy and Maintenance			
C-Level Financial Advice and Strategic Planning			✓
Succession Planning, Exit Consultation			✓
Annual Business Valuation			✓
Annual Corporate Governance, Meetings		✓	✓
Annual Fee*	**$4,320**	**$7,560**	**Custom**
Monthly Fee*	$360	$630	Custom
	(prorated based on onboarding date)		

Custom! Unlike the modern-day new car packages where you have to spend $8,000 for the moonroof, our Business Advisory Service plans can be customized specifically for you. The array above is simply a starting point. If you need more from us, let's chat about it!

Tax Patrol Services

We also have Tax Patrol! This is a wonderful tax service for those who don't need all the business advisory bells and whistles above, but from time to time want some love from an experienced tax consultant and business advisor. Have a quick tax question? Need to know the depreciation rules as you buy that new car? Wondering what your April tax bill is going to be in August? Tax Patrol is like ski patrol... you might not use it, but you sleep better knowing you have it.

Tax Patrol	Keystone	Copper	Breck
Individual Tax Prep)	✓		✓
Business Entity Tax Prep		✓	✓
Tax Planning, Tax Projection Worksheets	✓	✓	✓
Estimated Tax Payments Calcs	✓	✓	✓
Tax Resolution, IRS Audit Defense	Add-On	Add-On	Add-On
Complimentary Quick Chats (CQC)	Routine	Routine	Routine
Annual Fee	**$1,500**	**$2,100**	**$3,180**
Monthly Fee	$125	$175	$265

(prorated based on onboarding date)

[intentional white space]

Accounting and Payroll Services

Accounting fees are based on 2 bank account with less than 250 monthly transactions and include the QBO fee from Intuit. Custom quote is available if you have a lot going on such as third-party integrations (POS, time billing system), accrual accounting method, extensive benefits packages and / or industry specific issues (e.g, job costing in construction).

Employee payroll can be added to shareholder payroll for $100 per month if already using our Business Advisory Service plans above (e.g, Vail), or $175 for standalone. Custom quote for more than 5 employees and a referral to therapy.

Accounting, Payroll

Monthly Accounting	starting at $500 / month
Bi-Monthly Accounting	starting at $250 / month
Quad-Monthly	starting at $150 / month
Sales Tax, Personal Property Tax	typically $75 / month, or $150 / quarter
Employee Payroll (up to 5, bi-weekly)	1 employee, $100 / month 2-5 employees, $175 / month

Prorated Fees

Some more things to consider- when a partial year remains, our usual annual fee is pro-rated to not charge you for services you didn't use (like payroll and consultation). However, a large chunk of our annual fee is tax preparation which is typically a built-in fixed amount of $1,600 (both business entity and individual tax returns). Whether we onboard you in January, July or December, we have to prepare a full year tax return. This increases the monthly fee for the remaining months of 2021 but the monthly fee will later decrease in January of 2022 to reflect the amounts above. Yeah, we make it sound like 2021 is just around the corner.

Payroll Processing

We make very little profits on payroll processing... we offer it as a convenience to our clients. One throat to choke with a single call can be reassuring but if you want to run your payroll, go for it! Everyone thinks payroll is a piece of cake; write a check and done. Nope... we see a lot of mistakes being made by clients especially the handling of health insurance and HSA contributions since there are special rules for greater than 2% S Corp shareholders. Then again, we don't mind fixing what was broken.

Tax Returns
You can prepare your own individual tax return as well... but the benefit WCG preparing both individual and business tax returns is that we slide things around depending on income limitations and phaseouts.

> **Note:** An individual tax return is what the IRS calls Form 1040 and refers to the entity filing the tax return (you, the individual, are the entity). However, a married couple are deemed to be one entity for the sake of an individual tax return. So, when we say we will prepare your individual tax return, it is meant to include your spouse in a jointly filed tax return.

Break-Even Analysis (does an S Corp make sense?)
Break-even analysis is based on our annual fee of $4,320. If an S corporation saves you 8% to 10% (on average) in taxes over the garden-variety LLC, then $4,320 divided by 9% equals $48,000 of net ordinary business income after expenses and deductions.

More sales pitch! Keep in mind that our fee of $4,320 includes your individual tax return which you might already be paying another tax professional to prepare. WCG has a handful of clients who are right at the break-even point of $48,000 but leverage an S Corp and our services to get tax preparation, tax planning and consultation.

You can always find someone to do it for less- we know that. At the same time, we have a vested interest in your success and provide sound tax and business consultation as a part of our service. Here is a link to our Periodic Business Review agenda that we cover throughout the year so our consultation to you is comprehensive-

wcginc.com/PBR

We also have written a webpage on end of year tax planning-

wcginc.com/EOY

And, to see our entire fee structure (transparency)-

wcginc.com/fee

No more shameless promotion... at least for a while.

New S Corp Puppy, What Do I Do Now

The following is a reprint from a blog post and is a quick glance at some of the housekeeping that is required after bringing home your new S Corp puppy.

Open a Business Checking Account

You will need a separate business checking account for two big reasons. First, most payroll processors (ADP, Paychex, Gusto, etc.) require this per Bank Secrecy Act and Homeland Security rules. Second, compartmentalizing your personal and business worlds is just good accounting practice. If necessary, WCG can rebuild your financial statements and prepare tax returns based on bank statements. If your Nordstrom's is mixed in with Staples, it gets messy.

Yet another reason for the compartmentalization is preserve the separation of you, the personal, from the business. This might, heavy on "might," help you in a lawsuit or legal matter.

Set Up Payroll Accounts and Processing

As a shareholder of an S corporation, you wear two hats. One as an investor, and another as an employee. Well, that's a lie. As a business owner, in general, you wear a million hats... but two of them are investor and employee. Therefore, the IRS requires all S Corp shareholders who materially participate in the business activities to be paid a reasonable salary.

A salary is more than simply writing a check or making a transfer from your business checking account to your personal checking account. With a corporation or LLC taxed as S corporation those payments are owner draws and are now considered shareholder distributions. Payroll is payroll... complete with quarterly payroll filings (941s) and annual payroll filings (940, W-2 and W-3). Let's not forget the state equivalents.

Of course, WCG can handle all this for you, but if you choose to process your own payroll, we strongly recommend ADP or Gusto. WCG uses ADP.

Alert Clients to Payment Changes

You might have been receiving payments under your name and / or into your personal checking account. You will want to notify your clients or customers accordingly. You will also want to supply a W-9 to them alerting them that as an LLC or corporation taxed as an S corporation, you do not need to be issued a 1099-MISC or 1099-NEC (unless you are an attorney... seriously).

However, this is not a rock you want to push up that hill. If a client or a customer, or some ambitious accountant on the other end of the email thread wants to issue a 1099 to your S

Corp, don't fight it. Simply ensure they are using the business's EIN and not your SSN. It's just not worth the brain damage to convince someone otherwise.

Understand Mileage, Home Office, Cell Phone, Internet Expenses
If you previously reported your business activities on Schedule C of your Form 1040 individual tax return, there are some things to understand. As we just mentioned, as an owner of an S corporation you are both investor and employee. Investors cannot typically deduct mileage, home office, cell phone and internet expense. And! Employees can no longer deduct these expenses as well thanks to the Tax Cuts and Jobs Act of 2017 (Form 2106 as part of Schedule A was eliminated).

As such, your S Corp must reimburse you, the employee, for these expenses through an Accountable Plan reimbursement program. While it sounds fancy, the big takeaway here is that these expenses were commonly deducted on your individual tax return, but with an S Corp, these expenses are now employee reimbursements and are deducted on your business entity tax return. We will spend a lot of time on this and Accountable Plans in a bit.

Why does this matter? We commonly prepare and file a business entity tax return just to later have the shareholders want to deduct mileage, home office, cell phone and internet expenses on his or her individual tax return. This is a problem and requires amending the business entity tax return. Yuck.

Please don't wait until the preparation of your individual tax return to let us know that you have mileage expenses or a home office to deduct.

Understand SEP IRA / 401k Limits and Handling
This can be a big surprise, so please pay attention on this one (pretty please). With business activities reported on Schedule C, SEP IRAs and 401k company contributions are based on net business income after expenses. With an S Corp, they are based on W-2 wages paid to the shareholders. Big difference!

One of the reasons for leveraging the tax benefits of an S corporation is to reduce the amounts of Social Security and Medicare taxes (self-employment taxes)... and that is accomplished by paying a reasonable shareholder salary which is less than the net business income (see our wonderful Chapter 9 on Reasonable Shareholder Salary). Here is some math-

A business reported on Schedule C earns $100,000 after expenses. A SEP IRA contribution is based on this $100,000 and generally will be close to $18,587 for the sake of argument (20% of net business income after deducting the employer portion of self-employment taxes and adjusting for the contribution factor).

Next assume that this same business being taxed as an S Corp pays out a $40,000 salary to the shareholder. Your SEP IRA contribution is now limited to 25% of W-2 wages, and would be limited to $10,000.

So, if you are used to putting away large chunks into a SEP IRA, you will be in for a surprise.

Sidebar: SEP IRAs are old school and were used in crisis mode since solo 401k plans had to be set up during the tax year. Thanks to the SECURE Act, solo 401k plans can be set up in March, but contributions may be made and deducted as if the plan existed the year prior. Also! Keep in mind that solo 401k plans are way better than SEP IRAs with higher contributions (basically solo 401k = SEP IRA + $23,000 for the 2024 tax year). See our Chapter 12 on Retirement Planning (Using a 401k Plan in Your Small Business Retirement Options, page 359).

Wait! There's more. Similar to mileage, home office, cell phone and internet expenses, SEP IRA and 401k company contributions are deducted on the business entity tax return. Read that again. Before your corporation or LLC became taxed as S Corp decision, you might have been used to calculating a maximum SEP IRA contribution on your individual tax return; with an S Corp, this calculation and the decision to deduct the contribution is done on the business entity (S Corp) tax return.

Know the Filing Deadlines, Business Tax Payments
March 15. There it is… and this seems to sneak up on small business owners who have not filed a business entity tax return in the past. S Corps (Form 1120S) and partnerships (Form 1065) tax returns are due March 15, or the next business day. C Corps (Form 1120) tax returns are due April 15, or the next business day.

Also, your individual tax return cannot be filed until the business entity (S Corp or Partnership) tax return is completed. Why? An S Corp or Partnership tax return creates a K-1 which must be reported on your individual tax return. Therefore, if you are a DIYer and prepare your own Form 1040, please do not file until you've added the K-1 to the tax return.

Some states have a franchise or corporate tax that affects S corporations and other business entities. For example, if you were a sole proprietor last year and this year you created an entity in California and elected to have that taxed as an S Corp, the business will be required pay a franchise tax on April 15. The business might also pay estimated tax payments throughout the year for California's franchise taxes. Texas also has a franchise tax which is due May 15. Other states have other rules.

Again, there are a bunch of additional due dates and whatnot that might come with your new S Corp puppy.

Attention Late S Corp Filers
Things change a bit if you are filing a late S Corp election during the first few months of the year. Let's use some dates-

February 1	Send late S Corp election (Form 2553) to IRS
March 15	S Corp tax return (Form 1120S) is due
May 1	IRS gives you the green light for S Corp status
May 2	S Corp and individual tax returns are efiled
July 4	IRS ruins weekend with late S Corp filing penalty

Note the problem here... you cannot electronically file the S Corporation tax return (Form 1120S) on-time since you do not have approval from the IRS by March 15. No biggie! One option is to paper file the tax returns, but we've seen a ton of problems with that. The other options that WCG uses often is this-

Electronically file a tax return extension on March 15 which is naturally rejected (since the S Corp doesn't exist yet as a tax election).

▲ Mail a paper extension to the IRS on March 15 which is probably tossed by an otherwise friendly IRS agent.

▲ Electronically file the S Corp tax return when greenlighted by the IRS.

▲ Wait for the nastygram from the IRS saying we were late.

▲ Submit documentation to the IRS showing the sequence of events, and ask for first time penalty abatement. WCG is batting 100% for over a decade on this.

Your mileage might vary, but this gives you a broad perspective of the sequence when we are close to filing deadlines.

Adjust Estimated Tax Payments
One of the primary reasons, if not the only reason, to elect S Corp status is to reduce self-employment taxes (Social Security and Medicare taxes). If your previous accountant or tax return created estimated tax payments based on the previous year's data, and before your LLC taxed as S corporation election was made, those vouchers will include the full amount of self-employment taxes. In addition, with an S Corp election and the processing of payroll,

self-employment taxes now become Social Security and Medicare taxes and are handled directly through payroll processing.

As such, your estimated tax payments will be way too high and will need adjustments; in most cases, we can eliminate the need of estimated tax payments completely and handle all estimated income tax payments within payroll processing by inflating your withholdings to land on tax neutrality (more on that in a bit).

Accounting, Recording Financial Activity
This is an easy one since whatever you've done in the past to memorialize your business transactions remains the same. No, you do not need to instantly add a QuickBooks subscription to your world. While we love QuickBooks Online (QBO) since we can collaborate directly with you, if you have historically used Excel, bar napkins or some other accounting platform, then keep on keeping on.

Nothing changes from an accounting perspective with an S Corp. Yes, there are some minor differences when it comes to Capital Stock and the recording of employee reimbursements, but we can chat about that at tax time.

Let's dive into this a bit more.

Accounting Method
Many business owners ask if they should be cash or accrual when selecting the accounting method within their accounting platform such as QuickBooks Online. Simply put, the accrual-basis method recognizes revenue when earned (not when paid) and recognizes expenses when obligated to pay (but not necessarily paid). Conversely, the cash-basis method recognizes revenue when cash is received and recognizes expenses when cash is paid (mailing a check on 12/31 or swiping your credit card on 12/31 is considered paid in the current year).

There is also a modified cash-basis method of accounting for those who have inventory where generally you are using cash-basis for recording transactions but record all inventory transactions using accrual-basis. Which method should you use?

Yes, there are all kinds of exceptions, rules, thresholds, etc. and other nauseating details. Let's skip those now. Most small businesses can operate just fine using the cash-basis method of accounting; when cash comes in, it's revenue. When cash leaves, it is usually an expense or a shareholder distribution (or loan payment or capital expenditure on a monster truck for the office). Easy.

Phantom Income
Cash-basis method also prevents phantom income or paying taxes on bad income. What do we mean?

If you send an invoice on 12/31 but the client never pays, and you forget this, you will pay taxes on phantom income. Or, you send an invoice for $10,000 on 12/31 but the client only pays $6,000 on 7/1 because of a negotiated write-down; you paid taxes on $10,000 and now you must wait until the following year to recognize the $4,000 bad debt expense and subsequent reduction in taxable income. $4,000 times your tax rate might not be a big deal; $40,000 times your tax rate might be a killer since you didn't get the cash to pay the taxes.

Another scenario is where you invoice a client on 12/31 but because of norms in the industry, they don't pay for six months. If this is a large invoice you will have fronted the taxes generated by it on April 15 but not get paid until July 1. That can really suck the cash out of your flow.

Cash-basis method of accounting takes the mystery out of this stuff.

Bad Debts in Cash World
One question we get all the time... literally all the time... "I built a website for this dude and he never paid me. Can I deduct the amount he owes me?" It depends. If you are cash-basis then No since you never recognized the income nor paid taxes on it. If you are accrual-basis where you invoiced the dude and recognized the income as taxable, then Yes. To recap, you can only deduct a bad debt if you previously recognized the income, dude or no dude.

Here is another example to hopefully take this home. You are a landlord. Your property is vacant for two months; your taxable rental income is naturally reduced by this vacancy and as such creates a built-in tax reduction (not deduction... reduction... with an r).

Keep in mind that over time accrual-basis and cash-basis converge for most small businesses that are stable and not growing. From year-to-year things might be different, but after a decade or more, historical net income is virtually identical between accrual and cash. Sure, there are probably extreme and rare examples where this statement fails, but generally speaking it holds.

Accruals in Cash World

There are some nuances that we must take care of in a cash-based world. Four scenarios tend to repeat themselves often-

▲ You intend to make a 401k employer contribution by March 15. Cash hasn't left the checking account yet, however, you want to deduct the 401k contribution on your tax return. We would record the 401k Contribution expense (debit) with a corresponding 401k Liability (credit).

▲ You swipe your credit card for a bunch of expenses in December. You pay the credit card bill in January. The IRS, and the accounting industry, says you can recognize these expenses at the time of credit card swipe. However, cash has not left your checking account by December 31. As such, we record the expenses (debits) with a corresponding Credit Card Payable (credit).

▲ Your client, on the advice of their smart CPA, sends you a check on December 31 and you receive it on January 2. The 1099-MISC that is issued to you also includes this payment. We align top-line revenue with the total of all 1099s received, and then record a "timing difference" so that part of this revenue is not recognized as taxable income.

▲ You are part of a multi-entity arrangement where the mothership pays out a fee for service to the baby S Corps. However, December 31 comes and goes, and the final year-end accounting (bookkeeping) has not been done until February. Since the obligation existed on December 31, we record a Fee for Service expense (debit) and corresponding Payable (credit) so that net business income (profit) is reduced correctly.

1099-NEC Issued to Your SSN

Let's back up and talk about the 1099-NEC versus 1099-MISC. The 1099-NEC which stands for non-employee compensation was last used in 1982 until the IRS revived it for the 2020 tax year. Why? No one really knows, but the IRS pawned off the excuse of varying filing deadlines within the 1099-MISC, and to simplify, they spun off the 1099-NEC again.

Receiving a 1099-NEC is another minor inconvenience. Generally, we nominate the income to the business so we can change the color of money, and dictate which amounts are subject to self-employment taxes (Social Security and Medicare taxes). Mechanically we bring the income into your individual tax return (Form 1040) so it is reported correctly, but then make an adjustment along with notations to assign the income to your S corporation tax return (Form 1120S).

Ideally, S Corps should not be receiving 1099-NEC's at all. You can alert your clients or customers accordingly by completing and submitting a W-9 to each of them (and cross your fingers).

There are certain businesses such as insurance agents, investment advisors, realtors and consultants that might be precluded from receiving income and the subsequent 1099-NEC tax form in the business name and EIN. In other words, your Social Security number is being used to report the income to the IRS.

For certain people in the financial advisory sector, the tides are changing. More and more of these professionals are creating registered investment advisor (RIA) firms, and as such FINRA, the SEC and the higher ups at investment banks are allowing for 1099-NECs to be issued to the business's EIN instead of your personal SSN. This certainly simplifies things.

Please review Chapter 2 (Fleischer Tax Court Case, page 82) for more details on this conundrum.

Take Money Out of the S Corp
Remember, payroll taxes (Social Security and Medicare taxes) are the same as self-employment taxes. But they also include unemployment taxes, state disability insurance (such as California's state disability insurance) and other odd-duck local taxes. We discussed this in Chapter 4 (Additional Payroll Taxes, page 140).

As an S Corp shareholder, you are taking money out of the business in various ways-

Source	Payroll Taxes	Income Taxes
Reasonable S Corp Salary	Yes	Yes
Shareholder Distributions	No	No
Reimbursements (Accountable Plan)	No	No
Funding Retirement Accounts	No	Deferred
Self-Rental (not home office)	No	Maybe
Adding Children to Payroll	Yes	No
Shareholder Loans	No	No

Reasonable S Corp Salary
This is a bit obvious, right? Paying yourself a reasonable shareholder salary is a quick way to pull money out of the business. We've already touched on reasonable salary theories in Chapter 9 (Reasonable S Corp Salary Theory, page 217). We will explain payroll processing, tax planning, withholdings and cadence in a bit.

Shareholder Distributions (versus Income)

When you write a check to yourself or transfer money from your business checking account to your personal checking account, you are taking a shareholder distribution. However, you are not taxed on shareholder distributions nor are they a deduction to the business- you are taxed on income (net ordinary business income after expenses and deductions).

Here is a story to drive home this point- **WCG CPAs & Advisors** has an S Corp client who had accumulated about $400,000 in her business checking account over the years. No big deal. Cash is king, right? Her husband called and wanted to know the tax consequences of moving the $400,000 into their personal checking account since they were buying a house. We said None. You already paid taxes on the income that aggregated to $400,000 over the past three years. Huh?

Let's say your S Corporation earns $100,000 after shareholder wages and expenses, and you magically also have $100,000 in the business checking account. You transfer $60,000 to your personal checking account as a shareholder distribution. $40,000 is left behind in the business checking account.

What is your taxable income? $100,000. Good.

Next year, your business is a bit slower and you only earn $50,000 and therefore you have $90,000 ($40,000 + $50,000) in the business checking account. You transfer $80,000 to your personal account leaving $10,000 in the business account.

What is your taxable income? $50,000 even though you transferred $80,000 from the business to you. Cash is cash and income is income. As mentioned earlier, over time, aggregated historical cash should be very close to aggregated historical incomes for a stable business. This is mostly true even after accounting for depreciation since this is a mechanism to offset cash outflow for purchases.

This cash is cash and income is income thing can be a real bummer at tax time too. For example, you have $100,000 left over at the end of the year and your taxable income is coincidentally $100,000. You took $70,000 in shareholder distributions as a return on your investment, leaving $30,000 behind for business growth (the reinvestment).

If you are taxed at 24%, you will pay $24,000 ($100,000 x 24%) in taxes on $70,000 worth of net economic benefit from your business- suddenly this becomes painful and a near-35% tax rate ($24,000 divided by $70,000). Something to think about. Keep in mind that this is short-term pain since you are growing your business and hopefully increasing your net economic benefit from it (and adding to your shareholder basis which reduces capital gains should you sell).

We have more information about shareholder distributions including cadence in another section (Taking Shareholder Distributions, page 259).

Reimbursements (Accountable Plan)

We encourage businesses to create an Accountable Plan which allows employees to turn in expense reports for various reimbursable items. The typical reimbursed expenses through an Accountable Plan are home office use including depreciation, mileage or business-use portion of automobile expenses, cell phone and internet.

All these expenses have one thing in common- they are mixed used, both personally and business. Mixed-use expenses should be paid by the employee and later reimbursed. Conversely, anything that is 100% business use should be paid for directly by the business.

This is also expanded in a later section (Accountable Plan Expense Reimbursements, page 262) with some fun journal entries too, Exciting!

Funding Retirement Accounts

Not only can you make contributions to retirement accounts, the business can also fund your SEP IRA, solo 401k plan, profit sharing plan, defined benefits plan, cash balance plan, and other retirement plan mechanisms. We have Chapter 12 which is dedicated to retirement planning within your small business.

Self-Rental

We've already discussed self-rentals in Chapter 3 (Three Types of Income, page 130) and how you can pull money out that is only taxed at the income tax level. Here is a re-print of that information-

It is common for a business owner who relies on machinery or equipment to have two business entities. One entity is an LLC that owns the assets. The other entity is an S corporation which leases the assets from the LLC to use in the business. This directly reduces the S Corp's net operating business income, and might possibly reduce the amount of salary required to be paid by the business to the shareholders. Good news.

Here is an example-

	S Corp Owns Building	LLC Owns Building S Corp Rents from LLC
Gross Income	100,000	100,000
Rental Expense	0	30,000
Net Income	100,000	70,000
Reasonable Salary (assumed at 40%)	40,000	28,000
Payroll Taxes	5,640	3,948
Savings		1,692

This is an overly simplified example and leaves out depreciation, etc., but you get the idea. In addition, we used a 40% salary calculation simply for the sake of presentation. Your actual salary might be different in your situation. Regardless, the apples to apples comparison shows a nice little savings of $1,692. As mentioned in Chapter 2 (Real Estate Holding Company and Operating Company, page 44) the arrangement also allows you to have different partners in each entity allowing you to expand ownership in the operating entity while retaining full ownership in the leased asset (building).

Here is another self-rental situation. You find a business connection for renting space in your home for 14 days or fewer. Client parties and presentations are good examples. Board meetings for closely held businesses is a bad example (or at least one that is tough to defend). Your business enters into a lease arrangement at market rates. The business deducts the amounts paid as rent and issues a 1099-MSIC to you. On your tax return, the amount of rent is reduced to zero with a one-time expense adjustment under Section 280A in the amount of rent.

Adding Children to Payroll

This is another tool in the toolbox to pull money out of your S Corp. You pay your child $14,600 (for the 2024 tax year) or whatever the standard deduction is for that tax year and they spend it on college or gift the money back to you (or they fund a Roth IRA and save the rest for their first home). This is a deduction to you at your tax rate but is tax-free to the child. However, the child pays 7.65% in Social Security and Medicare taxes and the S Corp pays the same.

This usually works well when the parents tax rate is 22% or higher to provide a large enough delta between 15.3% (mandatory payroll taxes) and the parent's tax rate plus tax credit considerations (since chores are a snap, why not have them work too?).

We expand on this more in Chapter 11 (Putting Your Kids on the Payroll, page 334), but you can also read our Reducing Taxes summary article here-

wcginc.com/6177

Shareholder Loans

These are generally frowned upon. To truly be a shareholder loan where the S Corp lends money to the shareholder, there must be loan terms including payment, amortization and imputed interest. Shareholder loans have a purpose, but it is narrow and must be carefully implemented.

Processing S Corp Payroll

In this section we will discuss establishing the salary amount, payroll cadence, tax planning and withholdings, and adjustments.

Establishing the Salary Amount

We've discussed the theory behind calculating a reasonable S Corp shareholder salary in Chapter 9 (Reasonable S Corp Salary Theory, page217). You are also aware of the benefits of an S corporation such as K-1 income being taxed at the income tax level only, and not subjected to payroll taxes such as Social Security, Medicare, unemployment or disability taxes. This is one of the reasons you are using an S Corp election (probably the only reason).

As the theory of S Corp salary suggests, the amount to pay as a reasonable wage is dependent on you but also on the health of the business. Here's what we do at **WCG CPAs & Advisors-**

▲ During the initial onboarding, we review your qualifications and projected net ordinary business income after expenses and deductions for the year. From that information, we determine a reasonable salary amount. Not too high. Not too low. Goldilocks style.

▲ Next, we adjust the income tax withholdings to account for your overall income tax obligations as a household. Our goal is to land on tax neutrality which we define as a $1,000 refund from the IRS and a $500 refund from the state. This requires tax planning, which is only done in May, June, July, November and December (the other months are shockingly filled with tax return preparation).

As such, if we fire up payroll in Q1 or Q3, then we SWAG it (yes, accountants can SWAG things) and mark our calendars to tighten up the income tax withholdings once the tax plan is done (see Tax Planning below).

▲ We establish a cash needs number for processing payroll. A general rule of thumb is about 10% over the recommended salary for employer related payroll taxes. For example, let's say a reasonable shareholder salary is $60,000 or $5,000 per month. The cash that is necessary to be in your business banking account each month is about $5,500 ($5,000 + 10%).

▲ WCG uses ADP for payroll processing, and our platform is called "Run Wholesale." Not sure why. But the clever thing here is that we get to say your payroll is on "Run and Done" similar to "Set it and forget it." Keep in mind future tax planning and adjustments, which we will discuss in a bit. We know, it's super riveting and you just can't wait.

Another consideration is a late S corporation election with equally tardy payroll events. Let's say it is October and we want to go back to January 1 with a late S Corp election, and we also establish a reasonable shareholder salary of $60,000. There are only 3 months remaining, so each month will be $20,000 in salary amounts to account for the entire year. There might be some tinkering with the cash needs if you've already paid a bunch of estimated tax payments for the year.

Payroll Cadence
WCG recommends processing shareholder payroll for your S corporation monthly unless you already have a team on a payroll cadence such as bi-weekly or semi-monthly. Some accountants will simply run S Corp payroll once a year in December. In our opinion, this is bad for three big reasons-

▲ This contradicts your intention to establish a salary based on your credentials, work patterns, complexity of the business, etc. All those theoretical things the IRS and Tax Court use to determine a reasonable salary (we discussed separately in Chapter 9). To the best of your ability and circumstance, salaries should be forward-looking or contemporaneous, at least have the appearance.

▲ Running payroll once a year is a horrible budgeting tool. By processing payroll monthly, we ease you into your tax obligations throughout the year. We also tie estimated tax payments into payroll which further helps you budget (more on that when we get into the nuts-and-bolts examples later in this chapter). A $60,000 one-time salary event in December could easily require over $25,000 in cash for tax withholdings. We are all humans first, and budgeters second. Spreading the pain throughout the year helps your cash flow budget and subsequent decision-making (should you buy a new car or a used car).

▲ Some states will close payroll accounts if you file more than two quarterly payroll filings in a row without salaries or wages. Processing shareholder payroll monthly avoids this issue.

Tax Planning and Withholdings
Estimated tax payments change as well when you have an S Corp, especially the first year. Generally, you are required to pay at least 100% of your prior year tax liability or 90% of your current year tax liability whichever is lower. If you earn over $150,000, you must pay 110% of your current year tax liability. How do you keep that straight?

Here is some more WCG elegance (yeah, we're bragging a bit)- we calculate and pay your quarterly estimated tax payments through your payroll withholdings. No more writing separate checks or using online payment portals, and tracking due dates. We do this by manually entering your federal and state withholdings accordingly to reflect the tax liability for your W-2 income and your K-1 income, plus other household sources. Beauty!

Technically we are not paying estimated taxes, but we are sending money off to the taxing agencies via payroll.

For example, let's say you have a net ordinary business income (profit) after expenses and deductions before shareholder salaries of $150,000 and a reasonable salary of $60,000. From there, we look at all household income sources such as your spouse's income and withholdings, rental income, pension income and anything else that is material to your tax world.

Then we create a mock tax return (the tax plan). That's right! We extrapolate all this data, pump it into a tax return and determine your current year tax obligations. We do this periodically throughout the year. Nothing is as accurate as a mock tax return. Yes, you can use Excel or other online estimators, but a tax return is the best tool.

Then we crunch some more numbers. Here is a summary from our internal work paper with some assumptions-

Taxable Income	184,718
Income Tax Calculation	33,606
Less Other Withholding Sources	-8,000
Household Tax Deficit	25,606
Less W-2 From S Corp	-26,500
Less Estimated Tax Payments	0
April Tax Obligation (Federal)	-874

What the heck are we showing you here? The taxable income is making some assumptions such as spousal income, itemized deductions, exemptions, etc. The $184,718 is just a number. Please accept as is.

The tax related to this income is $33,606 according to the mock tax return and your spouse has withheld $8,000 on his or her W-2. The resulting household tax deficit in this example is $25,606. If we simply entered $60,000 into the payroll system and let payroll tables figure out the withholdings it might come up with $7,000ish. This would be a tax surprise in April since you would owe $18,000ish. Yuck. Bad news is OK. Surprises are bad.

This is because the payroll computer does not know about your K-1 income. The net ordinary business income after expenses and deductions from your S Corp tax return. Generally, when you have multiple income sources, especially ones without a withholding component such as K-1's and rentals, relying on payroll tables to determine withholdings is woefully inaccurate.

You could also have income disparity. For example, let's say you earn $150,000 and your spouse earns $30,000. When your spouse's employer computes tax withholdings, the payroll system does not understand that the household income is $180,000. It can only make basic assumptions. In this disparity, even if the $30,000 spouse claims 0 exemptions on a W-4 (max withholdings), the taxes withheld will not be enough when combined with the $150,000.

Our tax planning and income tax withholdings adjustments fix this.

To summarize, we compute your household tax liability and subtract external withholding sources to determine the amount of tax to be withheld from your S Corp payroll. No more estimated payments (usually). No more underpayment penalties. This is a nice way of reducing some chores in your world.

Payroll Adjustments

There are various payroll adjustments throughout the year. Let's say you onboard with WCG in February. We are going to do a quickie calculation of the reasonable salary and income tax withholdings to get things launched. However, in May, June or July (tax planning months) we are going to dig into the details, prepare the tax plan and make an adjustment to your payroll processing.

Another common scenario is where you might not be able to accurately predict your business activity for the year. For example, a real estate agent in March has no idea how much he or she will earn for the year. But in October and November, there is enough history to predict the future. What we do with this is use a small salary such as $500 per month to check the box, and then make adjustments in July and certainly in November.

Yet another situation is the S Corp owner who is experiencing rocket growth. If we use the previous year as a proxy for the first half of the next year (which is common), a large adjustment must be made in July to account for the growth. The adjustment is not necessarily about salary as it is about tax planning and income tax withholdings.

A common question is "Does it look bad if my salary changes throughout the year?" The answer is simply No. Think of sales and commissions or bonuses. Many professionals and other employees see varying incomes throughout the year. Also, the IRS looks at things in aggregate, and assumes that income and taxes withheld were evenly paid throughout the year. Big swings in income from year to year is certainly a trigger for audits, but a mid-year salary adjustment is not that.

Estimated Tax Payments

Our goal is to increase income tax withholdings to account for your overall household tax obligations. However, there are times when this doesn't work well, and separate estimated tax payments are necessary. There are two primary reasons for this.

First, you have a low salary relative to your solo 401k plan contribution. For example, a reasonable shareholder salary of $36,000 is determined. You are 52 years old, and want to defer $23,000 (for the 2024 tax year) plus catch-up of $7,500 for a total of $30,500. That leaves $5,500 for Social Security, Medicare and income tax withholdings. Never going to happen, so a separate estimated tax payment will be needed.

The other reason is similar to the above; your shareholder salary is low compared to your K-1 (which is net ordinary business income after expenses and deductions). For example, your W-2 is $100,000 but your K-1 is $500,000. Yes, you have employees so you are not being limited on the Section 199A qualified business income deduction. No, you don't have enough "room" on your paycheck to increase income tax withholdings to cover the taxes associated with $600,000 in gross income. Even if your effective tax rate with the IRS and the state was only 20%, which is low, it still doesn't work with a $100,000 W-2.

Unemployment and Workers Compensation
We addressed these issues in Chapter 4 (Additional Payroll Taxes, page 140). Please review. Here is a summary of the topics-

▲ FUTA and SUTA- unemployment tax. Unavoidable. You might be able to opt out, and as the Minnesota example illustrates, there is a tax savings.

▲ SDI- state disability insurance. Might be able to opt out for single-owner corporate officers such as California and New York.

▲ Workers Compensation Insurance- has nothing to do with unemployment or state disability insurance, and is not interchangeable with those terms. This is purely insurance coverage for on-the-job injuries and is provided by private insurance such as State Farm, All State, Farmers, etc. Ask your local insurance agent if you can opt out. Typically, you can since you don't plan no suing yourself for a paper cut or a rogue paperclip stabbing.

Salary First, Distributions and Loans Second
We wanted to throw this at you as well. Shareholders must be paid a salary before any shareholder distributions are paid out or loans are advanced to shareholders. This requirement is a technicality. You can take a shareholder distribution as an S Corp owner prior to paying a salary to yourself throughout the year. At the end of the year, however, you must have W-2 income if you received shareholder distributions.

If the business cannot afford to pay salaries, it is not necessarily required to do so. There is some gray area involving large depreciation expenses and other non-cash reductions in business income. So, if you have a pile of cash but experience a loss due to large depreciation, for example, you might still be required to pay salaries. If you believe your business won't be profitable, then we suggest deferring the S Corp election to another tax year. Remember there are provisions allowing a late S Corp election beyond the customary 75-day limitation- take advantage of this option by delaying your election if you are unsure.

Minimum Payroll with December Bonus
Small business owners can face some payroll challenges. First, it can be difficult to determine a salary amount for you on January 1st, because salary amounts are somewhat dependent on your business' financial health, and that in turn can be impacted by seasonal or unpredictable revenue. Think of a realtor whose sales can vary depending on the time of

year, and the roller coaster that is the real estate market. You don't want to overpay shareholder salaries since every $10,000 in salary is potentially $1,500 in unnecessary payroll taxes. That's problem #1.

Second, cash flow might be lumpy and bumpy, and therefore monthly payroll processing might strain cash reserves. This is common with realtors, like the example above, but it is also common for a lot of consultants or similar professions where you rely on contracts, invoices, purchase order approvals, partial or installment payments, and all the madness in between. Problem #2.

Last, payroll processing cannot be skipped since some states will close your payroll accounts if you do not process "enough" payroll during the quarter. This in turn creates a mess. Additionally, it is inefficient to turn payroll on and off from month to month. Problem #3.

One solution is to pay a minimum salary of $500 per month to the shareholders on an autopilot system. This solves all the problems listed above. Yay! Next, an off-cycle bonus is paid in December using hindsight to "true up" reasonable salary for the entire year.

Also, the beauty of payroll processing and leveraging it to pay income taxes in lieu of estimated tax payments is that the IRS and the state assume salary and income taxes were paid evenly throughout the year regardless of when payroll was processed and the amounts. This approach prevents underpayment penalties but provides flexibility with your cash plus the ability to earn some interest income.

Here is a summary of how minimum payroll with a December bonus works with WCG-

▲ We get "mins payroll" going and set on autopilot.

▲ We chat and determine a high and low business profit expectation so we can loosely determine a tax plan for the year. A payroll plan is also created showing the anticipated annual shareholder salary including the big December off-cycle bonus (what we call the OCB).

▲ Using the tax plan, we determine a "safety percentage" that you set aside when commissions or payments are received. For example, you receive a $10,000 commission check into your business. You set aside or earmark 25% (let's say) or $2,500 for the December bonus.

▲ The remainder is used to pay business expenses and can be taken out as a shareholder distribution. You can also "prepay" your 401k employee contribution to leverage dollar cost averaging (but there is some danger here that we can discuss).

▲ In November, we chat again and use year to date business profit plus the tiny predicted remaining business profit to help update the reasonable shareholder salary for the entire year. From there, we process the OCB.

Having said that, we prefer to have routine and even salary amounts each month if possible. Minimum payroll processing takes discipline to pay out the December bonus.

Taking Shareholder Distributions

The IRS and Tax Court do not like to see you use your business as an ATM machine. This is not because you just said automated teller machine machine. This is because the spirit of a shareholder distribution is to be a return on investment, and if it is magically tied to personal living expenses it looks bad. Think of it this way- you wouldn't call up Google and demand a dividend because baby needs new shoes, or the boat payment is due. Same thing here.

Another perspective- Apple shareholders are routinely upset because of the cash that Apple hoards. There are two ways to get a return on investment- capital appreciation (and subsequent sale) and dividends. If there are piles of cash and there aren't immediate or mid-term needs for the cash, shouldn't that be returned to investors who helped build the cash to begin with?

What do you do? One option is to take systematic shareholder distributions throughout the year, and flush out the remainder once a quarter or annually. Another option is simply distribute large chunks periodically without any cadence or basis that can be tied to personal living expenses. WCG prefers the first option. Looks clean. Defensible.

> Sidebar: Lenders do not like to see a bunch of cash in your S corporation bank account. If you are looking to buy a house in the next six months, drain your business bank account down to the operational minimum. Lenders see $100,000 in the business account and they assume the business needs this. You roll up and say you are going to take it all out for a down payment. Now the sales prevention team (i.e., underwriting) thinks your business will suddenly fail which cuts off your ability to service your debt. Next thing you know we must write letters explaining that your business won't fail because of this cash drain, and it becomes a big headache for everyone.

Here is another consideration. If you pile up money for a handful of years, and then flush it all out in one year, the relationship between income, reasonable shareholder salary and distributions will be unbalanced. Keep in mind that one of the criteria the IRS and the Tax Court use to test the reasonableness of a shareholder salary is the comparison between salaries and distributions. You don't get rollover credits for all those years where you didn't take out distributions, and while you can demonstrate the problem in support of your salary why have the conversation at all?

Bottomline- do not leave cash laying around in your business. Earmark it for future short-term purchase, put that money to use immediately, or put it in your personal savings account or retirement fund. Business owners routinely use their business checking account as a personal savings account. Bad. Don't do it. Run your business like a business, and make sure retained cash has a purpose! Idle business cash has very little upside unless you have a capital expenditure or some other near-future use.

We recently had a client who had a particularly good year. For sake of discussion, let's say the client had net business income (profit) of about $250,000 before a reasonable shareholder salary. He had a one-and-done project that boosted his net business income to over $800,000. His salary was $90,000, and remained unchanged, leaving about $710,000 in distributable cash (he didn't have a Section 199A QBI optimization problem).

During our planning meetings, everyone felt uncomfortable distributing more than about $200,000. However, he didn't want the remaining $510,000 to be idle as cash. Had he taken the full $710,000 out as a shareholder distribution, he was going to invest about $500,000 of it anyway. As such, the recommendation was to leave $510,000 in the business and invest this cash the same way he was planning, but in the name of the business. The plan will be to slowly redeem his investments and distribute this windfall over a handful of years (versus all at once). Same result. Much lower IRS risk.

A common question that is also asked is "If I take too much out, can I return some of the shareholder distribution back to the business?" Yes, you can. This is very common actually. Not elegant or ideal, but common. Things happen. No, this is a shareholder loan or additional paid in capital. It is a return of excess distributions. Keep it simple.

Reclassify Shareholder Distributions

Since payroll might be late to the S Corp party during the first year, at times we need to re-classify prior shareholder distributions as shareholder wages (and perhaps employee reimbursements).

Here is a sample journal entry for an S Corp shareholder who took out $20,000 as a shareholder distribution, but later reclassified the transaction as shareholder distributions, wages and employee reimbursements.

	DR	CR
Shareholder Distributions		8,950
Shareholder Wage Expense	7,000	
Employee Reimbursements	1,950	
Totals	8,950	8,950

When the original distribution took place, there was a debit to Shareholder Distributions for $20,000 and a credit to Cash for the same. We are simply reducing the $20,000 by $8,950 so the actual distribution reflects $20,000 less $8,950 or $11,050.

In other words, Shareholder Distributions was a negative $20,000 in the equity section of your business's balance sheet. After increasing Shareholder Wage Expense by $7,000 and Employee Reimbursements by $1,950, net ordinary business income is reduced by $8,950. This naturally reduces equity by the same amount therefore Shareholder Distributions must be reduced so equity remains unchanged. No adjustment is made to Cash. Make sense? Don't worry... we can provide these journal entries as necessary. We are just geeking out on our own silly accounting fun.

[exciting white space]

If we were putting this transaction into the books together from the start, it would look this starting with the shareholder distribution-

	DR	CR
Shareholder Distributions	11,050	
Cash		11,050
Totals	11,050	11,050

Then the Shareholder Wage Expense and Employee Reimbursements-

	DR	CR
Shareholder Wage Expense	7,000	
Employee Reimbursements	1,950	
Cash		8,950
Totals	8,950	8,950

Everything would end up in the same spot- Shareholder Distributions at $11,050, Owner Wage Expense at $7,000 and Employee Reimbursements at $1,950. Cash spent would be $20,000. The only difference is the first example is a correcting or reversing entry.

This sample is a slight over-simplification since there would also be a Payroll Tax Expense entry for the business's portion of Social Security, Medicare, Unemployment, etc. but you get the idea.

Accountable Plan Expense Reimbursements

An Accountable Plan, under IRC Section 1.62-2(C)(2), allows a business to reimburse an employee for expenses incurred in connected with the performance of duties for the business provided proper substantiation is followed (receipts, mileage logs, home office proof, the usual stuff). The substantiation rules are the same for taxpayers in general, but with an Accountable Plan, the "enforcer" is technically the business.

Here are some expenses from the Internal Revenue Code, Chapter 1, Subchapter B, Part VI: Itemized Deductions for Individuals and Corporations that you might find interesting-

Trade or business expenses	Section 162
Interest expense	Section 163
Taxes	Section 164

Bad Debts	Section 166
Depreciation	Section 167
Cost recovery	Section 168
Amortization of lease acquisition costs	Section 178
Section 179 expensing	Section 179
Start-up expenditures	Section 195

This is a very abbreviated list.

The typical reimbursed expenses through an Accountable Plan are home office use including depreciation, mileage or business-use portion of automobile expenses, cell phone and internet. All these expenses have one thing in common- they are mixed used, both personally and business. Mixed-use expenses should be paid by the employee and later reimbursed. Conversely, anything that is 100% business use should be paid for directly by the business.

The following is saying the same thing, but in bullet form-

▲ 100% business- Paid by the business, from the business checking account.

▲ 100% personal- Paid by you, from your personal checking account.

▲ Mixed- Paid by you, and reimbursed by the business for the business portion.

Of course, if you are reaping some huge cash back or travel deals with your personal credit card, then by all means charge the 100% business use items to your personal card and run those expenses through an Accountable Plan.

> Sidebar: The IRS and credit card businesses are butting heads over the rebate programs. It is an ascension of wealth and could technically be taxable income. Whoa! Yup, and the IRS would like 1099s to be issued to show the income. Today, these credit card rebates are considered a reduction in purchase price. This will be battled for the next decade for sure.

Remember that as an S corporation owner, you are both a shareholder and an employee. Therefore, when you are being reimbursed you are being reimbursed as an employee and not as a shareholder.

Also, recall that with the Tax Cuts & Jobs Act of 2017, unreimbursed employee expenses and anything else that was deductible subject to the 2% adjusted gross income limitation are gone after 2017. Therefore, some of this argument is moot and essentially makes deducting expenses at the S corporation level by being reimbursed all that more important… well, since it is the only option.

An Accountable Plan is easy to do, is a great way to pull money out of the business and reduces the amount of taxes paid. Keep in mind too that by reducing your overall net ordinary business income you are also reducing one of the criteria for the reasonable salary testing, and this in turn possibly decreases your salary (and subsequent Social Security and Medicare taxes). A win-win scenario.

Make life easy, get an Accountable Plan. Make life even easier, have us prepare this corporate document and the associated corporate governance documents. WCG charges $150 which includes consultation on how to leverage the most from it.

Accountable Plan Requirements

The Accountable Plan is usually drafted as a business policy and later adopted through Corporate Minutes, if your underlying entity is a corporation, and the plan satisfies three basic IRS requirements: a business connection; substantiation; and return of excess amounts-

Business Connection

The expense must have a business connection. Typically, expenses incurred by an employee while doing his or her job usually have a business connection. It might be a good idea to list some examples of things such as home office, cell phone, internet, mileage and meals. Health insurance premiums should be paid by the business directly; however, some states might require premiums to certain state-sponsored plans to be paid individually. In this case, these would be reimbursed through an Accountable Plan.

You could also list conditions and parameters for reimbursement. Must answer phone calls outside the office to claim a cell phone reimbursement. Or only mileage to and from client meetings, delivering product, running errands for supplies, etc. The more comprehensive the allowable business connections, the safer your plan will be.

Proper Substantiation

The employee must adequately account for the business for expenses within a reasonable time. Adequate accounting means completing expense reports and providing the business with receipts, invoices, and other documentary evidence of the expenses. Using a separate credit card and requesting credit card statements is a great recordkeeping technique.

There are special substantiation rules for meals, business gifts and anything considered "listed property." We can help you with these situations if necessary.

Return of the Excess Reimbursement
The employee must return to the business any excess reimbursements within a reasonable time. While this is not an issue if you are reimbursed only for what you request (what we accountants call after-the-fact reimbursements), you should still detail this policy in your Accountable Plan. Many businesses provide a monthly stipend to cover expenses, and employees are required to return unused portions.

Here is a timeline according to the IRS-

▲ An advance may be received within 30 days of the time of the expense.

▲ The employee furnishes an adequate account of expenses within 60 days after they were paid or incurred.

▲ The employee returns any excess reimbursement within 120 days after it was paid or incurred.

The Accountable Plan should address the above issues, and it should be drafted as business policy for all employees. While different employee groups and individual employees can have different plans, you should draft this policy while distancing it from any favoritism towards the shareholder employees.

For a sample Accountable Plan Excel template and other goodies that you can review please see-

wcginc.com/APlan

Shareholder Distributions as Reimbursements
We would prefer that employee reimbursements through an Accountable Plan be done as a single check or transfer from the business checking account into your personal checking account (as the employee). This makes the accounting very straightforward- you debit Employee Reimbursements and credit Cash. If you are using QuickBooks, you categorize the check or transfer as Employee Reimbursements with splits for each sub account (home office, mileage, cell phone, internet, etc.).

This is the most elegant.

Otherwise, the processing of an Accountable Plan can be done at the end of each quarter to basically reclassify owner or shareholder distributions as employee reimbursements. For example, let's say you took out $20,000 over the quarter as distributions. But after completing the Accountable Plan Reimbursement, the business owed you $5,000. We would make an entry to reflect the reimbursement, and your shareholder distributions would be re-classified as a $15,000 distribution (taxable) and a $5,000 reimbursement (non-taxable).

Here is a sample journal entry for an S Corp shareholder who took out $20,000 as a shareholder distribution, but later re-categorized the transaction as distributions, wages and employee reimbursements.

	DR	CR
Shareholder Distributions		8,950
Owner Wage Expense	7,000	
Employee Reimbursements	1,950	
Totals	8,950	8,950

When the original distribution took place, there was a debit to Shareholder Distributions for $20,000 and a credit to Cash for the same. We are simply reducing the $20,000 by $8,950 so the actual distribution reflects $20,000 less $8,950 or $11,050. No adjustment is made to Cash. Make sense?

If we were putting this transaction into the books together from the start, it would look this starting with the shareholder distribution-

	DR	CR
Shareholder Distributions	11,050	
Cash		11,050
Totals	11,050	11,050

And then the Owner Wage Expense and Employee Reimbursements-

	DR	CR
Owner Wage Expense	7,000	
Employee Reimbursements	1,950	
Cash		8,950
Totals	8,950	8,950

Everything would end up in the same spot- Shareholder Distributions at $11,050, Owner Wage Expense at $7,000 and Employee Reimbursements at $1,950. Cash spent would be $20,000. The only difference is the first example is a correcting or reversing entry.

This is a slight over-simplification since there would also be a Payroll Tax Expense entry for the business's portion of Social Security, Medicare, Unemployment, etc. but this should be illustrative enough.

The "look back" at the end of the quarter might not work if you provide a stipend or some other advance to your employees throughout the period. This is due to the time limits imposed on the substantiation requests and returns of excess reimbursements. Try to avoid the advance or stipend approach.

While the single check or bank transfer is ideal and elegant as we mentioned earlier, Accountable Plan reimbursements are commonly done at tax return preparation. Just like the example above, we reclassify some shareholder distributions as employee expense reimbursements.

The downside to this approach, and why the quarterly method is preferred, is that it throws off tax planning. If we are bouncing along thinking you are going to earn $100,000 but in reality it is $80,000 after Accountable Plan expenses are reimbursed, this could easily swing your tax obligations by $4,000 to $5,000. Sure, it would be in your favor as a tax refund, but it is still not ideal tax planning.

S Corp Tax Return Preparation

An S Corp must file a corporate tax return (Form 1120S) by March 15 and there are additional financial reporting requirements. Since an S corporation is a pass-through entity whereby the tax consequences are passed through to the shareholders, the individual tax returns (Form 1040) of the shareholders cannot be completed until the S Corp tax return is completed (both can be filed simultaneously). However, if you use **WCG CPAs & Advisors** to prepare your tax returns, we'll make it seamless and pain free. Ok, taxes and pain free don't really go together, but you get the idea.

Balance Sheet (Schedule L)

S corporations file a Form 1120S and this in turn creates K-1s for all the shareholders. Unlike many other tax professionals, we always create a balance sheet, and we always reconcile equity accounts (capital stock, additional paid in capital, retained earnings, shareholder distributions and basis). This can be challenging for us, but we feel it is important for you, the client, and for long-term reporting accuracy.

Creating a balance sheet is also just good accounting practice, and it contributes to the overall tracking of your business's worth. Lenders and investors will also want to see this information if you need leveraged financial assistance for business growth. Recently, a business owner was gifting away chunks of her business to her sons, and her basis needed to be calculated and transferred for gift tax filings. Her balance sheet information was a mess and needed fixing. We are retained frequently to put humpty dumpty back together and build historical balance sheet information.

Business succession, exit strategies, asset sales, business valuation, buy-sell agreements, etc. are topics rarely considered by most small business owners, and that is okay. But as accountants and business consultants, it is our job to keep you out of future trouble by putting things on the right track today. That starts with your corporate tax returns being comprehensively and accurately prepared, which includes Schedule L (the balance sheet). While we don't look for ways to complicate the heck out of things, demand that your tax professional prepare a balance sheet with your tax returns.

Shareholder Basis

When you own an S corporation, you are both employee and investor. If you invested $100 into Google, you could only lose $100. Nothing more. The same with your S Corp as an investor. For example, if you invested $10,000 into your business, but your business lost $20,000, your K-1 will show a $20,000 loss but you are only allowed to deduct the loss to the limit of your basis which is $10,000. Without tracking this information, you could be incorrectly deducting losses in the current year instead of carrying them forward to future years.

More importantly, without shareholder basis information, there is no way to determine the gain on your future business sale. Just like stock sales, when you sell your business for a zillion dollars the IRS will consider all that to be capital gain unless you can prove otherwise.

We'll dig a little deeper into shareholder distributions in excess of basis, and the problems that occur next.

Distributions in Excess of Basis

Sounds ominous doesn't it? It can be a big ol' pain in the tax butt frankly. What the heck are we talking about?

We described this in Chapter 4 (Distributions in Excess of Shareholder Basis, page 157) in good detail but the simple nuts and bolts of shareholder distributions in excess of basis goes like this- let's say you inject $1,000 into your business as startup capital, and your business has a net ordinary business income after expenses and deductions of $20,000. Your shareholder basis is $21,000. However, due to some interesting accounting dynamics, your business has $30,000 in cash and you distribute $25,000 as shareholder distributions.

You just triggered a shareholder distribution in excess of basis by $4,000 ($25,000 less $21,000), and this creates a capital gain and associated taxes.

Two of the top three reasons this occurs are depreciation and loans which separately create a cash greater than income situation. And the third reason shareholder distributions in excess of basis is bad historical basis data.

Please refer to Chapter 4 for more details. Keep in mind that a shareholder distribution in excess of basis is not always a bad thing; it is taxed as a capital gain which might be leveraged well on a tax return for certain taxable events and positions.

Minimize Tax or Maximize Value (Economic Benefit)

As mentioned elsewhere in this book, we encourage people to focus on building wealth and if they can save taxes along the way, then that is just icing on the cake. What do we mean here? Often, we see business owners who want to minimize their tax obligation rather than maximizing their business value, and this can be problematic in two areas; lending and selling.

Lending is more straightforward so we will tackle that first. If you are prone to pump a lot of personal expenses such as cars, computers, business trips that have a huge personal component, and other deductions through your business, your taxable income will be decreased. So, when the IRS shakes you down, you calmly say, "all these deductions have a business purpose and are considered ordinary and necessary." Then you go visit the bank, and you calmly say to the lender, "all these deductions really aren't business related and as such they shouldn't affect my credit worthiness or ability to pay a loan."

Can you see the pickle you are in between minimizing tax and maximizing value?

Selling a business is slightly different. To determine the value of a business, most valuations need to determine seller's discretionary cash flow (SDCF) which is also considered the net economic benefit. One technique is to start with taxable income, and then make adjustments such as adding back interest expense, depreciation and amortization. Officer compensation and perquisites (the fancy word for perks) are also checked for reasonableness; so, if personal expenses are being rifled through the business, these expenses are added back as well to increase SDCF. There are other adjustments as well, but these are the biggies.

It gets sticky again when the seller provides a general ledger of all his or her transactions, and starts highlighting a ton of stuff "reversing" tax deductions and reclassifying them as personal expenses. A few things here and there are fine, but if there are several material adjustments to SDCF at the request of the seller arguing that the expenses are truly a form of economic benefit to the seller (and future buyer) the credibility of the data starts to wane.

To recap, lenders want net economic benefit to support debt service. Buyers want net economic benefit because that is what he or she is essentially buying (future cash flow / economic benefit). As such, be careful how much you focus on minimizing tax versus maximizing value if you intend to leverage your business for lending purposes (even buying a house counts) or selling purposes.

Tracking Fringe Benefits

Before we go too far down the road, your business needs to track the amounts paid for fringe benefits so they may be included as Officer Compensation on Line 7 of your S Corp tax return and Box 1 of your W-2. Specifically-

▲ Self-employed health insurance premiums,

▲ Health Savings Account (HSA) contributions made by the business

▲ Health Reimbursement Arrangement (HRA) reimbursements, and

▲ Personal use of business assets such as automobiles and airplanes.

There are others, but these are the biggies. If you are using accounting software or even Excel, each of these should be a separate category. If you wanted to get fancy, you could have an account labeled "Officer Compensation" with sub-accounts being Wages, health insurance, HSA, HRA and Other.

In QuickBooks-ese, it would look like this-

Officer Compensation : Wages
Officer Compensation : Health Insurance
Officer Compensation : HSA
Officer Compensation : HRA
Officer Compensation : Other

At tax time, your profit and loss statement would then be framed and hung on our smart client wall. Yes, we have a not-so-smart client wall too which is thankfully much smaller since it is temporary until we give you the "see… how it works is…" tutoring during a Periodic Business Review.

Other Tricks of the Trade with S Corps

The big theme with S Corps is payroll for shareholders, and what constitutes a reasonable salary. Here are some tricks that you can consider to help reduce, lower or avoid self-employment tax, or Social Security and Medicare tax burdens-

A Shareholder Who Has Other W-2 Income

If you have other W-2 income then you are that much closer to reaching your Social Security wage limit. This in itself is not a trick. But, if you have a business partner who doesn't have W-2 income, then you can lop side the salary to the shareholder who does. This is especially helpful with a husband and wife team since office politics won't get in the way. For example, the wife has another job and earns $120,000. Her S Corp salary may be much higher than the husband's since she is closer to the Social Security cap (which is $168,600 for the 2024 tax year).

Huh? Let's say the S corporation had to pay out $70,000 in shareholder wages. The employer portion of Social Security and Medicare taxes are a sunk cost regardless of who is paid. However, if the spouse with outside income is paid and he or she exceeds the Social Security limit for the employee's portion of Social Security taxes, that overage is refunded to the taxpayer.

Of course, salaries must be commensurate with each shareholder's skill level, hours worked, value to the business, etc. but there is some grey area to work with.

Husband and Wife Team with High Income

Let's say a husband and wife couple work in the IT field, and combined they earn $600,000. The S Corp could have just one shareholder, let's say the wife, and the husband is merely a volunteer employee. The wife's salary could be higher than the husband's since she is running the business and is the only shareholder. She would reach the Social Security cap much sooner, but this only works if the husband's salary can remain below the cap.

Let's illustrate this further-

▲ Option A- Pay husband and wife $120,000 each for a total of $240,000. All $240,000 would be subjected to Social Security and Medicare taxes.

▲ Option B- Pay wife $200,000 and husband $40,000. Only $168,600 (for the 2024 tax year) plus $40,000 for total of $208,600 would be subjected to Social Security and Medicare taxes. This $31,400 difference in income subject to Social Security and Medicare taxes between Option A and Option B equates to about $4,800 in cash in your pocket savings.

Again, salaries must be commensurate for the work performed. A cool thing about making the wife the sole shareholder is that the business could gain benefits from being minority owned or considered "disadvantaged" although those benefits are becoming rarer.

Be mindful of the possible reduction in future Social Security benefits from a smaller salary.

Put Your Kids on the Payroll

You can also reduce the business's overall profits by paying your children to work at the office and paying them a wage. You already have to perform payroll, so you can simply add them to the list. See earlier sections of this chapter and Chapter 11 (Putting Your Kids on the Payroll, page 334) on fringe benefits and tax deductions for expanded information about putting your kids on the payroll.

Family Management LLC

Similar to above, however, the S Corp pays a management fee to another LLC that is reported on Schedule C of Form 1040 (not an S Corp). Since this garden-variety LLC is not an S Corp, Social Security and Medicare taxes do not have to be paid on wages to children. $9,800 must be paid to the child(ren) to break-even on the costs. IRS risk is moderate since the business connection between the S Corp and the Family Management LLC might not be arms-length or in good faith.

You can also read our Reducing Taxes summary article here-

wcginc.com/6177

Income Splitting as Gift

You can make someone in a lower tax bracket a shareholder in your S Corp to give them money. For example, you are taking care of your Mom and need to give her $10,000 each year to help with expenses. You would need to earn $13,000 or more just to be able to write a check for $10,000. However, if your Mom is in a lower tax bracket, as a shareholder she would pay fewer taxes to pocket the $10,000. And when your Mom eventually passes, her ownership can transfer back to you.

Yes, you could justify not paying Mom a reasonable salary since she is not performing any work for the business. She is simply an investor. However, just like paying your children to work for you, there might be a tax savings by having Mom work- her marginal tax rate could be dramatically lower than yours. Good luck with the "Hey Mom. Want a job?" conversation. What goes around comes around.

Just remember, putting family members on payroll is heavily scrutinized. Make sure the basics such as job descriptions, pay rates, time records, etc. are all in very good order. Memories fade, so document it today!

Adding Your Spouse to Payroll

We get a lot of calls and emails from business owners who ask about adding their spouse to payroll. There are several reasons where this might make sense, but there are also some pitfalls and things you need to be aware of. Here is a quick list of benefits we will get into, and right after this we'll discuss the problems.

▲ Expenses such as meals, business travel, mileage, cell phones, etc. have more deduction capability.

▲ Increase 401k plan or SEP IRA contributions as a household.

▲ Social security arbitrage.

▲ Dependent care credits.

▲ Leverage the minority owned small business benefits (usually with government contracts). Becoming more rare these days.

▲ Reduce income base for operating spouse and subsequent reasonable salary testing (huh? Don't worry... we'll explore this more).

Problems with Adding Spouse to Payroll

The biggest problem to adding your spouse to payroll is the additional payroll taxes. Before we jump too far into that, let's talk about how we would determine a reasonable salary if we were adding your spouse to payroll. One of the ways we determine reasonable shareholder salary is by the value of the tasks and duties being performed by the shareholder. This is similar to a market approach analysis that RCReports performs (see Chapter 9 which is dedicated to reasonable shareholder salaries).

So, we take some of those tasks and duties, split them up between spouses and then we maintain the same total Officer Compensation between two people. Huh? Ok, let's say Susan is being paid $100,000 by her S Corp. Her husband comes along and does some of Susan's tasks like bookkeeping and licking stamps. Stamp licking is high-end work. We would then pay Susan $80,000 and her husband would be paid $20,000 for a total of $100,000. Let's call her husband Mark, the chief stamp licker. There are worse things to be, Mark.

Think of Officer Compensation or reasonable S Corp salary like a pie, and we are just chopping it up into different pieces, some small, some large.

In this example, Social Security and Medicare taxes would be the same between paying just Susan, and paying Susan and Mark together. However, if Susan is being paid $190,000 and we now allocate $20,000 of that to Mark, we just generated an extra 6.2% x $20,000 in Social Security taxes on Mark because Susan's original salary already exceed the Social Security cap for the 2024 tax year of $168,600. Therefore, this would create unnecessary Social Security taxes... that is bad in case you were wondering seeing how reducing Social Security is one of the pillars of our book.

Also, unemployment is determined on each employee. So, Susan's unemployment tax is unavoidable and might amount to $350 to $500 depending on her state. Unemployment is similar to Social Security since it has a wage limit, and several states are very low such as $11,000 or so. By adding Mark to the payroll, we suddenly add $350 to $500 in unemployment insurance tax. That too is bad... but not too bad as compared to the possible tax benefits (be patient, we are getting there).

To make things worse, some states have a state disability insurance like California. This piles on to the unemployment insurance tax problem explained above.

Don't forget that if your spouse is already working somewhere else and receiving a W-2, he or she will be "contributing to" unemployment all over again by being added to the family business. However, there might be some tax arbitrage explained below.

Business Tax Deductions and Fringe Benefits
Dinners with your spouse could be booked as a business meeting making your meals expense 50% deductible (the 100% deductibility ended in 2022). You likely talk about the business all the time, right? Keep in mind that what makes business meals deductible is that you were meeting to discuss business regardless, and a meal happened to be consumed at the same time. Business purpose first, meal second in terms of the impetus.

Business travel to conferences or other business-related trips can be 100% deductible when your spouse is also an employee. Business trips to Fiji? Probably not. There are rules on extravagance.

What is the break-even on this? Assuming $500 of additional payroll taxes and a marginal tax bracket of 32%, you need $1,600ish of additional expenses that would otherwise be non-deductible. A $100 meal every two weeks gets you to $2,600. You were already spending the $100 every two weeks, and not it becomes deductible. Nice!

Please refer to Chapter 11 on tax deductions and fringe benefits.

401k Plans, SEP IRAs and Social Security
401k plan contributions and other benefits could be extended to your spouse. Currently, employees can defer $23,000 (for the 2024 tax year) plus another $7,500 if they are 50 or older. So, using our example before and assuming Susan is 50, she can defer $30,500 into her 401k. The business could also add another $25,000 (25% of $100,000) as a discretionary contribution for a total of $55,500. Not bad.

If we add Mark to the mix, this $55,500 becomes $86,000 ($55,500 plus $30,500) and it only "cost" you about $300 to $500 in additional payroll taxes. Said in another way, Mark could contribute $30,500 at a 32% marginal tax rate and defer over $9,760 in taxes, and it cost him $300 to $500 in insidious payroll taxes to do so. Not bad.

How would the salaries look in the scenario? We would pay Susan $65,000 and Mark $35,000. They each defer $30,500 into the 401k plan. The business adds another 25% of the combined salaries into the 401k (so, that doesn't change in either scenario).

Table time!

	Option A	Option B	
	Susan	Susan	Mark
Salary	100,000	65,000	35,000
401k Deferral	30,500	30,500	30,500
Business Contribution	25,000	16,250	8,750
Total 401k	55,500	86,000	

Also recall that solo 401k plans often allow spouses to pool their assets (some even allow separate accounts). If you need help with this, let us know. Contrary to some belief, you do not need two solo 401k plans and you don't need the full version company-sponsored 401k plan unless you hire a person besides the spouses.

We sometimes consider solo 401k contributions and retirement planning as more qualitative than quantitative. Remember, pre-tax retirement contributions are only tax deferrals- IOU's to the IRS that they patiently wait to collect when you retire. Therefore, when you withdraw retirement money you have to pay taxes. As such, the six-million-dollar question is what are marginal tax rates today versus marginal tax rates in retirement.

The theory is that you take these interest-free IOU's and parlay them into building wealth. Don't forget the benefit of deferring state taxes that you might not ever pay back if you relocate for retirement (Pennsylvania has caught on to this trick, and does not give you a tax deferral for 401k plans... no wonder the Eagles stink).

While **WCG CPAs & Advisors** defers to your financial planner, we strongly recommend Roth contributions into your 401k plan. High contribution amounts ($23,000 + $7,500 catch-up) and no income phase out like a typical Roth IRA. Is it easier to work today to pay a little bit more in taxes, or is it preferred to pull money from savings during your retirement years to pay for taxes? We discuss this more in Chapter 12 (Roth 401k Versus Traditional 401k Considerations, page 370).

Each spouse can be contributing to his and her respective Social Security basis and obtain Medicare coverage independently. Some people especially in their 50s and perhaps 60s want to contribute to their Social Security basis. Sounds crazy, but each situation is unique and requires careful planning. So, perhaps this benefit is more of a qualified benefit.

Health Insurance
Some states require businesses to have a "plus 1" on payroll to be compliant on health insurance. Last time we checked on this, Texas was still one of them. As far as we understand the rule, as an S Corp you need to have "you plus 1 other" on payroll to be compliant with the state's health insurance rules. Adding your spouse might satisfy this.

You might also find that having separate health insurance policies is the way to go... better coverage, lower premiums, or both. But only the health insurance on those who are greater than 2% shareholders can be deducted as an adjustment to income (dollar for dollar) versus a crummy limited deduction on Schedule A. Therefore, in this case, your spouse not only needs to be added to payroll but he or she must also be added as a member or shareholder to get the full deduction of the health insurance premium.

Dependent Care Credit
To qualify for dependent care (like a childcare facility or pre-school) tax credits, both parents must be working, looking for work or be full-time students, or a combination. Therefore, creating a viable job description and having your spouse receive a paycheck allows you to be eligible for dependent care tax credits.

Social Security Arbitrage
There might be a situation where a bit of tax arbitrage can be taken advantage of. Let's say Susan is being paid $120,000 by her S Corp. Her husband, Mark, makes $180,000 elsewhere. If Susan's salary is reduced to $80,000 and Mark is added to payroll at $40,000 there will be a $2,480 savings in Social Security taxes. How? Magic.

As an employee, your wage limit for Social Security taxes is $168,600 (for the 2024 tax year). If for some reason (like two jobs) you have wages that were taxed for Social Security taxes in excess of $168,600, you get that refunded on your individual tax return. Only the employee gets the refund, not the employer(s).

So, throughout the year Mark will have $40,000 in wages that were taxed for Social Security taxes by the S Corp. Susan will have $40,000 less in wages being taxed for Social Security taxes. In other words, we essentially take the Social Security taxes that Susan was going to pay and we make Mark pay them, but he has other W-2 income that exceeds the wage limit, so these taxes are refunded.

$40,000 x 6.2% is $2,480. Boom!

Yes, Mark would need to actually do work and be valuable (a stretch, we know), and all those things, but you get the idea.

Spouse As Independent Contractor
Paying your spouse or your children for that matter as contractors can open a can of worms. First, they probably aren't truly a contractor. Generally, a contractor is someone who holds themselves out to the public as a person in that particular line of work or trade. Second, in the case of an S Corp you are now converting some income that was otherwise not subjected to Social Security and Medicare taxes, and making it so. In other words, you are changing the color of the money but in the wrong way.

Comingling of Money
We've mentioned this previously, and we'll do it again here. Rule #1- Please get a separate checking account for your business, preferably with the same bank as your personal checking account so transfers (shareholder distributions) are easy. Rule #2- Do not pay for personal expenses or any mixed-use expense with business funds.

This is bad for several reasons- the IRS hates it. It erodes the corporate veil which is already dangerously thin since you are a closely held corporation. Lastly, if you need to re-construct your financials because of a QuickBooks disaster or some other calamity, having your business transactions compartmentalized within a bank account makes life better. All money coming in is income. All money going out is an expense or a distribution (or equipment purchase or loan payment).

Read Rule #2 again. It is imperative to keep an arms-length perspective on you, the employee, and relationship with the S corporation. If you worked for Google or Ford, you wouldn't be able to get the business to buy your groceries or pay your mortgage directly. Same thing with your business. Please refer to Chapter 11 on tax deductions and fringe benefits for a nice table.

Chapter 11
Tax Deductions, Fringe Benefits
(updated November 2023)

Chapter Introduction
Ahh.. the good stuff. Yes, you work hard. Yes, you want to be able to get a little extra from your hard work and your business. Yes, you want this to be tax-advantaged. We get it. This chapter will discuss the 185 tax deductions you cannot take, explain how to position yourself on allowable small business tax deductions, and then get into hot topics such as automobiles, home offices, deducting MBAs, Cohan rule and other fun things.

This chapter is long, but it might be the most worthwhile (or at least sought after).

Four Basics to Warm Up To
Before we get into which tax deductions and tax moves you can take, there are some basic concepts to help formulate your thinking.

Marginal Tax Rate
Quick lesson on small business tax deductions. When you write a check and it has a tax savings element (office expense, 401k, IRA, charity, etc.) it is not a dollar-for-dollar savings. For example, if you are in the 22% marginal tax bracket, you must write a check for $4,000 just to save $880 in taxes. Keep this in mind as you read this information on tax deductions. Also keep in mind that cash is king, and that perhaps paying a few more taxes today with the added flexibility of cash in the bank can be comforting. More on this later in the chapter.

Cash Savings or Tax Savings
You can save $50,000 today! Yes, today! You just need to write a $150,000 check to your church. Huh? That might not sound like the best idea to a lot of people since so much cash is leaving. Another way to look at this is this- most people say "I want to save taxes" but really what they are saying is "I want to save cash."

In other words, most people are in the cash-saving business not the tax-saving business. If we can do both, great. However, most tax-savings moves take cash, and cash is what you want to keep. Please keep this concept in mind as you review business deductions below.

287

Building Wealth

At the end of your life, you'll measure your financial success on the wealth you built not the tax you saved. We agree that a part of wealth building includes tax savings, but be careful not to sacrifice wealth for the thrill of a tax deduction (or deferral). Here is an example- let's say you stuff all your available cash into a tax-advantaged retirement account such as a 401k. A few years go by and a great rental comes on the market but your cash is all tied up in a 401k. So, you sacrificed potential building of wealth by not having an intermediate investment strategy for the sake of tax deferrals.

The Trick

Here's the trick. The Holy Grail if you will. You need to find a way to deduct money you are already spending. Read that again. For example, if you have a travel budget then you are already comfortable with a certain amount of money leaving your person. Let's find a way to deduct it through your business.

Automobile depreciation? Same thing. You are already comfortable with automobiles losing thousands of dollars in value especially in the early years, so let's a find a way to make this degradation in value a tax windfall.

The remainder of this chapter is written to help educate yourself so the money you are already spending can be positioned in such a fashion that it becomes a legitimate small business tax deduction. Remember that the greatest trick the devil ever pulled was convincing the world he didn't exist. The second greatest trick was finding a way to deduct the expense. You gotta love The Usual Suspects. Classic!

Section 199A Deductions – Pass Through Tax Breaks

Section 199A deduction also known as the Qualified Business Income deduction arises from the Tax Cuts & Jobs Act of 2017. This is a significant tax break for small business owners but there are rules and limits of course.

Section 199, without the A, is the section covering Domestic Production Activities Deduction. Section 199A is seemingly modeled after this (or at least a portion was ripped off by legislators) since the mathematics and reporting is similar between Section 199A and Section 199.

Section 199A Qualified Business Income deduction is a deduction from gross income on Line 13 on Page 1 of your individual tax return (Form 1040) for the 2020 tax year. Please recall that it is a deduction on your tax return since there are personal limitations. Therefore, two owners of the same business might have different results.

Calculating the Qualified Business Income Deduction

The basic deduction is 20% of net qualified business income which is huge. If you make $200,000, the deduction is $40,000 times your marginal tax rate of 24% which equals $9,600 in your pocket. Who says Obamacare isn't affordable now? Here is the exact code-

(2) DETERMINATION OF DEDUCTIBLE AMOUNT FOR EACH TRADE OR BUSINESS. The amount determined under this paragraph with respect to any qualified trade or business is the lesser of-

(A) 20 percent of the taxpayer's qualified business income with respect to the qualified trade or business, or

(B) the greater of-

> (i) 50 percent of the W-2 wages with respect to the qualified trade or business, or

> (ii) the sum of 25 percent of the W-2 wages with respect to the qualified trade or business, plus 2.5 percent of the unadjusted basis immediately after acquisition of all qualified property.

This is just a primmer... or if you've read this book from the beginning then you already know this. For more crazy details refer to Chapter 7 and 8 which are dedicated to the Section 199A deduction.

185 Business Deductions You Cannot Take

Similar to the 185 reasons to not elect S corporation taxation, there aren't 185 small business deductions that you cannot take. However, we want to start with the crazy things small business owners try to do since it is such a good springboard for discussion.

100% Cell Phone

Most small businesses operate on a cell phone. However, most small business owners also use his or her cell phone as a personal phone. The minute you get the "Hey honey... we need milk and eggs" text message to your cell phone, it drops from 100% business use to something else.

If you attempt to deduct 100% of your cell phone as a small business tax deduction, the IRS will claim 0% and then force you to demonstrate why it should be something else. Conversely, if you approach this from a position of being reasonable it is extremely challenging for the IRS to argue otherwise. What is reasonable?

We usually start with a single phone line cost of about $150 per month in 2020 dollars. While it might only take $10 to add another line, you would still need to spend $150 for yourself. From there it becomes a preponderance of the facts and circumstances. Some people say there are 40 hours in a work week and there are 168 available hours (24 x 7).

However, this calculus assumes your personal use "density" is the same as your business use "density." For most business owners, this is not true. You probably talk longer with clients and business associates, than you do friends and family.

Anywhere from 50% to 80% is a good jumping off point. Since this is a mixed-use expense between personal and business, the cell phone charges should be paid by you personally and then reimbursed by the business for the business use portion through an Accountable Plan. See Chapter 10 on operating your S Corp for more details (Accountable Plan Expense Reimbursements, page 262).

We feel compelled to hammer this point home- if the expense is mixed-use, such as cell phones, the bill is paid for with personal funds, and then the business portion is reimbursed to you by the business. Same with automobiles that are shared between personal and business use (we'll remind you in a bit). Yes, it feels better using business funds, but No, you shouldn't unless the expense is 100% business.

Automobiles
Automobiles will be discussed in nauseating detail later in this chapter, and there is a decision tree as well to help determine if you should own it or the business. In keeping with the business tax deductions that are disallowed, claiming your only automobile as 100% business use is a tough sell.

Home Office Improvements
You cannot spend $30,000, finish your basement, plop your desk in the middle of it and deduct the $30,000 for two reasons. First, the entire space must be regularly and exclusively used as a home office. This means the theater room must be a conference room, and the wet bar must be the office kitchen. Might be tough in the world of small business tax deductions.

Second, even if the entire basement is designated business use, the $30,000 represents an improvement. Therefore, it must be capitalized as an asset and subsequently depreciated over 39 years. From there, only the business use portion of mortgage interest, property taxes, insurance, HOA dues and utilities are deductible. And if you have an S corporation, then this business expense is reimbursed to you by the business through an Accountable Plan (and therefore deductible by the business as an employee reimbursement expense).

Don't worry, the projection TV with the non-glare screen was still worth it. We'll talk more about home offices especially with multiple locations later in this chapter.

Food

More bad news. You cannot deduct your business meals unless you fall under one of two situations-

▲ You are entertaining a client, prospect or other business associate (or a small group such as 12), and discussing business matters, or

▲ You are away from your tax home where you require substantial rest (such as an overnight trip), and that trip has a business purpose.

As such, if you cruise through the Starbuck's drive-through and grab your triple grande vanilla breve on the way to your day meeting, no good. However, if you are traveling away from your tax home when on a business trip, then order the venti. Live a little.

Your small business tax deduction is limited to 50% under both circumstances (the 100% that we enjoyed for all meals was only for the 2021 and 2022 tax years, so we are back to the same old same old).

The theory on this is straightforward- you have to eat regardless of owning a business or not. In other words, your meal is not contributing directly to the operations or success of your business. The IRS is clever- they don't mind giving you a tax deduction today on something that eventually will result in taxable business income through growth and profits in the future. Think of it this way- if you had a regular W-2 job, you wouldn't be able to deduct your meals. Why would that change with your shiny new business or S corporation?

In reference to overnight travel or travel away from your tax home, your tax home is the location where you earn income. Here is the word for word description from IRS Publication 17-

To determine whether you are traveling away from home, you must first determine the location of your tax home.

Generally, your tax home is your regular place of business or post of duty, regardless of where you maintain your family home. It includes the entire city or general area in which your business or work is located.

If you have more than one regular place of business, your tax home is your main place of business.

If you do not have a regular or a main place of business because of the nature of your work, then your tax home may be the place where you regularly live.

If you do not have a regular or a main place of business or post of duty and there is no place where you regularly live, you are considered an itinerant (a transient) and your tax home is wherever you work. As an itinerant, you cannot claim a travel expense deduction because you are never considered to be traveling away from home.

Main place of business or work. If you have more than one place of business or work, consider the following when determining which one is your main place of business or work.

▲ The total time you ordinarily spend in each place.

▲ The level of your business activity in each place.

▲ Whether your income from each place is significant or insignificant.

There you have it. Overnight travel away from your tax home will create a nice business deduction for that beer sampler with pretzels and mustard dip. Spicy of course.

Here is a link to IRS Publication 17 (Your Federal Income Tax)-

wcginc.com/5324

Tax homes can get tricky especially if you travel a lot or have multiple job locations. More details are coming up in this chapter when we discuss home offices. Also, we can always help sort through it to find the best tax position.

Also, note the word "itinerant" above. Here is a snippet of the snippet-

If you do not have a regular or a main place of business or post of duty and there is no place where you regularly live, you are considered an itinerant (a transient) and your tax home is wherever you work. As an itinerant, you cannot claim a travel expense deduction because you are never considered to be traveling away from home.

WCG CPAs & Advisors have a lot of Certified Registered Nurse Anesthetists (CRNA) who travel all over the country putting people to sleep on short-term contracts, or stints if you are Formula 1 fan. Unless you return periodically to a place where you regularly live, you will not have a tax home. Without a tax home a lot of travel, lodging and meals deductions go away.

> Sidebar: CRNAs certainly take the cake on fun business names like Sleepy Times Ahead LLC and Passing Gas with Class LLC. Either they are clever, or some of the gas meant for the patient was accidentally inhaled by the medical professional. Perhaps it wasn't accidental. Who uses gas anymore? We digress...

Per Diem

Sole proprietors including single-member LLC owners, and partners are allowed to deduct the federal per diem rate for meals. Lodging can only be deducted using the actual cost of lodging. Where are S corporations? You are not going to like this. Employees of corporations are eligible for per diem allowances, reimbursements and deductions **unless** this same employee owns more than 10% of the corporation.

This means that most S corporation shareholders are hosed, and can only deduct (or get reimbursed) for actual meal costs. IRS Revenue Procedure 2011-47 has this limitation and IRS Publication 463 states in part "A per diem allowance satisfies the adequate accounting requirements for the amount of your expenses only if...you are not related to your employer."

You are related to your employer if-

▲ Your employer is your brother or sister, half-brother or half-sister, spouse, ancestor, or lineal descendant,

▲ Your employer is a corporation in which you own, directly or indirectly, more than 10% in value of the outstanding stock, or

▲ Certain relationships (such as grantor, fiduciary, or beneficiary) exist between you, a trust, and your employer

Therefore, the question becomes, if you are an LLC being taxed as an S corporation, are you a corporation where you own stock or an limited liability company where you own a membership interest. We believe these are one in the same in this context. Don't fret. You can still deduct 50% of your meals when traveling; you just need to use actual expenses and not per diem allowances.

Country Club Dues
Nope. The IRS does not care how many times or how much you entertain your clients, prospects and business associates at your country club. The membership dues are not allowed. However, the specific out-of-pockets expenses associated with qualifying meals incurred at your country club are deductible. There are some other devils in the details, but this is the general gist. Also, recall that since the Tax Cuts and Jobs Act of 2017, entertainment is no longer deductible.

Don't confuse this with other types of dues such as Chamber of Commerce or other professional organizations such as BNI. Those dues are 100% deductible although there is some scuttle butt about BNI since a portion of the dues are likely for meals.

Client Gifts
Yuck, more IRS publications stuff on the way. In IRS Publication 463, here is the blurb on client gifts-

> You can deduct no more than $25 for business gifts you give directly or indirectly to each person during your tax year. A gift to a business that is intended for the eventual personal use or benefit of a particular person or a limited class of people will be considered an indirect gift to that particular person or to the individuals within that class of people who receive the gift.

> If you give a gift to a member of a customer's family, the gift is generally considered to be an indirect gift to the customer. This rule does not apply if you have a bona fide, independent business connection with that family member and the gift is not intended for the customer's eventual use.

> If you and your spouse both give gifts, both of you are treated as one taxpayer. It does not matter whether you have separate businesses, are separately employed, or whether each of you has an independent connection with the recipient. If a partnership gives gifts, the partnership and the partners are treated as one taxpayer.

$25 is the maximum per year per person. The second paragraph explains you cannot give $100 to a family of four (as an example), unless you have a separate bona fide relationship with each family member. Here is the link to IRS Publication 463 (Travel, Entertainment, Gift, and Car Expenses)-

wcginc.com/5330

In a recent IRS audit that we represented, the client presented a $1,000 receipt for forty $25 VISA gift cards along with forty names of clients, prospects and business associates, including the business connection to each. Excellent documentation frankly. The IRS agent accepted the business deduction as is, yet quietly we wondered if any of those names actually received the gift cards. We didn't bring it up. Interesting indeed.

Keep this in mind as well- note that the IRS refers to individuals in their little pontification above. Gifts to another business are limitless. So, if your client is a business and you want to express your gratitude, theoretically there is no limit provided an individual is not the designated recipient.

Promotional items that are under $4 in unit cost and have your business name or logo on them are not considered gifts and do not contribute to the $25 maximum.

Commuting Expenses
It is unfortunate, but expenses associated with your commute to work are not deductible. Tolls and parking are the common ones small business owners attempt to deduct. There is a subtle difference to be aware of- driving from a work location to your client's place of business is not commuting. Commuting is driving from your home to your office or client's place of business.

You can solve a lot of problems surrounding commuting expenses by qualifying for a home office. Then your commute is from the bedroom to the home office. If you shower, then the commute is from the bathroom to the home office.

All kidding aside, or least most of it, the tax benefit of the home office deduction is not too low, not too high. In our experience, about $250 or so of cash in your pocket benefit comes from the additional deductions associated with a home office. But! Where the big benefit comes from is the deduction of travel expenses; without a home office, your mileage or automobile expenses to your first client is not tax deductible. However, with a home office, this drive is now considered travel between work locations. Huge difference!

We do a deep dive into the home office deduction in a bit.

Professional Attire
The tax code is very clear on this. Anything that you can convert to everyday use is considered personal, and therefore not tax deductible. Many business owners want to deduct dry cleaning expenses or Men's Warehouse purchases, but they usually cannot. We know you are rocking it in the double-breasted vest without a coat look, but the IRS doesn't

have fashion sense and therefore doesn't care. However, there are some exceptions (of course there are).

WCG CPAs & Advisors prepares several tax returns for pilots, flight attendants, military personnel, nurses and firefighters. These uniforms are not suitable for everyday use and / or are protective in nature (such as steel-toed boots), and therefore are small business tax deductions. We also have a handful of models and actors as clients, and their clothing is considered theatrical costumes not suitable for everyday use.

Many small business owners will embroider a nice golf shirt or something similar. This can be deducted as either clothing not suitable for everyday use or advertising depending on the IRS agent who is bent out of shape about your tax returns.

The maintenance such as alterations and laundering of deductible clothing is also tax deductible. Shoes, socks, nylons, haircuts, watches and the like are all disallowed. Forget about it. In Mary A. Scott v. Commissioner, Tax Court Summary Opinion 2010-47, a Continental Flight Attendant was denied shoes, socks, nylons and hair product as unreimbursed employee business expenses. Here is the link-

wcginc.com/2010

It's a fun case and a quick read.

Loan Payments
Many businesses have loans, either for automobiles, business equipment or lines of credit. However, having an expense category of "Loan Payment" is a dead giveaway that the business owner doesn't understand that only the interest portion of the loan payment is deductible.

Think of it this way- if you lent your buddy $50,000 and he or she shockingly pays you back the $50,000 plus $10,000 in interest, only the $10,000 would be income to you. The $50,000 would be what we nerdy accountants call a return of capital.

Yet another way to look at this- your small business tax deduction must be recognized as income by another entity (either business or person), unless that entity is a charity. So, for the IRS to allow you to deduct mortgage interest on your home mortgage as an example, the lender must recognize the interest as income. Your deduction = someone else's taxable income.

Zeus and Apollo

Let's say you are a hotshot private investigator driving a red Ferrari 308 GTS in Hawaii. Can you deduct two Dobermans as business expenses? Possibly. We recently worked with a client who is a criminal defense attorney where we demonstrated that the need for security dogs was a bona fide occupational qualification. In other words, the dogs provided security to the criminal defense attorney so he was able to perform his job. Stop laughing, it was L-E-G-I-T. Not because of the creativity, but because of the argument's position.

Another way to look at these obscure examples- the IRS allows you to deduct most things if they eventually lead to the generation of taxable income. Think of investment fees. Think of Zeus and Apollo who allowed the attorney to continue taking on high-risk, high-profit (taxable) defense cases.

Conclusion

Enough about the stuff you can't do, or at least enough of the business deductions you need to carefully position yourself with, let's talk about the stuff you can do. There are several small business tax deductions that are common, yet overlooked or misapplied.

Depreciation

Before we get into the exciting world of automobiles, home offices and traditional business expenses, let's explore the concept of depreciation. How it works, how it can help, and how it can bite.

There are three basic types of depreciation available to small business owners-

▲ Section 179

▲ Bonus

▲ MACRS (or other suitable schedules)

Section 179

Section 179 of the tax code allows you to instantly depreciate assets up to $1,160,000 (for the 2023 tax year).

Not all property qualifies for Section 179 depreciation, namely real estate. Some property is considered Listed Property which has special rules and limits, namely automobiles and computers. To deduct Section 179 depreciation, your business must have net income and / or sufficient shareholder basis to absorb it, otherwise whatever is unused is carried forward to later years.

Bonus

Bonus depreciation is also enhanced. It was 50%, but it jumped up to 100% for 2018 through 2022 tax years. Bonus depreciation is now descending to 80% for 2023, 60% for 2024, 40% in 2025 and 20% in 2026. There are all kinds of rules and interplay between Section 179 and Bonus depreciation.

Now that bonus depreciation is coming back down to earth, Section 179 is becoming sexy again. Even during the good ol' days of 100% bonus, there were times where Section 179 depreciation yielded a better overall strategy especially given the interplay with Section 199A.

MACRS Etc

MACRS is not a depreciation schedule designed for bourbons. Frankly, bourbon shouldn't be sitting around long enough to depreciate... or spoil as us accountants would say. At our office, Maker's Mark seems to deplete long before it depreciates or spoils. All kidding aside, MACRS is Modified Accelerated Cost Recovery System which is the default depreciation schedule for most property. So, if you do not use Section 179 or Bonus depreciation, you will be utilizing MACRS depreciation (generally speaking). You can also elect other suitable schedules too but those choices and justifications get more complicated.

If you really want to complicate things, Generally Accepted Accounting Principles (GAAP) does not recognize accelerated depreciation. Therefore, if you have audited financial statements, there will be a difference between "book" depreciation and "tax" depreciation. 99% of the small businesses out there don't have audited financial statements (or the need for them). But you might run across this if you are buying or selling a business. WCG also does business valuations for divorce cases or economic damages lawsuits, and the "book" to "tax" and vise-versa becomes an important valuation component.

Tax Planning with Depreciation

We are shocked every time a client walks into our office demanding to pay fewer taxes. We smile and tell them that they are the only one. Most people want to pay more taxes, so we find it refreshing when someone wants to pay less. Yes, we're kidding.

Tax planning with depreciation must be carefully considered. Everyone wants the bird in the hand versus the two in the bush. We get it. But let's run through some scenarios which might expand your thinking and horizons.

Let's say you buy a piece of equipment for $200,000 and you deduct the whole thing in the first year using Section 179 depreciation. If your marginal tax rate is 12%, you saved yourself

$24,000 ($200,000 x 12%). Nice job. In the next year, your business is growing and you find yourself in the 22% marginal tax rate but you don't have any depreciation left, so no savings.

Here is a table illustrating Section 179 depreciation-

	Allowed %	Depreciation	Tax Savings
Year 1, Savings at 12%	100%	200,000	30,000
Year 2, Savings at 12%	0%	0	0
Year 3, Savings at 22%	0%	0	0
Year 4, Savings at 22%	0%	0	0
Year 5, Savings at 24%	0%	0	0
Year 6, Savings at 24%	0%	0	0
Totals	**100%**	**200,000**	**30,000**

Here is the exact same scenario using MACRS as your depreciation schedule (as opposed to using Section 179)-

	Allowed %	Depreciation	Tax Savings
Year 1, Savings at 12%	20.00%	40,000	4,800
Year 2, Savings at 12%	32.00%	64,000	7,680
Year 3, Savings at 22%	19.20%	38,400	8,448
Year 4, Savings at 22%	11.52%	23,040	5,069
Year 5, Savings at 24%	11.52%	23,040	5,530
Year 6, Savings at 24%	5.76%	11,520	2,765
Totals	**100%**	**200,000**	**34,291**

That is a $4,300 difference! However, this is overly simplified comparison given that $200,000 spans at least two marginal tax brackets. We used this dramatic disparity to drive home the point that you might be leaving money on the depreciation table.

Also, we concede that the time value of money is not at play in these examples. If you take your $30,000 tax savings and invest it wisely, it will outperform the lost tax savings. At a 6% rate of return compounded annually the savings are $10,147 compared to $4,300. But, this means you must invest it and not spend your tax savings on a cruise boat.

Before you call your tax accountant and franticly decline the Section 179 depreciation method, consider your income projections. The illustrations above only prove a point if your marginal tax rate is increasing. If you are experiencing an exceptionally good year, and the next few years will have less taxable income, then perhaps using the instant depreciation benefits of Section 179 make sense. Plan! Plan! Plan!

Tax Planning with Depreciation Recapture
Please understand that depreciation is a tax deferral system rather than a tax avoidance system. Huh? When you sell or dispose of an asset, you might have to pay tax on the portion that was depreciated.

For example, you buy a $200,000 piece of machinery and use Section 179 depreciation to deduct the entire $200,000 in the first year. Five years later you sell the equipment for $150,000 because you slapped some new paint on it and you are a shrewd negotiator with your buyer. You will now have to recognize $150,000 of taxable ordinary income. Yuck. But there is a silver lining- depreciation recapture is taxed at your marginal tax rate up to a maximum of 25% tax rate. So, you could have depreciated your asset during 37% marginal tax rate years just to pay it all back at 25%. Bonus. Tax planning is a must! How many times have we mentioned that?

You can kick this depreciation recapture can down the road with a Section 1031 exchange (also referred to as a like-kind exchange). Perform your favorite internet search on this topic- way too involved to explain here except that a Section 1031 exchange allows deferral of depreciation recapture and capital gains. And if you think you know what a 1031 exchange is, try learning about a reverse 1031 exchange- where you buy the replacement property first. Yup. It exists.

Keep in mind that 1031 like kind exchanges are now limited to real property with the recent tax reform.

What if you think you can be clever, and not deduct depreciation on your asset? IRS is way ahead of you. Way ahead. There is a little known rule called the allowed versus allowable rule and it can bite you in the butt. And it's not a nibble, it is potentially quite the bite, like Jaws-size ("You're gonna need a bigger boat").

Several Tax Court rulings will have a statement similar to "Tax deductions are a matter of legislative grace." Nice. When have you ever felt the grace of a legislator as you pay taxes? Never. At any rate, let's extend this statement a bit, and one can infer that tax deductions are not required to be taken which is completely true. And some tax planning can involve not taking tax deductions on tax returns in certain cases (seems weird, but there are narrow examples).

But the IRS assumes that you have deducted depreciation expense in the past so when you dispose or sell your asset, you MUST recapture depreciation even if you didn't deduct it in the past. That is a big Yuck. We commonly see this when taxpayers own rental properties and prepare their own tax returns. Tax preparation is a profession, not a hobby. Yeah, we said it! We have to, it's our chosen profession.

There are ways to fix this of course. One way is using Form 3115 Application for Change in Accounting Method. This form is used for a variety of things, and one of the things is to bring your depreciation current through a Section 481(a) adjustment. One of the problems with slapping a whole bunch of depreciation in one tax year is revenue and expense matching-this is one of the cornerstones of accounting principles, so these adjustments need to be detailed correctly. And with rental properties specifically, you might get into passive loss limit problems.

By the way, you can opt out of depreciating real property in Canada. Who knew?

We digress. Back to the chapter's topic- Tax Deductions, Fringe Benefits!

Small Business Tax Deductions Themes

There are some over-arching themes and concepts for all small business deductions. The business expense must be-

▲ Ordinary and necessary (IRS Publication 334), and

▲ Paid or recognized in the current tax year, and

▲ Directly related to your business, and

▲ Reasonable, and not lavish or extravagant (IRC Section 162 and IRS Publication 463).

Let's break these down. An ordinary expense is one that is common and accepted in your field of business, trade, or profession. A necessary expense is one that is helpful and appropriate, although not necessarily required, for your business. In Samp v. Commissioner, Tax Court Memo 1981-706, an insurance agent had a handgun since he traveled to an area with a recent unsolved murder. The Tax Court responded with "A handgun simply does not qualify as an ordinary and necessary business expense for an insurance agent, even a bold and brave Wyatt Earp type with a fast draw who is willing to risk injury or death in the service of his clients."

You must appreciate a Wyatt Earp reference from a Tax Court judge. Ouch. Clean up on aisle Allstate.

The expense must be paid or recognized in the current year. Expenses that were paid but not deducted in previous years cannot be "caught up" by deducting them today without amending your prior tax returns (which are easy to do, and should be done if there is money to be had). There is some wiggle room by paying expenses in advance. Under the Code of Federal Regulations (CFR), Title 26 (Internal Revenue), Chapter 1, Subchapter A (Income Tax) or 26 CFR 1.263(a)-4 for short, there is a rule called the 12-month rule. This allows you to deduct in full an amount where the benefit received from paying the expense spans two tax years.

Here is the exact wording allowing the immediate deduction of prepaid expenses for "any right or benefit for the taxpayer that does not extend beyond the earlier of-

▲   12 months after the first date on which the taxpayer realizes the right or benefit; or

▲   The end of the taxable year following the taxable year in which the payment is made."

Here is the link to the Code of Federal Regulations on the 12-month rule-

wcginc.com/5415

You'll need to search for Prepaid Rent, or scroll through a bunch of hoopla.

An example you see often is a one-year rental lease that starts July 1 and ends June 30 the following year. If you pre-paid the entire lease amount, you can deduct the entire amount since the benefit (the use of the rental space) is 12 months. However, let's say the lease term started February 1 of the following year, but you prepaid the entire amount December 31 of the current year. Since the benefit extends past the end of the following tax year, none of it is deductible in the current year and only a portion is deducted the following year.

Just because you can deduct an expense in one lump sum, doesn't mean that you should. Remember the conversation about depreciation, tax planning and increased marginal tax rates in the future? Also, this small business tax deduction scheme is usually reserved for those using cash-based accounting.

The expense must be related to your business- that seems obvious. Finally, the expense must not be lavish or extravagant. IRS Publications 463 states "You cannot deduct expenses for entertainment that are lavish or extravagant. An expense is not considered lavish or extravagant if it is reasonable considering the facts and circumstances. Expenses will not be disallowed just because they are more than a fixed dollar amount or take place at deluxe restaurants, hotels, nightclubs, or resorts." The IRS hasn't updated to remove the word "entertainment" but you get the idea.

The link for IRS Publication 463 (Travel, Entertainment, Gift, and Car Expenses) is below-

wcginc.com/5330

So, your Board of Directors meeting might spend $500 on catering but a $5,000 expenditure to hold your board meeting in Fiji might be considered lavish and extravagant. Be reasonable out of the gate, and it will be hard for the IRS to knock you off your perch.

Value of a Business Tax Deduction

Here is another concept that small business owners miss. Tax deductions only reduce taxable income. If you spend $1,000 and your marginal tax rate is 22%, then you only save $220 by spending $1,000. Every December, we field hundreds of phone calls and emails from clients asking if they should buy something to save on taxes. Our response is a simple flowchart-

▲ Do you need the item you are considering? If No, then stop. Don't buy anything. If Yes, then continue to the next question.

▲ Is the current year's income unusually high, or do you expect to earn more next year?

Without sound snarky, why would you buy something on December 31 if your tax rate will only increase the following year? Wait 24 hours, buy the cool thing you need and get a better yet delayed tax deduction. And if you don't need it, why would you spend money unnecessarily only to get a portion of that back in tax savings? Another way of saying this is- keep some tax deductions in your pocket for next year. You don't want to be in a position where you ran out of perfectly good deductions in a year of increased taxable income.

Conversely, if your current taxable income is unusually high and you expect it to go down next year then perhaps you should accelerate your timelines for major purchases. WCG can help with the tax modeling and planning.

All too often we hear people at cocktail parties say something silly like "Don't worry, it's a write-off." Remember that money is still leaving your person, and the money you are getting back in the form of a tax deduction is substantially less. Just because it is a "write-off" or a business tax deduction doesn't mean that you are using Monopoly money. Yes, it is easy to spend someone else's money but calling it a write-off doesn't change who owns the money.

Tax credits are in contrast to tax deductions. Tax credits such as $7,500 for buying a cool Porsche Taycan or $13,400 for adopting a child are a dollar-for-dollar reduction in your tax due. For example, if the computed tax liability is $20,000 and you max out your adoption credit of $13,400, you will only have a tax liability of $6,600. However, if you spend $13,400 in office furniture you will save taxes based on your marginal tax rate- 22% tax rate equates to $2,948. See the difference?

Tax deduction versus tax credit. There are very little tax credits for small businesses, but here are most popular-

▲ Alcohol Fuels

▲ Alternative Motor Vehicle

▲ Disabled Access

▲ Employer Provided Childcare

▲ Reforestation

▲ Qualified Research Expenses (models, patents, environmental testing, etc.)

▲ Pension Plan Start Up Costs

▲ Work Opportunity and Welfare to Work

Look these up. These are like college grants and other obscure things that most people don't chase down. There might be easy money for things you are already doing.

Deductions the IRS Cannot Stand

Here is a quick list of the small business tax deductions that the IRS cannot stand. That isn't phrased correctly. The IRS actually likes these tax deductions since most business owners either incorrectly deduct them or cannot substantiate an otherwise qualified deduction for lack of proper record keeping.

The IRS plays pot odds on the following business deductions since the recovery of taxes is probable and therefore profitable for the government. In poker, if it costs you $10 to bet and there is $100 in the pot, then you can be wrong 90% of the time and still break even. This is the essence of the pot odds: You're paying a fraction to win a larger sum, and the IRS is no different.

Here we go-

▲ Meals (shocker)

▲ Car and Truck Expenses, Mileage Logs (another shocker)

▲ Travel (abused regularly)

▲ Home Office (probably not as much anymore)

There are others, but these are the biggies. This should not have a chilling effect on you deducting these expenses. You should not be afraid of an audit. You should not be afraid of losing an audit. You should only be afraid of having an unreasonable or indefensible position. Sure, easy for us to say.

At the same time, if you have legitimate expenses and you can back them up with proof, then happily deduct them. Like Muhammad Ali once said, "It's not bragging if you can back it up." Well, the same can be said of small business tax deductions that are at higher risk of audit. If you can back it up then deduct it!

Automobiles and LLCs, S Corps

A question we entertain almost daily is "I want to save taxes. Should I have the business buy me a car?" Our auto-attendant replies with, "Do you need a car?" If you answer with "Yes" the auto-attendant replies with, "Hold please." If your "Yes" is not quick or mumbled, or if there is any recognition of hesitation, the auto-attendant is unhappy.

We digress. There are only a few questions you need to ask yourself when considering a car purchase. Are you the type of person who buys new? How long do you typically keep your cars? Is the car 100% business use? How many miles do you plan to drive? There is a decision tree at the end of the automobile section.

Back up for a bit. Remember our previous discussions about tax deductions, and how only a fraction of the money you spend is returned to you? So, back to our auto-attendant, "Do you need a car?" If the answer is "Yes" because your bucket of bolts is getting exceedingly dangerous, then Yes, buy a much-needed car out of a sense of safety. If the answer is "Not really, but I want to save taxes," then don't.

Two rules to live by-

▲ Cash is King (keep it!)

▲ Depreciation is a tax deferral not a tax avoidance system (typically)

There might be some other external forces at play. For example, if you need a car next year but your income is ridiculously and unusually high in the current tax year, then reducing your income now makes sense. Again, tax modeling and planning is critical.

Ok, you've chatted with your car-loving buddies at WCG and we've determined that a car purchase should be in your near future, now what? There are all kinds of issues here, so, buckle up as we go through this stuff. There are four scenarios-

▲ Business Owned Automobile (mixed bag)

▲ You Own the Automobile, Get Reimbursed By The Mile (clean and elegant)

▲ You Own the Automobile, Take a Mileage Deduction (silly in an S Corp... oh and by the way, gone with the Tax Cuts and Jobs Act of 2017)

▲ You Own the Automobile, Lease it Back to Your Business (exotic)

We'll start with the crowd favorite- Business Owned Automobile. As we go through these, please excuse our interchange of vehicle, automobile and car. They all mean the same thing. If you are being chastised by Tina Watson's sister for bringing food into her Toyota 4Runner then Turi would use the word "vehicle," with stark over-annunciation of each syllable like she was talking to someone who doesn't know English. Then again, there are so many grammatical errors in our book, who are we to complain?

Business Owned Automobile
If the business truly owns the car, then it should be titled in the business's name. Having said this, loan and lease terms might be crummy. Another concern is higher insurance rates. It appears that most auto policies will charge a higher premium for cars owned by a business for business purposes. While the insurance businesses are regulated and must demonstrate the need for the premiums being charged, the higher amount appears to be a money grab.

Some insurance businesses will allow you to title in the business name and your name as joint tenants with rights of survivorship (JTWROS). This satisfies the IRS's need for titling, and it might allow you to insure the automobile with a personal insurance policy. Talk to your insurance agent.

If you buy the automobile yourself and then transfer it to the business, you might be on the hook for sales tax twice (technically) although recently Departments of Motor Vehicles are understanding that a transaction did not take place. Also, your title might have a lien on it making it challenging to change titling and names.

Under Section 163(j) there is some relief. The automobile may be listed as an asset on the business's books (balance sheet). Specifically, and in the case of a Partnership or S Corp, since the taxpayer owns both the pass-through entity and the asset, the taxpayer is both the legal and equitable owner of the asset. Therefore, depreciation expense may be deducted, and loan interest may be deducted even if the loan is in the individual's name.

Section 179 and Bonus Depreciation

Let's talk about the Hummer Loophole since that is where most taxpayer confusion comes from. Yes, at some point, long ago, in a galaxy far far away, businesses could buy heavy trucks and deduct them 100%. Was this a loophole of sorts? Yes. Does Congress and the IRS like loopholes? Not really, unless it benefits them. Did Congress change the Hummer Loophole? Yes. What is the current state of affairs after the Tax Cuts and Jobs Act of 2017 (TCJA)? Good question, read on (sneak peek, we are back to 100% for heavy trucks... Hummers for everyone Oprah!).

Switching gears to which business automobiles are eligible for 100% Section 179 deduction under the current tax laws after the TCJA. The following trucks and business automobiles qualify for 100% deduction in Year 1-

▲ Automobiles that can seat nine-plus passengers behind the driver's seat (i.e.: Hotel / Airport shuttle vans, etc.).

▲ Automobiles with: (1) a fully-enclosed driver's compartment / cargo area, (2) no seating at all behind the driver's seat, and (3) no body section protruding more than 30 inches ahead of the leading edge of the windshield. In other words, a classic cargo van.

▲ Heavy construction equipment will qualify for the Section 179 deduction, as will forklifts and similar.

▲ Typical "over-the-road" Tractor Trailers will qualify.

This is straight from the Section179.org website who does a fantastic job of explaining this stuff. So, what are the Section 179 deduction limits for passenger automobiles and heavy trucks that don't meet the list above? That is another really good question!

The following is directly from the IRS website speaking in reference to the TCJA-

> The new law changed depreciation limits for passenger vehicles placed in service after Dec. 31, 2017. If the taxpayer doesn't claim bonus depreciation, the greatest allowable depreciation deduction is:
>
> $10,000 for the first year,
> $16,000 for the second year,
> $9,600 for the third year, and
> $5,760 for each later taxable year in the recovery period.
>
> If a taxpayer claims 100 percent bonus depreciation, the greatest allowable depreciation deduction is:
>
> $18,000 for the first year,
> $16,000 for the second year,
> $9,600 for the third year, and
> $5,760 for each later taxable year in the recovery period.
>
> The new law also removes computer or peripheral equipment from the definition of listed property. This change applies to property placed in service after Dec. 31, 2017.

Where do some of these limits come from? The $10,000 for the first year comes from the Section 280F limitation. The $18,000 for the first year comes from the Section 280F limitation plus applying Section 168(k) bonus depreciation. There was a hiccup in the tax code that disallowed depreciation in subsequent years if accelerated depreciation was taken. But just like in 2011, the IRS released IRS Revenue Procedure 2018-25 which provided safe harbor for depreciation in subsequent years.

Again, these numbers are based on luxury passenger vehicles; in other words, vehicles that weigh 6,000 pounds or less. Why is this important... keep going!

You say, "so, my heavy SUV doesn't qualify for a 100% deprecation deduction under Section 179 because of the seating and configuration of the cargo hold, so now what?" Another really good question! Keep 'em coming! We have the answers.

The order of depreciation is Section 179 Deduction, then Bonus Depreciation and then regular depreciation. This means you apply limits, subtract the allowance and then apply subsequent laws to the remaining amounts. A truck or SUV that weighs more than 6,000 pounds is not considered a luxury automobile and therefore is not limited by Section 280F in the same way.

As such, the first-year depreciation deduction for your heavy business automobile would be-

▲ $25,000 under Section 179 (actually it is $26,200 for the 2023 tax year according IRS Revenue Procedure 2022-38 which makes inflation adjustments), plus

▲ 80% Bonus Depreciation (for the 2023 tax year) under Section 168(k).

So that $90,000 Ford F-250 truck that comes in around 6,700 pounds would be fully deductible in Year 1. Wow! That is good news, right? Right! The Hummer Rule is back baby! Do I have to buy a new heavy truck to qualify for the bonus depreciation? No. The old rule was Yes, but the TCJA changed that too. Here is the blurb from the IRS website-

- The taxpayer didn't use the property at any time before acquiring it (read, new to you not "brand" new or never been used, emphasis emphatically added).

- The taxpayer didn't acquire the property from a related party.

- The taxpayer didn't acquire the property from a component member of a controlled group of corporations.

- The taxpayer's basis of the used property is not figured in whole or in part by reference to the adjusted basis of the property in the hands of the seller or transferor.

- The taxpayer's basis of the used property is not figured under the provision for deciding basis of property acquired from a decedent.

There you go. The problem still remains with luxury passenger automobiles weighing under 6,000. Those limits are $20,200 (for the 2023 tax year) for the first year under Section 168(k) bonus depreciation according to IRS Revenue Procedure 2023-14.

Subsequent years are much lower. If you want to read IRS Revenue Procedure 2011-21 for nauseating examples, then go for it.

The bottom line is this- to maximize your Section 179 deduction for the business automobile purchase, buy an automobile that weighs over 6,000 pounds. Or… instead of driving Miss Daisy, drive a sumo wrestler to push you over 6,000 pounds (kidding!).

Leasing or Financing
If your business leases the automobile, the business portion of the lease amount is expensed. However, there are limits to how much can be expensed, especially for expensive or what the IRS would consider luxury automobiles. The disallowed lease payment is called a lease inclusion and is detailed in IRS Revenue Procedure 2016-23. The amount is added back into income and taxed, leaving only the IRS allowed portion as a deductible lease expense. So before you lease that brand new 911, call us. We'll determine a plan after the joint test-drive.

Also consider that leases are generally bad, especially on business automobiles over $80,000 for three really big reasons. First, the residual value offered on a 36-month lease will be about 60% or $48,000. This is essentially what the leasing business believes the automobile will be worth after 3 years. Yuck #1.

Second, they take the degradation in value ($80,000 minus $48,000) and apply a capitalization rate of 8% to 12%. This is essentially your interest rate. Yuck #2.

Third, they put ridiculous mileage limitations such as 10,000 miles per year with heavy penalties for going over the limit. 10,000 miles is laughable for most modern-day business owners or families. Yuck #3.

Sure, if you lease a more economical automobile such as a Subaru Crosstrek for $30,000 then Yuck #1 goes away. But Yucks #2 and #3 remain. Also, automobile leases are generally not capitalized leases (they do not have a bargain purchase option) and therefore they cannot take advantage of the Section 179 deduction or Bonus Depreciation. Contrast that with your leased copier with a $1 buy-out option… this is considered "financing" or a capitalized lease, and the asset can be listed on your balance sheet, depreciated, painted purple, etc.

Liability
Another consideration- if you are driving the business car and get into an accident, the business might get into a liability rodeo just based on ownership. Proving that at the moment you were driving the car for personal reasons might not matter. We are not attorneys, but this scenario is not beyond possibility.

Personal Use
Lastly, and this is yet another big deal, any personal use must be considered taxable income as an employee of your S corporation. Don't laugh, it's true! How do you calculate the amount of imputed income? The easiest and most widely accepted way is to use the Annual Lease Value Table in IRS Publication 15-B Employer's Tax Guide to Fringe Benefits.

For the 2023 tax year, the lease value of a $50,000 automobile is $13,250 annually. If you use the business-owned automobile for personal use 10% of the time, then $1,325 will be added to your W-2 and taxed as compensation (including Social Security and Medicare taxes, and all the taxes you would expect). Here is the link to IRS Publication 15-B-

wcginc.com/5337

Under the "Cents-Per-Mile Rule," you can also use the mileage rate of 65.5 cents, but there are strong limitations such as the fair market value of the automobile must be below $60,800 (for the 2023 tax year). That will preclude some automobiles. But let's run the math anyways.

For example, you drove 15,000 miles and 5,000 miles were personal. You would need to add 5,000 miles x 65.5 cents (for the 2023 tax year) which equals $3,275 to W-2 income. And here's the personal use kicker- if you are operating your car for less than the standard mileage rate (and you usually do), you will artificially be inflating your income.

Having a mixed use (personal and business) automobile be owned by the business sounds like a lot of work. Everyone at our office likes French fries, but we won't run a mile for just one. Let's make sure it's worth it. Will the tax benefit of depreciation in the first two years offset the additional imputed income? Perhaps.

Keep in mind that it is difficult to justify 100% business use of an automobile if it is the only automobile you own- perhaps in Manhattan, but not for most Americans. Even if you have another automobile at your disposal, it still might not make sense to have your business own it. The question boils down to how many miles you will drive versus your ability to accelerate your depreciation versus your marginal tax rate today and the following years. At the end of this section on automobiles is an overly simplified flowchart to help you decide (or confuse the situation more).

LLC Owned But Using Standard Mileage Rate
If you are operating an LLC without the S corporation election, you might be tempted to use the standard mileage rate. Typically, this would be ill-advised- if you are using the standard

mileage rate you are probably better off owning the automobile personally and be reimbursed by the LLC. However, there are situations where this might make sense.

Let's look at the myriad of rules where using the standard mileage rate method is not allowed.

According to IRS Publication 463, you cannot use the standard mileage rate when you-

▲ Use five or more cars at the same time (such as in fleet operations), or

▲ Claimed a depreciation deduction for the car using any method other than straight line (such as MACRS), or

▲ Claimed a section 179 deduction on the car, or

▲ Claimed the special (bonus) depreciation allowance on the car, or

▲ Claimed actual car expenses for a car you leased, or

▲ Did not use the standard mileage deduction during the first year of use.

This makes sense. The IRS does not want you to exploit the system by claiming huge amounts of depreciation in the first year, and then switch to the possibly more lucrative standard mileage rate deduction. Here is the link for the IRS Publication 463 (Travel, Entertainment, Gift, and Car Expenses)-

wcginc.com/5330

Again, if your LLC owns the automobile but is using the standard mileage rate and your LLC elects S corporation status for taxation, this asset needs an adjusted cost basis for depreciation within the corporation. Why? As an S Corp where the business owns the automobile, the business can only use actual expenses and depreciation is a part of that.

The calculation for determining the basis of the automobile is quite simple since the IRS publishes the depreciation amount within the standard mileage rate.

Here's the math from IRS Notice 2022-03-

Purchase Price, 2020	50,000
2021 Depreciation @ $0.26 per Mile for 10,000 Miles	2,600
2022 Depreciation @ $0.26 per Mile for 10,000 Miles	2,600
2023 Depreciation @ $0.28 per Mile for 10,000 Miles	2,800
Adjusted Cost Basis end of December 2023	42,000

In this example, if the LLC elects S corporation status on January 1, 2024, an asset would be created on the S corporation's balance sheet with an adjusted basis of $42,000. The depreciation schedule for an automobile is typically five years, but when you switch from standard mileage rate to actual expenses (e.g., LLC electing S Corp status) the IRS requires you to estimate the remaining useful life. This is another conundrum. In this example, somewhere between two years and five years would be reasonable.

We just went over a ton of stuff under the Business Owns the Automobile section. Please look at a quickie decision tree later in this chapter.

You Own the Automobile, Get Reimbursed By The Mile

This might be the best option, especially if Section 179 depreciation is not going to benefit you much and/or you use the automobile personally more than you use it professionally. As the owner of the automobile, you would submit expense reports in the form of mileage logs. If you are a smart automobile owner, you would also use a smartphone app to keep track of your miles for you. Keep in mind that the IRS wants corroborating evidence to support your mileage logs, so keep those Jiffy Lube receipts or other service records showing odometer readings near the beginning and end of the year (so extrapolation can occur). Just whippin' out a pretty color-coded spreadsheet during an IRS examination is not enough.

The business would reimburse you according to your mileage log submission. This can be a great option for a lot of reasons. First, you are reducing the net income of your business, and if you are an S Corp the lower business income could decrease the amount of reasonable salary you must take as a shareholder. Second, most automobiles generally operate for less than the federal mileage rate.

Let's look at some numbers-

Business Miles	12,000
Miles Per Gallon (MPG)	25
Gallon of Gas	$4.50
Cost of Gas	2,160
Maintenance, Biz Portion	3,000
Total Cost	5,160
Reimbursement at $0.655 (2023)	7,860
Difference	2,700

As such, you just took home $2,700 tax-free. All legit. All legal. AAA might consider these operating costs to be too low, but then again this would be representative of an older or thrifty automobile. Why is that?

For the 2023 tax year, the IRS designated $0.28 of the $0.655 standard mileage rate to be depreciation of your automobile (almost half) according to IRS Notice 2022-03. Therefore, if you have a $5,000 POS which will be worth $5,000 ten years from now, you are getting reimbursed for depreciation that never happens. Cool! 10,000 miles would be $2,800 in your pocket (but you will reduce your basis in the automobile from $5,000 to $2,200).

Let's not forget that you took money out of the business tax-free, and you reduced your business's overall taxable income through legitimate small business tax deductions. Therefore, if we are using net business income after expenses as one of the proxies for determining a reasonable S corporation salary, that salary starts off at a lower number and subsequently reduces Social Security and Medicare taxes (among others). Win win!

Time to pump the brakes a bit. There is some confusion out there about getting reimbursed for actual expenses. For example, a business owner will own the automobile personally but also wants to get reimbursed for actual expenses. This same business owner will use the business credit card for gas and oil changes. This is bad. If you want to get reimbursed for actual expenses, it must be a pro-rated amount. If you drive 18,000 miles and 12,000 are business miles, then the business should only reimburse 75% of all actual expenses.

If you have leased your automobile and you use the standard mileage rate for reimbursement, you must continue with that method for the entire lease term.

Your business must have an Accountable Plan to take advantage of the You Own the Automobile, Get Reimbursed scenario. As a general rule, any payment of an allowance or reimbursement of business expenses for which the employee does not provide an adequate accounting (i.e., substantiation with receipts or other records) is considered to have been provided under a non-Accountable Plan and is required to be treated as taxable wages for purposes of federal, state, and local (if applicable) income tax withholding, Social Security and Medicare taxes, and federal and state unemployment taxes. Yuck!

As a reminder, please please please use your personal funds at the gas station and service center. If you want to be reimbursed for mileage, the business will absolutely pay for nothing except the reimbursement itself. You can certainly have the business pay for all automobile expenses, but then that becomes a business owned vehicle situation described above (Business Owned Automobile, page 298).

You Own the Automobile, Take Mileage Deduction

This is dead for S Corp shareholders. Thanks to the Tax Cuts and Jobs Act of 2017 all miscellaneous deductions that were once subjected to 2% adjusted gross income limits and then deducted on Schedule A are gone. Obtaining a tax deduction through a mileage deduction on your individual tax return was always a bad idea anyway with the Form 2106 and Schedule A limitations, and now it's just a memory.

If your business is not taxed as an S Corp, you are still able to deduct mileage on Schedule C of your Form 1040 tax return, or as Unreimbursed Partner Expenses (UPE) on Page 2 of Schedule E. We discuss this elsewhere, but for partners in a multi-member limited liability company who are used to this deduction, electing S corporation status will wreck your world a bit. Rather it being a deduction, it becomes a reimbursement from the business. In turn, that adds some office politics on who is spending what and for what.

You Own the Automobile, Lease It Back to Your Business

This might take a bit of getting used to so we will start with a similar situation. If you owned and operated a landscaping business, you might own the heavy equipment personally, and lease it back to the business. This is very common, and is considered a self-rental. Please refer to Chapter 3 (Three Types of Income, page 130) to refresh yourself on self-rentals and the handling of the income. As you know, self-rentals are perfectly fine as long as the lease rates being charged are considered market rates and cannot be considered remuneration of services provided (i.e., owner compensation).

The same thing can be accomplished with your automobile. You would lease a car that you own back to your business. This is not considered the same as the business leasing the car from a dealer. This is creating a self-rental arrangement between you and your business. And why would you want to do that?

The usual reason- it might prove to be a better tax position since you are reducing the income of your LLC which is subjected to self-employment taxes. Since we also use the ability to pay salaries as one of components in determining a reasonable salary for you as a shareholder in an S Corp, the leaseback option might influence a small reduction in your salary.

The income tax angle is a wash. A big table is coming up. First, let's talk about some basic assumptions.

Keep in mind- this arrangement will benefit an LLC through the reduction of self-employment taxes much more than an S corporation. You might be asking why not just elect S corporation status to solve your SE tax troubles? Perhaps your LLC is not generating the $30,000 in net business income after expenses to warrant the S Corp election.

Every year, AAA publishes the annual cost of driving an automobile, and the costs are broken down by small sedan, medium sedan, large sedan, sport utility vehicle and a minivan. From there, costs are established for 10,000 miles, 15,000 miles and 20,000 miles.

Small sedans are Chevy Cruze, Ford Focus, Honda Civic, Hyundai Elantra and Toyota Corolla. Medium sedans are Chevy Impala, Ford Fusion, Honda Accord, Nissan Altima and Toyota Camry. No numbers for a Porsche 911. Sorry. We're sure the operating costs aren't too bad, and we've recently heard that 911s never depreciate and the service checks are free.

There are certain fixed costs such as insurance, registrations and financing. There are certain variable expenses such as gas, tires and maintenance. Then there are some quasi-variable expenses, namely depreciation. Depreciation accelerates as the mileage per year increases. Think about Kelly Blue Book, Edmund's or lease rates- the reduction in value due to mileage gets more severe as the mileage exceeds 15,000. Sort of a curvilinear equation.

The lease rate needs some discussion too. If you have a newer, more expensive automobile, you might be able to fetch $600 per month. If you have an older car or a car that is more economical, a market lease rate might be $400. It can be a challenge to determine the market rate. Is it the rate a rental car agency would charge such as Hertz or Avis? Is it the rate a dealer would charge? Something in the middle? Don't forget the IRS Publication 15-B (Employer's Tax Guide to Fringe Benefits) where the lease value is determined by the IRS based on the value of the car. The benefit of ambiguity is the ability to pitch an argument on most numbers.

More tables. More numbers. Yes, tables are only meaningful to the table designer yet consider the following in a non-S Corp situation-

	5,000	10,000	15,000	20,000
Business Miles	5,000	10,000	15,000	20,000
Personal Miles	5,000	5,000	5,000	5,000
Total Miles	10,000	15,000	20,000	25,000
AAA 2014 Costs for Small Sedan	0.597	0.464	0.397	0.360
less Depreciation, Finance	0.288	0.204	0.161	0.106
Actual Operating Costs	0.309	0.260	0.236	0.254
Mileage Rate Method				
2015 IRS Mileage Rate	0.575	0.575	0.575	0.575
Mileage Deduction on Sched C	2,875	5,750	8,625	11,500
Savings of SE Tax	406	812	1,219	1,625
Savings of Income Tax @25% MFJ	719	1,438	2,156	2,875
Total Savings	1,125	2,250	3,375	4,500
Lease Method				
Annual Lease @ $400/month	4,800	4,800	4,800	4,800
less Depreciation ($3,160 Year 1)	-3,160	-3,160	-3,160	-3,160
Biz Use Expenses Using Actual Costs	1,545	2,603	3,544	5,076
Savings of SE Tax	897	1,046	1,179	1,395
Savings of Income Tax @25% MFJ	1,586	1,851	2,086	2,469
Gain on Net Rental Income @25% MFJ	410	410	410	410
Total Savings	2,073	2,487	2,855	3,454
Delta on Mileage Rate Method	-948	-237	520	1,045

Tilt!

We haven't updated this for 2023 numbers. Out of **WCG CPAs & Advisors** client base of 2,800, we only have one business doing this. Have some fun with this, but in the end the other scenarios won't hurt the brain as much.

The first question is the break-even. That number is 11,875 miles for a small sedan. That means if you drive fewer miles, then a lease arrangement might be a good idea. Conversely, if you drive more miles than 11,875, then using the mileage rate deduction is better. Yes, this is a middle of the road number. Pun intended.

Second question is depreciation and finance. Since you are charging a lease to your business for the use of the automobile, you cannot also add depreciation and finance charges. Those figures make up a large part of AAA's cost of ownership. You can only pass operational costs proportioned to business use. However, those expenses might be deducted on Schedule E of your individual tax returns, similar to rental properties.

How does the break-even move around? Good question. Frankly, AAA tends to be heavy-handed on the costs. So, if the average costs to operate an automobile go down or is less than what the AAA thinks, the break-even point decreases. If the market lease rate increases from the $400 used above, the break-even mileage increases.

In other words, as the mileage increases, you are amortizing the same fixed costs across more miles, whereas the IRS is giving you a flat rate of 57.5 cents for the 2015 tax year. Low miles? Lease arrangement might make sense since the mileage rate is lower than the actual costs. High miles? Your actual costs are being spread thinner, but the IRS still gives you 57.5 cents. Things to consider.

How does this arrangement reduce my self-employment taxes? Wow. Another good question- you are full of them. Leasing a car back to your business has the most benefit in the garden variety LLC or partnership where all the income is being subjected to self-employment taxes. As you know, an S Corp already sanitizes a bunch of income in the form of a K-1 which is not subjected to self-employment taxes.

So, to reduce your K-1 income in favor of non-passive self-rental income is basically moving money from your right pocket to your left pocket. Both income sources are only taxed at the income tax level. Net zero. But we've already discussed that reducing S corporation income through self-rentals might help reduce your reasonable salary. However, this is more apparent in self-rentals or lease arrangements that are not automobiles. The reimbursement allowances, depreciation limits and business use calculations on automobiles versus other self-rental items makes it less lucrative.

Conversely, in an LLC or partnership where self-employment tax is a concern, the automobile lease arrangement is a business expense and directly reduces the income, and therefore reduces self-employment taxes. This arrangement might be a good idea if you are unable to use an S Corp election (foreign investor) or if it doesn't make sense to (below break-even income).

There is some danger with the lease back to your business option. The biggest challenge is estimating the actual costs to operate your automobile, and the second challenge is estimating your mileage. So, if you are close to the break-even point it might not make sense. And engaging in revisionist history is not an ideal situation either.

Some more commentary. The AAA rate is published each year by the American Automobile Association and takes into account fuel prices, average insurance, registrations, etc.

The previous table assumes a 25% marginal tax rate. This is not a huge consideration, but as marginal tax rates increase the break-even point decreases. For example, on a small sedan, a jump from 25% to 32% in marginal tax rate increases your savings by $400 annually for a person who drives 15,000 miles for business and elects to use the mileage deduction and not the lease arrangement.

Medium sedans. With a slight increase in operating costs and subsequent market lease rates, the break-even is about 13,000 miles. Again, that might be low to some business owners. Hassle versus reward.

What is the net-net?

▲ The lease arrangement seems like an OK idea with low business miles.

▲ It seems exotic. It seems like a cool thing to drop at a party as a genius idea. But in the end, it might not be all that. But looking smart can be better than being smart.

▲ With one automobile, it only works well in an LLC or partnership where self-employment taxes are being applied to all income.

▲ With several automobiles (fleet) or machinery, lease-backs can prove to be smart tax planning.

To confirm, however, WCG can model your specific situation.

Automobile Decision Tree

In deciding whether to own the automobile personally or through your S corporation, here is a set of examples to help you make a decision. It is not a hard and fast set of rules, but will provide some guidance.

First, let's establish the bookends. On one end is the $80,000 luxury auto that you barely drive, and you recycle automobiles every 2-3 years. This is clearly business owned.

On the other end is the $30,000 modest automobile that you drive a tone of miles, and you keep automobiles for at least 5 years. This is clearly individually owned and reimbursed.

Armed with that information, here we go-

Example 1
You like big fancy cars that cost $80,000 and you only drive 5,000 miles for the business. Degradation of value is a way of life simply based on time so this automobile will go down in value, and as such you might as well get a tax deduction for it. Ergo, have the business own it. In other words, if you have already budgeted for the degradation of automobile value you might as well get a tax deduction for it, right?

Example 2
You are frugal and therefore you like to buy used Subaru's costing around $20,000... and, you drive the wheels off the thing because you are a real estate agent. Degradation in value is not as severe as example 1, so in this example the small business owner should own the automobile personally and get a mileage reimbursement from the business.

Example 3
You like big heavy trucks that cost $80,000 and you drive 12,000 miles for the business. You would like to save some taxes this year as well (shocking). This is a great example of using Section 179 plus 100% Bonus Depreciation to deduct the full amount of the truck.

Example 4
Same as example 3, but you expect your income to dramatically increase next year versus this year. In this case, have some patience and purchase the truck next year to match the excellent tax deduction against the higher income. We know, patience stinks. Our job is to build your wealth, and save taxes over your lifetime... not just today.

Example 5
You buy a lightly used SUV that weighs over 6,000 pounds for $50,000 and you drive it 6,000 miles per year. Yuck. This is right in the middle of "no man's land" where the decision is not obvious. Yes, you can deduct the full amount of $50,000 since the Section 179 deduction is not based on a new automobile, just new to you.

But recall that depreciation is a tax deferral... if you sell your business automobile for $40,000 a few years later, you will have depreciation recapture on the $40,000 taxed at ordinary income tax rates up to 25% tax rate. To make matters worse, Section 1031 Like-Kind

Exchanges no longer apply to automobiles since the recent tax reform so you can't trade it in to kick this depreciation recapture can down the road.

It might behoove you then to own this automobile personally and get a mileage reimbursement from the business. Then again, if you have an unusually high income this year perhaps deducting it in full today makes sense. Again, "no man's land" since the decision now has a ton of variables and what-ifs.

Example 6
Same as example 5 but you keep the automobile for 10 years and drive 15,000 miles. This changes the narrative. Since you will be owning it for so long with so many miles, the mileage reimbursement option is the way to go. In other words, own it personally and get reimbursed for the business miles you drive.

Let's flip this around. Let's say you buy fancy vehicles and you recycle them every 2-3 years. Typically, this should be owned by the business regardless of mileage since you are taking large degradations in value simply based on time with little consideration to miles. A $100,000 vehicle might be worth $70,000 after 2 years so use this depreciation in value as a tax benefit by owning it in the business.

We have a questionnaire that you can complete, and we can review together to find the best course of action. Here is the link-

wcginc.com/8120

Home Office Deduction
Is there a way to have the business reimburse, compensate, or otherwise pay for my home office? Can I still take a home office deduction with an S corporation? Yes, there is a way to claim a home office deduction with an S Corp.

Prior to the IRS making a recommendation to use the Accountable Plan and subsequent reimbursements to the employee (or shareholders), taxpayers would charge their corporation rent and declare the rent as income on Schedule E. Ok, but not elegant.

In the garden variety LLC world, the beauty of this was to take money out of the business as passive income. Since you were changing the color of money from earned income to passive income you were also sidestepping self-employment taxes. In the S corporation world, the beauty of this was to reduce the S Corp's overall income, and therefore reduce the reasonable salary heuristics or thresholds for shareholders while still taking money out of the business as passive income (again reducing self-employment taxes).

The IRS got sick of this (among other things of course).

The new school way is to use an Accountable Plan and reimburse the employee (you) for expenses associated with the home office. Remember, if you are an S Corp owner, you are both shareholder and employee. Imagine yourself as an employee of Google- the relationship would be arms-length, and you would submit expenses to Google just like you should with your own S corporation. Maintaining an arms-length perspective in your dealings as an employee of your S Corp will help you in the long run.

Your business must have an Accountable Plan to take advantage of this scenario and the basic housekeeping must be satisfied.

Section 280A of the Internal Revenue Code reads in part, "Except as otherwise provided in this section, in the case of a taxpayer who is an individual or an S corporation, no deduction otherwise allowable under this chapter shall be allowed with respect to the use of a dwelling unit which is used by the taxpayer during the taxable year as a residence."

So, what are the exceptions?

▲ Certain business use (typical home office, and discussed more here)

▲ Certain storage use

▲ Rental use (tax free... 14-day "Master's" or "Augusta" rule)

▲ Providing day care services

Section 280A continues by reading-

Subsection (a) shall not apply to any item to the extent such item is allocable to a portion of the dwelling unit which is **exclusively** used on a **regular** basis-

(A) as the **principal place of business** for any **trade or business** of the taxpayer, or

(B) as a place of business which is used by patients, clients, or customers in ... the normal course of trade or business,

(C) in the case of a separate structure which is not attached to the dwelling unit, in connection with ... trade or business.

We highlighted the buzzwords intentionally. Let's define these more carefully-

▲ Exclusive means the identifiable space or room is used only for business purposes (so let's not have a bed in your home office).

▲ Regular is a squishier since it is a facts and circumstances evaluation. Spending 4 hours a month selling Etsy stuff online probably won't win too many arguments.

▲ Principal place of business was once a hot topic but has been tightened up with this language right out of the tax code- "For purposes of subparagraph (A), the term "principal place of business" includes a place of business which is used by the taxpayer for the **administrative or management activities** of any trade or business of the taxpayer if there is no other fixed location of such trade or business where the taxpayer conducts substantial administrative or management activities of such trade or business."

▲ Trade or business has been defined in Commissioner v. Groetzinger, 480 U.S. 23, and reads in part, "to be engaged in a trade or business, the taxpayer must be involved in the activity with continuity and regularity and that the taxpayer's primary purpose for engaging in the activity must be for income or profit. A sporadic activity, a hobby, or an amusement does not qualify."

▲ Administrative or management activities include a nice list from IRS Publication 587 such as billing customers, clients, or patients, keeping books and records, ordering supplies, setting up appointments, forwarding orders or writing reports (we list more below).

Multiple Work Locations
You can have multiple work locations. The IRS states that if you use a home office as your primary location for substantial administrative activities you are allowed to essentially have two work locations. For example, you own a landscaping business and you have an office in your shop.

You perform all your administrative activities such as hiring and firing employees, accounting, balancing your checkbook, talking to your attorney, chatting it up with your Colorado Springs CPAs at WCG, etc. in your home office, that office counts as a work location in addition to your office in your shop. Here is the play-by-play blurb from the IRS-

> You can have more than one business location, including your home, for a single trade or business. To qualify to deduct the expenses for the business use of your

home under the principal place of business test, your home must be your principal place of business for that trade or business. To determine whether your home is your principal place of business, you must consider:

1. The relative importance of the activities performed at each place where you conduct business, and

2. The amount of time spent at each place where you conduct business.

Your home office will qualify as your principal place of business if you meet the following requirements.

1. You use it exclusively and regularly for administrative or management activities of your trade or business.

2. You have no other fixed location where you conduct substantial administrative or management activities of your trade or business.

This also works well for the consultant who works out of his or her home office, but also spends a ton of time on site with the client.

Don't forget that commuting miles between your residence and your office are not deductible, but if you have a home office suddenly these miles become business miles and therefore deductible. Boom! The use of Boom! is apparently out of fashion. Whatever.

You can read the full IRS Publication 587 (Business Use of your Home) by using the link below-

wcginc.com/5322

We will discuss the question, "What is my tax home?" (Tax Home, page 322).

Get Reimbursed for the Home Office

The expense report should detail the space used as a home office or storage of business items (inventory, supplies, etc.) as a percentage of overall square footage of the home. This percentage is then applied against rent, mortgage interest, property tax, utilities, HOA dues, insurance and repairs to determine the expense amount to be reimbursed. Depreciation must be reimbursed as well. The reimbursement can be monthly or quarterly or annually- your choice.

Keep in mind that two major expenses associated with a home office are mortgage interest and property taxes. These expenses are already 100% deductible on Schedule A (assuming your state and local taxes (SALT) do not exceed $10,000), so for most taxpayers the home office deduction or reimbursement is relatively small. And you must reduce your mortgage interest and property taxes being deducted on Schedule A by the amounts reimbursed by your business. No double dipping.

Here is quick table on what we mean-

Total Home Size	2,500
Home Office Size	150
Home Office %	6.00%

Expense	**Amount**	**Reimbursed**	**Schedule A**
Mortgage Interest	15,000	900	14,100
Property Taxes	2,500	150	2,350
Hazard Insurance	1,100	66	NA
Utilities	3,600	216	NA
HOA Dues	600	36	NA
Depreciation ($400,000 building)	10,256	615	NA
Totals	33,056	1,983	
Total Non Sched A	15,556	933	
Savings @ 22%		205	
Savings @ 37%		345	

What are we showing here? Good question! The $933 number above represents a reimbursement to you and a deduction to the business that would otherwise not have been deductible except through an Accountable Plan reimbursement. In essence with a home office you are deducting portions of Hazard Insurance, Utilities, HOA Dues and Depreciation.

So, a home office reimbursement as a business deduction might put $200 to $350 in your pocket. Might be worth it based on that alone, but where the home office has a ton of weight is now your commute is from the bedroom to the basement or den, and all travel from your home office is business travel.

Here is another consideration. For those taxpayers who are seeing Schedule A deductions being phased out due to high income, SALT limitations and / or Alternative Minimum Tax

(AMT), using the home office reimbursement is a way to ensure these deductions are not reduced.

This can be a huge swing in taxes. This is one of the largest compelling reasons to have us prepare both your corporate and individual tax returns- we can move things around to ensure the maximum deduction is obtained.

There are other examples. A quick example would be where you own an office building 100% through an LLC and the business is operating as a separate LLC or S Corp. The rent must be market rent- we suggest using Zillow or a realtor to periodically update your comparables for market rent analysis. This is outside the home office world (see our chapter on self-rentals).

Home Office Safe Harbor

There is a safe harbor provision for home office deductions where you can deduct $5 per square foot. This would be on Form 8829 for LLCs without an S Corp election. However, for S Corps where you choose to reimburse yourself for the use of the home office, you cannot use the safe harbor method.

According to IRS Revenue Procedure 2013-13 which reads in part-

> 02 Reimbursement or other expense allowance arrangement. The safe harbor method provided by this revenue procedure does not apply to an employee with a home office if the employee receives advances, allowances, or reimbursements for expenses related to the qualified business use of the employee's home under a reimbursement or other expense allowance arrangement (as defined in § 1.62-2) with his or her employer.

An expense allowance arrangement is synonymous with an Accountable Plan which we discuss in detail in Chapter 10 (Accountable Plan Expense Reimbursements, page 262) Therefore, you must use actual expenses! This is in stark contrast to the mileage reimbursement since the IRS simply gives you a rate per mile regardless of what you spend.

For disregarded LLCs and sole proprietors, there are some real advantages for using the safe harbor method such as being able to use all mortgage interest on Schedule A instead of a proration. But there are also some limitations that need to be considered. We typically optimize for both methods in these situations.

Home Office Issues with Multiple Owners

We broached this concern in Chapter 2 (Multi-Member LLC That Issues Invoices, page 52) but we'll tackle it again here. Let's say you and another person own a business together, and you elect to have the entity taxed as an S Corp. You also create an Accountable Plan to reimburse home office expenses among other things.

As you have learned, you cannot use the simplified method and therefore only actual expenses are reimbursed. No biggie right? Well, perhaps. However, what happens if your home office is smaller as a percentage of your overall home size? In other words, your room is 150 square feet and your house is 3,000 square feet... this is 5%. But your business partner has 180 square feet within a 2,500 square foot house... or about 7.2%.

Perhaps we are splitting hairs... but wait... there's more! What if your property taxes are substantially lower than your business partner's? HOA dues? Insurance? Housekeeper? We could go on and on.

You could limit your Accountable Plan expense reimbursements to a certain dollar amount, but doesn't that hose the other guy? You could reimburse without regard to limits or amounts, but doesn't that hose the guy with a smaller reimbursement? We'll find a new word for hose.

Yes, all those things are true except finding a synonym for getting hosed. One solution is to split up into a multi-entity arrangement as shown in Chapter 2 (Multi-Member LLC That Issues Invoices, page 52). Talk to us and we can help!

Home Office With Partnerships
If you are a partner in partnership (member of a multi-member LLC) that is not being taxed as an S corporation, you might be able to reduce partnership income through a tax mechanism called Unreimbursed Partnership Expenses, or UPE for short. UPE is a slamma-jamma version of old school Form 2106 unreimbursed employee expenses, and is a singular line on Schedule E Page 2 reducing partner income.

Here is the blurb from the IRS website on completing Schedule E if you can't get enough-

> You can deduct unreimbursed ordinary and necessary partnership expenses you paid on behalf of the partnership on Schedule E if you were required to pay these expenses under the partnership agreement. You only can deduct unreimbursed expenses on Schedule E that are trade or business expenses under section 162. Don't report unreimbursed partnership expenses separately if the expenses are from a passive activity and you are required to file Form 8582.

If your partnership agreement or operating agreement allows for it, partners can deduct UPE. However, an Accountable Plan-esque method must be used to create the workpapers and math behind the calculation since it is one big fat number without supporting statements or supplemental forms on your individual tax return (Form 1040).

Home Office Depreciation
Similar to rental properties (among other things), depreciation on a home office is required by the IRS. Here is a Q&A from their website under Sale or Trade of Business, Depreciation, Rentals > Depreciation & Recapture.

> Question- I have a home office. Can I deduct expenses like mortgage, utilities, etc., but not deduct depreciation so that when I sell this house the basis won't be affected?
>
> Answer- No. All allowed or allowable depreciation must be considered at the time of sale. You can generally figure depreciation on the business use portion of your home up to the gross income limitation, over a 39-year recovery period and using the mid-month convention. As long as you determine actual expenses and the correct amount of allowed or allowable depreciation, the depreciation reduces the basis of your home accordingly, whether or not you actually claim it on your tax return.

Note that last phrase, "whether or not you actually claim it on your tax return." That is the kicker. Truth be known, when a client sells their primary residence most tax professionals do not ask if it was ever used as a home office. Right, wrong or indifferent, it is often overlooked.

Additionally, home office depreciation is tough to track within a tax return. Sure, if you are a disregarded LLC or sole proprietor and reporting your business activities on Schedule C, you will use Form 8829 to generate the home office deduction and that form helps track home office depreciation. Easy.

If you use the simplified method for the home office deduction, you do not have a depreciation recapture problem since you do not have to depreciate your home office. Easy again. But as you know, using an Accountable Plan for reimbursing the S Corp shareholders (recall the two hats- employee and investor) requires actual expenses for home office reimbursement including depreciation.

What makes matters worse is that the depreciation deduction for home office reimbursement is truly done at the business entity level (Form 1120S or 1120). The individual tax return (Form 1040) is not affected, but when the home is sold, depreciation recapture is picked up as income by the individual who was reimbursed.

The tax theory goes like this- if you are reimbursed for depreciation then the cost basis of the asset is reduced by the amount of depreciation. When the asset is sold your reduced cost basis could increase your taxable capital gain (for houses, Yes, for automobiles and other things, probably No).

> Sidebar: Having your S corporation reimburse you for business mileage also reduces the cost basis of your automobile by 28 cents per mile (for the 2023 tax year). If you think home office depreciation is often overlooked, the reduction in cost basis for your automobile because of reimbursed mileage is flat-out ignored by most.

WCG CPAs & Advisors tracks home office depreciation within an individual tax return (Form 1040) by creating an out-of-service asset, and updating the historical depreciation each year. Not ideal, but at least it is contained within the owner's individual tax return for tracking, eventual sale and recapture.

Tax-Free Rental of Your Home

This is the so-called Masters Rule or Augusta Rule depending on your geographical vernacular which stems from Internal Revenue Code Section 280A(g). It is a unique rule in which homeowners who rent out their property for 14 days or fewer in a tax year are not considered to be engaged in the activity for profit, and therefore do not have to claim the rental income.

Therefore, you find a business connection for renting space in your home for 14 days or fewer. Client parties and presentations are good examples. Board meetings for closely held businesses is a bad example (or at least one that is tough to defend). Having said that, let's say you have multiple owners and while it appears closely-held, you need a nice place to chat about the business and be off-campus for privacy. An owner's home makes perfect sense.

Your business enters into a lease arrangement at market rates. The business deducts the amounts paid as rent and issues a 1099 to you. On your individual tax return (Form 1040), the amount of rent is reduced to zero with a one-time expense under Section 280A in the amount of rent.

WCG has a client who sells Pampered Chef, and she hosts demonstrations and parties once a month for a $1,000 per event. Her S Corp deducts $12,000 in rental expense but the cash received is considered tax-free. She legitimized this with competitive rate offers from banquet halls and the like, plus a contract between her and her S Corp. Perfect!

Additionally, your property's mortgage interest and property taxes are still deductible. Yeah baby! They call it the Masters Rule allegedly from those who rent out their homes for the Masters Tournament in Augusta, Georgia.

Tax Home

We often get the question What is my tax home? It is a tricky question... and it is one that a lot of taxpayers are very interested in since your tax home is where you will generally pay taxes and commuting to your tax home is not deductible.

One of the best ways to illustrate the issue is a quick review of a recent Tax Court case, Barrett v. Commissioner, Tax Court Memo 2017-195. Barret was a video producer in Las Vegas, Nevada (this is getting good already). His employer constructed offices in Washington, D.C., which required Barrett to travel to and from several times a year. His average stay in Washington was about two weeks.

Barrett claimed about $55,000 in travel expenses and the IRS challenged arguing that his tax home was in Washington and not Las Vegas. However, the Tax Court disagreed with the IRS because Barrett proved that he did substantial work for his employer in Las Vegas in addition to the work in Washington. As such, his tax home was considered Las Vegas and not Washington.

This allowed him to deduct his travel expenses including lodging and meals since he was not commuting to his tax home. A win for Barrett. But... he eventually lost since he could not substantiate his expenses. So while he was allowed to deduct associated expenses, his recordkeeping was shoddy. Shocking.

Another variant of the tax home issue for business income is the deduction of business expenses. We have yet another Tax Court case that is eerily similar to the Barrett case above. In Bigdeli v. Commissioner, Tax Court Memo 2013-148, the taxpayer was an oral surgeon living in Pennsylvania who traveled 130 miles to New York where he worked at a dentist office.

His personal home was Pennsylvania and his tax home was New York. His $55,950 in travel expenses for the two years in question were disallowed because a) they were personal non-deductible commuting expenses and b) his work location and subsequent tax home did not meet the temporary work location rules.

What if Bigdeli had a home office where he performed administrative functions in addition to his primary work functions outside the home? No dice.

There is a derived (some would say contrived) 50-mile radius rule. It is derived from IRC Section 162(h) which defines the local area for state legislators as 50 miles. The federal government defines metropolitan area for IRS employees as 50 miles from an IRS office as detailed in the Internal Revenue Manual 6.550.1.1.7 (revised December 2009). There are other references to 50 miles, so it is a good rule of thumb to use.

How does the 50-mile rule factor into your home office world? To eliminate commuting using an administrative home office argument, your home office must be within 50 miles of your tax home. This is per Revenue Rulings 99-7 and 93-86, including Chief Counsel Advice 200027047 (CCA's are the IRS's own attorneys' recommendation and interpretations).

Some caution here! This is an administrative home office argument... where you primarily do your work outside the home, and regularly and exclusively use a space in your home for administrative duties such as accounting, speaking to your attorney, invoicing, reviewing contracts, etc.

If you perform your primary work functions in both your home office and a work location outside the home, then your tax home will be the location where you spend the most time, perform the most critical functions and earn the most revenue. This is referenced in Chief Counsel Advice 200020055 which refers to Revenue Ruling 93-86 and 75-432, plus Markey v. Commissioner, 490 F.2d 1249 (6th Circuit 1974). Yeah, some old references but current tax law.

So, if you want to deduct travel, lodging and meals expenses associated with multiple work locations, either a) have your home office be within 50 miles of your tax home, b) do the most work in your home office with the outside-the-home work being secondary or c) have the assignment be temporary (under one year in duration).

How about having a W-2 job in Worcester, MA and running a business in New York City? In Sherman v. Commissioner from 1951, the Tax Court ruled that Worcester was Sherman's tax home and the expenses of travel, lodging and meals associated with his secondary business in New York City were deductible. Win for the taxpayer! A massive one.

Keep in mind the IRS definition of itinerant-

> If you do not have a regular or a main place of business or post of duty and there is no place where you regularly live, you are considered an itinerant (a transient) and your tax home is wherever you work. As an itinerant, you cannot claim a travel expense deduction because you are never considered to be traveling away from home.

As mentioned previously, **WCG CPAs & Advisors** have a lot of Certified Registered Nurse Anesthetists (CRNA) who travel all over the country putting people to sleep on short-term contracts, or stints if you are Formula 1 fan. Unless you return periodically to a place where you regularly live, you will not have a tax home. Without a tax home a lot of travel, lodging and meals deductions go away.

Business Travel Deduction

Let's start off by saying the IRS despises business travel deductions. They view it as a way to rifle personal expenses through the business, and on some levels they are correct. But then again, the rules allow for it under some circumstances. The easiest way to explain business travel as a small business tax deduction is to run through some examples.

You travel to Tahoe to look at rental properties. None of the expenses associated with this trip is deductible. If and when you purchase a rental property in Tahoe, the expenses associated with your travels will be considered an acquisition cost and added to the basis of the purchased property. Upon sale you will realize the tax benefit of your travels through a smaller capital gain.

You travel to Las Vegas on Tuesday for a conference. At night you take in the sights, attend the conference on Wednesday and return home the same day. Travel is deductible at 100%, hotel is deductible at 100% and meals are deductible at 50% (the normal deduction).

Same Las Vegas trip but you return on Friday, with Tuesday and Wednesday being the only days you attend the conference. Since the business portion of the trip did not exceed half of the overall trip, none of the travel is deductible. However, Tuesday's and possibly Wednesday's hotel and meal costs are deductible.

Same Las Vegs trip, but the conference is from Tuesday to Thursday, and you still return home on Friday. Travel is deductible at 100%, and hotel is deductible at 100% provided you demonstrate that returning home on Thursday was not economically feasible. Meals would follow suit with the hotel but at 50% (the normal deduction).

You travel to Miami on Thursday for a conference that starts Thursday and ends on Friday. You also schedule business meetings on Monday. You do not return home on Saturday since it was not economically feasible. Travel is deductible at 100%, hotel is deductible at 100% (including the Saturday and Sunday stay) and meals are deductible at 50%.

This is a generalization, but you get the idea. There are additional exceptions for travel outside the United States and additional rules about side trips (such as seeing Mom on the way home from a business trip). See your Mom (that's important) we'll worry about the deduction later!

If your spouse and / or children are employed by the S corporation, and have a genuine need as you for business travel then he or she follows the same rules above. Where business owners get into trouble is the employment part. Your spouse and / or children must have a legitimate position with the business, and a genuine reason for business travel.

Having Junior stuff envelopes is fine, but bringing Junior to a riveting conference on the "evolution of the market economy in the early colonies" probably won't work. Or have Junior attend a seminar where Vickers argues that Gordon Wood "drastically underestimates the impact of social distinctions predicated upon wealth, especially inherited wealth." Gotta love that epic bar scene from Good Will Hunting.

Deducting Business Meals

We chatted about business meals earlier in the chapter. The Tax Cuts and Jobs Act of 2017 (TCJA) redefined meals and entertainment. In a nutshell, entertainment was removed as a deduction and meals were left in limbo (bad law writing). As such, the IRS released Notice 2018-76 which essentially restores meals, but not entertainment, back to old law.

IRS Notice 2018-76

Now with the clarification offered by IRS Notice 2018-76, 50% of business meals may still be deducted (100% was only for the 2021 and 2022 tax years) if you follow these guidelines as outlined in the notice-

1. The expense is an ordinary and necessary expense under § 162(a) paid or incurred during the taxable year in carrying on any trade or business;

2. The expense is not lavish or extravagant under the circumstances;

3. The taxpayer, or an employee of the taxpayer, is present at the furnishing of the food or beverages;

4. The food and beverages are provided to a current or potential business customer, client, consultant, or similar business contact; and

5. In the case of food and beverages provided during or at an entertainment activity, the food and beverages are purchased separately from the entertainment, or the cost of the food and beverages is stated separately from the cost of the entertainment on one or more bills, invoices, or receipts. The

entertainment disallowance rule may not be circumvented through inflating the amount charged for food and beverages.

Here is an example of a business meals tax deduction that is allowed (straight from the wizards at the IRS who label everyone as A and B)-

Taxpayer A invites B, a business contact, to a baseball game. A purchases tickets for A and B to attend the game. While at the game, A buys hot dogs and drinks for A and B.

The baseball game is entertainment as defined in § 1.274-2(b)(1)(i) and, thus, the cost of the game tickets is an entertainment expense and is not deductible by A. The cost of the hot dogs and drinks, which are purchased separately from the game tickets, is not an entertainment expense and is not subject to the § 274(a)(1) disallowance. Therefore, A may deduct 50 percent of the expenses associated with the hot dogs and drinks purchased at the game.

There are more examples in the IRS notice, but you get the idea. Old school is now the same school, just make sure you disconnect the meal from the entertainment. And no boosting the meal bill to reduce the entertainment bill just to be able to deduct it- "this hot dog cost $100, but it came with a free baseball ticket." Ummm... Nope! See #5 above.

Other considerations that are commonly forgotten-

▲ You can deduct 50% for meals with employees when business is discussed. Common deduction when you add your spouse on payroll (and he or she actually does work).

▲ You can deduct 50% of the cost of transportation to and from the venue where the meal is consumed. Denver to Aspen on United to eat at Ellina or Campo De Fiori. Yum! Seems reasonable.

▲ You can deduct 50% of the costs associated with the meal such as taxes and tips, keeping in check with lavish or extravagant. Tipping $500 at McDonald's for the extra cheese on your whopper, and then asking for a kickback out back behind the dumpster is probably not good. If you do, get a receipt... we're sure you paid a commission on the kickback (kidding!).

This is a trick. McDonald's sells big macs not whoppers.

For business discussions during a meal, you must have a clear business goal in mind, the discussion must be substantive beyond casual conversation, and you must have an expectation of income or benefit to your business from the meeting. The meeting's main purpose should be business related with the eating of food being incidental or secondary.

Entertainment has been removed from Section 274 thanks to the Tax Cuts and Jobs Act. Here is a short list of the entertainment activities where the IRS would historically deny a business conversation effectively took place- nightclubs, theaters, sporting events, large social gatherings, hunting or fishing trips, pleasure boating, and Yes, golf outings. The theory is simple- you must be discussing business matters, and in the eyes of the IRS these activities don't allow for that. Not our argument, so don't blame us.

You may also deduct as a business tax deduction the cost of meals for business discussions that occurred before or after the meal. For example, after a lengthy day of negotiating a business transaction you take the associate out for a nice dinner to relax. While eating your dinner nothing is discussed about business. Since these two events are so closely related, the cost of the dinner is deducted as a meals expense. The business discussions before or after the meal must be substantial and closely connected (nexus).

Everyday Business Meals

Business owners try to deduct meals they eat while traveling throughout the day. This is not a tax deduction. The theory on this is straightforward- you must eat regardless of owning a business or not. In other words, your meal is not contributing directly to the operations or success of your business. The IRS is clever- they don't mind giving you a tax deduction today on something that eventually will result in taxable business income through growth and profits in the future.

Be careful about becoming Sutter. See Sutter Rule, page 329.

Spouse Business Meals

What happens if your spouse tags along to a business meeting over dinner? Or if the client or business associate brings his or her spouse? Do you have to split the bill up between business and non-business participants? No. The IRS considers the spousal attendance to the meeting to be incidental.

Can your spouse be considered a business associate as an employee? Of course. Before you get all excited about trips to Gallagher's in Time Square with your spouse to discuss business, we encourage restraint and reasonableness. If the occasional business discussion occurs during a meal, and the meeting's original intent was business, then this becomes a small business tax deduction at 50%. Position yourself carefully, and Yes, your spouse needs to be an employee.

Office Parties
Now we have three rules.

▲ You can deduct 100% of the meals you provide your employees if the meal is for the convenience of the employer, such as working lunches, and provided on the business premise.

▲ You can deduct 100% of the meals you provide related to employee recreation such as holiday parties and picnics (assumed to be off the business premise, and for WCG CPAs & Advisors at Fuzzy's Taco Shop).

▲ You can deduct 50% of the meals provided on the business premise where the meals "promote goodwill, boost morale or attract prospective employees" according to IRS Publication 15-B. In addition, the employees cannot include officers, shareholders and anyone who owns 10% or greater interest in the business. So, a one-person S Corp shareholder cannot deduct 50% of his or her meals under this rule. Nice try! Someone did. Someone was caught. Rule was written.

De Minimis Meals
The IRS is generous. They also say that meals, such as coffee and donuts, provided under de minimis rules are not considered imputed income to the employees. How nice?! Here is the blurb form the IRS-

In general, a de minimis benefit is one for which, considering its value and the frequency with which it is provided, is so small as to make accounting for it unreasonable or impractical. De minimis benefits are excluded under Internal Revenue Code section 132(a)(4) and include items which are not specifically excluded under other sections of the Code. These include such items as:

- Controlled, occasional employee use of photocopier. "Bob, making copies."

- Occasional snacks, coffee, doughnuts, etc. Glazed only.

- Occasional tickets for entertainment events (we'll see if this gets removed after TCJA).

- Holiday gifts

- Occasional meal money or transportation expense for working overtime

- Group-term life insurance for employee spouse or dependent with face value not more than $2,000

- Flowers, fruit, books, etc., provided under special circumstances such as your 103-year-old grandmother died.

- Personal use of a cell phone provided by an employer primarily for business purposes. Don't even go there on this one!

In determining whether a benefit is de minimis, you should always consider its frequency and its value. An essential element of a de minimis benefit is that it is occasional or unusual in frequency. It also must not be a form of disguised compensation. Therefore, routine dinners with your business partner are not de minimis. It might not qualify for the 50% either unless a business purpose is germane to the meal.

Sutter Rule

The Sutter rule allows the IRS to disallow a portion of your business meals when they consume a large part of your normal living expenses. In other words, if every meal you eat is a justifiable business meal, it might not matter under the Sutter rule. This rule was created in Richard Sutter v. Commissioner, 21 Tax Court 170 (1953), where Sutter expensed his lunch every day but the court found that "the deduction for the cost of lunches was apparently almost entirely payment for petitioner's own meals when he attended such functions as meetings of the Chamber of Commerce. There is no evidence that these costs were any greater than expenditures which petitioner would have been required to make in any event for his own personal purposes. They must consequently be disallowed."

Sutter was audacious- he deducted everything he could think of. It is a great read.

Again be careful. Business meals are low hanging fruit for the IRS. We've seen thousands of dollars in tax savings disappear before our eyes during an examination because the client could not demonstrate the business purpose. To not lose an audit, make sure you keep receipts beyond relying on the credit card statement. In addition, keep a log or journal of the person(s) you met with and the topics of discussion. Be very specific. Memories fade, so if you intend to reconstruct this evidence upon receipt of your examination notice from the IRS, think twice. IRS agents are no dummies on meals.

Remember this; pigs get fed and hogs get slaughtered. Be reasonable, people!

Cohan Rule

Let's briefly discuss record keeping, and then jump into a famous New York entertainer named Cohan who ultimately provided a nifty rule that can be used during an IRS audit. To be able to demonstrate a business deduction you need to show the date, the amount and the person or business you paid. A bank or credit card statement, or canceled check, satisfies this. The second element is the business purpose must be documented either through a logbook, planner or accounting software. Proof of payment plus business purpose equals tax deduction.

Do you need receipts? Yes and no. For travel, gifts and meals, if the amount is under $75 then you only need to document the event and business purpose in a logbook or planner. However, if you spend $10 at Costco for some paper, then you need proof of payment plus business purpose documentation. Seems a bit onerous and even contradictory, but it is true.

Enter Cohan vs. Commissioner, 39 F. 2d 540 (2d Cir. 1930). Yes, 1930 and we still use it today. George Cohan gave us "Yankee Doodle Dandy" and "Give My Regards to Broadway", and he gave us a tax deduction rule. His rule is simple- you can approximate your business expenses and ultimately your business tax deduction. What?! No, it is not that simple.

You must have corroborating evidence that demonstrates your expense. For example, as a Colorado Springs CPA firm, WCG can demonstrate that we prepare so many tax returns which are so many pages in length, and therefore we can approximate our paper costs. Temp. Regs. Sec. 1.274-5T(c)(3) also gives latitude to the IRS to allow substantiation of a business expense by other means.

We have successfully used the Cohan rule in IRS examinations. We have also implemented it during tax preparation when records are incomplete or missing (i.e., one hot mess). Having said that, using estimates and approximations looks bad. Keep good records, please. Do not rely on the Cohan rule or some treasury regulation to save your butt.

The Cohan rule or any type of estimation cannot be used for travel, business gifts and meals. All the good stuff needs strict record keeping habits. Section 274(d) of the U.S. Tax Code also states that listed property must be substantiated with proper documentation. Listed property includes automobiles, and equipment generally used in entertainment such as cameras and stereo equipment. Seems a bit outdated, but there you go. So, if you are a photographer who drives a car for business while entertaining guests, you will be a master at recordkeeping.

A logbook or planner is very influential during an audit. When a client can show contemporaneous records in a planner that coincides with travel, meals and home office use, the audit lasts about 90 minutes as opposed to four hours with a deficiency notice at the end. Contemporaneous comes from Latin, and means existing or happening during the same period. In other words, as things happen in your world, write them down in a logbook or planner.

Girls are better at this than boys because of purses, which is why we now have European shoulder bags for boys. Yet boys still stink at record keeping. If you are a boy, keep in mind that your DNA precludes you from multitasking. You might be doing two things at once, but that in no way is multitasking. Your contemporaneous record keeping might be more sequential.

Capital Leases versus Operating Leases

One of the problems facing small business owners is disguised purchase payments. This happens often when a business leases a copier (for example) for 60 months and then has an option to own the equipment after the lease term expires. We'll talk about that in a second.

The other issue with operating leases is that you cannot depreciate the asset. The most common situation is a leased automobile for the business. Since your automobile lease does not typically qualify as a capital lease, then it is considered an operating lease. The good news is that your lease payment contains the reduction in value (the difference between sales price and residual value), and as such you are receiving some "depreciation" in heavy air quotes with your tax deducted lease payments. The downsides are- a) they are limited to the degradation in value only and b) they are not accelerated.

Back to the capital lease situation. A true lease payment is deductible in full each month, but an installment purchase payment is only deducted to the amount of finance or interest charges.

Here is the blurb from IRS Publication 535-

> Lease or purchase. There may be instances in which you must determine whether your payments are for rent or for the purchase of the property. You must first determine whether your agreement is a lease or a conditional sales contract. Payments made under a conditional sales contract are not deductible as rent expense.

> Conditional sales contract. Whether an agreement is a conditional sales contract depends on the intent of the parties. Determine intent based on the provisions of

the agreement and the facts and circumstances that exist when you make the agreement. No single test, or special combination of tests, always applies.

However, in general, an agreement may be considered a conditional sales contract rather than a lease if any of the following is true.

- The agreement applies part of each payment toward an equity interest you will receive.

- You get title to the property after you make a stated amount of required payments.

- The amount you must pay to use the property for a short time is a large part of the amount you would pay to get title to the property.

- You pay much more than the current fair rental value of the property.

- You have an option to buy the property at a nominal price compared to the value of the property when you may exercise the option. Determine this value when you make the agreement.

- You have an option to buy the property at a nominal price compared to the total amount you have to pay under the agreement.

- The agreement designates part of the payments as interest, or that part is easy to recognize as interest.

There's no real value added by exploding all these factors into drawn out explanations. The most common lease problem is the $1 buyout or something similar- be careful what you are getting into with leases that might be disguised as purchases. Not a huge deal, but the accounting and subsequent business deduction will be different.

In the accounting world we call this example a capital lease (as opposed to an operating lease).Here are some more signs of a capital lease to noodle on-

▲ The ownership of the asset is shifted from the lessor to the lessee (you) by the end of the lease period; or

▲ The lessee (you) can buy the asset from the lessor at the end of the lease term for a below-market price; or

▲ The period of the lease encompasses at least 75% of the useful life of the asset (and the lease is non-cancellable during that time); or

▲ The present value of the minimum lease payments required under the lease is at least 90% of the fair value of the asset at the inception of the lease.

Note all the "or's". Again, don't get too caught up in the technicalities. Just understand that you might have a capital lease that needs further investigation and special handling for your accounting records. Operating leases are simple and deducted in their entirety (such as office rent).

Here is the link to the IRS Publication 535 (Business Expenses)-

wcginc.com/5334

One final word; under GAAP accounting, the rules are different for those who are required to follow special accounting procedures. Here is a blurb from RSM (a big fancy accounting and auditing firm) that explains it a bit-

> Under the old guidance (ASC 840), operating leases were not recorded on the balance sheet, but under ASC 842 operating leases are required to be recorded on the balance sheet, which results in the addition of more assets and liabilities on the balance sheet. Finance (capital) leases will continue to be recognized on the balance sheet. Certain types of assets are excluded from the new standard–leases relating to inventory, intangibles, and some natural resources. The recognition, measurement, and presentation of expenses and cash flows from a lease will continue to depend on its classification as a finance or operating lease. The classification criteria in ASC 842 does not impact the classification for most leases, however, the bright-line classification of ASC 840 was replaced with a principles-based approach.

Don't get hung up on this. Most small businesses do not have a GAAP requirement... this news is just for gee-whiz cocktail conversation. The reason for all this? Operating leases are obligations that are not required to be presented on the balance sheet. An automobile lease here and there, no biggie. A fleet of Boeing 737s is certainly a different situation, and as an investor you would want to know the impact on the balance sheet from these legal obligations.

Putting Your Kids on the Payroll

Should you pay Junior to vacuum? Perhaps. While most parents can't get their children to clean a counter or put away dishes, perhaps putting them to work at the office is a good option.

Tax Advantages

There are some minor tax advantages to paying your children- for example, you can pay your child $14,000 in wages, and since the standard deduction is $14,600 (for the 2024 tax year) the child will not have any taxable income. They can also gift this money back to you, or help pay for groceries.

Kidding aside, for you to give your child $14,600 to save for college or pay for college, it take probably takes $18,000 or more in parental income because of the income taxes.

However, there are some pitfalls. If you are paying them through an S Corp, you must also pay Social Security and Medicare taxes at 15.3%. Therefore, your marginal tax rate needs to be 22% or higher for this to make sense. Conversely, if you pay yourself this income through a shareholder distribution and you are in the 10% tax bracket, you will unnecessarily pay about $636 in general taxes (since payroll taxes are 15.3% and your tax savings is 10%, 5.3% x 14,600 is $734).

You could also pay your child more money since their tax bracket is probably lower than yours.

For regular LLCs, if your child is under 18, the business does not have to pay employment taxes such as Social Security and Medicare. You can also avoid Unemployment taxes until the child turns 21. But for S Corps and C Corps, Social Security and Medicare taxes are paid regardless of age.

However, you can set up a Family Management LLC (there are other branded or marketing terms for this) where the S Corp pays a fee to an LLC which then turns around and processes payroll for the children. You can read more here-

wcginc.com/6177

Your children are going to take your money anyways- might as well make it tax-advantaged.

Retirement Accounts

Your child can contribute to a retirement account and reduce your taxes. Seriously? Seriously!

For example, a 14-year-old can have an IRA or a Roth IRA and contribute 100% of earned wages up to the maximum contribution. And since the wages to the child are a direct business expense, this reduces your overall taxable income (lower S Corporation income, lower pass-through income, and lower shareholder taxes).

Consider this-

IRA Scenario		Roth Scenario	
Junior's Earned Income	21,600	Junior's Earned Income	14,600
Junior's Standard Deduction	14,600	Junior's Standard Deduction	14,600
Junior's IRA Contribution	7,000	Junior's Roth IRA Contribution	7,000
Taxable Income	0	Taxable Income	0
Payroll Taxes @15.3%	3,305	Payroll Taxes @15.3%	2,234
Mom/Dad Savings @10%	-1,145	Mom/Dad Savings @10%	-774
Mom/Dad Savings @22%	1,447	Mom/Dad Savings @22%	978
Mom/Dad Savings @37%	4,687	Mom/Dad Savings @37%	3,168

The standard deduction and IRA limits are for the 2024 tax year.

There are several things at play here. First, Junior must actually work, and this is the biggest bone of contention with the IRS. So, get that squared away. Second, Junior can still have tax-free income although Mom and Dad are claiming him as a dependent on their individual tax return (Form 1040). This generally preserves certain tax credits.

Another issue to consider is support and claiming Junior as a dependent. If Junior is going to college and Mom and Dad are paying him to work at the family business, for Mom and Dad to claim Junior as a dependent they must provide over half of the Junior's support. This includes the amounts spent to provide food, lodging, clothing, education, medical and dental care, recreation, transportation, and similar necessities.

This creates an interesting conundrum. If Junior makes $30,000 working for the family business, but socks all the money away into savings while Mom and Dad continue to pay over half of the support such as rent, food and education, they can still claim Junior as a dependent.

Yet another caveat to this is education credits. At times Mom and Dad's income is too high to be eligible for certain education credits. By paying Junior, and having Junior claim the education credit (and he would have to pay for college too, but gifting can assist), the overall household might win.

So, there might be real savings and, in the example above, Junior is saving for retirement.

A Roth IRA contribution is not deductible while an IRA contribution is, which is why the IRA scenario can have a higher salary. There is not a minimum age for an IRA or Roth IRA- you simply need to have earned income to contribute. And Yes, the money is the child's so when Junior turns 18 and wants to blow it on a new car, it's gone plus penalty. You can't fix everyone.

Company-Sponsored Retirement Plan
A company-sponsored plan could be a SIMPLE, SEP or 401k plan. The usual age for these types of plans is 21, but the plan may be created or adopted to be as low as 14 years of age. Therefore, if you hire your 14-year-old and you also have a 19-year-old working for the business, that 19-year-old suddenly becomes eligible if your company-sponsored plan allows 14-year-olds. There are hours of service thresholds you could implement as well.

But setting up the 401lk plan correctly allows your child to contribute $23,000 (for the 2024 tax year) to a 401k or the maximum limits on SIMPLE's and SEP's which can be significant. In turn the business gets an instant deduction, and the kid gets your money, albeit a bit early.

Conceivably, your child could have a $44,600 salary and contribute all kinds of money to his or her 401k plan and IRA. Here is a table-

IRA and 401k Plan Scenario

Junior's Earned Income	44,600
Junior's Standard Deduction	14,600
Junior's 401k Contribution	23,000
Junior's IRA Contribution	7,000
Taxable Income	0
Payroll Taxes @15.3%	6,824
Mom/Dad Savings @10%	-2,364
Mom/Dad Savings @22%	2,988
Mom/Dad Savings @37%	9,678

The standard deduction, 401k and IRA limits are for the 2024 tax year.

The rule is this- if you are covered by a retirement plan at work (what the IRS calls active participation), and you earn less than $73,000 (for the 2023 tax year) adjusted gross income (which Junior does), you can contribute both to a 401k plan and IRA, and get the IRA deduction.

Here is a link about the various options for small business owners to set up retirement-

wcginc.com/401k

Education Credits

You can also create some tax due to take advantage of the American Opportunity Tax Credit. Huh? Mom and Dad make too much money and cannot take advantage of the AOTC education credit. But Junior, with a little bit of tax due on their 1040 tax return from a $30,000 salary (for example), can get all the tax back as a credit plus the refundable portion. There are some things to navigate through such as claiming them as a dependent, the work needed for a $30,000 salary, etc. but it is something to consider.

IRS and State Concerns

You must be mindful of child labor laws, and as far as the IRS is concerned there are some rules too.

First, the child must actually perform work. Some argue that cleaning bathrooms and stuffing envelopes are different since cleaning bathrooms is non-essential to the business operations and therefore not qualifying. The counter argument is that having your child clean bathrooms replaces your third-party janitorial expense. Our advice is to be as legitimate as possible- create a job description, list of expectations, etc. Ensure that the work they do has a business connection.

Also, the pay must be consistent, and the pay must be reasonable relative to what you pay others for similar work. Basically, you need to treat them like any other employee to avoid troubles. Lastly, you need to keep detailed records such as timecards and job descriptions (of course you do!). This must be perceived as an arms-length relationship.

Many states have labor laws that dictate the age your child can work, even for Mom and Dad. For example, Indiana allows a 14-year-old to work with a permit. Minors under 14 may work as newspaper carrier, golf caddy, domestic service worker in a private residence (sounds like chores) or farm laborer. Minors under 12 in Indiana can only be farm laborers. Again, in Indiana, there is no need for a work permit if the work is outside school hours of 7:30AM to 3:30PM. We bring these examples to light so you understand to check your state or local laws about hiring your kids.

WCG CPAs & Advisors will not process payroll for any child under the age of 12 unless there are special circumstances. For example, we have a client who has twin 9-year-old daughters who do quite well recording Tik Tok videos. We continue to be amazed at how people make money, and what the public is willing to pay for the efforts.

Mom and Dad (your parents)
The concepts above could also be applied to supporting your Mom and Dad. Aside from possibly making them minority owners and providing them with shareholder distributions, there could be some scenarios where a salary could make sense as well. Other sources of income and tax brackets of course all need to be considered.

Education Assistance with an S Corp (Section 127)
There are two types of education- one that is open-ended and has no business connection to your trade or profession, and one that helps you improve a current work skill.

Open-Ended Education Assistance
Your LLC or S Corp can pay up to $5,250 (for the 2023 tax year, and has not changed for a while) of an employee's tuition and education expenses including your children who work for you. But there are some rules for your child. He or she must-

▲ Be age 21 or older,

▲ Be a legitimate employee of the LLC or S Corp,

▲ Not own more than 5% of the LLC or S Corp, and

▲ Not be your dependent.

The Age 21 rule stems from attribution rules whereby a child under the age of 21 is deemed to own the same percentage as his or her parents. So, if you own 100% and your child is 20, your child is considered to be a 100% owner for this benefit (and many others), which obviously exceeds the 5% rule.

For your amusement, 26 USC 1563(e) Constructive Ownership reads-

> (6) Children, grandchildren, parents, and grandparents
> (A) Minor children
> An individual shall be considered as owning stock owned, directly or indirectly, by or
> for his children who have not attained the age of 21 years, and, if the individual has

not attained the age of 21 years, the stock owned, directly or indirectly, by or for his parents.

And, 26 USC 127(b) Educational Assistance Programs-

(3) Principal shareholders or owners
Not more than 5 percent of the amounts paid or incurred by the employer for educational assistance during the year may be provided for the class of individuals who are shareholders or owners (or their spouses or dependents), each of whom (on any day of the year) owns more than 5 percent of the stock or of the capital or profits interest in the employer.

Therefore, your kids essentially (a) have constructive ownership until 21 year of age, (b) are considered a 5% shareholder and (c) are ineligible for education assistance. And as mentioned through this book, special rules kick in for a 2% shareholder (or 5% shareholder in this case) triggering tax consequences for benefits received. Therefore, the benefit might kick in around senior year in undergraduate school, and certainly for any graduate or post-degree education.

Under Section 127, reimbursable education includes any form of instruction or training that improves or develops the capabilities of an individual, and is not limited to job-related or degree programs. However, qualified expenses do not include meals, lodging and transportation.

A written plan must be drafted, and employees must be notified of the benefit. Therefore, we suggest having each employee sign a notice that explains the benefits, and that they have read and understand the benefits. And no other benefits can be offered as an alternative- in other words, you cannot provide additional pay or bonus for employees who do not use the educational assistance program.

Improving Current Work Skills
To be able to deduct education expense as a small business tax deduction, the education must either-

▲ Maintain or improves skills required in your existing business, or,

▲ Is required by law or regulation to maintain your professional status through continuing education credits such as attorneys, accountants, real estate agents, mortgage lenders, etc.

So, can you deduct your MBA? Perhaps. In Lori A. Singleton-Clarke v. Commissioner, Tax Court Summary Opinion 2009-182, the court ruled in Lori's favor. She was an established nurse, and she went back to school to obtain an MBA in Health Care Management. She was already in charge of quality control from a management perspective, and the MBA did not lead to an additional and discernable skill. Additionally, the court stated that the MBA improved her current work skill as a quality control coordinator. Subtle difference.

Here are some more-

Mary Colliver v. Commissioner, Tax Court Summary Opinion 2017-93. Mary held a Bachelor's degree in speech pathology and was offered a position with a hospital doing similar work. The hospital position required Mary to obtain her Master's degree in speech pathology, but the hospital allowed her to complete her studies while performing the tasks of the position. Specifically, the Master's degree allowed her to be a medical speech pathologist.

Mary subsequently deducted about $8,500 in qualified education expenses, and upon examination the IRS disallowed the deduction. The Tax Court also agreed and their summary concluded that the tasks and activities before and after the additional education were different enough to qualify as a new trade or business. In other words, Mary could not work in hospitals without the Master's degree, and her education allowed her to do so. The Court found this convincing enough to deny the qualified education expense deduction.

Our take is that this is certainly splitting hairs. Mary was a speech pathologist before and after, and she simply improved her current work skills as a speech pathologist to become a better one. It wasn't like she was a high school counselor who wanted to become a medical speech pathologist. So, be wary that the Tax Court is creating very low thresholds for making the leap of "new trade or business."

Here's another, similar crummy deal in our opinion-

Czarnecki v. U.S., 120 AFTR 2d 2017-5372. Jerry Czarnecki was an engineer for most of his adult life and held a Bachelor's degree in engineering and a Master's degree in applied mathematics. In 1998 he started a Doctoral program at MIT. Yeah, total nerd, ridiculously smart and probably super rich. Calm down ladies, we're sure he had a third eye and was married with a gaggle of unruly children who would drive you nuts.

In 2007 he started to work for the U.S. Navy as a Systems Engineer Level 3 ensuring that submarines wouldn't crumple under water and to study the effects of submarine vibration on batteries. Again, super high-tech stuff. During 2010 he was a licensed professional engineer but was not as a structural engineer. Jerry deducted $8,712 in qualified education expenses on his 2010 amended tax return (first mistake... give an IRS human a reason to say, "yeah right.").

His second mistake was not demonstrating how his Doctoral studies improved his current work skills. The Court said it was not enough to simply make the assertion as a global argument; the Court wanted very specific links between what Jerry did today and how his education improved his current set of skills.

As a result his deduction was disallowed

Before you drop $50,000 a semester for Wharton or Stanford, be careful. In our experience there is enough case law on either side of the MBA deduction issue to be wary. Having said that, get an MBA because you want the education, degree and ultimately more opportunities. If we can find a way to deduct it, great. If not, you still have improved yourself.

Summary of Small Business Tax Deductions

This chapter is huge, and has a ton of information in it and perhaps it is overwhelming. To reiterate information from the beginning of this chapter there are some over-arching themes and concepts for all small business deductions.

The business expense must be-

▲ Ordinary and necessary (IRS Publication 334), and

▲ Paid or recognized in the current tax year, and

▲ Directly related to your business, and

▲ Reasonable, and not lavish or extravagant (IRC Section 162 and IRS Publication 463).

We want to give you this table to help summarize the business deductions that are clearly not allowed (black), the ones that clearly are allowed (white), and the gaggle of exceptions (grey).

Business Expense	Deduction?
401k Plan	Get $500 tax credit from IRS for starting one. Great way to defer taxes. We can set this up.
Advertising	Yes.

Business Expense	Deduction?
Automobiles	Business use only. Use decision tree to see if you should own it or the business. Depends on price, turnover, miles driven, business use and marginal tax rates. Personal use added to W-2 Box 1, 3 and 5 using Lease Value rates in IRS Pub 15-B.
Business Travel	All kinds of rules. Mix pleasure with business under some circumstances.
Business Meals	50% if business discussion with client, prospect or associate. 50% if traveling away from your tax home on business. 100% for business social gatherings or convenience of the employer (lunch).
Cell Phone	Business use only. Never 100% unless you have second phone. Reimbursed through Accountable Plan.
Client Gifts	Max $25 per recipient per year.
Commissions	Yes.
Commuting Expenses	No. If you have a home office, then commuting becomes business travel and subsequently Yes.
Copier Lease	If the lease can be considered a capital lease, then No. If the lease is an operational lease, then Yes. Depends on the facts and circumstances.
Country Club Dues	No. Don't throw the book. Not our fault.
Defined Benefits Plan	Get $500 tax credit from IRS for starting one. Great way to defer taxes. We can set this up.
Education	Only if improves your current work skills or necessary for professional credentials (see Tax Court cases above).
Food	50% if business discussion with client, prospect or associate. 50% if traveling away from your tax home on business. 100% for business social gatherings or convenience of the employer (lunch).
Golf Outing	No. Seriously. Let it go.
Guard Dogs	If you are a high risk defense attorney on the East Coast and need a security detail, then Maybe. Must be a bona fide occupational qualification.
Health Reimbursement Arrangement (HRA)	Yes. Need a HRA plan. There are rules. Added to your W-2 Boxes 1, 16 and 14.
Health Savings Accounts (HSA)	Business contributions, Yes. Added to your W-2 Boxes 1, 16 and 14.

Business Expense	Deduction?
Home Office	If regularly and exclusively used for business then Yes. Multiple locations OK provided home office is primarily used for substantial administrative activities. Reimbursed through Accountable Plan.
Insurance	Business liability insurance, Yes. Auto insurance, Yes if the business owns the car. Health insurance, Yes and added to W-2 Box 1. Dental insurance, Yes and added to W-2 Box 1. Eye insurance, Yes and added to W-2 Box 1. Long Term Care insurance, Yes but limited. Disability insurance, No. Otherwise your benefits become taxable income. Life insurance, No. Only in C corporations where the corporation is the owner and beneficiary (no S Corp election!).
Kids On Payroll	Great way of reducing tax liability for the same amount of cash. Must do it correctly and follow state child labor laws.
Legal, Professional Fees	Yes.
Merchant Card Fees	Yes.
Per Diem	Maybe. If employees own more than 10% of a corporation, then No. Sole proprietors and single-member LLCs including partners in partnerships, Yes.
Professional Attire	If the clothing is suitable for everyday use then No. If the clothing is a uniform then Yes. Possible advertising expense. No dry cleaning unless clothing otherwise qualifies.
Profit Sharing Plan	Get $500 tax credit from IRS for starting one. Great way to defer taxes. We can set this up.
Retirement Plan	Get $500 tax credit from IRS for starting one. Great way to defer taxes. We can set this up.
Taxes	Sales tax, Yes. Payroll tax, Yes for business portion. Estimated tax payments, No. Nice try.
Utilities	No, unless you have a separate office location. If using home office, utilities is a part of the deductible basis.
Website	Yes.

There you go. There are tons of variations, exceptions, rules to follow, interpretations, positioning, and many more modifiers that we can't think of right now. Please contact us if you have any questions or concerns- we love to run through small business tax deductions with owners. And like a good parent, we try to find ways to say Yes. Yes, you can go to

Johnny's house right after you clean your room. Yes, you can deduct that expense provided you document it this way.

Business Tax Return Preparation

We get asked often, "What do you need to prepare my business tax returns?" Or, "what should I be recording or keeping track of throughout the year?" We created a template called the Simplified Business Operations (SBO) Worksheet. While spreadsheets and templates are only meaningful to the spreadsheet designer, you might find value and some helpful hints.

Here is the link to our SBO-

wcginc.com/21

Here is also a checklist of all the things we need beyond revenue and expenses for the preparation of your business tax return-

wcginc.com/2

Even if you don't use **WCG CPAs & Advisors**, you might find these tools helpful.

Comingling of Money

We've mentioned this previously, and we'll do it again here. Rule #1- Please get a separate checking account for your business, preferably with the same bank as your personal checking account so transfers (shareholder distributions) are easy. Rule #2- Do not pay for personal expenses or any mixed-use expense with business funds.

This is bad for several reasons- the IRS hates it. It erodes the corporate veil which is already dangerously thin since you are a closely held corporation. Lastly, if you need to re-construct your financials because of a QuickBooks disaster or some other disaster, having your business transactions compartmentalized within a bank account makes life better. All money coming in is income. All money going out is an expense or a distribution.

Do you get the feeling that we've said these words before? Like déjà vu? Ever have vuja de? It is the feeling that this has never happened before- opposite of deja-vu. Yes, we did mentioned this before in Chapter 10 on operating your S Corp. Here it is again.

Read Rule #2 again. It is imperative to keep an arms-length perspective on you, the employee, and relationship with the S corporation. If you worked for Google or Ford, you wouldn't be able to get the business to buy your groceries or pay your mortgage directly. Same thing with your business.

Here is another quick table to help you out with the "Which debit card should I use?" question.

Cash Outflow	Checking Account To Use
Car Lease	Personal, unless lease is in business name.
Gas for Car	Personal, unless owned / registered by business
Estimated Tax Payments	Personal, since an S Corp is a pass-through entity
Cell Phone	Personal, reimbursed through Accountable Plan
Home Utilities	Personal, reimbursed through Accountable Plan
Home Office Renovations	Personal, possible partial reimbursement
DSW, Banana Republic	Personal, but it would be nice
Shareholder Distribution	Business
Self-Employed Health Insurance	Business
Out of Pocket Medical	Personal, unless you have an HRA
Accountable Plan Reimbursements	Business
401k Contribution	Business
SEP IRA Contribution	Business, but you should use a 401k instead

Please read Chapter 10 on operating your S Corp and specifically the section on Accountable Plans for more information on getting reimbursed as an employee of your S Corp for those expenses that are both personal and business such as cell phones, home offices, internet, etc.

Reducing Taxes

One of our primary focuses at **WCG CPAs & Advisors** is ensuring you are paying the least amount of taxes allowed by law. Some of our other primary focuses are helping you build wealth and leverage the most of your financial worlds for you and your family. However, these focuses or objectives are not isolated; they are very much related to each other and intertwined.

Before we run through several tax reduction and tax avoidance ideas, let's talk about some basic concepts-

There is not a secret tax deduction club that only a few people know about. If there were, it would be like fight club, right? But trust us when we say no one is intentionally not talking about a tax deduction club.

Most people are interested in saving cash when they say they want to reduce or avoid taxes, but saving cash and reducing taxes are not necessarily the same.

Two households, making the exact same income, might have wildly different tax liabilities based on the myriad of variables such as children, mortgage interest, charitable donations, available tax credits, and, Yes, the proficiency of the tax professionals involved. So, just because your neighbor or produce clerk pays x does not mean you will too.

As household incomes travel through the ranges, a lot of things happen. The first $100,000 in income for most households is well-sheltered with itemized deductions and low tax brackets. The next $100,000 in income sees certain tax credits go away, higher tax brackets and fewer available tax deductions such as IRAs and other things (what we call income phase-outs).

In other words, if you go from $100,000 to $200,000 in household income, you will pay way more than double in taxes (you could easily see 2.5 to 3.0 times more). YUCK! The next $100,000 and beyond is completely naked, and is generally purely taxable (unless some tax reduction tactics are deployed). Super yuck!

Tax deductions and tax deferrals are not the same. Tax deferrals are tax bombs later in life; little IOU's to the IRS and they will eventually call in the chit. But if you use the immediate tax savings to build wealth, then a tax deferral is worth it. Deferring taxes to pay for a cruise vacation might not always be the best approach (then again, live a little!).

You want to match the highest tax deduction to the high income. Let's say it's December and you are considering buying a piece of equipment. If next year's income is going to be significantly higher, wouldn't it make sense to wait until January to complete the purchase? Probably.

Tax deductions commonly need separation with cash. For example, you can save $2,500 (for example) in taxes right now if you write a check for $10,000 to a charity. That might not make sense if you are more interested in cash than taxes, right? Tax deferrals commonly need separation with cash as well, but at least you get it back. IRA's and 401k plans (among others) come to mind.

Ok, here we go on those tax reduction and tax avoidance headlines. Some of this might not make sense purely based on the headline. We expand on each of these tax reduction strategies on our webpage (**wcginc.com/6177**).

▲ Sell Stock Losers to Offset Gains

▲ Borrow Against Your Unrealized Stock Gains

▲ Budget Review, Business Connection

▲ State Deferrals, Arbitrage

▲ 401k, SEP IRAs, and IRAs

▲ Health Savings Accounts (HSA)

▲ Advanced Tax Planning for IRA's, Roth IRAs and Roth Conversions

▲ Donor Advised Fund, Qualified Charitable Distribution

▲ Optimized Shareholder Salary

▲ Pass-Through Entity (PTE) Tax Deduction

▲ Profit Sharing, Defined Benefits Pensions (Cash Balance)

▲ Accountable Plan Reimbursements

▲ Prepay Expenses

▲ Depreciation Optimization

▲ Switching to Accrual Accounting

▲ Adding Spouse to Payroll

▲ Adding Children to S Corp Payroll

▲ Adding Children to Payroll Family Management LLC

▲ Consider Yourself a Passive Business Owner

▲ Short-Term Rental (STR) Loophole

▲ Cost Segregation on Real Estate

▲ Real Estate Professional

▲ 1031 Exchanges (Like-Kind) on Real Estate Transactions

▲ Tax Free Rental of Your Home

▲ Medical C Corp

▲ Permanent Life Insurance Plans

▲ Conservation Easement

▲ Captive Insurance

▲ Family Limited Partnerships (FLP) and LLCs

▲ Discounted Roth Conversions

▲ GRATs, GRITs, and Private Annuities

If you want to know about these bulleted items, please visit-

wcginc.com/6177

Chapter 12
Retirement Planning
(updated November 2023)

Retirement Planning Within Your Small Business

Most people have a pretty good handle on personal finance and basic retirement savings, and while the principles are generally the same in the small business world, a lot of business owners have a deer caught in your headlights at 2:00AM look when it comes to leveraging their business for retirement. And there is good reason- retirement planning within your small business carries a bunch more options and potential pitfalls (sounds like life in general, doesn't it?).

Reasons for Small Business Financial Planning

There are three major wealth considerations for small business owners (or anyone for that matter)-

▲ Accumulation (fun and exciting part)

▲ Preservation (the tricky part)

▲ Transfer (the necessary evil part)

Each of these major wealth considerations are interwoven, needs comprehensive focus to ensure the necessary dots are connected, and should have no gaps or holes exist during transitions. That is where financial planning comes into play.

Accumulation is easy. Most people think if they toss some money at a mutual fund they are planning for retirement. Nope.

Preservation gets tricky since we need to have our money outlast our lives. And with people living well into their 90s, this can be tough. Let's put it another way- if you work for 40 years, from age 25 to 65, you need to save enough to live for another 25-30 years. That is incredible. If you are spending $100,000 at age 55, you better be making $180,000 and putting the $80,000 into a moderate growth retirement vehicle.

Preservation also includes proper insurance, asset protection through trusts, pro-active maneuvering and other tools in the toolbox.

Transfer of wealth is automatic. We have yet to see a hearse with a trailer hitch. Or, said in a completely starker way, every life comes with a death sentence. How it is executed is partially up to you. Did we just ruin your appetite? Sorry.

Transfer of wealth can also be tricky. The current federal estate tax exemption is $12.92 million (for the 2023 tax year) per person, and a passed spouse can posthumously port his or her exemption to the surviving spouse. Not bad. And most people don't have over $26 million in estate value. Rich people problems (now referred to as high net worth... the most over-used and water-downed phrase today).

> Sidebar: According to a November 2019 Forbes article, over $30 trillion in wealth will be transferred by baby boomers. Furthermore, according to a 2018 study from Bankrate.com, millennials are less inclined to invest in the stock market. So, where this wealth goes is certainly unclear.

These federal exemption amounts are indexed each year, and while Congress can always vote to repeal, this estate tax exemption was written in stone with passing of the American Taxpayer Relief Act of 2012. However, various states have much lower exemptions. For the 2022 tax year, Connecticut was $9.1 million, Hawaii was $5.5 million, among other examples.

Nebraska does not have an estate tax, but they do have an inheritance tax (the recipient pays depending on relationship and could be as high as 13%). California, the class favorite, is one of 33 states that do not impose an inheritance tax. Apparently, you've been taxed to death and there is nothing left to tax when you die in California.

Therefore, just because you are out of woods federally, doesn't mean the transfer your wealth is free of taxation. Get a plan.

What about your business? Does it have an exit strategy or wealth transfer strategy? Businesses are like marriages; easy to get into, hard to get out. Add this to the plan.

The reasons for financial planning are-

Goals and Objectives
Define your goals and objectives, determine your current position and discover unmanaged risks. This sounds simple and makes sense, but defining goals and objectives is a fluid concept. They change. And as they change, the plan needs to be malleable enough to adapt.

Financial plans are modified annually or whenever a major life change as occurred, whichever is more frequent. This is important.

The Plan
Financial plans also create a blueprint and chart a course on how to reach goals and objectives while managing risk. Again, this sounds simple. But even the most basic house needs a blueprint for framers, plumbers, electricians and even inspectors to review and implement. And in the case of a financial plan, these same players are your financial advisors, tax professionals, attorneys and insurance specialists.

Accountability
Financial plans also provide confidence, measure success and hold everyone accountable. If everyone agrees that your financial plan will ensure financial security in your life, then it becomes a measuring stick for determining success along the way. Anyone can throw some money at an investment, but what does it mean? And does it fit the plan? And is the selection of that investment meeting the plan's objectives.

WCG CPAs & Advisors can always assist you with retirement and financial planning as it relates to your small business and taxation. If you need a referral for a financial advisor, we might be able to help with that too. However, we have fallen out of favor with a lot of the assets under management fee schedules, so we have trouble endorsing an advisor since most charge a percentage based on your asset values. We are not quite sure how the size of your portfolio translates into time and expertise, and in turn the value for services provided, but we digress.

Small Business Retirement Plans Comparison
We are going to put the carriage in front of the horse, and show you a comparison of basic small business retirement plans before explaining each plan. We cheated, and used Pacific Life's online calculator to demonstrate these differences. Why re-invent the wheel? And frankly, they do a fantastic job at this type of stuff. Here is their link-

wcginc.com/6103

We took a handful of salaries (for corporations including S corporations) and net incomes (for sole proprietors and partners in partnerships) and plugged them into Pacific Life's calculator, and came up with the following table based on the 2023 tax year limits-

Salary/Income	Entity	Max 401k	Max SEP IRA	Max SIMPLE
60,000	Sole Prop / Partner	33,652	11,152	17,162
60,000	Corporation	37,500	15,000	17,300
125,000	Sole Prop / Partner	45,734	23,234	18,963
125,000	Corporation	53,750	31,250	19,250
150,000	Sole Prop / Partner	50,381	27,881	19,656
150,000	Corporation	60,000	37,500	20,000
174,000	Sole Prop / Partner	54,848	32,348	20,321
174,000	Corporation	66,000	43,500	20,720
232,000	Sole Prop / Partner	66,000	43,792	21,928
232,000	Corporation	66,000	58,000	22,460
264,000	Sole Prop / Partner	66,000	50,106	22,814
264,000	Corporation	66,000	66,000	23,420
346,000	Sole Prop / Partner	66,000	66,000	25,000
346,000	Corporation	66,000	66,000	25,400

Note the bolded $66,000 number. This is the maximum defined contribution amount permitted in 2023 per plan (and Yes, you can have two plans- we'll talk about Greg and his two plans in an example later).

Crazy! The following are some quick observations-

▲ In 2023, the maximum you can contribute to a qualified retirement plan is $66,000 ($69,000 for the 2024 tax year). You can go above this with a defined benefits pension (cash balance)- more on that later.

▲ Partnerships (those required to file Form 1065) follow the same limits as Sole Prop above.

▲ $174,000 in W-2 salary from your C Corp or S Corp is the magic number for maximizing your 401k. After that, any increase in salary does not help. Your fastest way to reach your contribution limit is through a 401k plan.

▲ $264,000 in W-2 income from your S Corp is the minimum salary for a max SEP IRA contribution.

▲ $346,000 from your small business or K-1 partnership income from your Schedule E as reported on your individual tax return is the magic number for maximizing your SEP IRA contribution. SEPs are old school and used for crisis management rather than planning (more on that too).

▲ Earned income from a sole proprietor is net profit minus 50% of your self-employment (SE) tax minus your contribution. Since the contribution actually adjusts the maximum contribution, this can be a circular reference. And No, 401k or SEP contributions do not reduce SE tax.

▲ 401k max is computed by taking $22,500 employee (you) contribution, plus 25% of your W-2 or earned income (as adjusted). This is for the 2023 tax year. The $22,500 goes to $23,000 for the 2024 tax year.

▲ SEP IRA max is computed by taking 25% of your W-2 or earned income (as adjusted).

▲ Max SIMPLE 401k is basically $15,500 plus 3% of your W-2 or earned income (as adjusted). Don't spend too much time thinking about SIMPLE 401k plans. This increases to $16,000 for the 2024 tax year.

▲ You can add $7,500 for catch-up contributions if you are 50 years old or older.

Let's talk about each of these qualified plans in turn, starting with the 401k. Out of the box, or non-traditional retirement plans will follow (profit sharing plans, defined benefits pensions, cash balance plans, Section 79 plans, etc.). Exciting!

Self-Employed Retirement Plan Basics

There are two plan basics, either a defined contribution plan or a defined benefits plan.

A defined benefit plan is a benefit that is payable to you upon retirement. It is usually based on formulas to compute the periodic payments made to you during retirement. These are sometimes referred to as a pension or annuity since a benefit is defined, and the paid to you. For example, military personnel who meet certain obligations are paid a recurring benefit for the rest of their lives. It might be indexed each year for cost-of-living increases and it might have survivor benefits. Either way it is a guaranteed payment based on a formula. If you live to 100, you might "beat the system." If you die at 55, the pension payment ends, and the money set aside for you is lost.

In contrast, a defined contribution plan specifies how much money will be contributed to a retirement plan today. This is precisely how 401k plans work. It removes a lot of the guesswork and risk from guaranteeing a certain defined benefit to you upon retirement. Rather, the risk is all yours- the amount you invest, how long you invest and how you invest it will dictate the retirement benefit. This benefit might be projected with planning software, but it is not technically defined or guaranteed.

Because of guaranteed payments and life expectancy issues, employers have scaled back on defined benefit plans. The cool thing is this- as a small business owner you are the employer and defined benefit plans might have a real place in your retirement planning. One of the examples is a cash balance account which is technically a defined benefits plan, but you can see the account balance like a defined contribution plan. More on that later.

Some terminology clarification. We use the word deferral when referencing employees and contributions when referencing businesses. When an employee is putting money into a retirement plan, he or she is deferring a portion of compensation hence our use of deferral. This has nothing to do with deferring taxes since deferrals into Roth 401k plans do not reduce taxes.

As a side bar deferred compensation plans include pension plans, retirement plans and employee stock option plans. For now, let's go back to the defined contribution plan and run through some of the basics.

Retirement Questions to Ask

If financial planning is being skipped, then you need to boil things down a bit. There are three very simple questions that need to be asked and, in most cases, the last question is the most important.

Retirement Goals and Objectives
When do you want to retire? Will it be transition-style or cliff-style? Is it better to burn out than to fade away (Rock of Ages anyone?)? And then all the issues of how much and for how long.

What type of legacy do you want to leave behind for your heirs? Do you want the check to the mortician to bounce?

Investment Risk
The quintessential question for all financial planning is investment risk so retirement plans and products can be matched with the investor's level of risk tolerance.

Show Me the Money
How much money can you give up temporarily? This is the most important question. This will single handedly dictate 401k versus SEP IRA versus IRA versus defined benefits pension versus whatever. Perhaps not single-handedly, but the amount of cash you can stomach separating from as a small business owner will be a compelling factor in your decision making.

For example, if only have $7,000 to spend, an IRA is all you might need assuming 2024 IRA contribution limits. Having said that, a solo 401k plan which also has a Roth option to it, might be better even if you only put in $7,000. More on that in a bit.

And as any small business owner will explain, most extra dollars are invested back into the business. This is a simple math equation- many small business owners believe in and perhaps even realize a larger return on investment with a dollar invested back into the business versus the stock market or real estate.

In many cases, a small business will be a huge source of retirement income either through residual income (such as an insurance agent or a financial advisor), shareholder or partnership income such as guaranteed payments, or from the sale of the business.

This might not be as true for the one-person consultant of course, but you get the idea of pressure between growth and retirement.

Tax Savings and Tax Deferrals
Many taxpayers walk into our offices at **WCG CPAs & Advisors** and tell us they want to pay fewer taxes. Who doesn't? We usually chuckle, and tell the client that he or she is the only one and it is sooooo refreshing to hear someone want to pay fewer taxes. Sorry for being

snarky, but taxes are a way of life. Yes, our job is to have you pay the least amount of taxes permitted by law and not a dollar more, but that isn't the only objective.

Tax savings comes in four variants- you can lie, cheat and steal, or you can understand the allowances, deductions and credits alongside the wiggle room afforded by the IRS code. We prefer the latter of course although the audit rate risk of 0.4% for S Corps and partnerships makes it all too tempting. Darn laws and ethics!

However, notice how 401k plans, IRAs, and other tax-deferred vehicles are not listed as one of the four ways to save taxes within self-employed retirement plans. A tax deferral is not automatically a tax-savings technique- it might be. It might not be. In true accountant fashion, it depends.

This is a real-life case- we have two Boeing engineers who saved about $1 million in the company 401k plan. The employee deferrals were all pre-tax, so they avoided about $250,000 in taxes since they were in the 25% marginal tax rate. Not bad.

However, they currently have four children, a house mortgage, and the usual tax deductions of a household of this size and age. When this couple retires in 2025, their marginal tax rate will increase to 32% due to their pension income and other income sources, and the dramatic reduction in tax deductions and credits.

So, they saved at 25% and they will pay it back at 32%. Bummer. But wait! There is more to the story. Just like Paul Harvey, there is a page 2, or in the case of this book, on the next page. Yes, we are dating ourselves by referring to Paul Harvey but when that is all your parents listened to in the car, it is hard to forget.

What about all tax deferrals? Where does that money go? Usually to buy stuff like cars, vacations, food, and other consumables which don't offer a return on investment. But what if this same couple invested the current tax deferrals into a conservative portfolio which yields a nice 5% rate of return (after tax consequence)? Things tilt in their favor- so we are back to having a tax benefit from tax deferrals. Huh?

The following is a ridiculously overly simplified table to demonstrate what we are talking about. Here are the assumptions-

▲ Defer $23,000 (for the 2024 tax year) per year for 10 years.

▲ Marginal tax rate is 22% during wage earning years.

▲ Rate of return on investing tax deferral savings is 5% net of taxes.

Here's the table-

Year	Defer	Tax Savings @ 22%	Growth at 5%
1	23,000	5,060	5,313
2	23,000	5,060	10,892
3	23,000	5,060	16,749
4	23,000	5,060	22,900
5	23,000	5,060	29,358
6	23,000	5,060	36,139
7	23,000	5,060	43,258
8	23,000	5,060	50,734
9	23,000	5,060	58,584
10	23,000	5,060	66,826
Totals	230,000	50,600	66,826

A quick recap- you deferred $230,000 and deferred $50,600 in taxes. That deferral grew to $66,826 because you invested it in a safe 5% investment portfolio. Great. What does this do?

Here is the realized savings for a 22% marginal tax rate during retirement-

Withdrawals Taxed at 22%	50,600
Growth on Tax Savings	66,826
Realized Savings (difference)	16,226

If your marginal tax rate remains the same at 22% you still see a savings of $16,226 as shown above. Again, this is predicated on you taking the tax you normally would have paid and investing it wisely. Not all of us are this disciplined.

But if your marginal tax rate increases from 22% to 35%, your savings is zero. Granted, to jump 13% in marginal tax rate between wage earning years and retirement years seems rare, but you get the point.

The moral of the story is this. Yes, tax deferrals can lead to tax savings, but you must work the system and be disciplined. Not just today, but for several years, and you need a jump in marginal tax rate that is 9% or less (in general). Assuming you have an increase at all. See below-

Withdrawals Taxed at 32%	73,600
Growth on Tax Savings	66,826
Realized Loss (difference)	-6,774

The bummer of this table is the leap from 22% to 32% marginal tax rate. Recall that you deferred tax at the 22% marginal tax rate. If you pay it back at 22%, then you are golden. You pay it back at 32% (the next marginal tax rate), then you lose money.

What should you do? Financial planning and review with your financial advisor are a must. Generally, we see people in the 10 and 12% marginal taxes doing post-tax (Roth). We see people in the 32, 35 and 37% marginal tax rates doing pre-tax. Then, we see people in the 22 and 24% marginal tax rates doing a mixture of post-tax and pre-tax retirement contributions.

We'll talk about the built-in hedge with the employer (your business) contributions which must be pre-tax. In other words, your 401k deferrals are Roth (post-tax) and your employer contributions are pre-tax. This combination is a great hedge.

There is also the RMD angle. RMD is a common TLA (three letter acronym) tossed around at bingo parlors and country clubs, and stands for required minimum distributions. In a nutshell, the IRS forces you to take out a portion of your pre-tax retirement savings every year so they can collect on the IOU you gave them several years ago.

RMD calculations are simple. You take your age, find your life expectancy factor and divide that into your aggregate pre-tax account balance. Do you remember science class and discussing a molecule's half-life? RMDs are very similar- over the course of retirement, you must withdraw pre-tax retirement dollars, but the calculus doesn't force you to take it all out over your lifetime. It always has some factor of your age, and depending on your frugality you might die with a pile of money since the minimum leaves behind a lot.

The IRS released updated life expectancy tables and distribution periods in November 2020. The last time this was done was nearly 20 years ago! Here is snippet of the IRS RMD table which can be found in the appendix of IRS Publication 590-B (the most recent is for the 2022 tax year)-

Age	Factor
72	27.4
75	24.6
80	20.2
85	16.0
90	12.2

So, if you are 75 years old and had $1M in pre-tax money, your RMD would be $40,650 ($1,000,000 divided by 24.6).

What does this have to do with tax deferrals becoming tax savings? At some point you die, and if you only take out the minimum amount from your accounts, you will die with money in the bank. And this now-inherited IRA, for example, is taxed at your heirs' rate. Under the new SECURE Act from December 2019, distributions from inherited IRAs to individuals other than spouses must be fully distributed in 10 years. There are some exceptions and other issues such as disabled individuals and minors, but that is the general gist.

The IRS wants to collect your previous IOU to them, like a Vegas bookie, and they don't want to watch you keep kicking the can down the road.

So, for you there is tax savings built into the RMD system since not all the money is taken out and taxed. If you add in your heirs' marginal tax rates, perhaps this changes from a "family unit" perspective. Heck, you're the dead person- let your kids worry about your taxes by assuming them as their own. It takes a while to payback for all those sleepless nights and stinky diapers, but eventually it happens.

All kidding aside, here is something to consider- with life expectancy well into the 90s, your children might be retired too when you pass. Crazy but realistic, especially if you had kids before you had a career.

Using a 401k Plan in Your Small Business Retirement Options

A 401k plan is a defined contribution plan. Specifically, the name 401k refers to the section in the IRS code that allows for retirement plan contributions to give you an instant tax savings.

Technically it is Title 26, Chapter 1, Subchapter D, Part I, Subpart A, Section 401, Subsection K.

Subchapter D deals with deferred compensation. Part I deals with pensions, profit sharing, etc. Subpart A deals with the general rule. Section 401 deals with qualified pensions, profit sharing, etc. And Subsection K deals with deferred arrangements. Who knew?

But from there, the 401k plan has several variants and options. We'll be exploring-

▲ i401k, Solo 401k, Solo K, Uni K, Owners Only 401k (and all the marketing terms)

▲ Company-Sponsored 401k (when you have a staff)

▲ Safe Harbor Provisions for 401k Plan Testing

▲ Roth Options with a 401k Plan

▲ Two Plans, Rolling Old Plans

▲ 401k Plans and Roth IRA Conversions

▲ Loans and Life Insurance

▲ Age Based or Tiered Profit-Sharing Add-On to a 401k Plan

▲ Defined Benefits Pension / Cash Balance Add-On to a 401k Plan

▲ SIMPLE 401k (not the same as SIMPLE IRA)

The Owners-Only 401k Plan

The i401k, solo 401k, solo k, uni k, or owners-only 401k (or whatever marketing name a bank or securities firm is selling) is a great small business retirement plan for-

▲ a one-person show,

▲ a one-person show with a spouse who also works for the business, or,

▲ a group of members in a multi-member LLC that does not have any employees. The Economic Growth and Tax Relief Reconciliation Act of 2001 modified the contribution limits and rules, and allowed for an emergence of the owners-only 401k plan.

Due to special tax rules, you can contribute more to this type of plan than other comparable retirement plans. The previous table in the beginning of this chapter illustrated this point with real life numbers. Under the usual rules for defined contribution plans such as SEP IRAs and profit-sharing plans, the deductible contribution is capped at-

▲ 25% of your salary or 25% of your earned income (as adjusted), or

▲ $69,000 for the 2024 tax year (plus $7,500 for catch-up) whichever is more restrictive.

But your deferrals as an employee into your solo 401k plan do not count towards the 25% cap, and this rule extends to your spouse. This is why the owner-only or solo 401k plan allows for the largest contribution because you have three sources of funding-

▲ You at $23,000 (for the 2024 tax year) plus $7,500 for catch-up (employee deferral), and

▲ Ditto for your spouse, and

▲ The business contribution up to 25% of your compensation, and

▲ The funding is independent of each other (deferrals are deferrals, and contributions are contributions).

Read that again. Let's say you have a $60,000 salary, $39,000 to invest into retirement savings and you are married. If only one person draws a salary, he or she can only defer a maximum of $23,000. But if a married couple pays a $30,000 salary to each person, then the total retirement deferral can be $46,000 without having to increase salaries to allow for a larger business contribution.

With a SEP IRA, in contrast, you would need a 4 x $46,000 or $216,000 salary to make the same retirement contribution (alternative math is $46,000 from the example above divided by 25%). The increase in payroll costs would wipe out your returns for at least two years. Not good. We'll talk more about why a SEP IRA is used for crisis management and not for self-employed retirement plans (although the recent passage of the SECURE Act makes this moot, but we'll explain anyway).

Here is an illustrative table showing this concept in a different way from Chapter 10 (Adding Your Spouse to Payroll, page 273) where we show Susan earning $100,000 versus Susan earning $65,000 and Mark earning $35,000.

	Option A	Option B	
	Susan	Susan	Mark
Salary	100,000	65,000	35,000
401k Deferral	30,500	30,500	30,500
Business Contribution	25,000	16,250	8,750
Total 401k	55,500	86,000	

Deferrals and contributions are discretionary, so you can cut back as cash flow and objectives change. The deadline for funding the business (employer) matching or non-elective contribution to your solo 401k plan is the tax filing deadline for your business including extensions. So, if you are an S Corp, the business tax return (Form 1120S) is due March 15. But with a tax return extension you could delay the funding until September 15. However, sole proprietors have until April 15 (the tax return filing deadline) or October 15 (if you file an extension) to make his or her deposits.

Employee deferrals for corporations (such as an S Corp) must be deposited by the 15th of the following month. So, a March 27 paycheck for Q1 would require you to deposit employee funds by April 15, which is typically a slow day around the WCG office (kidding, we're celebrating at the local taco bar).

These deadlines are true for all 401k plans (solo, company-sponsored, Roth option, Safe Harbor provision, etc.). However, there is more wiggle room and less scrutiny for when employee deferrals are deposited since discovery is a challenge (in other words, you won't rat on yourself). To keep things simple and elegant, we recommend following the same schedule as "big person" 401k plans.

Side Note: There is nothing saying you cannot wait until the last few months to make all your deferrals into your 401k plan, or any other quarter where perhaps a little bit of market timing or dollar cost averaging might be beneficial. Being the boss gives you flexibility with your small business retirement options.

Sidebar to the Side Note: Be careful about running out of room on your last few paychecks of the year. If you are paying yourself $60,000 a year or $5,000 a month, your November and December paychecks will be $10,000 and will not have enough room for a one and done $23,000 (for the 2024 tax year) employee 401k deferral.

Then again, nothing that a bunch of payroll amendments can't solve. Yeah, that sounds cheap and easy.

Unlike company-sponsored 401k plans, the individual or solo 401k plan does not need to perform discrimination testing of highly compensated employees (HCEs). More on that in a bit.

Solo 401k plans are also very economical to administer, allow for attractive retirement savings for you and your spouse, and remain simple enough to avoid all the hassles of a full company-sponsored plan. A company-sponsored plan (in contrast to a solo 401k plan) will cost about $1,000 to $1,500 per year (as of October 2023, **WCG CPAs & Advisors** has 47 team members and our 401k plan with Sure401k, a sister company to SurePayroll, was about $1,500 annually).

However, most solo 401k plans only charge for the commission or sales charge of the investments. For example, if you invest in A share mutual funds, there is a one-time sales load or commission of 5.75% (which might vary a bit between funds and fund classes). On that particular investment there are not any additional commissions, and the account fees are very small or non-existent. A shares (as opposed to C shares) are desirable for long-term investing since the commission paid is a one and done, and this cost is essentially amortized over several years.

The only downside is you cannot have a solo 401k or an owners-only 401k if you have employees. Even one part-time admin might blow this up depending on their hours and years of service (see below).

Having Staff with a Solo 401k Plan

If you have a staff, but you do not want to deploy a company-sponsored 401k plan, you can still maintain an owners-only self-employed 401k plan by excluding employees.

▲ Your plan can exclude any employee who has not reached the age of 21.

▲ If the employee is 21 years old, and during a calendar year, the plan year (which is usually the calendar year) or any rolling 12-month period does not work at least 1,000 hours, he or she may also be excluded.

If one of these conditions is true, then you can maintain your solo 401k plan.

Don't go out and try to make your admin an independent contractor. In most states, to maintain independent contractor status, the person must hold themselves out to the public as a contractor in that trade or profession. We don't see too many full-time, dedicated, one-client admins running around with business cards and websites advertising admin services.

There is wiggle room. First, there are PEO (professional employee organizations) which allows you to hire the leased employees, but the PEO runs payroll and handles all the human resource functions. There is some mounting pressure on PEOs since they help small business owners avoid or reduce a lot of things such as unemployment compensation insurance, workers compensation premiums, fringe benefits, health care, and in some cases, retirement plans.

You can also have everyone in your office be licensed. For example, insurance agents, financial advisors or real estate agents might work together as a team, but with revenue sharing capabilities an independent contractor status can be maintained while effecting certain "control." This gets tricky and is a narrow example.

Self-Directed 401k Plans

There are 401k plans that allow you to invest in non-traditional investments such as real estate or buying a business. A common phrase you hear in a ROBS 401k which stands for Rollover for Business Start Ups. It is beyond the scope of this chapter, and frankly it can be a very bad idea although it sounds hip at your next cocktail party. Rob is certainly the operative word since we see a lot of these ideas rob people of their retirement money.

A self-directed IRA is easier to set up and maintain, while a self-directed 401k plan is much more challenging. While these two self-directed vehicles share similar problems and gotchas. Here is a recent post on the pitfalls of self-directed IRAs and 401k plans-

wcginc.com/6133

If you want more information, we have worked with Equity Trust and New Direction IRA who can create and help maintain these accounts and plans.

Company-Sponsored 401k Plan

Typically, an employee must be allowed to participate in the 401k after obtaining 21 years of age and one year of service. One year of service is defined as 1,000 hours in any calendar year, plan year or rolling 12-month period.

Plans can be modified to have less restrictive eligibility requirements, and the recent SECURE Act has allowed part-time employees to enroll into a 401k plan without being counted towards plan testing.

401k plans cost around $1,000 to $1,500 annually for the plan administration from a TPA (third party administrator) and there are asset management fees of 0.5% (index funds) to 1.5% (managed mutual funds) as well.

Therefore, you will have two vendors with a traditional or company-sponsored 401k plan. You will have a 401k plan administrator and you will have a custodian / asset manager. These are oftentimes handled together but have several clients who custody the assets with Vanguard, for example, yet maintain the plan administration, like filing Form 5500, themselves. Seems like a lot of work.

Be very leery of ADP, Paychex and Wells Fargo. These are the top 401k plans that are lost to competitors who offer better customer service, better choices and overall better plans for you and your employees. Wells Fargo is notorious for offering "free" 401k plans, and once you are committed, you discover that the plan is very limiting and underperforms. Free? Really? When was the last time you received something for free that was worth keeping (besides an office doughnut)?

You don't work for free, so be careful of those who claim to.

401k Plan Safe Harbor Provision

Solo 401k plans do not need a safe harbor provision- this is reserved for company-sponsored 401k plans. Regardless, we believe you should understand the rules.

Congress and the IRS want to ensure that self-employed 401k plans do not favor highly compensated employees (HCEs). To be a highly compensated employee you must

▲ either own more than 5% of the business or

▲ earn more than $150,000 in salary (for the 2023 tax year) and was in the company's top 20% in terms of pay.

Therefore, nearly all small business owners are HCEs from an ownership perspective regardless of salary. There are three tests-

▲ You cannot defer more than 2% above the average deferral of non-HCEs. Take a standard deviation curve, go out 2%, and draw a line in the sand. This is the ADP test (Actual Deferral Percentage).

▲ Another test looks at matching contributions from the employer (your business). This is the ACP test (Actual Contribution Percentage).

▲ Lastly, the top-heavy test ensures that HCEs don't have more than 60% of the entire plan's value.

As a small business owner, it is easy to fail any of these tests and more likely all three. A common example is where you have several plan participants, but only your HCEs are deferring close to the maximum. This creates a top-heaviness to your small business 401k plan, and the tax code will fail your plan by suggesting it discriminates in favor of a few highly compensated employees. Not your fault of course since you cannot force your staff to make deferrals into the 401k plan, but if the cookie crumbles that way the plan fails.

If your 401k fails the ADP or ACP testing, there are two methods to bring the 401k plan back into compliance. One method is to make an employer contribution for all non-HCEs. The second method is more individualized where each HCE is refunded a portion of their contributions and those amounts are also contributed by the employer to all non-HCEs. Messy and complicated. Read IRS Revenue Procedure 2013-12 for more information.

But isn't that the point? Isn't the point of a self-employed retirement plan to give the people who are worth the most, the most of the business's benefits and resources (i.e., the owners)? Of course, it is. At the same time, we must play by the rules. So, help is on the way through the Safe Harbor provision. You can defer the maximum, and also have the business match it, without the HCE testing. What's the catch? There's always a catch in the "harbor."

A Safe Harbor plan must satisfy four requirements, with required contributions being the main one. This entails using one of the following formulas-

▲ Basic- Match 100% of the first 3% of compensation, plus 50% of the next 2% of compensation, or

▲ Enhanced- Match 100% on the first 4% of the compensation, or

▲ Non-Elective- Contribute 3% of compensation to all eligible employees

The first two options appear to be more in favor with small business owners than the third since you can take the chance that not all employees will contribute. In addition, the safe harbor 401k plan must have-

▲ 100% vesting for the required contributions,

▲ provide an annual notice to all participants, and

▲ contain withdrawal restrictions (no hardship withdrawals, for example).

However, if the business contributes more than the safe harbor amount, that portion may follow a vesting schedule.

Therefore, don't run out and make your 401k a 401k plan with safe harbor provisioning just because you think you need it. If you do not see a problem passing the discrimination tests, then skip it. For example, you have a small business, the disparity of salaries is low, everyone is participating well and you as the owner are not overloading the plan. Your 401k plan might pass testing as is without having to add the safe harbor provision. Remember, under the safe harbor provision, the employer is required to make contributions according to one of the options above. So, there's your catch.

One planning strategy is that if you require a 401k with safe harbor, you could use the required contribution to defer an annual raise. In other words, you could attempt to pass on an employee raise by contributing the obligatory 3% (for example) employer portion of a safe harbor 401k plan. Probably only one time though, unless you enjoy posting jobs and conducting interviews. Even the first attempt might be a bust.

As a side note, those employee groups that have a collective bargaining agreement can have a separate 401k plan. For example, airlines have pilots who are a large employee group and who have the most discretionary income among the other groups. Therefore, if the airline had one single 401k plan, it would probably fail ADP or ACP testing. Instead of electing safe harbor provisioning, the pilot group is allowed to have its own 401k plan under a collective bargaining agreement which isolates the plan from flight attendants, customer service, mechanics, etc. Who knew? I'll take 401k plans for $600, Ken.

Roth 401k Plans

If you want your retirement savings to grow tax free, you need a Roth IRA or Roth 401k. But don't get too hung up on the phrase tax free growth. Roth IRAs and Roth 401k's are not for everyone, and tax deferral today (non-Roth investments) might be the better answer as alluded to earlier (see Tax Savings and Tax Deferrals). Let's back up the truck a bit and chat about the Roth tag on an IRA or 401k. Yes, a Roth IRA is different than a Roth 401k. The words have dramatically different meanings.

The 401k and traditional IRA came about because it was theorized that you had a much higher marginal tax rate during your wage-earning years than you would during retirement. For example, you could easily be in the 22% marginal bracket when you are 55, but be in the 12% bracket when you are 70. So, you would save taxes at 22% and pay them back at 12%.

Not bad. This theory still holds true for hundreds of thousands of Americans but there have been some recent hiccups.

The data were shifting and suggested that the delta between wage earning marginal tax rate and retirement marginal tax rate was waning. So, some smart people got together and passed laws allowing the Roth IRA. Specifically, it was Senator William Roth from Delaware in 1997 who passed the legislation. Thankfully not much was going on in Delaware in the 90s and Senator Roth was able to create this excellent legislation. As you might be aware, the Roth IRA allows you to take after-tax dollars and invest it, and when you take the money out all of it is tax-free. Beauty!

So, the Roth IRA is not a tax deferral system like a traditional IRA. It is a pay tax now and avoid paying tax later system. But all that glitters is not gold as Robert Plant would say. A Roth IRA is only available to those who earn less than $230,000 per year for married filing joint taxpayers ($146,000 for single taxpayers) for the 2024 tax year, and a Roth IRA has very low contribution limits of $7,000 (for the 2024 tax year). Yuck. Now what?

Enter the Roth 401k which is a hybrid of a 401k and a Roth IRA, and can be a great selection among the small business retirement options. All the taste of a Roth IRA without the calories. Starting January 2006, many businesses amended their 401k plans and started introducing Roth options. So, even if your small business doesn't adopt a 401k plan, your spouse's job or your main job might benefit from the Roth 401k. Ask your benefits administrator to see if your other job or your spouse's other job offers the Roth 401k option.

A Roth 401k has no income limitations and employees (you) can defer up to $23,000 (for the 2024 tax year) or $30,500 with catch-up. But business contributions cannot be designated as Roth. Since the business (employer) matching or profit-sharing is a deduction to the business, these funds are considered pre-tax and will not enjoy tax free growth. In other words, your contributions as an employee may be designated as after-tax or Roth type contributions, and the business's contribution will be automatically designated as pre-tax or traditional type contributions.

In essence, the Roth 401k has two accounts which can be managed separately within the 401k plan; one after-tax and another pre-tax.

Since the biggest challenge in deciding on using a Roth IRA or Roth 401k pivots on your marginal tax rate during retirement, and crystal balls don't have the accuracy they used to, a good plan is to hedge against both. A Roth 401k has this feature built in. Your deferrals as an employee can be Roth (post-tax) which hedge against retirement tax rates being similar to wage earning tax rates. Conversely, business funds are traditional (pre-tax) and hedge against retirement tax rates being lower than wage earning tax rates. Got it? How about this-

Employee deferral into 401k	Pre-Tax (deduction to you)
Employee deferral into Roth 401k	Post-Tax
Business contributions into 401k	Pre-Tax (deduction to you vis a vis the business)
Business contributions into Roth 401k	Not allowed

The mix between the two is the challenging part. 80% Roth and 20% pre-tax? 60-40%? Truly depends on your vision of retirement and your income sources. Bunch of rental income and residual earned income? Rich parents leaving you with thousands of dollars in dividend income? Gotta coin to flip? Two out of three? As mentioned earlier, financial planning and tax projections are the starting point for an answer that will unfortunately take a lifetime to validate. We can see your headstone now- "Her tax projections hit a 95% confidence interval. Kids are proud." Small font or big stone. You decide.

Therefore, be careful of anyone telling you to always max out your Roth contributions without at least asking questions. Yes, there are zillions of calculators available on the internet- simply search for "ira versus roth ira calculator" and the inundation will be overwhelming. Or perhaps underwhelming.

Historically Roth options on a 401k plan used to be costly, but thanks to Adam Smith and his concept of economics, fierce competition has driven the pricing down. However, only a handful of custodians offer the Roth option to the 401lk plan. The recent consolidation of TD Ameritrade and Charles Schwab have made it worse. As of November 2023, here what we have for Roth options and loan options within solo 401k plans-

	Roth	Loans
Fidelity	No	No
TD Ameritrade / Schwab	No	No
eTrade	Yes	Yes
Vanguard	Yes	No

There might be other options, but those are the big ones. Many of WCG CPAs & Advisors small business owners leverage eTrade for their 401k plan.

Roth 401k Versus Traditional 401k Considerations

Two arguments abound when considering a pre-tax 401k contribution. The argument goes like this- your retirement tax rate will be lower than your wage-earning tax rate. For those in the 32%, 35% or 37% marginal tax brackets, this is likely true. However, those earning big bucks probably continue to earn big bucks during retirement from investments, real estate, consulting, etc.

The other argument is about the free loan from the IRS. If you contribute $30,500 to your pre-tax 401k and you are in the 32% marginal tax bracket, you just put $9,760 in your pocket ($30,500 x 32%). Sure, at some point the IRS wants it back when you withdraw it during retirement and will tax the original contribution plus whatever you earned on it. But this might fall into the let's worry about next time, next time category.

As such, the second argument is about using the IRS's money to build additional wealth. You take your $9,760 and do something good with it. Yeah, this argument sort of works. $9,760 annually might not move the needles much on your wealth building strategies. You would need $9,760 x 10 years at 6% rate of return just to afford a down payment on an average rental property.

Rather, most wealth is built with after-tax dollars. The leveraging of the IRS free loan concept sounds great on paper until you gain perspective on the size of the lever.

Another side argument is completely avoiding state income taxes by reducing your state income and therefore income tax with 401k contributions during your wage-earning years, and then establish residency in a tax-free or a tax-friendly state during retirement.

The theories above make sense; however, we ask a basic question- is it easier to pay taxes during your wage-earning years or during retirement? Sure, it depends how much you withdraw during retirement. Please consider that to spend $150,000 during retirement, you might have to withdraw upwards of $180,000 to account for the income taxes.

During your wage-earning years you might have the ability to work a little harder to pay for taxes now. Pick up an extra shift. Close an extra deal. Get a few more tax returns out of the door if you are a tax accountant. Whatever it takes, right? During your retirement years, especially mid-70s or older, you pay taxes with retirement savings (or at least it feels like you do depending on your cash sources).

Also, keep in mind that your primary objective in life is to build wealth. Your second objective is to save taxes, and what a lot of people forget about is saving taxes is not done in a vacuum or just one year; it is done over your entire lifetime.

Finally, consider that the law of 72 suggests that your investments will double every 8 years. Huh? The average rate of return for the S&P 500 is 9.2% since inception. If you take 72 and divide it by 9 (the rate of return) this equals 8, and suggests that your investment will double in 8 years. Where are we going with this? If you have 2 or 3 "doubles" coming up, to have that growth be tax-free upon retirement might be nice.

As mentioned elsewhere, **WCG CPAs & Advisors** recommends financial planning by a qualified planner to determine your objectives and model your particular scenario.

Two 401k Plans

Another twist. Let's say you have a side business and a regular W-2 job where you max out your deferrals into the 401k plan. You cannot make employee deferrals to your side business solo 401k plan since you are collectively limited to $23,000 (for the 2024 tax year) or $30,500 with catch-up, but your business can make a discretionary non-elective contribution up to $69,000 or $76,500 with catch-up (for the 2024 tax year).

Here is the word for word example from the IRS using 2016 limits of $18,000 as an example (occasionally they illustrate things well)-

Greg, 46, is employed by an employer with a 401(k) plan and he also works as an independent contractor for an unrelated business. Greg sets up a solo 401(k) plan for his independent contracting business. Greg contributes the maximum amount to his employer's 401(k) plan for 2016, $18,000. Greg would also like to contribute the maximum amount to his solo 401(k) plan. He is not able to make further elective deferrals to his solo 401(k) plan because he has already contributed his personal maximum, $18,000.

He has enough earned income from his business to contribute the overall maximum for the year, $53,000. Greg can make a non-elective contribution of $53,000 to his solo 401(k) plan. This limit is not reduced by the elective deferrals under his employer's plan because the limit on annual additions applies to each plan separately.

Good ol' Greg. From the employer or business perspective, a discretionary non-elective contribution is in contrast to a matching contribution. This means that a contribution can be without the employee making a deferral. This is key since in the tidy IRS example above, Greg has max'd out his deferrals at his regular job, so he cannot make additional deferrals with his side business. However, the business can make a non-elective contribution.

A non-elective contribution means that the business's contribution is not dependent on the employee's deferral. Seems counter-intuitive. In other words, you do not put anything into the 401k plan, but your business can contribute up to 20% of your income from the business as a garden variety LLC (or 25% of your W-2 from your business if electing S Corporation status). These are also referred to as discretionary contributions.

> Sidebar: The phrase profit-sharing contributions is sometimes used as well. However, this is like interchanging 401k and IRA. Technically, a profit-sharing plan is different than a 401k plan, and it can either be standalone or deployed in combination with a 401k plan.
>
> Therefore, if a company has excess profits (cash) and wants to make a contribution to the 401k plan, these are considered discretionary non-elective contributions and not profit-sharing contributions. This is because a 401k plan is being used and not a profit-sharing plan. Our apologies for splitting hairs and getting all nerdy on the nomenclature.

In summary, the $23,000 (for the 2024 tax year) limit is your limit as a person. But each 401k plan has a limit of $69,000 (see the last line of the IRS example on the previous page using 2016's limits) which can add a lot of muscle to your self-employed retirement plan.

No, you cannot add your W-2s together (main job and side job) and use that for the basis of your side job / business employer contribution. That would be nice though.

> Warning! Each year a handful of small business owners neglect to let us know they picked up W-2 income on the side, and they also forget to inform us that they contributed to their "side W-2 gig's" 401k plan. Yes, we ask. We ask often. Therefore, keep in mind that the $23,000 deferral limit into a 401k plan (for the 2024 tax year) is for all plans, combined.

Rolling Old 401k Plans or IRAs into Your Small Business 401k Plan

Other benefits of having a 401k within your business include being able to consolidate other plan assets such as profit sharing, money-purchase plans, traditional IRAs and SEP IRAs into your 401k plan. You can gain some elegance with this- for example, often times your IRA will have both deductible and non-deductible contributions. You could roll the deductible contributions into your solo 401k plan and roll the non-deductible contributions into a Roth IRA or Roth 401k (a Roth conversion). No, Roth IRAs cannot be rolled into your 401k unless the 401k has a Roth option.

Another benefit comes from backdoor Roth conversions. When converting a non-deductible IRA contribution to a Roth IRA, all your IRAs are considered even the pre-tax (deductible) ones. Your conversion is subject to "pro-rata" rules which is summarized by SmartAsset.com as "if your traditional IRA contains both pre-tax (deductible) and after-tax (non-deductible) contributions, the Pro-Rata rule dictates that your Roth conversion will be taxed proportionate to your pre- and post-tax percentages."

Therefore, a solution is to take all your pre-tax IRA contributions and roll them into your solo 401k plan. This leaves only the after-tax contributions behind which can then be converted to Roth without tax consequences.

Some words of caution. Rolling old IRAs and such into your shiny new self-employed 401k plan might not be the best idea. In some cases, the rollovers will be captive or trapped in the 401k plan. For example, let's say you have a $50,000 IRA and you move it into your 401k. Two years later you have a crisis and need to access the $50,000. Your 401k plan might not allow you to withdraw this money without a hardship provision, have an in-service rollover or allow loans against the plan assets. These features, or some would say are poorly documented limitations, vary among plan providers.

Another concern is the filing of a 5500-EZ tax form. This is not a massive problem, but once your 401k plan reaches $250,000 in plan assets, you must file a 5500-EZ each year.

Also, 401k plans (beyond the solo 401k plans) might have higher fees and fewer options. In our observation, many 401k plans have an annual asset management fee of 1.5% to 3.0% of assets, whereas most IRAs (and solo 401k plans) operate for less than 1.5% annually. There are kickbacks from the asset managers to the 401k plan administrators which is why you see some administrators like Wells Fargo offering free 401k plans.

401k Loans and Life Insurance

401k plans may have loan provisions. This means you can borrow up to 50% of the account balance with a 2024 tax year hard ceiling of $50,000 (or 50% of $100,000+). This limit has not changed for several years. You are basically paying yourself interest on the loan.

401k plans can also buy life insurance, which is a neat way of deducting your life insurance premiums since the money going into the 401k plan may be pre-tax. There are all sorts of rules and limitations, but you should be aware of this option.

401k Plans and Roth IRA Conversions

Let's lay some groundwork first. On your individual tax return, you have three basic IRA options-

▲ Traditional IRA, deductible

▲ Traditional IRA, non-deductible

▲ Roth IRA, not deducted

You probably knew this already, however, we want to focus on the traditional IRA that is non-deductible due to income limits. At some point in household income, a Roth IRA is unavailable. Bummer. Yet at another point, a deductible traditional IRA is unavailable leaving the non-deductible IRA contribution. Super bummer.

No biggie, right? You simply do a Roth conversion of the non-deductible traditional IRA. Not so fast. There is a little-known problem called aggregation where you must ratably convert both the deducted and non-deducted IRA pools simultaneously should you do any conversion.

For example, you have $90,000 in deducted IRA funds and $10,000 in non-deducted IRA funds for a total of $100,000. If you want to convert $10,000 into a Roth IRA, you will be converting $9,000 from the deducted IRA pool and $1,000 from the non-deducted IRA pool. The $9,000 will be a taxable event.

The solution is to roll your deducted traditional IRA funds into your 401k plan leaving your non-deducted IRA funds naked. Then in turn you convert these remaining funds into a Roth IRA.

Turbo Charged 401k Plans

Oftentimes business owners want to put away a ton of money in a small business 401k plan, but cannot due to inherit limitations within the plan. Or business owners want to keep most of the plan money for themselves, which is shocking yet natural. For example, to have the business make a 10% profit sharing contribution, every eligible employee will also receive a 10% contribution which is usually undesirable. You only thought having a staff was a pain because of drama and turnover. Add this dilemma to the list.

You work hard to make money, and you shouldn't have to work too hard to keep most of it. There are turbocharger kits you can add to your normally aspirated 401k plan. These usually work best with an underlying safe harbor 401k plan.

Here we go-

▲ Age-Weighted / New Comparability Profit Sharing Plan, and

▲ Defined Benefits Pension / Cash Balance Plan

Age-Weighted
A profit-sharing plan based on age allows older employees to receive more of the profits than younger employees (hence the tricky name of age-weighted). Another way to look at this is to consider those closer to retirement possibly needing the most assistance in saving for retirement. This also makes sense since older employees are usually more valuable, and therefore profit-sharing plans can be used to discriminate in their favor.

Age-weighted profit-sharing plans are designed to be top heavy, and two people earning the same salary can have very different profit-sharing contributions simply based on age which is perfectly acceptable. No, there is a not a weight-weighted formula where older employees are usually heavier and therefore get more of the profit sharing. That would be fun though. Brings a whole new meaning to a top-heavy plan. There are probably some more jokes in there, yet we digress.

How the formula works is beyond this book, but an age-weighted profit-sharing plan allows a business to contribute more to those employees who are older including owners.

New Comparability
The new comparability profit sharing formulas take age-weighted formulas one step further by grouping certain employees together such as officers, executives, clerical, etc. Officers are given a higher portion of the profit sharing, and within the officer group the older employees are given a higher portion. A double shot. For example, a crusty officer will have a much larger contribution than a new administrative assistant.

The new comparability method is also referred to as cross-tested, and will normally have underlying actuary consultants defending the plan's provisions and discrimination. Remember, discrimination is not bad as long as it can be justified and supported. Yes, this adds to the cost. But let's look at a real-life example that WCG worked on to see how this works first.

The following is a husband-and-wife business with over $600,000 in net profits from 2016. Yeah, it is a bit old but the illustration remains meaningful.

Employee	Age	Salary	Deferral	NEC	Profit	Total

					Sharing	
Mike	43	265,000	18,000	7,950	27,050	53,000
Susie	43	212,000	18,000	6,360	28,640	53,000
Linda	35	62,155	2,486	1,865	876	5,227
Aaron	29	39,868	1,595	1,196	562	3,353
Timothy	32	24,611	0	738	347	1,085
Blake	25	33,452	0	1,004	472	1,475
Jacqueline	31	34,411	1,376	1,032	485	2,894
Denise	23	27,529	0	826	388	1,214
Nate	32	22,104	0	663	312	975
Tony	26	22,086	0	663	311	974

Tilt. Analysis on the next page.

Here are some observations and clarifications-

▲ NEC refers to non-elective contributions, and in this example these are the contributions required under the safe harbor 401k plan provisions.

▲ Profit sharing is based on salary and age. Note the subtle differences for everyone except Mike and Susie.

▲ $53,000 was the maximum allowed under a 401k plan with tiered profit sharing for 2016.

▲ In this real case, the owners kept 75% of all monies put into the plan. Not shabby.

▲ The annual cost in 2016 to administer this plan was $2,500.

▲ The tax deferral savings was over $53,000 for these business owners including state income taxes too (based on 39.6% federal rate and 11% state rate). This was California, and the couple plan to retire in Nevada- instant 11% tax savings.

▲ Yes, those salaries for Mike and Susie are ridiculously high. Therefore, the increase in payroll taxes must be weighed against the savings and benefits. After $168,600 (for the 2024 tax year) only Medicare taxes are being "unnecessarily" paid at 2.9% plus the surtax of 0.9%. The benefits could outweigh this 3.8%.

Defined Benefits Pension / Cash Balance Plan

If the age-weighted or new comparability profit sharing plans supercharge a 401k plan, the defined benefits pension and cash balance plan turbocharges it. We can hear gear heads moaning all over the country above turbo and super charging your engine. Regardless, the defined benefits pension and cash balance plan adds a ton of meat to your 401k platter. Here we go.

A defined benefit is in contrast to a 401k plan since a 401k plan is a defined contribution. A defined contribution plan specifies the amount going into the plan and has nothing to do with how much will be available when you start taking withdrawals. It could be $0 or millions. A defined benefit is a calculus where some future benefit is defined and is usually a stream of payments similar to an annuity.

A cash balance plan is a form of a defined benefits pension, with one major difference. The participant can see his or her account balance grow over time similarly to an IRA or 401k plan. A cash balance plan can be considered a hybrid since it does not rely on formulas and salary histories although it falls under a defined benefits umbrella by definition.

This is important. Since it is a defined benefit, the business has an obligation to fund the plan. Unlike a defined contribution, defined benefit is a 3-to-4-year commitment and a business cannot adjust contributions into the plan based on performance or cash flow needs. There are provisions allowing a business to pause the plan, but that gets tricky really fast. We have heard of cases where the IRS has seized a business owner's house and assets until the pension was correctly funded. Ouch.

A cash balance plan is usually piggybacked onto a safe harbor 401k plan, and it truly is a separate plan (the latter is a defined contribution, and the former is a defined benefit). So why would a small business want a cash balance plan in addition to a 401k plan? The usual reason- put more money into a self-employed retirement plan for the owners' personal retirement and defer taxes.

Similar to age-weighted and new comparability profit sharing plans, cash balance plans use a person's age to determine the amount that can be contributed and use actuary consultation to defend the plan's discrimination.

Here is a quick list of the 2023 amounts that can be contributed into a cash balance plan based on age-

Age	401(k) only	401k with Profit Sharing	Cash Balance	Total	Tax Savings
70	30,000	73,500	398,000	471,500	188,600
65	30,000	73,500	321,000	394,500	157,800
60	30,000	73,500	309,000	382,500	153,000
55	30,000	73,500	241,000	314,500	125,800
50	30,000	73,500	188,000	261,500	104,600
45	23,500	66,000	146,000	212,000	84,800
40	23,500	66,000	114,000	180,000	72,000
35	23,500	66,000	89,000	155,000	62,000
30	23,500	66,000	69,000	135,000	54,000

Before you lose your mind on the tax savings (which is assumed to be at 40% total between federal and state), you need the cash to do so. To save $104,600 at age 50 you need to part ways with $261,500 in cash. Also, if your spouse is on the payroll, you can double it. We only showed ages in chunks of 5.

Here is a link to FuturePlan by Ascensus who provides a full table-

wcginc.com/6104

[intentional white space, please don't feel shorted]

Here is another real-life example that we consulted on in 2016 (outdated, but very illustrative and current in concept)-

Employee	Age	Salary	401k Deferral	Profit Sharing	Cash Balance	Total Contribution
Betty	45	265,000	18,000	35,000	75,000	128,000
Fred	47	115,385	18,000	35,000	0	53,000
Subtotals		380,385	36,000	70,000	75,000	181,000
Wilma	43	70,181	9,825	4,562	500	14,887
Dino	25	23,109	693	1,502	500	2,695
Pebbles	29	22,892	687	1,488	500	2,675
Barney	23	13,908	417	904	500	1,821
Mr. Slate	23	13,444	403	874	500	1,777
Arnold	26	11,670	350	0	0	350
Tex	51	7,088	213	0	0	213
Daisy	18	713	0	0	0	0
Subtotals		163,005	12,589	9,330	2,500	24,419
Totals		**543,390**	**48,589**	**79,330**	**77,500**	**205,419**

It is a lot to absorb, and we could have cut off the example after Pebbles but we wanted to give you a real case. More notes and clarifications-

▲ Betty and Fred are the owners, and were able to keep 92.5% of the money contributed to the 401k and cash balance plans. That is ridiculously good!

▲ Profit sharing can be on a gradual vesting schedule over 6 years (same holds true for standalone profit-sharing plans without the cash balance piggyback).

▲ Cash balance contributions can have a cliff vesting over 3 years (remember the 3 to 4 year commitment previously mentioned).

▲ Total tax savings was 51% since this case was also in California, or about $92,000 combined for just the owners' portion.

▲ The annual cost to administer this in 2016 was $1,750 for the 401k plan portion and $4,300 for the cash balance plan. Cash balance plans are pricey since actuary consultants are used to defend the plan's discrimination. Worth every penny.

Ok, so we've covered the basics of how to turbocharge your 401k plan to allow for more contributions and tax savings. What are some of the downsides?

The plan costs are not low. Sure, the tax savings is much higher than the costs, but those tax savings are actually tax deferrals. And in most cases tax deferrals become tax savings, but you must be disciplined on using those savings to grow your business or invest wisely (which might be the same thing).

Asset management fees range from 1.5% to 3% for Vanguard, American Funds, Nationwide, etc. 401k plans and defined benefits pension plans have two cost elements- the direct plan cost including a per participant charge, plus the asset management fees. Granted asset management fees are everywhere you turn- but small 401k plans usually have the highest. Having said that, small 401k plans are also nimble and completely customizable so your investment options are vast.

The commitment on a defined benefits pension and cash balance can be huge. And there are some devils in details such as minimum interest rate credits and other things that can be challenging. This is not your problem- the people you retain to manage your defined benefits pension and cash balance plan take on this responsibility.

If a handful of employees are older than the owners, this will adversely affect how much the owners can contribute into the plan for themselves. As mentioned, profit sharing and cash balance plans are age-based. Ideally the owners are 8-10 years older than the rank and file for this to work well.

Total holdings in the defined benefits pension plan are limited to about $3.1 million (for the 2022 tax year), enough to cover the maximum allowed payment in retirement of $345,000 a year (for the 2024 tax year). The IRS also has strict required minimum contribution rules and a steady source of income is fairly important. Therefore, you cannot be a contingency based attorney with a huge stockpile of cash today without being able to demonstrate the ability to support the plan next year and the following years.

SIMPLE 401k

If you have employees beside your spouse, a SIMPLE 401k might be a good option. Under a SIMPLE 401k plan, an employee can elect to defer some of his or her compensation. But unlike a traditional 401k plan, the employer must make either-

▲ A matching contribution up to 3% of each employee's pay up to $345,000 (for the 2024 tax year), or

▲ A non-elective contribution of 2% of each eligible employee's pay (non-elective means that the business must do it without fail to maintain the plan's integrity)

No other contributions, such as profit sharing, can be made and the employees are totally vested in any and all contributions. You can only have 100 or fewer employees, and no other retirement plan is allowed. SIMPLE 401ks are also not subjected to discriminatory testing of highly compensated employees (HCEs) unlike traditional 401k plans.

Contributions are $16,000 for the 2024 tax year plus $3,500 for catch-up.

SIMPLEs have fallen out of favor recently since the only real benefits were no testing and low costs- that has changed a lot lately since the landscape of 401k plan providers is much more competitive (low cost) and lawmakers have given us 401k with safe harbor provisions so therefore no highly compensation employee (HCE) testing.

We haven't seen these plans get deployed with any kind of regularity since Bush was president. As in the first one.

SEP IRA

Simplified Employee Pension Individual Retirement Arrangement. Yes, the A in IRA does not stand for Account, it technically is Arrangement but if you say Account, it's okay. We know what you mean. But if you call your IRA a 401k, our OCD does not allow us to let that one go. IRAs are not 401ks and 401ks are not IRAs. From what we understand, we can no longer say "our OCD." Our apologies. So many words and phrases we used to say... it's probably better that we don't anymore. We digress...

How about this? Our super highly stressful and highly technical profession coupled with the desire to be hyper accurate cannot let you call your 401k plan and IRA and vise versa. Bagels and donuts are both breakfast foods, but that is where it ends. Hopefully that explanation is better than the OCD reference.

Back to business. As an employee, you do not make contributions to a SEP IRA, the business does so on your behalf. Yes, it is a tax deduction to the business which is essentially a tax deduction to you. The business can contribute 20% of business income (for sole proprietors, single-member LLCs and partnerships) or 25% of your salary (for corporations such as S Corps). There are no catch-up provisions since the business is making the contribution.

All eligible employees must have a pro-rata employer contribution. So, if you make $100,000 and your assistant makes $30,000, if the business contributes 10% on your behalf it must do the same for your assistant.

Four reasons why these are fading (but there is a silver lining below)-

▲ SEP IRAs require much higher salaries to reach the $69,000 maximum retirement savings for the 2024 tax year,

▲ Pro-rata contributions strictly based on salaries is no more beneficial or less restrictive than a 401k with Safe Harbor, and

▲ The administrative costs of 401k plans have been reduced to that of a SEP IRA.

▲ Another consideration is that the SEP IRA does not allow for plan loans whereas 401k plans do (up to $50,000 for the 2024 tax year).

SEP IRA contributions are due with the associated tax return including extensions (similar to employer contributions in 401k plans). An interesting yet allowed tactic is to always file an extension for your tax returns. This allows you to file your tax returns any time up to the extension deadline, but not make the employer contribution until the extension deadline. Huh? Hang in there on this one. Here is another way of saying it-

You could file an extension on February 1. File your Form 1040 on March 1. And make the contribution on October 15. However, if you skipped the extension filing and simply filed your Form 1040 on March 1, your SEP IRA contribution is due April 15. Weird. Then again, we don't make the rules, we just tell you about them.

SEP IRAs are old school in favor of the 401k plan. Prior to the SECURE Act, 401k plans must be implemented before the calendar year is over, SEP IRAs can be used for crisis management after the fact. As such, December 31st can come and go blowing up your desire to have a self-employed 401k plan, but a SEP IRA can be created after January 1 and allow for previous year contributions and tax deductions.

However, with the SECURE Act, you can open a 401k plan in 2024, and make employer contributions in 2024 but have them earmarked for the 2023 tax year. Employee deferrals are not available in this fashion. So, your 401k plan is not "retro'd" back to the previous year, but the SECURE Act provisions allows for prior year contributions. Subtle difference. You can think of this similar to a SEP IRA which can be opened in 2024, contributed in 2024, but applied to 2023.

SEP IRA, Roth IRAs and the Roth Conversion

If you want your retirement savings to grow tax free, you need a Roth IRA or Roth 401k. If tax-free growth is generally preferred, you can accomplish this outside of the business. However, there are some problems, or at least potential problems.

A quick recap of the limitations of a garden variety Roth IRA- a Roth IRA is only available to those who earn less than $240,000 per year for married filing joint taxpayers ($161,000 for single taxpayers) for the 2024 tax year, and a Roth IRA has very low contribution limits of $7,000. What can be done? Two things- a Roth 401k, which grows tax free, can accept business profit sharing and has a much higher contribution limits of $23,000 (for the 2024 tax year) or $30,500 with catch-up as we've already discussed. That is option #1.

Another Roth like option involves two steps. You create a SEP IRA in 2023 and take your deduction on your 2023 tax return. You convert the SEP IRA into a Roth IRA in 2024, and this in turn creates a taxable event for 2024 but no penalty. You then create another SEP IRA in the same year to counter the tax consequence of the conversion. Imagine putting $69,000 (for the 2024 tax year) into a Roth IRA each year- amazing. Frankly the ability to convert might not last long, but we'll take advantage of it as long as we can. However, SEP IRAs can be viewed as the middleman, and we always want to cut out an unnecessary stop. Implementing a 401k plan circumvents this.

If you have a traditional IRA you can do the same thing. Be careful about shooting your income into the stratosphere in terms of marginal tax brackets. Too many financial advisors and taxpayers mess this up. Let us help. Let us model this taxable event.

Another option along the IRA lines is to make a non-deductible traditional IRA contribution and then convert that into a Roth IRA the following year. This has zero tax consequence since it was never deducted in the first place. Therefore, if you make too much money for a Roth IRA contribution you can contribute to a non-deductible traditional IRA and later convert it.

You are limited to one rollover or conversion per year per account (there is mild controversy within the IRS publications and industry practices on the number of allowed rollovers).

Controlled Groups

Another concern is controlled groups. If you think you are clever and create a holding company to only offer retirement savings plans to certain employees (like your family), the IRS says No. There are controlled group rules where a holding company that controls another business must offer the same retirement programs for both businesses.

Two general types of controlled groups might exist- a parent-child and brother-sister. The parent-child is where one business owns another. That's simple. It gets a bit more complicated with brother-sister where various individuals own multiple businesses. By definition, a brother-sister controlled group exists when five or fewer individuals, estates or trusts own a controlling interest (80% or more) in each organization and have effective control.

For example, you are smart and you connect with two other smart people to form a multi-member LLC. Since you have a revenue splitting scheme that varies from year to year, you use the multi-member LLC as a funnel and feed income to the underlying S corporations. Therefore, each person owns an S Corp that owns an equal interest in the multi-member LLC. Simple enough.

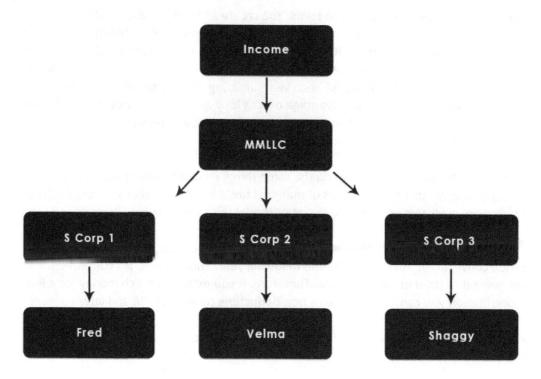

In this example, a 401k plan would be better implemented at the multi-member LLC level. Let's dive into the details shall we?

Affiliated Service Group Rules

Let's say a law firm is structured as a partnership similar to the schematic above. There are three partners. Each partner is separately incorporated as a professional corporation and taxed as an S Corp. Each corporation has a one-third partnership interest in the law firm

(MMLLC). The sole employee and sole shareholder of each professional corporation is an attorney who would otherwise be an individual partner of the law firm if he or she were not incorporated. Easy so far.

All billings for legal services are done by the law firm and partnership income is distributed among the corporate partners according to the Operating Agreement. The law firm is the First Service Organization (FSO) and each of the three S corporations is an A-Organization (A-Org) with respect to that FSO. The four organizations constitute an Affiliated Service Group (ASG). This is the "classic example" of an ASG and can create all kinds of problems with retirement plans.

How did we go from easy to yuck in just a few sentences? A business is automatically a First Service Organization (FSO) if it engages in one of the following fields-

▲ Accounting

▲ Actuarial Science

▲ Consulting

▲ Engineering / Architecture

▲ Health / Medicine

▲ Insurance

▲ Law

▲ Performing Arts

This list should look a little familiar; it was the basis for the specified service trade or business (SSTB) designations for Section 199A. While you do not see certain professions called out, such as Financial Advisors, the IRS and ERISA are more concerned with function over form. Accounting + Consulting + Insurance might equal Financial Advisor. So be careful on trying to consider this list to be strict from a definitions perspective.

If you are an ASG, then the employees of all of the ASG businesses are deemed to be employed by a single employer for purposes of meeting the retirement plan provisions outlined below-

▲ Non-discrimination rules, IRC Section 401(a)(4)

▲ ADP/ACP testing for 401k plans, IRC Sections 401(k) and 401(m)

▲ Compensation limits, IRC Section 401(a)(17)

▲ Participation and coverage rules, IRC Sections 401(a)(3), 401(a)(26) and 410

▲ Vesting rules, IRC Sections 401(a)(7), and 411

▲ Limits on contributions and benefits, IRC Sections 401(a)(16) and 415

▲ Top-heavy rules, IRC Section 416

▲ SEP and SIMPLE rules, IRC Sections 408(k) and 408(p)

How do the IRS and ERISA find out? Challenging for sure! We've seen businesses run around with an ASG for a decade without a problem. But let's say the IRS develops an app that allows them to peer over your shoulder. Aside from them telling you to floss more, they also notice your 401k plan.

Owner Only 401k Plans in MMLLC Environment

What if the structure did not have any employees and only had owners? This changes the rules a bit since now discrimination, or specifically, exclusions are allowed within 401k plan documents.

Let's also go back to our example and say that Fred and Shaggy all had created solo 401k plans for each respective S Corp. This works, but only if there are no other employees other than owner-employees.

Here is how it looks-

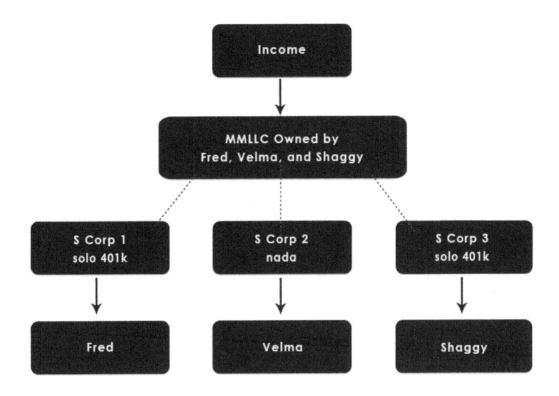

This would allow Fred and Shaggy's S corporations to pay W-2 shareholder wages and make employer 401k contributions at the S Corp level. Beauty! Why should Fred and Shaggy have to plan for retirement in concert with each other, or worse be limited by Velma's three ex-husbands who are bleeding her dry? You didn't know that about Velma, did you? Messy.

In other words, Fred could put away $69,000 (for the 2024 tax year) into his 401k plan while Shaggy only contributes $15,000 into his 401k plan. These plans are independent and are not cross-tested, and as such each owner can do his or her own thing.

As you can see Affiliated Service Groups and 401k plans don't defeat the beauty of the MMLLC – S Corp schematic, it just makes it a bit more complicated. There are more rules about FSOs, ASGs, A-Orgs and B-Orgs... nauseating. Just remember the possible issues and do the homework. WCG works with a handful of Third-Party Administrators (TPAs) who can give you deeper advice and defend the 401k and profit-sharing plans.

Here is a link to our referrals document-

wcginc.com/9500

401k plans are about $1,000 to $1,500 annually yet piggybacking a profit-sharing plan will add additional fees. You can custody the plan assets with any custodian who accepts outside retirement plans and TPA services.

Spousal Attribution and Controlled Groups

Spouses generally have attribution to the other spouse by virtue of marriage. For example, a 5% shareholder cannot receive educational benefits from a corporation and by virtue of marriage neither can your spouse.

However, spouses may have separate businesses with separate 401k plans without violating controlled group rules. This also allows each plan to be tested separately. For example, one spouse could have a business with employees and offer a 401k plan with safe harbor provisioning. The other spouse could also have a solo 401k plan for his one-person S Corporation.

Here is the snippet from 26 CFR 1.414(c)-4-

(5)Spouse -

(i)General rule. Except as provided in paragraph (b)(5)(ii) of this section, an individual shall be considered to own an interest owned, directly or indirectly, by or for his or her spouse, other than a spouse who is legally separated from the individual under a decree of divorce, whether interlocutory or final, or a decree of separate maintenance.

(ii)Exception. An individual shall not be considered to own an interest in an organization owned, directly or indirectly, by or for his or her spouse on any day of a taxable year of such organization, provided that each of the following conditions are satisfied with respect to such taxable year:

(A) Such individual does not, at any time during such taxable year, own directly any interest in such organization;

(B) Such individual is not a member of the board of directors, a fiduciary, or an employee of such organization and does not participate in the management of such organization at any time during such taxable year;

(C) Not more than 50 percent of such organization's gross income for such taxable year was derived from royalties, rents, dividends, interest, and annuities; and

(D) Such interest in such organization is not, at any time during such taxable year, subject to conditions which substantially restrict or limit the spouse's right to dispose of such interest and which run in favor of the individual or the individual's children who have not attained the age of 21 years. The principles of § 1.414(c)-3(d)(6)(i) shall apply in determining whether a condition is a condition described in the preceding sentence.

Drool. Let's cook the previous legalize down to two major bullets-

▲ Spouses don't have direct ownership in each other's business (mine is mine, yours is yours), and

▲ Spouses don't meddle in each other's business affairs.

Don't get too wrapped up in controlled groups or affiliated service groups- just understand the basic premise of what you offer in one must be offered in others if a controlled group exists. We can help identify the problem and then steer you to people smarter than us on this extremely narrow topic.

Non-Qualified Deferred Compensation Plan

We don't want to go too far down this road, but you should be aware of this option. It is usually reserved for highly compensated employees such as executives who can set aside more money, and it might allow a non-qualified deferral to help a qualified plan, such as a 401k plan, to conform to plan testing. 401k plans with profit sharing and defined benefits pension piggybacks usually eliminate the need for this.

Exotic Stuff

There are all kinds of exotic stuff out there. Be careful. If it sounds too good to be true, check it out. Do your research. Talk to us. Yes, there are several legitimate yet exotic plans out there. A lot of them use life insurance as the vehicle. Life insurance has many unknowns and can prove difficult to tease out the problems or issues. With life insurance there must be an insurable interest by the policy owner, and some of the life insurance-based plans cannot be used in a pass-through entity such as S corporations and disregarded entities such as single-member LLCs.

Here are some things that might be a good fit for you and your business-

Self-Directed 401k Plans

Self-directed 401k plans allow you to invest into non-traditional investments such as rentals, other businesses, etc. This is very similar to self-directed IRAs. However, similarly to self-directed IRAs, self-directed 401k plans have several pitfalls such as unrelated business taxable income (UBTI) and unrelated debt financed income (UDFI).

Please visit our website for more information-

wcginc.com/sdira

You can also review our previous chapters. Be careful with self-directed IRAs and 401k plans. Not always a bad thing, but being unaware can leave you with expensive lessons.

Employee Stock Ownership Plans

You can also set up an employee stock ownership plan (ESOP) where employees can purchase business stock over time, and the stock is held in trust. A cool feature is the tax deferral of this system- the employee-owned portion of the business profit's is added to the ESOP's overall asset balance, and is only taxed when the employee makes withdrawals similar to an IRA. Check out the National Center of Employee Ownership here-

wcginc.com/6110

Section 79

Internal Revenue Code Section 79 offers huge deductions of policy premiums and instant tax savings. A Section 79 plan is where life insurance is offered as a group policy, but employees are able to obtain more benefits that are taxable as income. However, there is cash value to the policies that allow for borrowing in the future. There is one inherent problem- when a life insurance policy for a business under ten employees is underwritten, no medical exam is necessary which means the policy has high risk. And to balance that, the policy will have poor cash accumulation. Short-term gains, potentially long-term failures. Are all Section 79 plans bad? No. Just do your homework and ask those pointed questions.

Captive Insurance Company

If you have high property and casualty insurance needs, you can create another corporation that is essentially in the insurance business by collecting premiums from your primary business and investing those premiums into quality investments. The primary business gets a massive tax deduction since insurance premiums are an expense, and if the premiums are less than $1.2 million per year, the captive insurance company only has to pay taxes on the investment income.

Read that again. The captive insurance company does not pick up any taxable income directly from the premiums paid. Eventually the money is returned to you at dividend tax rates.

Tax savings is difference between ordinary income tax rates and capital gains tax rates.

The use of a captive insurance company is disclosed on your tax returns as well. At present, WCG has about 30 clients who leverage this arrangement, and with recent tax court and federal court decisions, captive insurance is under severe scrutiny and is being lumped with other abusive tax shelters.

Controlled Executive Benefits and Endorsement Split-Dollar

These programs are similar in the sense that life insurance is used to retain key employees by controlling the access to the cash value. The tax deferral or tax savings might not be available with type of arrangement, and depending on how it is setup, the payout to the beneficiary might be taxable as well. This is very complicated, and your garden variety financial planner might not be comfortable with these. Your best bet is to speak directly to an advisor who works for a life insurance business such as Transamerica, Northwestern Mutual, New York Life, etc. Or at the very least get a second opinion.

Again, do your homework and ask around before jumping into a life insurance-based product. They have their place, and they can provide huge tax savings especially during high marginal rate tax years. But not all products and plans are the same.

Expatriates or Expat Tax Deferral Planning

For our small business owners or contractors working overseas, there is a consideration when it comes to tax deferred retirement planning. Currently the amount of foreign earned income that can be excluded from ordinary income tax is $126,500 (for the 2024 tax year). Therefore, if you qualify as an expat and your income is less than $126,500 all your income is excluded.

Fast forward, if you elect to defer some of your earnings into a tax deferred retirement account you might be creating a tax liability unnecessarily. In other words, if your income was already being excluded from income tax, why put money into a tax deferred retirement account just to pay tax on the money later when that money was never supposed to be taxed in the first place. Huh? Stay with us.

You make $126,500. You pay $0 in taxes. You put $7,000 in a normal trading account. This $7,000 was never taxed and never will be. You make $10,000 on it because you're smart. You sell the investments and recognize a $10,000 taxable gain all at capital gains rates.

Same situation, but with an IRA-

You make $126,500. You pay $0 in taxes. You put $7,000 (for the 2024 tax year) in an IRA. This $7,000 is not taxed. You make $10,000 on it because you're smart. You sell the investments, withdraw the money and recognized a $17,00 taxable gain, all at ordinary income tax rates.

There are more devils in the details of course, but you get the general idea. To put money away in a tax deferred retirement account when that income was already going to be excluded generally does not make sense. A Roth IRA in this situation would be more ideal.

Implementing a 401k plan doesn't solve any problems either. According to the IRS and specifically IRC 1402(a)(11), IRC 3401(a)(8), IRC 911 and Revenue Ruling 70-491, if all your income is excluded using the foreign earned income exclusion, then you cannot contribute to a 401k plan.

Revenue Ruling 70-491 sums it up from 1970 (when the foreign earned income exclusion was $25,000). An attorney established a profit-sharing plan and earned $40,000. The ruling stated only $15,000 was considered earned income for the purposes of Section 401 (which is where we get 401k plan stuff).

Small Business Retirement Planning Recap
There are also several options and combination of options, and we can work with you to settle into the best plans. Here are some jumping off points-

One Person Show or Husband/Wife Team
Solo 401k plan with Roth Option is the best bet. Very low cost, efficient contributions, and has a good mix of pre-tax and after-tax contributions to hedge against future income tax rate risk.

Second best option is SEP IRA which allows conversion to Roth IRA each year. But this is usually after the fact, or when you are in crisis management mode and want to save taxes.

Multi Owner Partnership or MMLLC
Owners-Only 401k plan.

Multiple Employees
Company-sponsored 401k plan with Roth and Safe Harbor provisions is the best bet. Similar benefits to Solo 401ks. However, Safe Harbor provisions forces the business to make contributions to avoid highly compensated employee (HCE) testing.

Piggyback the profit-sharing plan and cash balance plan to the 401k plan to super-size your contributions while retaining over 90% of the plan assets for the owners.

SIMPLE 401ks are not as attractive. While the non-elective business contributions are slightly lower than 401ks, the contribution limits are low in comparison. At $60,000 in salary, a 401k allows for a total plan injection of $38,000 ($23,000 + 25% of $60,000) whereas the SIMPLE 401k is only $17,300 for the 2024 tax year.

Multiple Entities
Company-sponsored 401k plan implemented at the multi-member LLC level and adopted at the subsidiary S Corp entity level. This would be an Affiliated Service Group and be subjected to controlled group testing.

Epilogue

WCG Fee Structure

We pride ourselves on being transparent and having a simple fee structure. Most business services and tax returns will fit into the fees described below. Sure, there's always the outlier or the unusual situation, but the following information gives you an idea of our philosophy. We only have time on this earth to sell, and we cannot inventory it. Our fees are an attempt to coincide with expected time spent.

Individual Tax Prep

Our starting fee is $800 for standalone jointly-filed individual tax returns (Form 1040). Most are $800 to $1,000. However, we also have FasTrac 1040 at $525 and a fee range of $250 to $400 for children and students depending on your tax footprint.

Small Biz, LLCs, Rentals Tax Prep

Small businesses are commonly reported on your individual tax return on Schedule C. Rental activities are reported on Schedule E. Typical fee range is $800 to $1,000 for those with 1-2 rentals or one side business.

Partnerships, Corps Tax Prep

Our starting fee is $1,500 for partnership (Form 1065) and corporate tax returns (Form 1120 and 1120S) depending on the quality of your accounting records (most are $1,500 to $1,800).

Business Formation

We can create a business or corporation for $625 plus the state filing fees. Includes Articles, EIN, Operating Agreement and S Corp election.

S Corp Election

We can elect your entity to be taxed as an S corporation for $450 (timely) or $600 (late), or $1,200 (super late, and this includes penalty abatement efforts).

Business Advisory Services

People want to know costs, and while this might seem like more shameless self-promotion, you still need to understand what you are getting into.

Sales pitch alert! WCG specializes in small businesses which have a small number of owners, and often just a one-person show. Did you know that 95% of all S Corps have only one shareholder, and 99% of all S Corps have three or fewer shareholders?

Common S Corp candidates and current clients for **WCG CPAs & Advisors** are consultants, attorneys, financial advisors, insurance agents, physicians, chiropractors, doctors, surgeons, anesthesiologists, nurse anesthetists, real estate agents, contractors, photographers (the profitable ones), online retailers, FBA retailers and good ol' fashion widget makers, among several others. We also have several medical groups and financial advisor teams operating multi-tiered entity structures.

The tax savings of an S corporation is not in dispute. But what does it cost to have tax preparation, payroll, tax planning and consultation done? Because small businesses are a core competency for us, we have created Business Advisory Services packages that includes the following-

Tax Planning and Preparation	Vail	Telluride	Aspen
Pro-Active Household Tax Planning	✓	✓	Advanced
Pro-Active Business Entity Tax Planning, PTET	Add-On*	✓	✓
Annual Tax Reduction and Deferral Analysis	✓	✓	✓
Small Business Tax Deductions Optimization	✓	✓	✓
Section 199A QBI Tax and Salary Optimization	✓	✓	✓
Estimated Tax Payments (done thru payroll)	✓	✓	✓
Business Entity Tax Prep	✓	✓	✓
Individual Tax Prep, One Owner	✓	✓	✓
Expat / Foreign Income Calcs, Forms	Add-On	Add-On	Add-On
Tax Resolution, IRS Audit Defense	As Req'd	As Req'd	As Req'd
Situational Tax Law Research (up to 3 hours)			✓

Payroll and Accounting Services	Vail	Telluride	Aspen
Reasonable Shareholder Salary Calculation	✓	✓	✓
Monthly Shareholder Payroll Processing	✓	✓	✓
Employee Payroll Processing	Add-On	Add-On	Add-On
Annual Payroll Processing (includes ten 1099s)	✓	✓	✓
Accounting Services (bookkeeping + analysis)	Add-On	Add-On	Add-On
Quarterly QuickBooks Consulting, QuickStart	Add-On	✓	✓

Business Advisory Services	Vail	Telluride	Aspen
Consulting			
Consultation, Periodic Business Reviews (PBR)	Annually	Routine	Routine
Complimentary Quick Chats (CQC)	Routine	Routine	Routine
Interfacing with Other Professionals		Routine	Routine
Financial Analysis			
Fractional Controller	Add-On	Add-On	Add-On
Financial Statements Analysis, Comparisons		Quarterly	Quarterly
Cash Flow Management and Analysis			Annually
First Research, Industry-Focused Consulting		Annually	Annually
National and Metro Economic Reports			Annually
KPI Analysis, Benchmarking, Trend Analysis			✓
Budgeting, Forecasting, Goal-Setting			✓
Strategy and Maintenance			
C-Level Financial Advice and Strategic Planning			✓
Succession Planning, Exit Consultation			✓
Annual Business Valuation			✓
Annual Corporate Governance, Meetings		✓	✓
Annual Fee*	**$4,320**	**$7,560**	**Custom**
Monthly Fee*	$360	$630	Custom
	(prorated based on onboarding date)		

Custom! Unlike the modern-day new car packages where you have to spend $8,000 for the moonroof, our Business Advisory Service plans can be customized specifically for you. The array above is simply a starting point. If you need more from us, let's chat about it!

Tax Patrol Services

We also have Tax Patrol! This is a wonderful tax service for those who don't need all the business advisory bells and whistles above, but from time to time want some love from an experienced tax consultant and business advisor. Have a quick tax question? Need to know the depreciation rules as you buy that new car? Wondering what your April tax bill is going to be in August? Tax Patrol is like ski patrol... you might not use it, but you sleep better knowing you have it.

Tax Patrol	Keystone	Copper	Breck
Individual Tax Prep)	✓		✓
Business Entity Tax Prep		✓	✓
Tax Planning, Tax Projection Worksheets	Streamlined	Pro-Active*	Pro-Active*
Estimated Tax Payments Calcs	✓	✓	✓
Tax Resolution, IRS Audit Defense	Add-On	Add-On	Add-On
Complimentary Quick Chats (CQC)	Routine	Routine	Routine
Annual Fee	**$1,500**	**$2,100**	**$3,180**
Monthly Fee	$125	$175	$265
	(prorated based on onboarding date)		

*The Tax Planning Asterisk

Yeah, we all dislike the little asterisk. The gotcha! The fine print! Well, here is one of those situations. Pro-active and Pro-active Biz are different. Pro-active tax planning is limited (for individuals and households) and does not include business-entity tax planning and payments (California's Franchise Tax, New Jersey's BAIT, Portland's overall madness, NYC, etc.), pass-through entity tax (PTET) calculations and payments, among other things. Not every business entity needs separate tax planning! Please see our Tax Planning Services webpage and Master Service Agreement for more information.

wcginc.com/msa

[intentional white space]

Accounting and Payroll Services

Accounting fees are based on 2 bank account with less than 250 monthly transactions and include the QBO fee from Intuit. Custom quote is available if you have a lot going on such as third-party integrations (POS, time billing system), accrual accounting method, extensive benefits packages and / or industry specific issues (e.g, job costing in construction).

Employee payroll can be added to shareholder payroll for $100 per month if already using our Business Advisory Service plans above (e.g, Vail), or $175 for standalone. Custom quote for more than 5 employees and a referral to therapy.

Accounting, Payroll

Monthly Accounting	starting at $500 / month
Bi-Monthly Accounting	starting at $250 / month
Quad-Monthly	starting at $175 / month
Sales Tax, Personal Property Tax	typically $75 / month, or $150 / quarter
Employee Payroll (up to 5, bi-weekly)	1 employee, $100 / month 2-5 employees, $175 / month

Prorated Fees

Some more things to consider- when a partial year remains, our usual annual fee is pro-rated to not charge you for services you didn't use (like payroll and consultation). However, a large chunk of our annual fee is tax preparation which is typically a built-in fixed amount of $1,600 (both business entity and individual tax returns). Whether we onboard you in January, July or December, we have to prepare a full year tax return. This increases the monthly fee for the remaining months of 2021 but the monthly fee will later decrease in January of 2022 to reflect the amounts above. Yeah, we make it sound like 2021 is just around the corner.

Payroll Processing

We make very little profits on payroll processing... we offer it as a convenience to our clients. One throat to choke with a single call can be reassuring but if you want to run your payroll, go for it! Everyone thinks payroll is a piece of cake; write a check and done. Nope... we see a lot of mistakes being made by clients especially the handling of health insurance and HSA contributions since there are special rules for greater than 2% S Corp shareholders. Then again, we don't mind fixing what was broken.

Tax Returns

You can prepare your own individual tax return as well... but the benefit WCG preparing both individual and business tax returns is that we slide things around depending on income limitations and phaseouts.

> Note: An individual tax return is what the IRS calls Form 1040 and refers to the entity filing the tax return (you, the individual, are the entity). However, a married couple are deemed to be one entity for the sake of an individual tax return. So, when we say we will prepare your individual tax return, it is meant to include your spouse in a jointly filed tax return.

Break-Even Analysis (does an S Corp make sense?)

Break-even analysis is based on our annual fee of $4,320. If an S corporation saves you 8% to 10% (on average) in taxes over the garden-variety LLC, then $4,320 divided by 9% equals $48,000 of net ordinary business income after expenses and deductions.

More sales pitch! Keep in mind that our fee of $4,320 includes your individual tax return which you might already be paying another tax professional to prepare. WCG has a handful of clients who are right at the break-even point of $48,000 but leverage an S Corp and our services to get tax preparation, tax planning and consultation.

You can always find someone to do it for less- we know that. At the same time, we have a vested interest in your success and provide sound tax and business consultation as a part of our service. Here is a link to our Periodic Business Review agenda that we cover throughout the year so our consultation to you is comprehensive-

wcginc.com/PBR

We also have written a webpage on end of year tax planning-

wcginc.com/EOY

And, to see our entire fee structure (transparency)-

wcginc.com/fee

More About WCG

Founded by Tina and Jason Watson, **WCG CPAs & Advisors** has provided worldwide tax preparation and business consulting from our Colorado Springs CPA firm offices since 2007. Given our unique expertise and the efficiency of virtual yet authentic relationships, we have pioneered the online tax accountant presence for over a decade. Our clients are primarily in California, Nevada, Colorado, Texas, the Midwest, Florida and the eastern seaboard. This makes sense given the largest GDP producers for the country reside in the same areas. We also have several expats operating domestic businesses from overseas!

Since the beginning of our firm, WCG has been using secure client portals to safely exchange financial information, giving you access to excellent service and advice, while saving you time and resources. In-person appointments are nice, even better with donuts, but are not required. Yes, hugs and handshakes cannot be replaced, but phone calls, emails, push notifications and direct interaction on your cell phone, chat service and video-conferencing allow great communication without chewing up a bunch of your time. Given our new landscape of public safety and security, a virtual relationship with your tax consultant and business advisor is essential. Over 80% of our business clients are outside of Colorado!

With over 45 tax and business consultation professionals including several CPAs and Enrolled Agents (EAs) on our team, WCG consults on corporation structures, business coaching, industry analysis, executive benefits, retirement planning, exit strategies and business valuations, income modeling and tax representation. Not all firms can say they offer this approach beyond the nuts and bolts of accounting and tax preparation. Here is some more information on our team-

wcginc.com/team

Consultative Approach

How are we different? Easy! We take a consultative approach to our client relationships. We have the experience of a big CPA firm without the stuffiness. WCG will be your advocate by putting you in a position to make informed decisions by leveraging our professional network of knowledgeable Colorado CPAs, corporate and estate planning attorneys, and Certified Financial Planners to work in concert for you. Why play messenger when we can bring this service spectrum under one roof?

Plus, WCG will be your point of contact as you travel through the cycles of your personal and business lives. Many tax accountants and business consultants are only compliance-oriented, and while government and IRS compliance is critical, being proactive through proper tax and business planning is equally important. Some firms have this depth, yet very few offer a consultative approach beyond the nuts and bolts of accounting and business tax return preparation. In other words, a tax return is simply the result of year's worth of discussions and planning sessions.

Let's not forget financial statement analysis! Bookkeeping is usually equated to bank reconciliations. We provide accounting services which we define as bookkeeping plus analysis (we do both!). What do the numbers mean? How can I get more out of my business?

Core Competencies

WCG consults with small business owners and tax clients on riveting topics like these-

▲ customized business structures for tax efficiency, flexibility and protection

▲ operating agreements, structuring deals with investors

▲ S Corp elections (even late S Corp election back to January 1, 2023, even in 2024)

▲ Section 199A Qualified Business Income Deduction and Specified Service Trade or Business Analysis

▲ reasonable shareholder salary determinations and defense

▲ accounting (bookkeeping + analysis), financial statement preparation and payroll processing

▲ tax advocacy, strategies and planning (bad news in August, OK... surprises in April, bad)

▲ business advisory services to leverage more from your business for you and your family (put more money in your pocket), including lovely yet detached children

▲ CPA Concierge services and customized service packages suited for your business

▲ industry analysis, KPI analysis, benckmarking and peer to peer comparison

▲ executive and fringe benefits

▲ retirement planning (SEP IRA v. 401k, defined benefits and cash balance plans)

▲ business valuations, buy-sell support and exit strategies

▲ financial expert testimony, divorce litigation support

▲ tax representation (happy happy joy joy)

Outside of typical business services (accounting and payroll), consultation and tax preparation, we have focused on these niche competencies for our group of Colorado Springs CPAs and business advisors.

▲ Small business advisory services and administration including S Corp elections and tax planning.

▲ CRNA contractor business consulting including others in the medical community.

▲ Rental properties, including real estate investing strategies and management consultation.

▲ State income tax nexus, physical presence and substantial economic presence issues including income apportionment.

▲ Pass-through entity tax deductions and SALT workarounds.

▲ Expatriates, or Expats for short, including foreign earned income exclusion, FinCEN 114 FBAR filings including Form 8938, Form 5471 and 5472 and other international tax matters.

WCG protects the fortress by not doing everything, but everything we do, we do very well. We also leave room for the individual tax client who does not own a business but has complex tax issues needing expertise, tax planning and wealth management.

In general, our client base is primarily comprised of consultants, engineers, financial advisors, physicians, chiropractors, doctors, surgeons, dentists, anesthesiologists, nurse anesthetists, insurance agents, photographers (the profitable ones), attorneys, online retailers, FBA retailers, real estate agents, real estate investors and good old fashioned widget makers, and several others. A lot of our clients are one-person bands... W-2 one day, 1099 the next.

We also have several medical groups and financial advisor teams operating a tiered entity arrangement where each individual owns an S corporation.

No BS
We are not salespeople; we are consultants. We are not putting lipstick on a pig expecting you to love it. Our job remains being professionally detached, giving you information and letting you decide.

We see far too many crazy schemes and half-baked ideas from attorneys and wealth managers. In some cases, they are good ideas. In most cases, all the entities, layering and mixed ownership is only the illusion of precision. As Chris Rock says, just because you can drive your car with your feet doesn't make it a good idea. In other words, let's not automatically convert "you can" into "you must."

Expectations of Our Clients

We select our clients on two important criteria. First, we expect our clients to be open, honest and responsive in communication. Second, we prefer to work with clients who view our partnership as a collaboration, where our challenges and successes are shared. Unlike transactional relationships, we'd rather work with you than for you. Having said that, we understand some people just want a transactional 'latte' and don't want to get too involved with steaming the milk- that is OK too.

Let us work together to develop and implement a proactive yet nimble plan for your future!

Final Words

We hope you enjoyed reading this book, and wish you the very best of luck in all your endeavors. If we can be of any assistance, please don't hesitate to reach out to us!

Made in the USA
Middletown, DE
14 September 2024

60922941R00243